传世经典
英美剧合集
精读篇

主 编　翟兆通　岳二趁

副主编　纪小军　祝莉丽

编 委　李 琛　施跃华　刘东昊

浙江工商大学出版社
ZHEJIANG GONGSHANG UNIVERSITY PRESS

图书在版编目（CIP）数据

传世经典英美剧合集. 精读篇 / 翟兆通，岳二趁主编.
— 杭州：浙江工商大学出版社，2017.11
　　ISBN 978-7-5178-1915-8

Ⅰ. ①传… Ⅱ. ①翟… ②岳… Ⅲ. ①英语—汉语—
对照读物②电视文学剧本—作品集—英国—现代③电视文
学剧本—作品集—美国—现代 Ⅳ. ①H319.4：Ⅰ

中国版本图书馆CIP数据核字(2016)第275316号

传世经典英美剧合集：精读篇

翟兆通　　岳二趁　主编

责任编辑	王　英　罗丁瑞	
封面设计	小鸟设计工作室	
责任印制	包建辉	
出版发行	浙江工商大学出版社	
	（杭州市教工路 198 号 邮政编码 310012）	
	（E-mail:zjgsupress@163.com）	
	网址：http://www.zjgsupress.com	
	电话：0571-88904980，88831806（传真）	
排　　版	北京沙漠之泉文化有限公司	
印　　刷	北京俊兴彩色包装有限公司	
开　　本	787mm×1092mm 1/16	
印　　张	23.5	
字　　数	597 千	
版 印 次	2017 年 11 月第 1 版　　2017 年 11 月第 1 次印刷	
书　　号	ISBN 978-7-5178-1915-8	
定　　价	45.00 元	

Preface 前言

　　中国学生对英语学习的感受是复杂的。一方面是所有的中国学生都知道英语作为当今世界最重要的国际通用语言，是我们了解世界、学习别人的窗口，也是我们与别人交流、沟通的工具，对我们提升自己的水平非常重要，所以每个人都有强烈的学好英语的愿望。但另一方面是残酷的现实：每个中国学生从小到大学习了十几年的英语，做过无数习题，参加了无数的考试，尽管分数可能不差，却是处在一种听不懂话、张不开嘴的状态。这其中的原因并不在于做学生的不用心，而是我们通过背单词、做填空学到的英语是死的。在我们的头脑中，单词的拼写与实际发音是分离的，语法、句型与真实的生活场景是脱节的；需要面对面的交流时，往往不知道该如何表达自己，学过的单词和句型也反应不过来，所以也就听不懂别人说的话。

　　其实，如果把那些听不懂的句子写下来的话，大多数人是可以明白它们的含义的。中国学生英语的语法基础不错，所欠缺的其实就是把已经掌握的知识点应用到实际场景中。针对这一点，观看英剧和美剧对我们有很大的帮助。

　　通过观看英剧、美剧学习英语，对不了解英国、美国社会的中国学生无疑是一个不错的途径，但如果以为看看电视剧就能学会一门外语可就大错特错了。看英剧、美剧学语言也是有方法的。首先，对那些热播的连续剧要有所选择，不是所有的热播剧都能帮你学英语。初学者可以从经典剧目如《老友记》《成长的烦恼》《人人都爱雷蒙德》等这些轻喜剧中选择一部自己喜欢的开始，有一定听力基础的学生可以根据自己的专业选择单词更难、语速更快的警探剧或史诗剧等。

　　选定剧目之后，可以先借助字幕把剧集快速看一遍，了解基本剧情和人物，这样既满足了好奇心，又避免在接下来的学习中被好看的情节分散了注意力，同时，也有助于了解剧中人物的性格和语言风格，帮助以后有重点的学习。当我们对剧情有了一个基本的了解，故事本身的情节不会对其中的英语语言产生干扰的时候，就可以真正开始学习了。需要强调的是对通过看剧来学习语言而言，只看一遍是不够的，必须反复观看、精听，直到完全

　　理解对话中的句子用词、含义，并能够复述那些典型句子，才能真正做到让英剧、美剧中的经典对白为我所用，所以同一剧集看个十遍八遍没有什么奇怪的。

其次，在学习英语的过程中，需要特别强调的是字幕这个特殊的工具。完全不依靠字幕，凭着自己逐个单词硬听，难度太大、效率太低，难以坚持下去。可如果一直看字幕，人会不自觉地通过中文字幕来理解英语，这样达不到听懂、理解、记忆、重复的学习效果，同样是在浪费时间。比较好的解决方法是运用中英文双语字幕。先借助中文字幕理解含义，再通过英语字幕掌握用词，遇到生词查一查字典，不熟悉的句型记下来，便于以后单独背诵。这样反复几遍之后，关掉字幕，再来听对白，就能很轻松地理解其含义。

听懂英剧、美剧的对白不是我们的目的，学习语言最终是要能够交流，要能够表达自己的想法。所以在英剧、美剧的学习中，最重要的是要能够跟读，而且要有意识的模仿人物的语音、语调、重音、节奏，包括连读、吞音、弱化、浊化，以及习惯用语、表达方式、俚语引文。在没有语言环境的时候，尽量模仿剧中人物的台词是我们能够学到地道发音的最简单的途径。跟读熟练到一定程度后，就是复述句子，这样经过一段时间的积累，我们就能掌握一定数量的句型，遇到相当的场景，把一些名词、形容词替换掉，就可以将我们自己的想法用正确的方式表达出来，这才是我们学习语言的真正目的。

此外，通过英剧、美剧学习语言还有利于对英国、美国文化及整个西方文化的理解。语言是思维的载体，学习了英音、美音只是皮毛，更重要的是这种语言背后的文化理念和思维模式。英美文化是和我们中国不一样的文化，要了解他们的思维方式才能知道他们在想什么，会去做什么，才能更好地与他们打交道，而这些文化的细节，大量蕴含在英剧、美剧中，使得英剧、美剧成为学习文化最好的媒介。

最后需要提醒大家的是，看英剧、美剧只是提供了学习英语的一种方法，而不是万能的捷径。任何语言的学习都不是一件轻轻松松就能够做到的事情。在看英剧、美剧的过程中，记录用的纸和笔是必不可少的。而且通过英剧、美剧提高英语表达能力也不是一朝一夕就能完成的，反复的听读、常年的积累才会有量变到质变的飞跃。但愿每一位用这本书的人都能完成这个飞跃。

最后，感谢编辑为本书所提出的框架设计，另外，本书在编写过程中还得到冷雨洁、蔡雨珈等同志的帮助，在此一并感谢。由于时间仓促，编者水平有限，书中难免有错误，恳请专家同行多提宝贵意见。

编　者

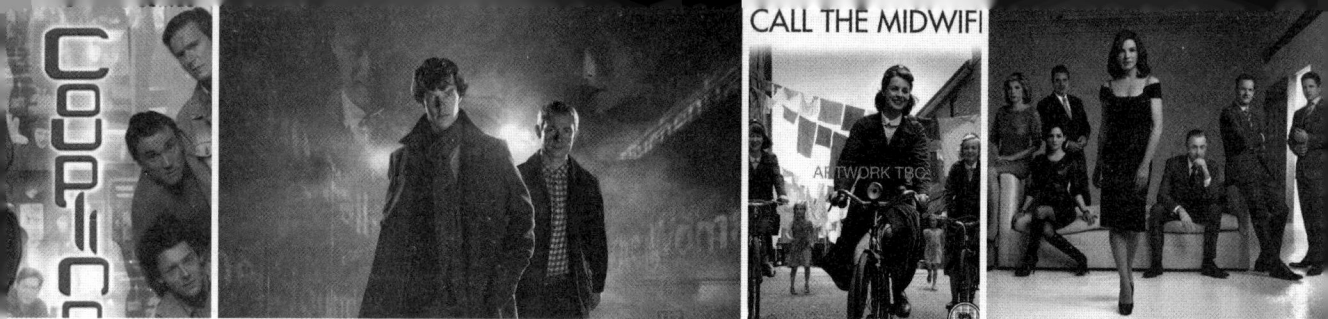

英美剧介绍

　　"美剧"是对美国电视剧的简称。20 世纪 80 年代，一部拍摄于 1970 年的《大西洋底来的人》(*The Man from Atlantis*) 成为敞开国门之后中国人了解美国的窗口，麦克·哈里斯脸上的蛤蟆镜一度成为时尚青年的标志。《加里森敢死队》(*Garrison's Gorillas*) 的热播、停播与复播更是中国人思潮迸发的晴雨表，影片中有血有肉的英雄形象与国内生硬的人物形象形成了鲜明对比。《成长的烦恼》(*Growing Pains*) 更是以轻松幽默、记录生活点滴的形式让中国人第一次知道了什么是情景喜剧。这部剧集让我们走进美国家庭，体验了代际沟通的可能及其背后的美国式幽默。凡此种种，都已成为那个年代的文化切片。

　　在长期的发展历程中，美剧的许多传统逐步得以确立，其中"季"的运营模式最为现在的中国观众所了解。"季"是各大电视网播出新作品的季节，每一季一般 22 集左右，这是由美国特有的播映方式决定的。美国商业电视以每年 9 月中旬至第二年 4 月下旬为一个播出季，时长约 30 周。新季以美国电视艺术与科学协会主办的"艾美奖"颁奖典礼为序幕。美国电视剧一般一个星期只播一集，因此 20 多集正好够播一季。美国的电视剧是边拍边播的，很注重收视率，一部收视率低的电视剧是无法生存的，只要吸引不了观众的注意力，那么不管该剧的情节进行到何处，都会被电视台毫不留情地撤下。每年秋季，美国电视网纷纷推出自己的新剧，或者延续之前已经获得成功的经典剧集。这段时间天气较冷，人们一般较少外出，电视收视率自然大幅提升。通过这种每年固定的播出时段，我们可以在许多"长寿"的美剧中找寻美国社会变迁的轨迹。从 2004 年《迷失》(*Lost*) 的播出开始，美剧真正走进了中国人的视野。它剧情紧凑，一点也不拖沓；跟亚洲的电视剧比较，其取材范围、拍摄水准和投资都大大胜出。由于 2011 年几大视频网站陆续在海外上市，许多优秀的美剧也出现在中国内地的电视屏幕上。

　　电视网是美国电视体系的主体，本质上是一家经营电视节目的大公司。通常，各大电视网在全国各地拥有许多电视台，他们向这些电视台提供节目内容。美国主要的电视网有以下几个。

① 哥伦比亚广播公司（CBS）

　　哥伦比亚广播公司，美国三大广播电视公司之一，主打警探剧，如《犯罪现场调查》(*Crime Scene Investigation*)、《犯罪心理》(*Criminal Minds*) 等。

② **全国广播公司（NBC）**

全国广播公司，美国三大广播电视公司之一，美国第一个全国性广播网，主要剧目有：《老友记》(Friends)、《法律与秩序》(Law and Order)、《白宫风云》(The West Wing)、《超能英雄》(Heroes) 等。

③ **美国广播公司（ABC）**

美国广播公司，美国三大广播电视公司之一，是从全国广播公司分离出来的，主要剧目有：《绝望的主妇》(Desperate Housewives)、《迷失》(Lost)、《波士顿法律》(Boston Legal)、《与星共舞》(Dancing With the Stars)、《实习医生格蕾》(Grey's Anatomy)、《丑女贝蒂》(Ugly Betty)、《复仇》(Revenge) 等。

④ **福克斯广播公司（FOX）**

福克斯广播公司，排名第四，主要剧目有：《识骨寻踪》(Bones)、《24 小时》(24 Hours)、《X 档案》(The X-Files)、《豪斯医生》(House M.D.)、《危机边缘》(Fringe)、《越狱》(Prison Break)，以及《别对我撒谎》(Lie to me) 等。

⑤ **哥伦比亚及华纳兄弟联合电视网（CW）**

哥伦比亚及华纳兄弟联合电视网，其代表剧目有《邪恶力量》(Supernatural)、《美眉校探》(Veronica Mars)、《超人前传》(Smallville)、《绯闻女孩》(Gossip Girl)、《吸血鬼日记》(Vampire Diaries)、《尼基塔》(Nikita) 等。

⑥ **家庭电视广播网（HBO）**

家庭电视广播网是时代华纳下属的付费电视网，出过一些质量很高的剧集，如《黑道家族》(The Sopranos)、《欲望都市》(Sex and the City)、《真爱如血》(True Blood)、《罗马》(Rome)、《兄弟连》(Band of Brothers)、《血战太平洋》(The Pacific) 等。

美国电视剧并非一块视觉文化的新大陆，它正以越来越考究的艺术品位、越来越奔放的自由创意，区别于日趋僵化的好莱坞。就像 20 世纪 80 年代初美国最优秀的影视作品，美剧正在为我们打开一个鲜活的、具有创造力的窗口。

法国《电影手册》甚至敏锐地认为，在工业化的电影制造领域，美国电视剧的成就已经超越了好莱坞的大多数电影（《骇客帝国》除外）。有人断言，美国电视剧正处于一个难得的黄金时代，电视剧工业给予创造者更多的自由，而这种情况在好莱坞几乎不存在。"当电影沦为儿童玩具，电视剧所提供的阅读快感将使它成为最后的成人读物。"

"英剧"是喜欢看英国电视剧的中国人为英国电视剧起的简称。英国人素以风格本土化、制作精良的剧集为傲。英剧的类型也很丰富，无论是展现方寸之间的情景喜剧，还是家长里短的剧情剧，都因其冷幽默及其人文气息，打上了"英国制造"的烙印。就拿絮絮叨叨几十年的肥皂剧《加冕街》(Coronation Street) 来说，连伊丽莎白女王二世都自曝是其拥趸。

　　英剧和美剧类似，也有"季"的运营模式。一年一季，每季大约有 3 到 9 集。在中国，美剧的传播率和受欢迎度现阶段在一定程度上大超英剧，但是作为戏剧的鼻祖，英剧是与众不同的，也是不容小觑的。现在美剧迷耳熟能详的《绯闻女孩》(Gossip Girls)、《同志亦凡人》(QAF) 及《都市侠盗》(Leverage Age) 等，都是分别从英剧《皮囊》(Skins)、英版《同志亦凡人 》(QAF) 及《飞天大盗》(Hustle) 中衍生而来的。如果把这几部放在一起做对比，即可看出美剧的价值观更符合普通思维，该紧张时紧张，该微笑时微笑，该煽情时也绝不手软，是最规矩的、最优秀的大众之作。但回到英剧，我们会发现，无论是流传甚广的《小不列颠人》(Little Britain)，还是经典的《IT 狂人》(IT Crowd)，或是独树一帜的《应召女郎的秘密日记》(Secret Diary of a Call Girl)，都看得出英国人注重小人物的真实生活再现和本土化的艺术气息的展示。

　　英剧善于在主角身上表现极致的夸张阴郁：不屑温暖，没空煽情，只要需要就不顾道德廉耻和主流价值观，傲慢到了一定程度。而就是这股洒脱的傲慢，让英国人满腔满腹的智慧和讽刺跃然荧屏，就算是最简单的情景喜剧也能刀刀见血，对人对己都毫不留情，无厘头和超现实达到了超高的程度。看完优秀的英剧后，绝非不痛不痒，在他们所营造出的独特的艺术气氛下想全身而退，简直不可能。

　　事实上，同美剧一样，英剧早就在国内流行了。《天线宝宝》(Teletubbies) 和《憨豆先生》(Mr. Bean) 都是英国出品。而现在，在视频网上，《欢喜冤家》(Coupling)、《神出鬼没》(Spooks) 等这些英国电视剧早已成为最热的"抢手剧"。你完全有理由相信，现在电视迷的必看剧目里，除了美国制造，还有英国制造。

　　总体来说，少了美式的饶舌与圆滑，英国式幽默使英剧突出重围，展现了自己独特的、清新的、自然的风格。

Contents 目录

◎ 英美剧介绍

Chapter 1 情景喜剧 Situation Comedy/Sitcom

Chapter 2 科幻剧 Science Fiction

Chapter **3** 警探剧 Detective Drama

Chapter **4** 律政剧 Legal Drama

Chapter 5 医务剧 Medical Drama

Chapter 6 剧情剧 Story Opera

Chapter 7 青春偶像剧 Tendy Drama /Idol Drama

Chapter 8 史诗剧 Epic Drama

Chapter 1

Growing Pains

情景喜剧
Situation Comedy/Sitcom

　　情景喜剧，也称处境喜剧，是一种喜剧演出形式，最开始出现在广播中，如今已成为最受欢迎的电视节目之一。情景喜剧有其特有的模式：一般都有一个中心场景，也就是由三面实墙布置出的一个半开放的空间，观众和摄像机在敞开的"第四面墙"外；剧中的大部分情节都在中心场景中发生；有相对固定的主演阵容，角色人物的个性特征也基本完整、稳定；剧集以系列轻喜剧的形式有规律的连续播放，单集多在 30 分钟左右；每集可独立成章，上下集之间又有联系，全剧则含有一条或多条故事线。与剧情片不同的是，情景喜剧的内容大多贴近日常生活，人物塑造讲究平民化，依靠诙谐、幽默的对白推动情节的发展，用巧妙的故事情节来制造笑料、吸引观众，有些情景喜剧还会在后期制作中加入录制的笑声，以加强其喜剧效果。

　　曾在 20 世纪 90 年代连续热播 10 年的美剧《老友记》，又称《六人行》，是此类情景喜剧的代表作。此外，早年风靡国内的《成长的烦恼》，以及近年流行的《人人都爱雷蒙德》《生活大爆炸》等，都称得上是此类剧目的经典之作。

The Big Bang Theory

《生活大爆炸》

1

入选理由：

《生活大爆炸》是一部少见的以"科学家"为主要人物的情景喜剧，由混迹好莱坞多年的老牌编剧查克·洛尔和比尔·普拉迪担任主创，2007 年 9 月一经推出便好评如潮，目前已经续拍到第九季，被誉为《老友记》以来最受欢迎的情景喜剧之一。

近年来，科学元素正成为好莱坞的流行时尚，科学家也变得越来越正面。与《老友记》中仅有罗斯一个人说话常咬文嚼字还饱受大家嘲笑不同，剧中的四位主演，满嘴的科学理论，却引发了人气的飙升。人们不仅欣赏他们科学而搞笑的生活模式，甚至将"科技宅男"列为婚恋市场的单身新贵，号召剩女们赶紧抢占这些有着大好前景的潜力股，正应了该剧的宣传口号："聪明是新的性感（Smart is the new sexy）！"

Section 1　剧情特点：

在普通人的印象中，科学家常常是古怪的、刻板的，有很多怪癖，不善与人交流、不修边幅、不太正常，总之是一群很没意思的人。而《生活大爆炸》一剧则颠覆了人们的普遍观念，剧中的四位科学家分别是实验物理学家莱纳德、理论物理学家谢尔顿、太空工程师霍华德（他只有硕士学位并为此饱受谢尔顿的嘲笑）、天体物理学家拉杰。这四人都是二十六七岁，在加州理工学院（CIT）工作（背景选在 CIT 大概是因为那里出过费曼的缘故）。这群高智商的理工天才离开了自己精通的领域后确实是些情商超低、对普通生活缺乏经验、不善与人交流的"宅男""极客"，但是他们超乎常人的敏捷思维和独特的行为方式却让人觉得他们是那么幽默、可爱。让这群宅男与现实发生联系的是公寓里新来的美貌性感的女邻居佩妮。佩妮是个梦想成为演员的女孩，但一直没能成功，平时只能在附近的一家餐馆里打工。她智力平平、追求时尚、待人友善，与科学家们是截然不同的两

2

个世界的人，最重要的是，她最近单身。莱纳德对佩妮一见倾心，在追求佩妮的过程中，一个美女和四个宅男的生活开始爆炸了……

Section 2　对白特点：

《生活大爆炸》适合有一定基础的英语学习者观看和学习。难以听懂是该剧对白最大的特点。由于主要人物都是高智商的科学家，因此该剧的对白语速很快，且用词大多生僻、专业，涵盖了物理、化学、生物、医学等学科的最前沿。更为可怕的是，宅男们说话动辄就冒公式和理论，要不就是引用科幻名剧的台词，非得有很强的理工科背景及对经典动漫、科幻剧达到耳熟能详的地步，才能理解其中的含义，否则基本就和剧中的佩妮一样，即使听懂了每一个单词，也仍然是一头雾水，不知所云。这无疑会给听力有一定基础的学生带来沉重打击。

唯一称得上安慰的是作为地道美国人的佩妮也一样听不懂他们的话，经常会问 "What does that mean"。所以，不要在开始阶段被这部剧的难词吓到，坚持听下来，一定会在听力上有突破性的提高。而且通过这部剧的学习，能够获得很多关于科学、科幻及动漫的背景知识，这样，在生活中与其他宅人聚会时就不用发愁没有话题了。

另外，值得一提的是，加州大学洛杉矶分校的物理和天文学教授大卫·萨尔兹伯格担任该剧的科学顾问，负责核实剧中对白所涉及的大量科技词汇及各个学科的背景知识。萨尔兹伯格是一位真正的物理学家，他的加盟保证了对白的严谨、准确及逻辑性。相信这部剧中的科学元素能给受困于繁难的专业词汇的理工科学生带来惊喜。

Section 3　角色分析：

谢尔顿·库珀 (Sheldon Cooper)：《生活大爆炸》一剧里，最抢镜的不是原定的男女主角，而是被网友们昵称为"谢耳朵"的谢尔顿·库珀教授。这位 IQ 高达 187 的天才理论物理学家，从小就是一名神童，小学 5 年级毕业就上了大学。他拥有一个硕士学位，两个哲学博士学位，15 岁时就成了教授。作为剧中笑料最多的人，他身上集中了关于科学家的一切刻板印象：不通世事、古怪顽固、偏执强迫、吹毛求疵、目中无人，拒绝相信世界上有比他聪明的人。但是所有这些让人抓狂的东西组合到他身上却形成了一种可以称之为"可爱"的效果，引发观众的热捧。从语言学习的角度来说，库珀博士是最可怕的人，除了他那让人抓狂的性格，打他嘴里说出来的怪词数量巨大且速度奇快，因此让人又爱又恨。

"Bazinga" 是最有"谢尔顿"特色的语言。令人难以想象的是像谢尔顿这样毫无幽默感的人也可以搞怪，他会一本正经的跟人讨论，等你相信他后，他会跟你说 "Bazinga"，意思是刚才的话是他杜撰出来逗你玩的，令人哭笑不得。查不到这个单词的出处，翻译成"骗到你了"比较合适。这个词可能就是编剧 "Bazinga" 出来的，但相信韦伯词典很快会加入这个词条。

莱纳德·霍夫斯塔特 (Leonard Hofstadter): 按照《生活大爆炸》编剧的最初设计，莱纳德应该是主角，他和佩妮之间的感情是全剧的主线。一个痴情傻博士，能理解宇宙的运作，却不懂怎么向喜欢的女孩表白——又一个俗套的美女与野兽的故事。但是，随着剧情的发展，谢尔顿越来越抢眼，与他的各种怪癖相比，莱纳德的书呆子气和宅男的内向、木讷简直就像白开水一样寡淡，产生的笑料不多。他也是几个宅男中最像正常人的一个，虽然他个子矮小、外貌不佳、视力奇差，默默爱慕着漂亮的女邻居却老是失败而归而常被几个室友嘲笑，但他朴实、善良，是唯一能够忍受谢尔顿各种怪癖的老好人；而且他说话好懂多了，语速又慢，用的难词、怪词是几个人中最少的。

佩妮 (Penny): 作为常与理工宅男和女博士们在一起的美女，佩妮想不当女主角都难。这个邻家女孩是个标准的"美国甜心"，金发性感，热爱社交购物和与各种性感男生约会，虽然智力和学识跟这些天才博士们不在一个档次上，但是热情、开朗。从她照顾生病的谢尔顿这一段上可以看出佩妮骨子里的善良温柔。其实佩妮还是很聪明的，经过莱纳德和谢尔顿等人的影响，从第三季起，佩妮开始听得懂关于尤达和克林贡的笑话了（分见《星球大战》和《星际迷航》）。

霍华德·沃尔维茨 (Howard Wolowitz): 《生活大爆炸》里的配角们几乎个个抢眼，组成科学四人组的还有犹太小个子工程师霍华德·沃尔维茨，以及印度来的拉杰·库萨帕里。霍华德是个极有喜感的角色：个头矮小、言语猥亵、爱穿紧身衣、健美裤、化烟熏妆、戴闪闪发光的蝙蝠侠皮带扣；三十多岁了还和老妈住在一起，需要人照顾饮食起居；自以为是泡妞高手、魅力非凡，其实只会用一些下流话跟那些根本不拿正眼看他的女人搭讪。这样的人居然有个可爱、甜美的博士女朋友乐意与之结婚，看来导演真的很喜欢这群宅男。霍华德的老妈也是个亮点，一个胖胖的大嗓门女人，总把儿子按十来岁的未成年人一样对待。其角色设计的独特之处在于她自始至终都没有正式登场，一直是只闻其声、不见其人，所有台词都是在后台用沙哑的嗓音大声喊出来的。

拉杰·库萨帕里 (Rajeshesh Koothrappali): 粒子天体物理学家拉杰·库萨帕里是个羞涩的印度男孩，在女性面前害羞得讲不出话来，只有酒精才能帮他克服语言障碍，可是喝多了又会丧失自控能力，常常误事。拉杰说的是带有印度口音的英语，听起来还不错，能分辨。编剧想得很周到，理工科的学生学习一些印度口音是必要的，要知道在美国的大学里，印度裔的教授特别多。

🔊 Passage 1 📹

剧情介绍:

（选自第 1 季第 11 集）谢尔顿感冒了，变得更加难缠，要求别人像照顾小孩子一样照顾他，为他提供各式服务。身边的几个宅男听说他病了都被吓跑了，无人过问的谢尔顿只好跑到佩妮工作的餐馆，还在餐馆里旁若无人地大声擤鼻涕、咳痰。这位智商高达 187 的自负天才想要喝汤，却被佩妮一句"为什么不叫外卖"问得哑口无言。尽管谢尔顿很讨人厌，但善良的佩妮还是送他回家，并照顾他，满足这个长不大的天才的各种荒唐的要求。

Scene 1: In the early morning, Sheldon found himself sick. He called Leonard for help, but Leonard fled even without putting on his pants and shoes.

清晨，谢尔顿发现自己病了，他大声呼唤莱纳德。而莱纳德闻声后落荒而逃，连裤子和鞋子都来不及穿好。

🔊 **Sheldon:** Leonard, I'm sick! Leonard? Leonard? Leonard? Leonard, my comforter fell down, and my **sinuses**[1] hurt when I bent over.

(Sheldon called Leonard.)

Sheldon: Leonard, where are you?

Leonard: I'm at work.

Sheldon: At 6:30 in the morning?

Leonard: Yes.

Sheldon: On Sunday?

Leonard: Yes.

Sheldon: Why?

Leonard: They asked me to come in.

Sheldon: I didn't hear the phone ring.

Leonard: They **texted**[2] me.

Sheldon: Well, as I predicted, I am sick. My fever has been tracking up **exponentially**[3] since 2:00

谢尔顿： 莱纳德，我病了！莱纳德？莱纳德？莱纳德？莱纳德，我的被罩掉了，我一弯腰鼻窦就疼。

（谢尔顿给莱纳德打电话。）

谢尔顿： 莱纳德，你在哪儿呢？

莱纳德： 我在工作。

谢尔顿： 早上六点半？

莱纳德： 是。

谢尔顿： 星期天？

莱纳德： 是。

谢尔顿： 为什么？

莱纳德： 他们叫我帮忙。

谢尔顿： 我没听见电话响过啊。

莱纳德： 他们发短信给我。

谢尔顿： 是这样，正如我预测的那样，我病了。我的体温从凌晨两点开始

注释
1. **sinuses** ['saɪnəs] *n.* 鼻窦 sinus 的名词复数
2. **text** [tekst] *v.* 短信联系
3. **exponentially** ['ekspənəʃ(ə)li] *adv.* 快速上升、呈指数倍数增长
4. **sputum** ['spjuːtəm] *n.* 痰

a.m. And I am producing **sputum**[4] *at an alarming rate*[1].

Leonard: *No kidding?*[2]

Sheldon: No, not only that, it has shifted from clear to milky green.

Leonard: All right. Get some rest and drink plenty of fluids.

Sheldon: What else would I drink, gases, solids, **ionized**[5] **plasma**[6]?

Leonard: Drink whatever you want.

Sheldon: I want soup.

Leonard: Then make soup.

Sheldon: We don't have soup.

Leonard: I'm at work, Sheldon.

(There was a dog when Leonard went downstairs, and its barking drew Sheldon's attention.)

Sheldon: Is that a dog?

Leonard: Yes.

Sheldon: In the lab?

Leonard: Yes, they're training dogs to operate the **centrifuge**[7], for when they need dogs to… operate the centrifuge for blind scientists. I have to go.

就呈指数曲线上升。而且我咳痰频率是惊人的。

莱纳德：没开玩笑吧？

谢尔顿：没有，不仅如此，痰的颜色已经从透明变成浑浊的绿色了。

莱纳德：好吧，多休息、多喝液体。

谢尔顿：不然，我还能喝什么？气体？固体？还是离子化的电解质？

莱纳德：想喝什么随便你。

谢尔顿：我想喝汤。

莱纳德：那就煲汤啊。

谢尔顿：家里没汤。

莱纳德：我在工作，谢尔顿。

（莱纳德下楼正遇到一只狗，电话里传来的狗叫声引起了谢尔顿的注意。）

谢尔顿：那是狗叫吗？

莱纳德：是的。

谢尔顿：在实验室里？

莱纳德：是的，他们在训练狗操作离心机，以备需要时让狗去……为盲人科学家操作离心机。我得挂了。

Scene 2: Leonard told Howard and Rajeshesh that Sheldon was ill, then the three friends decided to go to cinema to watch all-night movies in order to avoid Sheldon's disturbance. Without finding his three friends, Sheldon had to come to the restaurant where Penny worked.

莱纳德立刻告诉霍华德和拉杰谢尔顿得病的消息，三人决定溜到影院去看通宵电影来躲过谢尔顿患病的艰难时刻。找不到他们三人的谢尔顿只好来到了佩妮工作的餐馆。

Waitress:	Homeless, crazy guy at table 18.	同事：	有个疯子加流浪汉在 18 号桌。
Penny:	No, just crazy.	佩妮：	不，他只是个疯子。

(Sheldon was coughing continuously, blowing his nose and spitting...)

（一连串擤鼻子、吐痰等怪异行为……）

Penny:	Sheldon, what are you doing here?	佩妮：	谢尔顿，你在这里做什么?
Sheldon:	I'm sick, thank you very much.	谢尔顿：	我病了，这还得感谢你。
Penny:	How could you have gotten it from me? I'm not sick.	佩妮：	你怎么这么肯定是我传染给你的呢，我没病。
Sheldon:	You're a **carrier**[8]. All these people here are **doomed**[9]. You're doomed!!!	谢尔顿：	你是带菌者，这里所有的人都在劫难逃了。你们在劫难逃了!
Penny:	Sheldon, what do you want?	佩妮：	谢尔顿，你想要什么?
Sheldon:	I want soup.	谢尔顿：	我想喝汤。
Penny:	Why didn't you...Why didn't you just have soup at home?	佩妮：	为什么你不……那你为什么不在家弄汤喝?
Sheldon:	Penny, I have an IQ of 187, don't you imagine that if there were a way for me to have had soup at home, I would have thought of it?	谢尔顿：	佩妮，我的智商高达 187，你不想想，如果我在家有办法喝汤的话，我会来这里么?
Penny:	You can have soup delivered.	佩妮：	你可以叫外卖啊。
Sheldon:	I didn't think of that. Clearly, febrile **delirium**[10] is *setting in*[3]. Please bring me some soup while I still understand what a spoon is for.	谢尔顿：	我没想到。很明显，我已经处于发烧后的精神错乱状态了。趁我还知道汤匙是做什么用的，赶紧给我上汤吧。

> **Scene 3:** Penny had to ask for leave to send Sheldon home.
>
> 佩妮只好请假送生病的谢尔顿回家。

Sheldon:	Thanks for bringing me home.	谢尔顿：	谢谢你带我回家。
Penny:	It's OK. I didn't really need to work today. It's not like I have rent or car payments or anything...	佩妮：	没事，我今天也不是很需要上班。反正我也没有租金、车，或其他什么费用要付……
Sheldon:	Good, good.	谢尔顿：	那就好，那就好。

注释
5. **ionized** ['aɪənaɪzd] *adj.* 离子化的	8. **carrier** ['kærɪə] *n.* 带菌者
6. **plasma** ['plæzmə] *n.* 电解质	9. **doom** [du:m] *v.* 注定；判决；使失败
7. **centrifuge** ['sentrɪfju:dʒ] *n.* 离心机	10. **febrile delirium** 发热引起的谵妄

Penny:	OK, if you feel better.	佩妮：	好吧，祝你早日康复。

Penny: OK, if you feel better.
Sheldon: Wait! Where are you going?
Penny: Home, to write some bad **checks**[11].
Sheldon: You're going to leave me?
Penny: Sheldon, you are a grown man. Haven't you ever been sick before?
Sheldon: Of course, but not by myself.

Penny: Really? Never?
Sheldon: Well, once, when I was 15, spending the summer at the Heidellberg Institute in Germany.
Penny: Studying abroad?
Sheldon: No, visiting **professor**[12]. Anyway, the local cuisine was a little more sausage-based than I was used to, and the result was an internal **blitzkrieg**[13], with my lower **intestine**[14] playing the part of Czechoslivakia[1].
Penny: And there was no one there to take care of you?
Sheldon: My mom had to fly back to Texas to help my dad, because the house had slipped off the cinder blocks again.
Penny: Again?
Sheldon: It was **tornado**[15] season, and it was an aluminum **house**[16]. Anyway, the housekeeper in the **faculty**[17] residence didn't speak any English, when I finally managed to convince her I was sick, she said, "mochtest du eine darmspfilung?"
Penny: What does that mean?
Sheldon: Based on what happened next, I assume it means "would you like an **enema**[18]?"
Penny: Okay, sweetie.

佩妮： 好吧，祝你早日康复。
谢尔顿： 等等，你要去哪儿？
佩妮： 回家，去写些空头支票。
谢尔顿： 你就这样扔下我不管？
佩妮： 谢尔顿，你已经长大了，难道你之前没生过病吗？
谢尔顿： 当然生过病，但从没只有我一个人照顾自己。
佩妮： 真的？从来没有？
谢尔顿： 有一次，我15岁，暑假的时候在德国的海德尔堡理工大学。
佩妮： 留学？
谢尔顿： 不，客座教授。总之，当地的烹饪方法用的香肠比我习惯的多了一些，其结果就是我肚子里上演了陆军联合闪电战，我的大肠扮演的是捷克斯洛伐克。
佩妮： 当时那里没人照顾你吗？
谢尔顿： 我妈不得不飞回德克萨斯去给我爸帮忙，因为房子的煤渣砖又塌方了。
佩妮： 又？
谢尔顿： 当时是飓风季节，那是个临时房子。当时系里的公寓管家不会讲英语，当我终于让她相信我病了的时候，她说了一堆德语。
佩妮： 什么意思？
谢尔顿： 根据后来发生的事，我认为意思是你想要灌肠吗？
佩妮： 好吧，亲爱的。

注释
11. **bad checks** 会被银行拒付的支票，空头支票
12. **visiting professor** 客座教授
13. **blitzkrieg** ['bli:tskri:g] n. 闪电战，闪击战，（尤指）猛烈的空袭
14. **lower intestine** 大肠
15. **tornado** [tɔːˈneɪdəʊ] n. 龙卷风
16. **aluminum house** 指临时性的房子；**aluminum** 铝
17. **faculty** ['fæklti] n.（指学的）专科，系
18. **enema** ['enəmə] n. 灌肠

📖 文化背景

1. Czechoslivakia 捷克斯洛伐克

二战中遭受德军闪电战的攻击，全线溃败。

📷 常用表达

1. at an alarming rate 以惊人的速度

例：As the figures show, we appear to be falling out of love with pubs at an alarming rate.

如统计显示，我们正以惊人的速度，失去对酒吧的兴趣。

2. No kidding? 没开玩笑吧?

例：I'm not kidding; I'm serious.

我没开玩笑，我是认真的。

3. set in 到来，开始

例：The rainy season has set in.

雨季已经开始了。

Passage 2

剧情介绍：

（选自第 2 季第 4 集）一般人在取得个人成就之后会洋洋得意、四处炫耀，而别人获得成功并在自己面前炫耀的时候会产生难以克制的嫉妒。科学家也有普通人的一面！这回轮到拉杰了，由于发现太阳系的新星，拉杰获得人物杂志的提名。开始，朋友为他祝贺，但慢慢地，味道有些变了……

Scene 1: In the apartment, Lenard, Howard, and Penny were eating fast food taken from some Chinese restaurant.

公寓，莱纳德、霍华德、佩妮在吃从中餐馆叫来的外卖。

Lenard: Let's see, Rajesh was the Kung Pao Chicken.

莱纳德：让我们看看，拉杰是宫爆鸡丁。

Penny: I'm the **dumplings**[1].

佩妮：我的是饺子。

Howard: Yes, you are.

霍华德：没错。

Penny: **Creepy**[2], Howard.

佩妮：太恶心了，霍华德。

Howard: Creepy good or creepy bad?

霍华德：可爱的恶心还是纯粹的恶心？

Lenard: Who was the **shrimp**[3] with lobster **sauce**[4]?

莱纳德：谁点的鲜虾加龙虾酱？

Howard: That would be me. Come to papa, you **unkosher**[5] delight. I'm not necessarily talking to the food.

霍华德：那是我的。朝这里看，你这个脏脏的小美味。我这话可不光是对着食物说哦。

Penny: Sit over there.

佩妮：坐一边去。

(Sheldon comes in and draws out a sheet of baby wipe.)

（谢尔顿过来，从桌上的盒子里抽出一张纸巾。）

Sheldon: Sit over there. Baby wipe?

谢尔顿：坐一边去。你要婴儿纸巾？

Penny: Why do you have...?

佩妮：你为什么用……？

(Everybody tried to stop her, "Stop ! Stop asking him...")

（一众人等都拦着说：别，别问！）

Sheldon: I'll tell you why. I had to **sanitize**[6] my hands, because the university replaced the paper **towels**[7] in the rest rooms with hot air blowers.

谢尔顿：我来告诉你为什么。我必须消毒我的手，因为大学把厕所里擦手的纸巾换成了吹风机。

Penny: I thought the blowers were more sanitary.

Sheldon: Hot air blowers are **incubators**[8] and **spewers**[9] of **bacteria**[10] and **pestilence**[11]. Frankly, it un-kosherd be more **hygienic**[12] If they just had a **plague-infested**[13] **gibbon**[14] **sneeze**[15] my hands dry.

(Rajesh rushed in excitedly, wanting to announce a piece of good news. But he was tongue-tied at the sight of Penny…)

Rajesh: Hey, guys, I just got the most *amazing*[1] news…

Penny: Gosh, Rajesh, do you think you'll ever be able to talk in front of me without being drunk? Okay, well, I'll just, um, go eat by myself.

Lenard: Penny, you don't have to do that.

Penny: Oh, it's okay, between him not talking, him talking and him… I'm better off alone. Good-bye, you poor, strange little man.

Rajesh: She's so **considerate**[16].

Howard: So what's your news?

Rajesh: Remember that little **planetary**[17] object I **spotted**[18] beyond the **Kuiper Belt**[19]?

Lenard: Oh, yeah, 2008-NQSUB-17.

Rajesh: Or as I call it, planet Bollywood[1]. Anyway, because of my discovery, People magazine is naming me one of their 30 under 30 to watch.

H. and L.: Rajesh… congratulations. That's incredible.

佩妮： 我怎么感觉吹风机更卫生。

谢尔顿： 吹风机可以说是细菌和瘟疫的发源地。老实说，用吹风机的话，还不如让一只得了瘟疫的长臂猿打喷嚏打到我手上来得卫生呢。

（拉杰兴奋地冲了进来，要宣布一个好消息，结果一看见佩妮，马上张口结舌说不下去了……）

拉杰： 伙计们，我有一个天大的好消息……

佩妮： 天哪，拉杰，你如果不喝醉的话，是不是永远都不能在我面前说话？好吧，那我就自己一个人去吃了。

莱纳德： 佩妮，你不需要这样的。

佩妮： 没事，考虑到他不说话，他说的话，还有他……我最好还是离开吧。再见，你这个可怜的怪人。

拉杰： 她太贴心了。

霍华德： 你有什么大新闻？

拉杰： 还记得那个我定位的比凯伯带天体更远的那颗行星吗？

莱纳德： 哦，对，2008-NQSUB-17。

拉杰： 或者用我的叫法，宝莱坞星。总之，由于我的发现，《人物》杂志把我提名为三十岁以下的三十大焦点人物之一了。

霍和莱： 拉杰……祝贺，太棒了。

注释
1. dumpling ['dʌmplɪŋ] n. 饺子
2. creepy ['kriːpɪ] adj. <美俚> 恐怖的，恶心的
3. shrimp [ʃrɪmp] n. 虾
4. lobster sauce 虾酱，豆豉
   lobster ['lɒbstə] n. 龙虾 sauce [sɔːs] n. 调味汁
5. un-kosher 不符合犹太教规的食物
6. sanitize ['sænɪtaɪz] vt. 给……消毒
7. towel ['taʊəl] n. 纸巾
8. incubator ['ɪnkjuːbeɪtə] n. 培养器
9. spewer ['spjuːə] n. 喷出，涌出
10. bacteria [bæktɪərɪə] n. 细菌
11. pestilence ['pestɪləns] n. 瘟疫
12. hygienic [haɪ'dʒiːnɪk] adj. 干净的，卫生的
13. plague-infested 得瘟疫的
14. gibbon ['gɪbən] n. 长臂猿
15. sneeze [sniːz] v. 打喷嚏
16. considerate [kən'sɪdərɪt] adj. 体贴的
17. planetary ['plænɪtərɪ] adj. 行星的
18. spot [spɒt] v. 认出，定位
19. Kuiper Belt 凯伯带（数十亿颗在海王星轨道之外绕行的小型冰体构成的碟形带）

Sheldon: Excuse me, 30 what under 30 what to watch what?

Rajesh: 30 visionaries under 30 years of age to watch as they challenge the preconceptions of their fields.

Sheldon: If I had a million guesses, I never would have gotten that.

Rajesh: It's pretty cool. They've got me in with a guy who's doing something about hunger in Indonesia, and a **psychotherapist**[20] who's using **dolphins**[21] to **rehabilitate**[22] prisoners, and Ellen Page[2], star of the charming independent film, Juno.

Howard: Do I get an honorable mention for designing the telescope camera mounting bracket you used?

Rajesh: Sorry, it's not part of my heartwarming and personal **narrative**[23] in which a humble boy from New **Delhi**[24] overcame poverty and prejudice and journeyed to America to reach for the stars.

Howard: Poverty? Your father's a **gynecologist**[25]. He drives a **Bentley**[26].

Rajesh: It's a **lease**[27].

Sheldon: I'm confused. Was there some sort of **peer review**[28] committee to determine which scientists would be included?

Rajesh: Peer review? It's _People_[3] magazine. People picked me.

Sheldon: What people?

Rajesh: The people from _People_.

Sheldon: Yeah, but exactly who are these people? What are their **credentials**[29]? How are they qualified? What makes **accidentally**[30] noticing a hunk of rock that's been **traipsing**[31] around the solar **system**[32] for billions of years more noteworthy than any other scientific accomplishment made by someone under 30?

谢尔顿： 不好意思，三十岁以下的什么三十大人物的什么焦点？

拉杰： 三十岁以下的三十名值得关注的梦想家，因为他们对自己领域的一些传统臆断提出了挑战。

谢尔顿： 让我猜百万次我都不会想到是这样。

拉杰： 酷极了。他们让我和一个在研究印度尼西亚饥荒问题的人一起入选，还有一位精神治疗师，他在用海豚来感化囚犯，还有爱伦·佩姬，她是那部独立电影《朱诺》里的明星。

霍华德： 你会不会在采访中提到你用的那个望远摄像机的固定架是我设计的？

拉杰： 不好意思，这和我所要叙述的温馨故事无关，在我的故事里，我是一个从新德里来的傻男孩，克服了贫困和歧视，不远万里来到美国寻找星星。

霍华德： 贫困？你老爸是个妇科医生。他开的是宾利。

拉杰： 那是租的。

谢尔顿： 我有点搞不懂。是不是由什么行业审查委员会来决定选哪些人？

拉杰： 行业审查？这是《人物》杂志。人们选择了我。

谢尔顿： 什么人？

拉杰： 《人物》里的那些人啊。

谢尔顿： 确切地说，这些到底是什么人？他们有什么凭据吗？为什么他们有资格评选？偶然发现了一块在太阳系里慢悠悠地飘了几十亿年的大石头为什么就比其他三十岁以下科学家的成就更加杰出呢？

Rajesh: Boy, I'll bet Ellen Page's friends aren't giving her this kind of **crap**[33].

(Rajesh left angrily.)

拉杰: 天哪，我敢打赌爱伦·佩姬的朋友一定不会拿这样的废话损她的。

（拉杰愤而离开。）

Scene 2: Lenard, Howard and Sheldon came to Rajesh's office and said sorry for their bad behavior last night. Just then, Dr. Gablehauser came in.

莱纳德、霍华德拉上谢尔顿来到拉杰的办公室，为昨晚的恶劣表现道歉，正在这时，系主任盖博豪斯博士进来了。

Dr.: Dr. Koothrappali, Dr. Hofstader, Dr. Cooper, Mr. Wolowitz.

博士: 你们好，孩子们，库萨帕里博士、霍夫斯塔特博士、库珀博士、沃尔维茨先生。

Everyone: Dr. Gablehauser.

众人: 盖博豪斯博士。

Dr.: Boys, I've got a question for you. Who in this room discovered a star?

博士: 孩子们，我有个问题要问你们。这个房间里，谁发现了颗星星？

Rajesh: Actually, 2008-NQSUB-17 is a planetary body.

拉杰: 事实上，2008-NQSUB-17 只是颗行星。

Dr.: I'm not talking about you, I'm talking about me. You, my **exotic**[34] young friend, are my star.

博士: 我不是在说你，我是说我呢。你，我来自异国他乡的青年朋友，就是我的明星。

Sheldon: But you didn't discover him. You **merely**[35] noticed he was here, much like he did with 2008-NQSUB-17.

谢尔顿: 但他不是你发掘出来的。你以前都不会留意到他，就跟他也没怎么留意过 2008-NQSUB-17 一样。

Leonard: Sheldon...

莱纳德: 谢尔顿……

注释

20. **psychotherapist** [ˌsaɪkəʊ'θerəpɪst] *n.* 精神治疗医师

21. **dolphin** ['dɒlfɪn] *n.* 海豚

22. **rehabilitate** [ˌriːə'bɪlɪteɪt] *v.* 使恢复正常

23. **narrative** ['nærətɪv] *n.* 故事

24. **New Delhi** 新德里（印度首都）

25. **gynecologist** [ˌdʒaɪnɪ'kɒlədʒɪst] *n.* 妇科医生

26. **Bentley** 宾利，英国顶级豪华轿车品牌

27. **lease** [liːs] *n.* 租赁物

28. **peer review** 同行评审

29. **credential** [krɪ'denʃl] *n.* 凭据

30. **accidentally** [ˌæksɪ'dentlɪ] *adv.* 偶然地

31. **traipse** [treɪps] *v.* 在……游荡

32. **solar system** 太阳系

33. **crap** [kræp] *n.* 垃圾，废话

34. **exotic** [ɪg'zɒːtɪk] *adj.* 异国的

35. **merely** ['mɪəlɪ] *adv.* 几乎不

Sheldon:	Oh, sorry.	谢尔顿：	不好意思。
Dr.:	Boy, we've got to get you into a better office. Something more suited to your **status**[36].	博士：	孩子，我们真该给你换个好点的办公室。这才能能配得上你的名气。
Rajesh:	Really, you don't have to go to any trouble.	拉杰：	真的不用麻烦了。
Dr.:	How about if I put you in Von Gerlich's old office?	博士：	我把你安排到凡·格里奇以前的办公室怎么样？
Rajesh:	*I'd rather*[2] have Fishbein's. It's bigger.	拉杰：	我更喜欢菲什拜因的，它更宽敞。
Howard:	Wait a minute, I called dibs on Fishbein's office the day he started showing up at work in his bathrobe.	霍华德：	等等，自打菲什拜因穿浴袍出现在办公室那天，我就申请他的办公室了。
Sheldon:	He gets a new office; I can't even get paper towels in the men's room?	谢尔顿：	能给他换办公室，就不能在男厕所放点擦手巾？
Leonard:	Sheldon...	莱纳德：	谢尔顿……
Sheldon:	Damn, this is hard.	谢尔顿：	该死，真难为我了。
Dr.:	Let me ask you something. What do you think the business of this place is?	博士：	让我问问你们，你们觉得咱们的工作为的是什么？
Leonard:	Science?	莱纳德：	科学？
Dr.:	Money.	博士：	是钱。
Howard:	Told you.	霍华德：	告诉过你了。
Dr.:	And this boy's picture in *People* magazine is gonna raise us a pile of money taller than... Well, taller than you.	博士：	这孩子的照片上了《人物》周刊，能给我们带来多少钱！（拍着霍华德的脑袋）堆起来比你高。
Howard:	I have a master's **degree**[37].	霍华德：	我有硕士文凭的。
Dr.:	Who doesn't?	博士：	谁没有啊？

> **Scene 3:** After dinner, Rajesh showed off his glory to his friends and invited them to attend his reception, without noticing they were displeased. Anyway, thanks to alcohol, Rajesh could speak in front of Penny this time.
>
> 晚饭后，拉杰在跟几个朋友炫耀他的风光，并邀请朋友们周末出席为他举行的招待会，丝毫没察觉到朋友们的不爽。也许是喝酒了的缘故，这回他可以在佩妮面前说话了……

Rajesh:	So, Saturday night, can I *count on*[2] my **posse**[38]?	拉杰:	那就周六晚上了，就这么说定了。
Howard:	Gee, I'd love to, Rajesh, but I can't make it.	霍华德:	我很乐意去，拉杰，但我去不了。
Rajesh:	Oh, ok, Leonard?	拉杰:	好的，莱纳德，你呢？
Leonard:	No, I could… no.	莱纳德:	不行，我要……不行。
Rajesh:	Sheldon?	拉杰:	谢尔顿，你呢？
Sheldon:	I can make it. But I won't.	谢尔顿:	我能去，但我不想去。
Penny:	What are you guys talking about?	佩妮:	你们在说什么？
Rajesh:	There's a reception for my magazine article on Saturday.	拉杰:	周六有场为我的杂志文章举行的招待会。
Penny:	And you guys aren't going? I can't believe you. Rajesh is celebrating a **tremendous**[39] **accomplishment**[40]. And you're not even going to be there to support him?	佩妮:	你们这些家伙不准备去？真不敢相信。拉杰要庆祝他的惊人成就，你们甚至都不去支持他？
Sheldon:	A tremendous accomplishment would be if the planetary body he discovered were **plummeting**[41] toward earth and he **exploded**[42] it with his mind.	谢尔顿:	惊人成就应该是如果他发现一个行星体正急速撞向地球，他用意念摧毁了它。
Howard:	*That would be cool*[3]. I'd go to that reception.	霍华德:	那太酷了。那个招待会我得去。
Penny:	Come on, this is huge. Rajesh is gonna be in *People* magazine, and he didn't even have to knock up one of the Spears' sisters.	佩妮:	拜托，这很重大。拉杰上了《人物》杂志，他甚至不用搞大一个明星妹妹的肚子。
Rajesh:	Would you like to go with me?	拉杰:	你愿意和我一起去吗？
Penny:	Of course I would. I would be honored.	佩妮:	我当然愿意。我很荣幸。
Rajesh:	Really? Cool!	拉杰:	真的，太好了。
Penny:	*Shame on you guys*[4].	佩妮:	真替你们脸红！

注释 **36. status** ['steɪtəs] *n.* 地位	**40. accomplishment** [ə'kɒmplɪʃmənt] *n.* 成就
37. master's degree 硕士文凭	**41. plummet** ['plʌmɪt] *vi.* 骤然落下
38. posse ['pɒsɪ] *n.* 可能性	**42. explode** [ɪk'spləʊd] *vt.* 使爆炸
39. tremendous [trɪ'mendəs] *adj.* 巨大的	

文化背景

1. Bollywood 宝莱坞

宝莱坞是位于印度孟买的广受欢迎的电影工业基地的别名。印度人将"好莱坞"（Hollywood）打头的字母"H"换成了本国电影之都孟买（Bombay）的首字母"B"，把"好莱坞"变成了"宝莱坞"（Bollywood）。

2. Ellen Page 爱伦·佩姬

1987年出生的爱伦·佩姬在2007年制作的影片《朱诺》中担任主演，并因此红遍美国，被封为"国民偶像"。其实，早在《朱诺》之前，爱伦·佩姬已经是公认的演技派明日之星。2006年，在《水果硬糖》中的表演让整个好莱坞都对她称赞有加。而《朱诺》更为她获得了"金球奖喜剧类最佳女演员"的提名。一位好莱坞的监制评价道："爱伦·佩姬是2007年带给我们的最大惊喜。"在2010年的影片《盗梦空间》中，她出演了筑梦师阿里阿德涅（Ariadne）。

3. *People* 《人物》

自从1974年创刊以来，《人物》杂志已经成为美国文化的一部分。每个星期，《人物》都会以图文并茂的方式播报名人和普通人的故事。《人物》杂志最初的创办宗旨就是讲述平凡人的不平凡故事，但除了播报普通人，也播报明星，每期杂志的封面人物都是读者希望了解更多的人。

常用表达

1. amazing 令人吃惊的，不可思议的

例：Amazing!That's a tremendous accomplishment.

太神奇了！那可是一个巨大的成就!

2. Can I count on my posse? 用于征求朋友们的意见，表示"怎么样啊，大伙儿？"的意思。

例：Sunday night,can I count on my posse?

那就本周日晚上，大伙儿说如何?

3. That would be cool. 那可太酷了。

例：That would be cool if you can climb to the top of the mountain.

如果你能爬到山顶，那可就太酷了。

4. Shame on you. 不要脸！无耻!

例：She shouted "Shame on you" and drove away.

她大喊了一声"你真不要脸"，然后就驾车离开了。

Passage 3

剧情介绍：

（选自第 3 季第 14 集）到底是天才，谢尔顿连思考问题时的姿势都与普通人不同。先是背对黑板站着，频频快速回头，声称是想利用瞬时边缘图像激发上丘脑；然后在吃饭的时候用豆子摆成需要的形状，后来嫌豆子太小，干脆在屋子里用小球做实物模拟，害得别人一进屋就摔跤；不眠不休熬了三四天，甚至跑去佩妮工作的餐馆义务打工，借以开发思路。一句话，科学家也不是那么好当的啊！

Scene 1: In the early morning, Sheldon was pondering a difficult problem. He stood in front of a white board on which there were formulas, turning his head about frequently. Penny stepped in and looked at him confusedly.

清晨，谢尔顿在研究时遇到了一个难题，为此苦苦思索。不过他采取了一种非常特别的方式，他背对着黑板站着，频频快速回头，佩妮走出来，满腹狐疑地看着他。

Penny:	What are you doing?	佩妮：	你干什么呢？
Sheldon:	I'm attempting to view my work as a **fleeting peripheral image**[1] *so as to*[1] engage the **superior the colliculus of my brain**[2].	谢尔顿：	我在尝试以瞬时边缘图像来审视我的成果以激活我的上丘脑。
Penny:	Interesting. I usually just have coffee. You've been *up all night*[2].	佩妮：	真有趣。我一般喝点咖啡就行啦。你一夜没睡吗？
Sheldon:	Is it morning? Then I've been up all night.	谢尔顿：	早上了吗？那我就是彻夜未眠。
Penny:	And you're **stuck**[3]?	佩妮：	那你卡壳了？
Sheldon:	Why else would a person try to engage their superior colliculus?	谢尔顿：	要不然怎么会有人想要激活上丘脑。
Penny:	Oh, sorry, sweeties, I can't help you till I've had my coffee.	佩妮：	噢，抱歉，亲爱的，我喝完咖啡之前可帮不了你。
Lenard:	Penny, I told you if you don't put him in his crate at night, he just runs around the apartment.	莱纳德：	佩妮，我早就告诉过你，你要不把他关到他房间里，他会在公寓里上蹿下跳一整夜。

注释
1. fleeting peripheral image 瞬时边缘图像
2. superior the colliculus of brain 上丘脑
3. stuck [stʌk] *adj.* 卡住的、阻塞的

Penny: What is he doing now?

Lenard: Hmm, he's either **isolating**[4] the terms of his formula and examining them **individually**[5], or looking for the **alligator**[6] that swallowed his hand after Peter Pan cut it off.

Sheldon: Captain Hook's[1] hand was eaten by a crocodile, not an alligator. If you're going to mock me, at least get your facts straight.

Lenard: Aye, aye. Captain.

佩妮： 他这又是在做什么？

莱纳德： 嗯，他要么是在给他的公式做因式分解并单独检验，要么就是在寻找那只被彼得潘削掉之后又让短吻鳄吞噬的手。

谢尔顿： 虎克船长的手是被鳄鱼吃掉的，不是短吻鳄。要是你想损我，至少把事实先弄清楚。

莱纳德： 遵命，遵命，船长。

Scene 2: Lenard, Howard and Sheldon were sitting at the table in university dining hall. Actually, the other two were enjoying their lunch, while Sheldon was still thinking over his problem, having no appetite, dinner plate pushed aside…

莱纳德、霍华德和谢尔顿坐在大学的餐厅里，或者说那两个人在吃饭，谢尔顿仍然纠结他的难题，饭菜被推到了一边，面前铺满了书籍和笔记，一副食不甘味的样子，嘴里还念念有词……

Sheldon: Electrons move through **graphene**[7], act as if they have no mass…

Howard: How long has he been stuck?

Lenard: **Intellectually**[8] about 30 hours. **Emotionally**[9] about 29 years.

Sheldon: Unit cell contains two carbon **atoms**[10]… Interior **angle**[11] of **hexagon**[12] is 120 degrees.

Howard: Have you tried **rebooting**[13] him?

Lenard: No, I think it's a **firmware**[14] problem.

(Rajesh came in when they were teasing…)

Rajesh: Hey, it's Disco Night at the Moonlight Roller **Rink**[15] in Glendale tonight. Who's up for getting down?

谢尔顿： 当电子穿越石墨烯时，没有显示出质量反应……

霍华德： 他这样卡壳有多久了？

莱纳德： 这一次有 30 个小时。就感觉上而言，29 年他一直这样。

谢尔顿： 单元晶格上有两个碳原子……六边形内角为 120 度。

霍华德： 你有没有试过重启他一下？

莱纳德： 没，我觉得是硬件出了问题。

（两人一起坏笑，这时拉杰来了……）

拉杰： 嗨，格兰岱尔市的月光旱冰场今晚举行迪斯科之夜。谁要一起去啊？

Howard:	That's perfect. Bernadette's been **hocking**[16] me to take her roller skating.	霍华德:	太棒了。伯纳黛特老缠着要我带她去滑冰呢。
Lenard:	I think Penny likes to skate. The four of us could double.	莱纳德:	我觉得佩妮也喜欢滑冰。我们四个可以两两成对了。
Howard:	*What could be better?*[3] We're in.	霍华德:	再好不过了,我们去。
Rajesh:	Great. It's not like I brought it up because I wanted to go.	拉杰:	好啊。好像不是因为我想去才提出来的。
Howard:	You can come with us.	霍华德:	你可以一起来的。
Rajesh:	No, it's okay. I don't have to go. I'm happy just to **guide**[17] you and your ladies to suitable **entertainment**[18] choices. I'm a walking brown yelp.com.	拉杰:	不了,没关系。我没必要去。我很高兴给你们和你们的女士提了合适的娱乐建议。我就是个活生生的印度大众点评网。
Sheldon:	**Structure**[19], constant structure. One atom…	谢尔顿:	结构,常态结构。一个原子……
Howard:	Boy, he's really gone, isn't he?	霍华德:	伙计,他真的着魔了,对吧?
Lenard:	Yeah, this morning he used a stick of butter as the **deodorant**[20].	莱纳德:	是啊,早上他还拿黄油当香水来着。
Howard:	I thought I smelled **popcorn**[21].	霍华德:	我就说怎么闻到股爆米花味儿。
Sheldon:	**Pattern**[22] is the same as **fermions**[23] travels on the pathways, **Hexagonal**[24]…It's always hexagonal…	谢尔顿:	模式与费米子在轨道上的轨迹是完全一样的,是六边形的……一直是六边形的……
Lenard:	I haven't seen him this stuck since he tried to figure out the third *Matrix* movie.	莱纳德:	自从那次他尝试理清《黑客帝国3》以来,我还没见他这么卡壳过。
(Without noticing Lenard and Howard's mocking, Sheldon grabbed lima beans in Rajesh's dinner plate…)		(思考中的谢尔顿根本没听见莱纳德和霍华德的嘲讽,突然,谢尔顿一把抓起拉杰盘子里的豆子……)
Rajesh:	Hey, those are my **lima beans**[25]!	拉杰:	嘿,这是我的青豆!
Sheldon:	Not lima beans, carbon atoms.	谢尔顿:	不是豆子,是碳原子。
Rajesh:	But if I don't eat my lima beans, I can't have my cookie.	拉杰:	但是如果我不吃青豆,我就不能吃曲奇了。

注释

4. **isolate** ['aɪsəleɪt] *v.* (因式)分解
5. **individually** [ˌɪndɪ'vɪdʒuəlɪ] *adv.* 单独地;逐个地;分别地
6. **alligator** ['ælɪɡeɪtə] *n.* 短吻鳄
7. **graphene** ['ɡræfiːn] *n.* 单层石墨
8. **intellectually** [ˌɪntə'lektʃuəlɪ] *adv.* 真正意义上
9. **emotionally** [ɪ'məʊʃənlɪ] *adv.* 感觉上地
10. **carbon atom** 碳原子
11. **interior angle** 内角
12. **hexagon** ['heksəɡən] *n.* 六边形
13. **reboot** [ˌriː'buːt] *v.* 重新启动
14. **firmware** ['fɜːmweə(r)] *n.* 固件

15. **rink** [rɪŋk] *n.* 溜冰场
16. **hock** [hɒk] *v.* 纠缠
17. **guide** [ɡaɪd] *v.* 引导
18. **entertainment** [entə'teɪnmənt] *n.* 娱乐,消遣
19. **structure** ['strʌktʃə(r)] *n.* 结构
20. **deodorant** [diː'əʊdərənt] *n.* 有气味的东西,指香体剂
21. **popcorn** ['pɒpkɔːn] *n.* 爆米花
22. **pattern** ['pætn] *n.* 模式
23. **fermion** ['fɜːmɪən] *n.* 费米子(一种微观粒子)
24. **hexagonal** [heks'æɡənl] *n.* 六边形的
25. **lima bean** 青豆

Lenard: Here, you want my **peas**[26]?	莱纳德： 这儿，你想要我的豌豆吗？
Sheldon: The peas…perfect. They can be **electrons**[27].	谢尔顿： 豌豆……好极了。它们可以拿来做电子。
Howard: Want my corn?	霍华德： 想要我的玉米吗？
Sheldon: Don't be **ridiculous**[28]. What would I do with corn?	谢尔顿： 别傻了。我拿玉米做什么呢？
Lenard: So roller skating…should we all have a bite to eat first?	莱纳德： 那么滑冰的那件事……我们先在哪儿吃饭呢？
Howard: Good. P.F. Chang's? My mom has **coupons**[29].	霍华德： 好啊。那家中国餐馆如何？我妈有优惠券。
Lenard: Great. Your mom's not coming, right?	莱纳德： 好。你妈不会来吧？
Howard: Not this time, I promise.	霍华德： 这次不会了，我保证。
Rajesh: Okay, just to be clear, roller skating was my idea, and I'm very unhappy that you turned it into a double date. And I hope you both fall on your **asses**[30], and break your **coccyxes**[31].	拉杰： 好吧，先把话说清楚了，滑旱冰是我的主意，我很不高兴你们把这搞成双双约会，我巴不得你们都摔屁股墩，弄断尾椎。
Sheldon: The **plural**[32] of coccyx is coccyges.	谢尔顿： 尾椎的复数应该是 coccyges。
Rajesh: Screw you. Give me back my lima beans.	拉杰： 去你的。还我的青豆来。

Scene 3: Penny was working at the restaurant when Sheldon stepped out from the kitchen, aprons in his waist.

佩妮在餐馆里工作，谢尔顿突然系着围裙从后厨里走出来。

Sheldon: Behind you.	谢尔顿： 小心你后面。
Penny: Sheldon, what *the hell*[4] are you doing?	佩妮： 谢尔顿，见鬼，你在这干什么？
Sheldon: I'm trying to get these tables cleared. We're **slammed**[33].	谢尔顿： 正准备清理这些桌子。我们差点撞上。
Penny: No, wait, wait, no, wait. Wh… What are you doing here?	佩妮： 不，等等，等等，你……你在这干什么？
Sheldon: A reasonable question. I asked myself, what	谢尔顿： 这个问题很合理。我问自己，我

is the most **mind-numbing**[34], **pedestrian**[35] job **conceivable**[36], and three answers came to mind. That toll **booth**[37] attendant, and Apple Store Genius, and what Penny does. Now…since I don't like touching other people's coins, and I refuse to **contribute to**[38] the **devaluation**[39] of the word "genius", here I am.

Penny: You just, you just walked in and they hired you, just like that?

Sheldon: Oh, heavens, no. Since I don't need to be paid, I didn't need to be hired. I simply came in, picked up a **tray**[40], and started "working for the man." Let me get that plate out of your way.

Penny: Sheldon, this is ridiculous.

Sheldon: Is it? Just moment ago, I had a minor **epiphany**[41] regarding the **polymer**[42] degration phenomenon while scraping **congealed**[43] **nachos**[44] off a plate. Bernadette, table 10 wants their check.

Bernadette: Thanks, Sheldon.

Penny: Sheldon, wait, this isn't even what I do. I'm a waitress, not a **busboy**[45].

Sheldon: You're right. That is more **menial**[46].

(Sheldon gave the tray to Penny and walked forward to take the guests' order, leaving Penny stiffening there…)

能想到的最不需要用脑子、最没想象力的工作是什么，我脑海中浮现了三个答案：分别是收费站收费人员，在苹果专卖店工作的天才，还有佩妮的工作。现在呢……因为我不喜欢碰别人手里的钱，我也不想让"天才"这词加速贬值，所以我选了这儿。

佩妮： 难道你，你就这么走进来，就被录用了？就这么简单？

谢尔顿： 哦，当然不是。因为我不需要他们付工资，自然也不用被录用了。我仅仅是直接走进来，拿了个托盘，就开始"服务大众"了。我来收拾这个盘子。

佩妮： 谢尔顿，这太荒谬了。

谢尔顿： 真的？就刚才，当我在清理盘子上的玉米片的时候，我突然就想通了高聚物降解现象。伯纳黛特，10 号桌买单。

伯纳黛特： 谢谢，谢尔顿。

佩妮： 谢尔顿，等等，那压根就不是我的工作呀。我是服务生，不是勤杂工。

谢尔顿： 哦，对。你的工作更低等。

（谢尔顿把手里的托盘推给佩妮，直接走上前去为客人点餐，佩妮在一旁石化了……）

注释		
26. pea [piː] n. 豌豆		37. toll booth 过路收费亭
27. electron [ɪˈlektrɒn] n. 电子		38. contribute to 促成
28. ridiculous [rɪˈdɪkjələs] adj. 可笑的，荒谬的		39. devaluation [ˌdiːvæljʊˈeɪʃn] n. 货币贬值
29. coupons [ˈkuːpɒn] n. 优惠券		40. tray [treɪ] n. 托盘
30. ass [æs] n. 屁股		41. epiphany [ɪˈpɪfəni] n. 显现
31. coccyx [ˈkɒksɪks] n. 尾椎（复数形式是 coccyges）		42. polymer [ˈpɒlɪmə] n. 聚合物
32. plural [ˈplʊərəl] n. 名词复数		43. congeal [kənˈdʒiːl] v. 凝固
33. slam [slæm] v. 猛烈撞击		44. nachos [ˈnætʃəʊs] n. 烤干酪辣味玉米片
34. mind-numbing 头脑麻木		45. busboy [ˈbʌsbɔɪ] n. （美）餐馆工
35. pedestrian [pəˈdestrɪən] adj. 缺乏想象力的		46. menial [ˈmiːnɪəl] adj. 卑微的
36. conceivable [kənˈsiːvəbl] adj. 想得到的		

📖 文化背景

1. Captain Hook: 虎克船长

小飞侠彼得潘故事中的反面人物。

☎ 常用表达

1. so as to 以便，以致

例: The player had to fade back so as to have room to pass the ball.

这名运动员不得不后退，以便留出传球的空间。

2. up all night 彻夜难眠，整夜未睡

例: You stayed up all night to write that?

你熬了一整晚就写了这玩意儿?

3. What could be better? 这就最好不过啦!

4. the hell 用在问句中，表示加强语气。

例: What the hell are you doing?

你到底在干什么?

Growing Pains
《成长的烦恼》

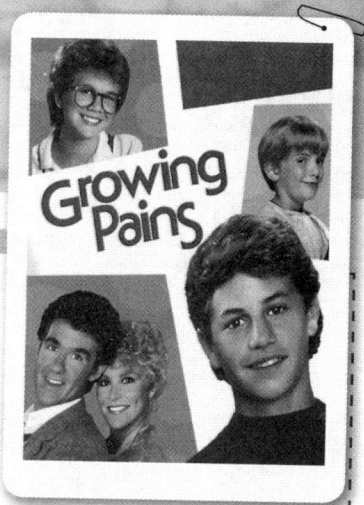

入选理由：

    《成长的烦恼》是由美国广播公司拍摄的大型情景喜剧片，共七季 166 集，20 世纪 80 年代曾红极一时，在长达 7 年的播出期间一直稳居收视率排行榜首位。该剧的创作和演员阵容堪称豪华，而且从该剧还走出了很多日后出色的演员，最有名的要算当今好莱坞片酬最高的男星之一———莱昂纳多·迪卡普里奥，他当年就曾在该剧集中扮演过一个小角色。

    《成长的烦恼》成功地向我们展现了一个美国郊区大家庭的幸福生活。作为一部以家庭为主轴的情景喜剧代表作，该剧不仅在美国创下了收视率纪录，还出口到多个国家，获得了世界各国观众的喜爱。

    该剧是中国内地引进的第一部美式情景喜剧，一经播出就引发了收视狂潮，曾在 90 年代风靡一时。剧中人物风趣幽默的对白令人耳目一新，使本剧深受观众喜爱，这对中国电视剧行业有很大的触动，据说第一部国产喜剧《我爱我家》就是受它的启发。而该剧对中国的影响已经不只限于电视领域，剧中美国父母对子女所采取的启发式教育方法及平等对话的沟通方式也启发了很多家长对如何教育子女进行了更深层次的思考，其影响可谓深远。

Section 1　剧情特点：

    《成长的烦恼》一剧主要讲述的是居住在纽约长岛的西维尔一家的日常生活。父亲杰森·西维尔是一名心理医生，母亲麦琪是一名记者，他们有三个孩子：迈克、凯萝尔和本。在故事的最后两季里为了丰富剧情，又新加了小妹克瑞斯和养子卢克，而卢克的扮演者就是如今大红大紫的好莱坞实力派明星莱奥纳多·迪卡普里奥。故事刚开始的时候，麦琪回电视台开始上班，而杰森则在家里开他的心理诊所，顺便照顾孩子们的生活。这位老爸可谓是影视剧中最早的"宅男"之一，心理医生的角色设定使得该剧在探讨孩子的教育方法和夫妻相处方面的情节设定更加真实可信。实际上，该剧这种以现实家庭生活为题材的情景喜剧成为 20 世纪 80 年代以来情景喜剧的创作主流，甚至左右了它之后的电视情景喜剧的发展方向。而且最难能可贵的是，作为一部喜剧，它并不一味的搞笑，有几集甚至可以说是悲剧，但这样的处理却又契合该剧的主题：成长并不总是那么美好。

Section 2　对白特点：

《成长的烦恼》非常适合初学者了解、学习美音。由于剧情设计以家庭为主，围绕着三个活泼淘气的孩子展开，所以对白也都是与家居、学校有关的内容，没有冷僻难解的词汇，剧中主要演员的对白，特别是三个孩子的语言非常生活化，值得反复听读。更重要的是，通过观看该剧，我们可以领略美国家庭教育和学校教育的风貌。该剧提供了一个了解、观察美国人的绝好视角。

Section 3　角色分析：

杰森·西维尔（Jason Seaver）：尽管美国没有那么多大男子主义的传统，女权运动又这么兴盛，但是作为一个大男人，自己居家当"煮夫"而让老婆去外面上班，也还是需要些魄力和能力的吧。毕竟男人会做饭、会做家务的不多，做得好的就更少了，这个可和主义真没关系，纯粹的生理问题。不过西维尔大夫可不一般，不愧是搞心理的，非常注重事件发生的细节及心理的微妙变化，知道人与人最重要的是沟通、交流，所以不论遇到什么问题都能平心静气的与对方交谈，不论孩子、老婆、亲人、病人全都搞定，是个了不起的老爸。

麦琪·西维尔（Maggie Seaver）：有勇气改变生活的不只是西维尔医生，还有他的妻子麦琪。作为一个已经当了十五年家庭主妇的女人，重新步入社会应该也是个不小的挑战。如何平衡工作和家庭的矛盾是每个职业女性必须要应对的课题，无论是在美国，还是在中国。而有勇气面对这一切困难的动力应该出自对生活的热爱，就像剧中麦琪所说的，"我不是必须去工作，而是我喜欢去工作"，奋斗的结果是令人欣慰的，麦琪从开始的三流小报的记者慢慢成了华盛顿的新闻官，孩子们也都长大成人，真是事业、家庭双丰收，而使这一切成为可能的是家庭成员彼此间浓浓的亲情。但愿现实生活中的每一个奋战在职场的白领丽人都能有麦琪这样的结局。

迈克·西维尔（Mike Seaver）：西维尔家的大儿子迈克是个功课不好却又整天搞恶作剧的淘气大王，让杰森夫妇大伤脑筋。剧中有一句经典台词，当杰森和妻子谈及迈克的未来，他忧愁地说：迈克除了会笑，还会干什么呢？可就是这个招牌式的微笑却让他迷倒了众多女孩（不论是戏里还是戏外）。长大后的迈克想当演员，可残酷的现实告诉他，光会微笑是不行的。受生活所迫，当年的学校里的淘气大王居然去补习学校，当起了代课教师，还把自己一个无家可归的学生带到家里来。真是个好老师。

凯萝尔·西维尔（Carol Seaver）：与淘气的老大相比，老二凯萝尔可是个品学兼优的好学生，虽然有点书呆子气，但每门功课都是 A 的成绩可不是随便得到的。不过，正因为在大家眼中她是个完美无缺的好孩子，所以她有时也很羡慕迈克——做什么都不用考虑后果，不用顾忌名声。凯萝尔虽然平时总是一副对自己很有信心的样子，但在她的心底却也有自卑的一面，认为自己不如其他女孩漂亮，不如其他女孩受欢迎。幸好有做心理医生的老爸耐心开导，凯萝尔顺利度过了成长危机，成为一个富有才华的孩子，未进入大学，就已经在出版公司当上了主管，她的未来必定是一片光明。

本·西维尔（Ben Seaver）：精灵古怪的小本是妈妈的小心肝和哥哥迈克的小跟班，因为在很长时间里都是家最小的孩子，会经常跟妈妈撒娇，会受到大哥大姐的呵护，当然也会跟在淘气哥哥的后面，干些不该干的事情。不过不会永远有人做庇护者的，当开始自己面对世界时，在一次次的失败、努力、再失败、再努力的过程中，这个孩子也在慢慢长大。

Passage 1

剧情介绍：

（选自第1季第4集）西维尔家的女儿凯萝尔是个成绩优秀的好学生，一直都是父母的骄傲，但是这回，凯萝尔为应聘学校报纸编辑而写的新闻稿可真不是一般的差。当记者的妈妈试图用非常婉转的方式告诉女儿，写报道应该怎样去写，可惜还是让自负的女儿感觉自尊心受到了伤害。然而现实远比妈妈说得更惨，校报的负责老师虽然聘用了凯萝尔，却把她的文章批得一文不值。凯萝尔一气之下拒绝了聘用，在妈妈的帮助下开始反思自己。

Scene 1: Maggie was reading the article Carol prepared for job application. Although Carol was conceited about her composition, it absolutely could not meet the requirements of news report. It was just a pile of fancy phrases, which made Maggie disappointed.

晚饭后，麦琪在厨房里阅读凯萝尔准备拿来应聘的文章，尽管凯萝尔自己对这篇文章很有信心，可实际上这篇文章根本不符合新闻报道的要求，完全是在堆砌词汇，看得麦琪直吸冷气。

Jason: Carol's paper can't be that bad.

Maggie: She wrote about guys who dig for **clams**[1].

Jason: Well, what's wrong with that?

Maggie: She called it "I clam, therefore I am"[1].

Jason: Did she?

Maggie: Listen to this. Night **abduces**[2] the **ismus**[3] **beneath**[4] its **odium**[5] **mantel**[6]. The **mollusks**[7] **imbibe**[8] one last **sip**[9], **betwixt**[10] their **valves**[11] and **expel**[12] the day's **muculance**[13].

杰森： 凯萝尔的文章难道就那么差吗？

麦琪： 她这篇文章写的是"挖蛤蜊的人"。

杰森： 这有什么不好？

麦琪： 题目是"我挖，故我在"。

杰森： 她这么做了？

麦琪： 念给你听听。"夜，展开了黑色的夜幕，笼罩了海峡，一条软体动物喝饱了最后一口海水以后，排出了全天的粘液。"

注释

1. **clam** [klæm] n. 蚌，蛤 v. （在沙滩上）挖蛤
2. **abduce** [æb'dju:s] v. 使外展；把……引开
3. **-ismus** 具体或抽象概念
4. **beneath** [bɪ'ni:θ] prep. 在……之下，在下方
5. **odium** ['əʊdɪəm] n. 憎恨，厌恶
6. **mantel** ['mæntl] n. 无袖外披斗篷
7. **mollusk** ['mɒləsk] n. 软体动物

8. **imbibe** [ɪm'baɪb] v. 吸收；喝
9. **sip** [sɪp] v. 小口喝，呷
10. **betwixt** [bɪ'twɪkst] adv. 在……中间
11. **valve** [vælv] n. 瓣膜；活门
12. **expel** [ɪk'spel] v. 驱逐；把……除名；排出（气体等）
13. **muculance** ['mju:kjʊələns] n. 粘液；黏液

Jason: She could be pushing a little?

Maggie: Jason, read this.

Jason: With the **dexterous**[14] **manipulation**[15] of his **digits**[16], the master clammer **extricates**[17] the **muculant**[18] mollusk from its **lepidious**[19] **menage**[20]. Well, look at it this way, we have a daughter who knows what muculance is. How many people know what muculance is.

Maggie: Nobody knows what muculance is. And that's the problem. Newspaper writing needs to be clear, accessible. Ah, Jason, what am I gonna to tell her? She asked for my honest opinion.

Jason: No kid wants your honest opinion. They want **unconditional**[21] **approval**[22].

Maggie: And *what if*[1] you don't approve?

Jason: Then you'll have a **significant**[23] **dilemma**[24] much like the one you're in now.

Maggie: Thank you, Dr. Seaver. Oh, come on, Jason, help me out here.

Jason: Well, if we want this to be a learning experience for her…

Maggie: Go on.

Jason: And all learning is based on **positive**[25] **reinforcement**[26].

Maggie: More.

Jason: See, if you want a pigeon to perform, you reward it with a **pellet**[27].

Maggie: What are you saying?

Jason: I'm saying we should have had pigeons. They are easier to raise.

Maggie: Jason, come on.

Jason: You just *start off*[2] by pointing out the strengths of the article. And then you show her how the article could be improved.

Maggie: You're right.

杰森： 她写得也太细了吧？

麦琪： 杰森，你读读。

杰森： "用灵巧的手指头，那挖蛤蜊的专家，把这个混身粘乎乎的软体动物，拉出它石灰质的家"。应该这样看，我们的女儿知道什么是软体动物，有多少人能知道这个概念呢。

麦琪： 没有人知道什么是软体动物，可问题就在这儿，报刊文章就应该写得明了易懂。噢，杰森，我该怎么跟她说呢？她要听我诚恳的意见。

杰森： 没有哪个孩子能听父母诚恳的意见。他们要的是无条件的赞成。

麦琪： 要是你不赞成呢？

杰森： 那样可就会进退两难了，就像你现在这个样子。

麦琪： 谢谢你，西维尔博士。噢，快点，杰森，快帮我出出主意。

杰森： 好吧，如果我们把这回就当成一次让她学习的机会……

麦琪： 说下去。

杰森： 而且所有学习的基础全在于得到正面的鼓励。

麦琪： 继续。

杰森： 你看，比如，你如果想让一只鸽子好好表现，你得先给它喂食。

麦琪： 这话什么意思？

杰森： 我们真该养一只鸽子，那可比孩子好养多了。

麦琪： 杰森，快说，你什么意思啊？

杰森： 你应该一开始指出她文章的长处，然后你再告诉她文章该怎么修改。

麦琪： 你说得对。

> **Scene 2:** Maggie had no idea how to tell Carol without hurting her that her article was not that good. She knocked Carol's door and went in, but didn't know how to speak when she found her daughter was eager for her judgment.
>
> 如何做才能既告诉凯萝尔她的文章不行，又不伤了孩子的自尊心呢？麦琪心里一点底也没有，她犹犹豫豫地敲开凯萝尔的房门，看到女儿正在等她来评价就更不知如何开口了。

Maggie: Carol.

Carol: Come in.

Maggie: Ha… Well, it's late; you must be tired. We can talk about this tomorrow…

Carol: No, Mum, I've been waiting for you. I read the article again; I think I can be more **objective**[28] now.

Maggie: That's a good thing to do. Put it away for a while, get some distance, often what you thought was perfect…

Carol: I know, I know…I've already changed it.

Maggie: You did?

Carol: Yeah.

Maggie: Ah…

Carol: The two "muculance" is in the same sentence…terrible. Make the second one "**pituitousness**[29]".

麦琪：凯萝尔。

凯萝尔：请进。

麦琪：嗨，好吧，已经很晚了，你也一定累了，我们明天再谈好了。

凯萝尔：不，妈妈，我一直等着你呢。我又把文章看了一遍，我认为现在我能客观点了。

麦琪：你这样做好处很多，把文章放一段时间，保持距离，经常这样做你往往会发觉原来……

凯萝尔：我知道，我知道，我已经修改过了。

麦琪：你修改过了？

凯萝尔：对。

麦琪：啊哈……

凯萝尔：同一句里有两个"软体动物"，太糟糕了，我把其中的一个改成"粘液动物"了。

注释

14. **dexterous** ['dekstrəs] *adj.* 机巧的，巧妙的
15. **manipulation** [mə'nɪpjuleɪʃn] *n.* （熟练的）操作
16. **digit** ['dɪdʒɪt] *n.* 手指
17. **extricate** ['ekstrɪkeɪt] *v.* 使摆脱困难，脱身
18. **muculant** ['mjuːkjuələnt] *adj.* 含粘液的
19. **lepidious** ['lepɪdɪəs] *adj.* 石头的
20. **menage** [meɪ'nɑːʒ] *n.* 家
21. **unconditional** [ʌnkəndɪʃənl] *adj.* 无条件的
22. **approval** [ə'pruːvl] *n.* 批准；认可；赞成
23. **significant** [sɪg'nɪfɪkənt] *adj.* 重大的；有效的；有意义的；值得注意的；意味深长的
24. **dilemma** [dɪ'lemə] *n.* 困境；进退两难
25. **positive** ['pɒzətɪv] *adj.* 积极的；肯定的
26. **reinforcement** [riːɪn'fɔːsmənt] *n.* 增援；加强
27. **pellet** ['pelɪt] *n.* 颗粒饲料
28. **objective** [əb'dʒektɪv] *adj.* 客观的
29. **pituitousness** [pɪ'tjuːɪtəsnɪs] *n.* [古语] 粘液

Maggie: Oh…

Carol: Are you proud of me, mum? The truth.

Maggie: Of course, honey, I am always proud of you.

Carol: You think I'll make the paper?

Maggie: Well, it's obviously you have **potential**[31]. Very few people could write like… this.

Carol: So, you do think I shouldn't change anything, Mum? It is great!

Maggie: Well, What I… What I…What I am saying is… I am…Carol, it's clear that you put a lot of time into this article. It's…well thought out, it's well **typed**[32], and … and I just love these **margins**[33].

Carol: But...

Maggie: Well, it's not so much a but…

Carol: It sounds just like a but.

Maggie: Well, what I am trying to say is…

Carol: *Cut to*[3] the "but", mum!

Maggie: But…it is just not newspaper writing, honey. Look, in any field there're rules, you just have to learn them. Newspaper writing has to be more **simple**[34], **straight**[35] **forward**[36].

Carol: So you think my article is **garbage**[37].

Maggie: Sweetheart, if I let you turn this in to Mr. Simmonds, he'd tell you the same things, only **meaner**[38].

麦琪：   哦……

凯萝尔： 你为我自豪吗？说实话。

麦琪：   那还用说，我一向都为你自豪。

凯萝尔： 你说我能编报纸吗？

麦琪：   不错，从文章看你很有潜力，很少有人能写出这样的文章。

凯萝尔： 这么说，你认为我一个字都不用改了？太棒了。

麦琪：   这个……我的，我的意思，我的意思是说，我，哦，凯萝尔，我可以看出你写这篇文章确实花了不少的时间。文章……，哦，构思非常好，打字也非常清楚，还有……还有我很喜欢你的这种格式。

凯萝尔： 但是？

麦琪：   噢，我并没有想说但是。

凯萝尔： 听起来你想说但是。

麦琪：   哦，我想说的是……

凯萝尔： 直接说"但是"吧，妈妈。

麦琪：   但是，报刊文章不是这么写的，亲爱的。你看，在任何领域里都有一定的规矩，你得学习它们。报刊上的文章应该写得更简单，直接明了。

凯萝尔： 所以你认为我的文章是垃圾。

麦琪：   宝贝，如果我让你把这篇文章拿给西蒙斯先生，他也会告诉你同样的话，而且只会更难听。

Scene 3: The school teacher criticized Carol harshly for her article. Carol rejected the job angrily. Maggie came upstairs to comfort her, only to find that Carol was dumping all her draft manuscript…

学校老师也批评了凯萝尔的文章。凯萝尔一气之下拒绝了老师的聘用，麦琪知道了忙上楼来安慰女儿，却看见凯萝尔正在把以前写的文稿都扔掉……

Maggie: Carol, how come you *turned* the job *down*[4]? I mean it really seemed like you had your *heart set on*[5] it.

Carol: Yeah! Well that was before I realized that there's nothing really **creative**[39] about **journalism**[40]. I mean all you do is **regurgitate**[41] facts. If I'm going to be a writer I'd rather do a novel. At least people don't train their puppies on *Moby Dick*[2]!

Carol: Carol, I can understand your being angry at me for my **criticism**[42] of your article.

Carol: Why should I be angry? Simmonds gave me the job!

Maggie: I know! I know. I guess, what I'm trying to say is, well, honey, it's always **tricky**[43] giving criticism to someone you love. And I guess I just didn't do a very good job. Obviously Simmonds was very happy with what you did. And I'm glad that I was wrong …

Carol: No!

Maggie: Pardon me?

Carol: I said no. Ok? Are you happy? He said everything you said, only worse. He said my article was replete with **stinkiocity**[44].

Maggie: But you said that you got the job.

Carol: Yeah, that was only because all the other articles were replete with stinkiocity.

Maggie: Oh, honey! I am so sorry.

Carol: He said he even didn't know what muculance was.

麦琪：　凯萝尔，你怎么能拒绝聘用呢？我的意思是说你不是一心想去报社工作吗？

凯萝尔：是啊，那时候我还没意识到，新闻工作并不需要创造性，只要把事实堆砌起来就行了。如果我要当作家的话，我宁可去写小说。至少人们不会拿《白鲸》去训练小狗。

麦琪：　凯萝尔，我理解你对我批评你的文章感到生气。

凯萝尔：我为什么要生气？西蒙斯已经决定聘用我了。

麦琪：　我知道，我知道，我想，我现在要对你说的话就是，噢，亲爱的，对一个所爱的人，提出批评是件很难的事情。而且我想也许是我没做好工作。显然，西蒙斯对你的成绩非常满意。我很高兴我的话说错了。

凯萝尔：没有!

麦琪：　你说什么？

凯萝尔：我说没有！你没有说错，你高兴吗？你的话西蒙斯全说了，而且说得更糟。他说我的那篇文章，充满了一股腐臭气味。

麦琪：　可是你说他已经聘用你了。

凯萝尔：他也只能聘用我了，因为别的文章也都充满了腐臭气。

麦琪：　噢，宝贝，我真是太遗憾了。

凯萝尔：他说他都不知道什么是软体动物。

注释
31. **potential** [pə'tenʃl] *adj.* 潜能；可能性
32. **type** [taɪp] *v.* 打字
33. **margin** ['mɑːdʒɪn] *n.* 书页边的空白
34. **simple** ['sɪmpl] *adj.* 简单的；单纯的；天真的
35. **straight** [streɪt] *adj.* 直的，直接的
36. **forward** ['fɔːwəd] *adv.* 向前的，易于……的
37. **garbage** ['gɑːbɪdʒ] *n.* 垃圾；废物
38. **mean** [miːn] *adj.* 刻薄的

39. **creative** [krɪ'eɪtɪv] *adj.* 创造性的
40. **journalism** ['dʒɜːnəlɪzəm] *n.* 新闻工作；报章杂志
41. **regurgitate** [rɪ'gɜːdʒɪteɪt] *v.* 机械地引用；刻板地重复；生搬硬套
42. **criticism** ['krɪtɪsɪzəm] *n.* 批评，批判
43. **tricky** ['trɪkɪ] *adj.* 棘手的，复杂的，难处理的
44. **stinkiocity** 臭味

Maggie: Well, that's just his stupidness, sweat heart. Everybody knows what muculance is.

Carol: I'll never be able to write like you.

Maggie: Oh, *hold on*[6], hold on, honey, that's just not true. Now maybe you were reaching a little... but you have great **natural**[45] **abilities**[46].

Carol: You're just saying that.

Maggie: Hey, hey. Didn't I establish myself last night as someone who isn't afraid to tell the truth?

Carol: Yeah. Even if it does mean **crushing**[47] a little kid's **ego**[48]. Do you really think that I might have natural ability?

Maggie: I dug this out of the **attic**[49] this afternoon. Well, I thought you might like to take a look at it.

Carol: A letter I wrote from **camp**[50] 5 years ago?

Maggie: Uh huh. Read it.

Carol: "Dear mum and dad, Camp is fun, except for the **rash**[51] I got when I tried to find out what **poison**[52] **sumac**[53] looks like, except for the kids **teasing**[54] anyone who is small, fat, left handed. Missing you and baby Ben, and even Mike a little, but don't tell. Bring my chemistry set and potato **chips**[55] on visiting day, love, Carol." That's not so good?

Maggie: Hey, Didn't we bring your chemistry set and your potato chips?

Carol: Yeah.

Maggie: Then you got your point across.

Carol: Yeah.

麦琪： 那是因为这个人太愚蠢了，宝贝。每个人都知道软体动物是什么。

凯萝尔： 我永远也没本事像你那样写作。

麦琪： 噢，挺住，挺住，宝贝，这并不是事实。现在你只是需要再努力一点儿，你的天赋很好。

凯萝尔： 你不过是说说的。

麦琪： 嘿，嘿，昨天晚上，我对你说的话还记得吗？我并不害怕讲真话。

凯萝尔： 对，即使这样做意味着毁掉一个小孩子的自我感觉。你真的认为我有很好的天赋吗？

麦琪： 这是下午从顶楼上找出来的，我想这封信还是让你好好看看。

凯萝尔： 这是五年前我从夏令营写来的信？

麦琪： 啊哈，念念吧!

凯萝尔： "亲爱的爸爸妈妈，夏令营很有趣，除了我在寻找漆树的时候染上了皮疹，还有就是男孩子们总取笑我是个矮矮肥肥的左撇子。想你们和弟弟本，也有点儿想迈克，但不要告诉他。来看我的时候带我的化学装置和土豆片来。爱你们，凯萝尔。"我写得并不好。

麦琪： 嗨，后来我们去看你的时候，给你带了化学装置和土豆片了吗？

凯萝尔： 带了。

麦琪： 那就说明你把自己的意思表达清楚了。

凯萝尔： 哦，我明白你的意思了。

注释

45. **natural** ['nætʃrəl] *adj.* 自然的；天生的
46. **ability** [ə'bɪləti] *n.* 能力
47. **crush** [krʌʃ] *v.* 粉碎；压榨
48. **ego** ['iːɡəʊ] *n.* 自我；自我意识
49. **attic** ['ætɪk] *n.* 阁楼；顶楼
50. **camp** [kæmp] *n.* 露营；扎营
51. **rash** [ræʃ] *n.* 皮疹
52. **poison** ['pɔɪzn] *n.* 有毒；毒药
53. **sumac** ['ʃuːmæk] *n.* 漆树（灌木）
54. **tease** [tiːz] *v.* 取笑；戏弄
55. **chip** [tʃɪp] *n.* 碎屑，碎片

📖 **文化背景**

1. 这是模仿法国哲学家笛卡尔的名言"我思故我在"（I think, therefore I am）。

2. Moby Dick 美国作家梅尔维尔的代表作，中文译为《白鲸》，记述一位捕鲸船老船长在同一条巨大凶猛的白鲸莫比·迪克搏斗中船破身亡的经历，被誉为 19 世纪美国最重要的作品。

☎ **常用表达**

1. what if 如果……怎么办？

例：What if he was faithless to his wife?

要是他对妻子不忠怎么办？

2. start off 开始，启程

例：What shall we start off this thing with?

我们该从哪儿开始谈这件事？

3. cut to 切换到

例：Cut to 2010, and group intelligence is fast emerging as the next frontier in this field。

转到 2010 年，团体智力成为在这个领域下飞速发展的一个新前沿。

4. turn down 拒绝

例：I thanked him for the offer but turned it down.

我谢绝了他的提议。

5. set heart on 渴望，决心

例：He has set his heart on pursuing his studies abroad.

他已下定决心到国外求学。

6. hold on 坚持，稍等

例：You helped me to hold on at times when I didn't think I could even go on trying.

在我认为自己甚至无法继续尝试的时候，你帮我坚持了下来。

Passage 2

剧情介绍：

（选自第 1 季第 18 集）老大迈克一直是个问题学生，整天淘气，不好好学习。可这次，他的历史居然考了 94 分，全班最高，老师在公布成绩时发现迈克把所有的答案都写在鞋底上。这样一来，所有人都认为迈克考试作弊了，学校通知西维尔夫妇到校见老师。在父母见老师之前，迈克解释了事情的经过，杰森向老师说明了情况，最后迈克获得了补考的机会，为自己恢复了名誉。

Scene 1: The exam was coming. Mike stepped into the classroom confidently because he had made some special preparation, while his classmates were cramming for the exam, such as Boner, his desk mate…

要考试了，迈克胸有成竹地"挪"进考场，因为他已经在考前做了特殊的准备，而其他同学都在紧张得看最后一眼书，比如他的同桌伯纳……

Boner:	The one thing I know is that I don't know this.	伯纳：	我唯一知道的事就是我对它一无所知。
Mike:	Oh, my man, you worry too much.	迈克：	哦，老朋友，你过度担心了。
Boner:	At least I'll have you for **company**[1] in summer school.	伯纳：	至少暑假补习班有你陪我。
Mike:	No, no, not this time. I got this thing **aced**[2].	迈克：	不，不，不是这次。我已经把事情搞定了。
Boner:	You mean to tell me you **actually**[3] studied the stuff?	伯纳：	你的意思是说，你实际上全都复习好了？
Mike:	Boner, Boner, Boner…so young, so **naive**[4].	迈克：	伯纳、伯纳、伯纳，你太年轻，太天真了。
Boner:	You got cheat notes!	伯纳：	你想作弊！
Mike:	You just let the people get the wrong idea.	迈克：	你说的会让别人误解的。
Classmate:	Where are they?	同学：	你藏哪儿了？
Mike:	Look, I don't know what you guys are talking about. Here, search me. Full body **strip**[5] search.	迈克：	看，我没有带你们这些家伙说的东西。这儿，搜我吧，全身都可以搜。

Classmate: No, thanks.

Classmate: teacher, teacher...

Dewitt: Alright people, I trust you all are **sufficiently**[6] **frightened**[7]. If not, you should be, because this test will count for a **quarter**[8] of your total grade.

Boner: A quarter? Only yesterday he said 25%!

Dewitt: This is **multiple**[9] choice, and you have 30 minutes and your papers will be graded before you leave. You may begin.

Mike: The **final**[10] Northern battle of civil **war**[11] was, A. battle of Wardroom, B. battle of Gettysburg, C. battle of network stars, Gettysburg[1]! I actually know this stuff!

(When the test results were released, the teacher was astonished by Mike's high grade because he was not such a good student in usual...)

Dewitt: Now some of your test result did surprise me. For instance, it was interested to learn from Mr. Stan Boner that general Grand's first name was Lu.

Boner: I can't look, I can't look! I've got to look! 67! Oh! All right!

Dewitt: And what is perhaps the biggest shock in my teaching career since boys started wearing earrings is that the highest grade in the class, 94, was earnt by Mike Seavor.

Mike: Ah, No. 1.

Dewitt: Mr. Seavor, before we **schedule**[12] a **press**[13] **conference**[14], I have to ask how does a student whose very name has become

同学：	不，谢了。
同学：	老师来了……
德沃特：	同学们，我相信你们都非常紧张。不紧张那是不对的，因为这次测验的成绩将占你们总分的四分之一。
伯纳：	四分之一？昨天他还说占 25%。
德沃特：	这次考试是多项选择题，时间 30 分钟，考卷会在你们离开前批改完。现在……开始!
迈克：	南北战争在北方的最后一战：A. 沃尔特战役，B. 葛底斯堡战役，C. 星际网络战，葛底斯堡! 嘿，实际上这些玩意儿我都知道!

（发成绩了，老师对平时成绩一贯很差劲的迈克突然考高分很是怀疑……）

德沃特：	现在，你们某些人的考试结果让我非常吃惊。比方说，从斯坦·伯纳同学那里了解到大将军名叫陆，这太有意思了。
伯纳：	我不看，我不看，我不得不看看，67，啊，太好了!
德沃特：	而我教书的生涯里，自从看见男孩戴耳环以外，最让我吃惊的可能就是这次全班最高分为 94，获得第一名的人是……迈克·西维尔。
迈克：	啊，第一名!
德沃特：	西维尔同学，在我们举行一个记者招待会之前我不得不提一个问题，一个平时总得差的学生，这

注释

1. company ['kʌmpəni] *n.* 陪伴
2. ace [eɪs] *n.* 发球得分，击败
3. actually ['æktʃuəlɪ] *adv.* 实际上，事实上
4. naive [naɪ'iːv] *adj.* 天真的，幼稚的
5. strip [strɪp] *v.* 脱去衣服
6. sufficiently [sə'fɪʃntlɪ] *adv.* 充分地；足够地
7. frightened ['fraɪtnd] *adj.* 害怕的；受惊的；受恐吓的

8. quarter ['kwɔːtə(r)] *n.* 四分之一
9. multiple ['mʌltɪpl] *adj.* 多重的；多样的；许多的
10. final ['faɪnl] *adj.* 最终的，最后的
11. civil war （美国）国内战争
12. schedule ['ʃedjuːl] *n.* 安排，计划
13. press [pres] *n.* 新闻；出版社
14. conference ['kɒnfərəns] *n.* 会议；协商

synonymous[15] with the phrase D minus manage such a grade?

次怎么会得到这样的分数？

Mike: What can I say, Mr. Dewitt? When you got it, I got it.

迈克： 我所能说的是，德沃特先生，答对了就是答对了。

(Mr. Dewitt spotted the answers Mike had written on the bottoms of his shoes.)

（德沃特先生看到了迈克写满答案的鞋底。）

Dewitt: Oh, and now I see where you got it.

德沃特： 哦，我现在知道怎么回事了。

Mike: Are you actually calling me a cheater?

迈克： 你是不是认为我作弊了？

Dewitt: Mr. Seavor, don't try to fool a Willie Dewitt! The shoes, now…

德沃特： 西维尔同学，你不要试图愚弄我，威利·德沃特先生！鞋子给我，现在。

Mike: Mr. Dewitt…

迈克： 德沃特老师……

Mr. Dewitt: Have your parents, **guardian**[16] or **Parole**[17] officer call for an **appointment**[18].

德沃特： 请你的父母、监护人或者假释官打电话约个见面时间。

Scene 2: Jason was enraged by Mike's cheating on exam, and he stood in the corridor alone, thinking over whether there was something wrong with his family education. Then came Maggie…

杰森知道迈克考试作弊后非常愤怒，独自一个人待在外边的走廊上，反思自己的教育方法有无失误。麦琪出来找杰森……

Maggie: Here you are. You're going to **freeze**[19] out here.

麦琪： 你在这儿？你在这儿会冻死的。

Jason: No, I've got my anger to keep me warm.

杰森： 不，我已经被怒火烧热了。

Maggie: Could you share some with me? Jason, I have something to tell you. I didn't want to tell you but since you're feeling **betrayed**[20] by Mike I **figured**[21] you needed some good news. You are not really Mike's father.

麦琪： 那你能帮我也暖和一下吗？杰森，有件事要告诉你。我本来不想说的，但是既然迈克的行为使你感觉被辜负了，我想你需要知道一点好消息。你不是迈克真正的父亲。

Jason: Well, you know what I've been thinking?

杰森： 好了，你知道我一直在想些什么？

Maggie: That when Mike looked you in the eye and lied, it made you question your whole

麦琪： 你看着迈克当着你的面撒谎，这让你对自己教育孩子要忠诚老实

approach[22] to teaching our kids the **value**[23] of truth and honesty. And you're **wondering**[24] if instead of encouraging them by example, a little fear or **punishment**[25] might have been a bit more effective. And you're probably remembering the time when Mike was eight and he lied about finger painting the new **rug**[26] and I wanted to **spank**[27] him but you **convinced**[28] me that **reasoning**[29] with him was better.

Jason: How do you do that?

Maggie: Oh, it's not all that **amazing**[30]. I **bet**[31] you know what I am thinking *right now*[1]?

Jason: Oh, you're probably thinking that no matter how disappointed we both are, we must support him because we love him **dearly**[32]. And we'll do our best to **mould**[33] him into an honest man. And that even if we fail he can always have a productive life in **politics**[34].

的方法产生了怀疑；你还怀疑除了自己以身作则外，对他们施加一点惩罚也许更有效；你还可能想起来迈克8岁那年，那次他说谎不承认他用手指头蘸颜料在新地毯上画画，我要打他屁股，但是你说服我要用讲道理的方式会更好。

杰森： 你怎么猜到这些的？

麦琪： 哦，这一点也不稀奇，我打赌你一定也想到我现在在想什么。

杰森： 哦，你在想无论我们俩怎么对迈克失望，我们都必须支持他，因为我们都深深地爱着他。而且我们要尽力把他培养成一个诚实的人。万一我们失败了，还可以让他去搞政治。

Scene 3: The Seavors were waiting for Mr. Dewitt in his office. Maggie was persuading Mike into admitting his mistake, while Mike still did not care at all.

西维尔一家在老师办公室里等着德沃特老师的到来，麦琪还在尽最后的努力试图劝迈克认错，而迈克还是那副无所谓的样子。

注释

15. synonymous [sɪ'nɒnɪməs] *adj.* 同义的；同义词的

16. guardian ['gɑːdɪən] *n.* 监护人

17. parole [pə'rəul] *n.* 假释

18. appointment [ə'pɔɪntmənt] *n.* 约定；预约

19. freeze [friːz] *v.* 冻结；冷冻；僵硬

20. betray [bɪ'treɪ] *v.* 背叛，出卖；辜负（期望等）

21. figure ['fɪgə] *v.* 考虑，认为

22. approach [ə'prəutʃ] *n.* 方法；途径；接近

23. value ['væljuː] *n.* 价值，价格；价值观

24. wonder ['wʌndə] *v.* 怀疑；想知道；惊讶

25. punishment ['pʌnɪʃmənt] *n.* 惩罚

26. rug [rʌg] *n.* 小地毯；毛皮地毯

27. spank [spæŋk] *v.* 打屁股

28. convinced [kən'vɪnst] *adj.* 使确信；说服

29. reason ['riːzn] *v.* 说服；推论；辩论

30. amazing [ə'meɪzɪŋ] *adj.* 令人惊异的

31. bet [bet] *v.* 打赌

32. dearly ['dɪəlɪ] *adv.* 深深地

33. mould [məuld] *v.* 浇铸；塑造

34. politics ['pɒlətɪks] *n.* 政治

Maggie:	Mike, Mr. Dewitt will go a lot easier on you if you just **admit**[35] what you did.	麦琪：	迈克，如果你承认了，德沃特老师会对你客气得多。
Mike:	I don't care.	迈克：	我才不在乎呢。
Jason:	But we do. Couldn't you at least **pretend**[36] that you care what we think?	杰森：	可我们在乎，你能不能至少假装重视我们的意见。
Mike:	Sure but nobody will believe me.	迈克：	可以，但是没人会相信我。
Jason:	Why should anyone?	杰森：	他们干吗不相信你？
Mike:	Because I didn't cheat… forget it, it doesn't matter.	迈克：	因为我从来都……算了，不说了。
Jason:	Why should we have believed you back in 7th grade when you tried to tell us that the D on your report card stood for **darn**[37] good?	杰森：	为什么我们要相信你，在你 7 年级的时候你就试着告诉我们，你成绩单上的"差"就是差一点满分？
Maggie:	And what about in the 8th grade when you told the school your name was Seavormen so you could *take* the **Jewish**[38] holidays *off*[2]?	麦琪：	还有你 8 年级的时候对学校说你是犹太人的后裔，所以应该享受犹太教节日的假期。
Jason:	Just this week…	杰森：	还有，这个星期……
Mike:	OK, OK, sometimes I lie, but there's a big difference between being a liar, and being a liar. I mean you guys should know when I'm telling the truth. I mean what kind of parents are you anyway?	迈克：	好了，好了，有时候我是讲假话，但是我讲过假话并不等于我老讲假话，我的意思是说当我说真话的时候你们应该知道，我想知道你们到底对我什么看法？
Jason:	Disappointed.	杰森：	失望。
Mike:	You want to know the truth? OK, I'll tell the truth. Yeah, I was going to cheat, and I figured it as the only way. So I was up half the night copying all that stuff onto my shoes, because I had to pass the test. But **somehow**[39] it didn't just go on my shoes, it got into my head too. Sure blew me away! But when it came time to look for the answers I didn't have to, I knew them.	迈克：	你们想知道真相？好吧，让我来告诉你们真相。是的，我本来是想作弊来着，也是因为没办法了。所以我花了大半夜时间把答案抄在了我的鞋子上，因为我必须通过考试。奇怪的是我不仅仅是抄在鞋上了，我也记在脑子里了。我记得很牢。反正在考试的时候，我根本就没有去看答案，因为我都知道。

Maggie:	Well, I'd like to believe you, Mike.	麦琪:	好，我相信你说的话，迈克。
Mike:	Yeah.	迈克:	是啊。
Jason:	Well you have to admit, you're not exactly[40] the type of guy who has a **reputation**[41] for knowing things like Abraham Lincoln was the 17th president?	杰森:	不过你也得承认，根据你的一贯表现，别人不会认为你是那种能知道林肯是第17届总统这样问题的人。
Mike:	Yeah, he was 16th president.	迈克:	对，他是第16届总统。
Jason:	Yeah, Grant was 17th.	杰森:	对，格兰特是第17届。
Mike:	No, Grant was 18th, Johnson was 17th, he became president after Lincoln was **assassinated**[42] on April 14th, 1865.	迈克:	不，格兰特是第18届，约翰逊才是第17届。他在1865年4月14日林肯被刺以后就任了总统。
Dewitt:	Dr. and Mrs. Seavor, I'm Willis Dewitt, glad you could come. Why don't we *get right down to business*[3]?	德沃特:	西维尔博士、西维尔夫人，我是德沃特，很高兴你们能来，我们开门见山地谈好吗？
Jason:	**Absolutely**[43]. Mike did not cheat on this examination, Mr. Dewitt, and it's important that we *clear* that *up*[4].	杰森:	当然。迈克在考历史的时候并没有作弊，德沃特先生，我们是特意来澄清这点的。
Maggie:	And it would have been so easy for him to do, what with all the answers written on the **bottom**[44] of his shoes.	麦琪:	如果他要作弊的话太容易了，因为答案都写在他鞋底上了。

(Mike was taking his make-up test.)

（迈克在补考。）

| Jason: | Thank you, Mr. Dewitt for letting Mike take this make-up test. | 杰森: | 谢谢你让迈克参加补考，德沃特老师。 |
| Dewitt: | No problem. | 德沃特: | 不，没什么。 |

注释

35. admit [əd'mɪt] *v.* 承认；容许

36. pretend [prɪ'tend] *v.* 假装，伪装，佯装

37. darn [dɑːn] *v.* 织补，缝补

38. Jewish ['dʒuːɪʃ] *adj.* 犹太人的；犹太族的

39. somehow ['sʌmhaʊ] *adv.* 以某种方法；莫明其妙地

40. exactly [ɪg'zæktlɪ] *adv.* 恰好地；正是；精确地；正确地

41. reputation [ˌrepjuˈteɪʃn] *n.* 名声，名誉；声望

42. assassinate [əˈsæsɪneɪt] *v.* 暗杀；行刺

43. absolutely [ˌæbsəˈluːtlɪ] *adv.* 绝对地；完全地

44. bottom ['bɒtəm] *n.* 底部；末端

📖 文化背景

1. Gettysburg 即著名的葛底斯堡

美国南北战争期间，北军在葛底斯堡击溃南军，成为内战的转折点。同年林肯在此发表了著名的葛底斯堡演说，提出建设"民有、民治、民享的政府"（government of the people, by the people, for the people）。

☎ 常用表达

1. right now 立即，此刻

例： Let's go right now before it gets too late.

我们马上就去，不然就太晚了。

2. take...off 请假，休假

例： She took two days off work.

她休了两天假。

3. get down to business 着手办正事，开始讨论实质问题

例： Stop kidding. Let's get down to business.

别开玩笑了，我们办正经事吧。

4. clear up 解决（问题），消除（误会）

例： During dinner the confusion was cleared up; they had mistaken me for Kenny.

误会在午餐时消除了；他们曾因为肯尼误会了我。

Passage 3

老三本如今已经是中学生了，需要独自去面对生活中的一些突发状况，比如这回，本在学校里被一个身高力大的男同学欺负了，为了能与之一决高下，不服气的本决定去学空手道。经过一番刻苦训练，本终于小有所成。但是，本并没有因此成为一个暴力男，而是真正领悟了空手道的真谛。

Scene 1: Ben came back home and told his parents that he would try to revenge because his new cap was grabbed by a punk in the school. As parents, how should they react to their bullied son?

本在学校里被一个霸道的同学夺走了新帽子，他气哼哼地回到家，跟父母说他要想办法报复。面对被人欺负的儿子，大人又该如何教育呢？

Ben: That's it! I've made my decision, and you're not talking me out of it. I want a gun.

Jason: (gasping) *Forget it*[1]!

Ben: Okay, you talked me out of it. Here's plan B: I want to take **Karate**[1] lessons.

Jason: Karate?

Maggie: Why?

Ben: You guys remember my brand-new $27 cap? Well, this **punk**[2] at school named Razor made me give it to him in front of Becka and everybody.

Jason: Come on, Ben, you've had to deal with **bullets**[3] before…$27 cap?

Ben: This kid is **dangerous**[4]. He is certified USDA mean.

Jason: Well, I think you should report this to the vice-

本： 就这样了，我已经下定了决心。你们不必再劝我了，我要支枪。

杰森： （抽了口气）别做梦了？

本： 好吧，你让我放弃了。这儿还有第二计划，我要去学空手道。

杰森： 空手道？

麦琪： 为什么？

本： 你还记得我那顶新买的27块钱的帽子吗？好啦，被那个叫瑞仁的小流氓给抢走了，当着贝卡和所有人的面。

杰森： 行了，本，在你不得不用子弹来处理之前……多少？27块钱的帽子？

本： 那小子特别厉害。全校没有一个人能碰他。

杰森： 这样的话，你应该去报告给副校长。

注释
1. **Karate** [kəˈrɑːtɪ] *n.* 空手道
2. **punk** [pʌŋk] *n.* [俚语] 小流氓，小阿飞
3. **bullet** [ˈbulɪt] *n.* 子弹
4. **dangerous** [ˈdeɪndʒərəs] *adj.* 危险的

principal.

Ben: Yeah? A kid tried that last year. Now he's living in **Nevada**[5] under an **assumed**[6] name.

Jason: There's got to be a better way to handle this, Ben. Why don't you just go…?

Ben: What's so about Karate? I mean, it's **philosophical**[7], it's **graceful**[8], and it teaches you how to put your foot through somebody's brain.

Maggie: Oh! Ben, if that's why you want to learn Karate, you can forget it.

Ben: Fine! Then let me go look in my closet to see if I have anything else in Razor's size.

Jason: Ben! Wait a minute, Ben. Maggie, maybe it's not such a bad idea to let him take a few Karate lessons.

Maggie: *No way*[2].

Jason: Well, you don't know what it's like. You've never had somebody **bully**[9] you around at school.

Maggie: Well, as a matter of fact, Didi Ribozo tried to keep me from using the girl's bathroom the entire **junior**[10] year.

Jason: So what did you do?

Maggie: I gave up liquids during school hours.

Jason: See, you gave in. That's not the way you want Ben to solve this.

Maggie: Well, I know that, Jason. But I also don't want him putting his foot through someone's brain.

Jason: Well, right now, someone's brain is inside Ben's cap. I don't like **violence**[11] any more than you do, but we're both gonna feel better if he knows how to protect himself.

Maggie: Yeah, but I just wish there was some way he could reason with this boy.

Jason: Maggie, it is my experience there are two kinds of people: those you reason with, and those named Razor.

本：去年有个同学试过了，结果他现在在内华达隐名埋姓呢。

杰森：那得找个更好的解决办法了，本。你为何不去学……

本：我不知道空手道有什么不好。我是说它能够启发思维，动作优雅，还教你如何用脚踢别人的头。

麦琪：噢，本，如果这是你想学空手道的原因的话，你就忘了这事吧。

本：好啊，那让我看看衣橱里还有什么瑞仁能够穿的。

杰森：本，你先等一等，本。麦琪，我看这主意不坏，就让他上几天空手道课吧。

麦琪：不行。

杰森：你不懂这里面的奥秘，你又没尝过在学校里让人欺负的滋味。

麦琪：事实上，在整个大学一年级的学期里，迪迪·瑞布都想让我用不成女厕所。

杰森：你怎么做的？

麦琪：我一到学校就开始戒水。

杰森：看，是你让步了，你不希望本也这样解决问题吧。

麦琪：我知道，杰森，可我也不希望他用脚踹别人的脑袋。

杰森：现在那个别人的脑袋正戴着本的帽子。我比你更不喜欢暴力，可他如果能保护自己，咱们俩都会觉得好受些。

麦琪：是啊，可我还是希望他能和那孩子讲道理。

杰森：麦琪，根据我的经验，世界上有两种人，一种人可以讲道理，另一种人就是瑞仁。

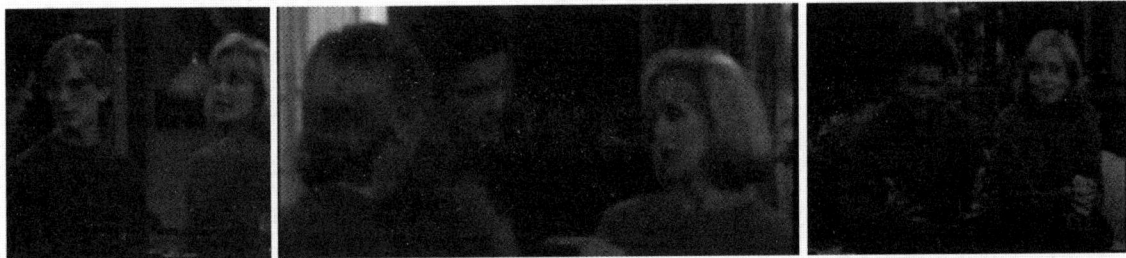

Scene 2: In the Karate club, Ben meant to show off his fighting skills but was beaten by Maggie, and was mocked by Mike when he got home, so he wanted to give up Karate lessons. Jason and Maggie did not want their little son give up easily, so they played a good cop/ bad cop routine instead of using a moralistic way.

在空手道馆里，本来想跟妈妈炫耀一下的本反而被妈妈打伤了，回到家还被哥哥迈克嘲笑，伤心的本想放弃空手道了。杰森和麦琪觉得不能让儿子这么轻言放弃，但是他们俩没有采用说教的办法，而是"一个白脸、一个红脸"地合作演出了一场双簧。

Jason: Hey, Ben. Your mom says you want to give up Karate lessons.

Ben: Look, dad. I tried; I failed; my life is **ruined**[12].

Jason: Come on, that eye's gonna be fine. But there's no reason why you can't go right back to karate class.

Maggie: Jason, what are you talking about? The next person he fights might not love him like I do.

Jason: Well, I don't want our son to give up just because he got **hurt**[13], Maggie.

Maggie: Jason, he wasn't just hurt. He was taken out, flattened, destroyed! By his mommy! I'm sorry, **pookie**[14], does it still hurt?

Ben: No! I've made peace with being a four-eyed **geek**[15], whose **butt**[16] was kicked by his mother.

Jason: Ben, I don't want you to quit, and I'm gonna tell you why.

杰森： 嘿，本，你妈说你想放弃上空手道的课？

本： 你看，爸爸，我努力了，但失败了，我的一生完了。

杰森： 得了，眼睛的伤会好的。可你没有任何理由不去接着上空手道课。

麦琪： 杰森，你在说些什么呀？下一个跟他打的人可能就不会像我这么爱他了。

杰森： 可我不想我们的儿子仅仅因为受伤就放弃，麦琪。

麦琪： 杰森，他不仅仅是受伤，他被摔出去，被打瘪了，被毁坏了，还是被他的妈妈。我对不起你，心肝，你还疼吗？

本： 不，我现在想要平静地做个四眼，尤其是被妈妈打了以后。

杰森： 本，我不想让你退出，我告诉你为什么。

注释	
5. Nevada 内华达，美国州名，位于美国的西南部	**11. violence** ['vaɪələns] *n.* 暴力
6. assumed [ə'sjuːmd] *adj.* 假的；假装的	**12. ruin** ['ruːɪn] *v.* 毁灭；使破产
7. philosophical [ˌfɪlə'sɒfɪkl] *adj.* 哲学的，冷静的	**13. hurt** [hɜːt] *adj.* 受伤的；痛苦的；受损的
8. graceful ['greɪsfl] *adj.* 优雅的；优美的	**14. pookie** 小可爱
9. bully ['bʊlɪ] *n.* 欺负；威吓	**15. geek** [giːk] *n.* 家伙，人
10. junior ['dʒuːnɪə(r)] *adj.* 大学一年级	**16. butt** [bʌt] *n.* 屁股

Ben:	Oh, please, dad. No pep **talks**[17].
Jason:	Oh, come on. I mean, you've been down before, Ben, and every time you've been down before, you've reached down deeper for some of that "**heck**[18], I can do it" Seaver **spirit**[19], right?
Ben:	And I thought you were gonna give me a pep talk.
Jason:	And what about the cap thing?
Maggie:	Oh, it's very **simple**[20]. From now on, we dress him in **plain**[21], **generic**[22] clothes that no other kid would be caught dead in.
Ben:	Wait a minute…
Maggie:	Jason, let him quit.
Jason:	Oh, we still gotta eat the cost of those karate lessons.
Maggie:	Well, Chrissy can take them.
Jason:	Ah.
Maggie:	Honey, we should just face it. It's **obvious**[23] that Ben doesn't have the **talent**[24], the drive, or the ability.
Jason:	God knows, he's a **klutz**[25].
Ben:	Okay, okay. I'm starting to feel that "heck, I can do it" Seaver spirit. Mom, dad, I'm going back to Karate. And you know, you guys used to be much better at this "good cop, bad **cop**[26]" thing.

本：	哦，求你了，别做讲演。
杰森：	哦，行了，我的意思是你以前也失败过，本，每次失败后你都会更加深刻地认识到"见鬼，我能做好这个"的西维尔精神，对吗？
本：	嘿，我还以为你要发表演说呢。
杰森：	帽子的事怎么样了呢？
麦琪：	哦，这很简单，从现在起我们就给他穿朴朴素素的、平平常常的衣服，就不会有人来抢了。
本：	等一等。
麦琪：	杰森，就让他放弃吧。
杰森：	哦，课程的全部学费我们都已经交了。
麦琪：	让克瑞斯接着学。
杰森：	好。
麦琪：	亲爱的，我们要面对现实。很明显，本既没有天分，也没有内驱力或者能力。
杰森：	上帝知道！他是个笨手笨脚的人。
本：	好了，好了，我开始认识到"见鬼，我能够做好这个"西维尔精神的含义了。妈妈爸爸，我要继续学空手道。要知道，以前你们一唱一和的表演要比这高明。

Scene 3: Ben got some achievements in his Karate lessons. Someday Ben ran into that bully in the school and the punk challenged him as usual. How should Ben, a martial artist now, react to his provocation?

本的空手道学得初有成效。这天在学校又和那个爱欺负人的同学撞上了，那个家伙一如往常的挑衅，武林高手该如何接招儿呢？

Razor: What are you **staring**[27] at, geek? Am I gonna have to **bust**[28] you one? I said give it to me now.

瑞仁：看什么呢，四眼？是想让我动手？我说了现在把衣服给我。

Ben: No. I'm not giving you this jacket, or anything else ever again.

本：不，我不会再给你夹克或别的什么东西了。

Razor: Whoa! Big man, huh? Big words. All right, geek, *c'mon*[3], let's throw. Show me what you've got, *tough guy*[4], huh! C'mon, let's go for it right here, right now! Go for it!

瑞仁：哇呜，了不起的人啊，说大话呢吧。好啊，四眼，来练两下，看看你都学了些什么，硬汉？不错，嗯，来吧。就在这练练，就现在，来吧。

Ben: He's wide open. The **dude**[29] will never see it coming. Control. Don't touch him unless you have to.

本：他一点都没防备，让那小子尝尝厉害。稳住，不到迫不得已不动手。

Razor: C'mon, geek, let's go for it. Huh! Huh!

瑞仁：来呀，四眼，咱们练两下，哈，哈。

Ben: I'm not gonna fight you.

本：我不想和你动手。

Razor: Did you hear that? He said he's not gonna fight me, huh. What am I supposed to do, huh? Stand on his feet, and use him like a punching bag[5]? (laughing) Look at the dude, he's frozen. Come on, baby, let's get out of here.

瑞仁：听见了吗？他说他不想动手。嗯？我该做什么呢，哈？站在他脚边把他当练功袋用吗？（大笑）这个傻瓜僵住了。来吧，宝贝，咱们离开这吧。

Luke: Hey, man, you were amazing.

卢克：嘿，兄弟，你真不错。

Ben: Thanks. I came real close to getting **ugly**[30].

本：谢谢。刚才我差点就和他动粗了。

Luke: Well, speaking of ugly, you can forget about Becka. She's not worth it.

卢克：是啊，说起粗鲁，你该忘掉贝卡，她不值得你这样。

Girl: Excuse me, Ben?

女孩：打搅一下，本。

Ben: Yeah?

本：怎么？

Girl: I really like the way you **handled**[31] that **creep**[32].

女孩：我真喜欢你刚才镇定的样子。

Ben: Thanks.

本：谢谢。

Girl: Save you a seat at lunch?

女孩：午饭给你占个位？

Ben: Sure. I'm always hungry.

本：好的，我总是觉得饿。

注释

17. pep talk 鼓舞士气的讲话

18. heck [hek] *ex.* 真见鬼（hell 的委婉说法）

19. spirit ['spɪrɪt] *n.* 精神；心灵；情绪；志气

20. simple ['sɪmpl] *adj.* 简单的；单纯的；天真的

21. plain [pleɪn] *adj.* 简单的；朴素的

22. generic [dʒəˈnerɪk] *adj.* 泛化的，通用的

23. obvious ['ɒbvɪəs] *adj.* 明显的；显著的

24. talent ['tælənt] *n.* 才能；天才；天资

25. klutz [klʌts] *n.* 笨手笨脚的人

26. good cop, bad cop: 一个红脸，一个白脸

27. stare [steə] *v.* 凝视，盯着看

28. bust [bʌst] *v.* 使破产；使爆裂

29. dude [du:d] *n.* 花花公子；纨绔子弟

30. ugly ['ʌɡlɪ] *adj.* 暴躁的，乖戾的；好吵架的

31. handle ['hændl] *v.* 处理；操作；运用

32. creep [kri:p] *n.* 爬行；蔓延；慢慢地移动

📖 文化背景

1. Karate 空手道

空手道来源于中国拳法，成型于琉球王国（今琉球群岛），是风靡于世界的一种武术。古琉球由于长年的禁武政策，武器一向被禁止使用，因此，人们不得不创出赤手空拳的格斗技术，以求得生存的自卫本领，尤其是 17 世纪初日本萨摩藩侵占琉球后，严禁武器的携带和保存，于是在上层阶级之间，参考中国拳法，创出了独特的格斗技术，这就是最初的空手道，称之为"唐手"，1935 年正式命名为"空手道"。现在作为竞技体育项目的空手道目的已不同于最初的格斗训练，它提倡最大化地发挥空手道特有的"一击必杀"威力，培养人们"不畏艰辛、敢于拼搏、不惧强大、增强自信"的武道精神的同时，使我们的身躯成为抗敌的真正"武器"。

✍ 常用表达

1. Forget it. 没关系，算了吧。

例：—I am sorry I broke your teapot.

— Forget it.

—对不起，我打破了你的茶壶。

—没关系。

2. No way. 没门，决不。

例：There's no way I'm agreeing to that!

这件事我决不同意!

3. c'mon 拜托，快来（come on）

例："C'mon, they are employees working for the government." Gadhafi said.

格达费说："得了吧，他们不过是政府雇来干活的。"

4. tough guy 硬汉，难缠的人

例：It's impossible to beat David. He is a tough guy.

想要打败大卫很难。他很强悍。

5. punching bag 沙袋，攻击目标

例：He resigned because his boss used him as a punching bag.

他辞职了，因为老板把他当成攻击目标。

Coupling
《欢喜冤家》

THE COMPLETE THIRD SERIES

CoupLing

入选理由：

　　这是一部由英国广播公司（BBC）2 频道于 2000 年正式推出的以青年人为题材和对象的系列情景喜剧，是一部经典的英国情景喜剧电视剧。剧中角色纯正的英国腔调，保证大家在观剧时可以把英式英语听个够，但同时也会担心他们会咬到自己的舌头。本剧在情节设计中所达到的精致和完美让人叹为观止，而六位当时并不算大明星的青年演员所展现的精湛演技更是具有顶尖演员的水平，无怪播出之后立刻走红大西洋两岸，在互联网电影资料库、亚马逊及 BBC 网站可以领略到其受欢迎的程度。2002 年底，第三季播完，故事情节基本告一段落。美国全国广播公司看到这部"英国版《老友记》"在英美两地广受欢迎，认为正好可以搬来做 2004 年终于要停播的《老友记》的接档剧目，于是在 2003 年大张旗鼓地决定翻拍。美国的粉丝本来以为这是件好事，没想到美国的翻拍采用了全台词照搬的方法，结果只播出一集就因为骂声太大而搁浅。英式的对白、英式的幽默，另有一番情趣。该剧于 2000 年 5 月在 BBC2 频道播出了第一季即获得广泛好评，这从互联网电影资料库 9.2 的评分可见一斑，该剧于 2003 年获得英国喜剧奖（BCA）"最佳电视喜剧"奖项。

Section 1　剧情特点：

　　本剧每集都是 29 分钟，主要是讲三男三女生活的场景，想到了什么？对了，《老友记》！同样的男女角色配备，同样是爱情喜剧，于是，《欢喜冤家》便被称作英国版的《老友记》。然而，一贯以制作精良而著称的英剧总是能给人惊喜，该剧的创意和编剧均由史蒂芬•莫法特（Steven Moffat）一人担当，在情节设定、人物表演、喜剧元素的设计和表现等诸多方面所达到的水平，要比《老友记》高几个档次。相比之下，《老友记》只能说是一部"业余"水平的好作品而已。当然总体来说，英剧的水准本身就高于美剧，这和英剧注重创意与编剧一体化是分不开的，美剧的创意一般也就展现在最初几集的编排上，以后主要的编剧工作都是由其他编剧根据最初的角色设定来自由发挥，编剧队伍的构成也是不断变化，老的走新的来，造成美剧情节连贯性差，甚至前后矛盾，故事往往缺乏深度，人物性格平面化，缺少发展。

本剧基本上每集都会有个小故事，但是上一个故事又与下一个故事环环相扣，密不可分，这些故事围绕以下多条主线展开：史蒂夫和苏珊之间逐渐确立起来的关系，杰夫寻找艳遇过程中的种种意外及后来和上司发展出来的一段关系，派崔克和萨利之间若有若无到情深难舍的感情发展，还有简在事业和异性关系中的各种奇事，等等。剧情的展开基本上采取了讲述的方式，而且往往是三个男生在这边讲，三个女生在那边谈，谈话的内容构成了故事的背景，所以大多数时候故事的前半段剧情都是倒叙的，而后半段该如何进展，则随着时间的推移展开，因而牢牢吸引了观众的眼球。有的时候一件事从不同人口中描述出来，就成了截然不同的样子，让人啼笑皆非。有的时候，是分角色进行讲述，直到看完了所有人的经历，你才能获得完整的剧情。所以说本剧的剧情设计得十分巧妙，时而调足了观众的胃口，时而让观众在捧腹的同时若有所思，让人觉得环环相扣，大呼过瘾。

Section 2　对白特点：

这是一部典型的英国情景喜剧，所以其中的对白时刻能彰显出独特的英式幽默。有些话听起来是那么离奇搞笑，显得无厘头，但是细细回味却觉得十分有道理。举个例子，"屁股是我们女人的天敌，它纠缠我们一生，总是跟在我们后面，而且不断壮大。我怀疑我的屁股在背着我偷偷吃零食"。这是这部剧中一个漂亮姑娘极其严肃地说出的一段话，而在这部剧里，这种让你喷饭的台词比比皆是。本剧的对话比较直接，很少有那种扭捏、拖泥带水之感，相对于美剧《老友记》的"温暖"，它的精妙的对白简直就是"风刀霜剑严相逼"。

Section 3　角色分析：

史蒂夫 (Steve): 是一个优柔寡断、性格不成熟的帅哥，但有时也会大发脾气，替所有男性同胞说出心声，但这是极少数的时候。与简相恋多年，分手后与苏珊相恋，决定与其相伴终生，并生下一个男孩。

杰夫 (Jeff): 他是史蒂夫的莫逆之交，举止语言古怪，思想天马行空，在聊天时突然会冒出一个与交谈内容毫不相关的词来，让大家啼笑皆非。总是说自己淡定从容，但是面对女孩总紧张得说不出什么好话来，常常越描越黑，有一次竟把自己说成了只有一条腿的残疾人，因此他很长一段时间没有找到女友，但是找到之后，对另一半非常专一。

派崔克 (Patrick): 是个头脑简单、外表性感的人，与他交往过的女性众多，他曾说过"基本你们认识的我都交往过"。一次去孕妇交流会，竟然被大多数孕妇认了出来。平时交谈时派崔克最沉默寡言，做事也是默默无闻，但是作为保守党的他谈论起政治来，却一发不可收拾。

简 (Jane): 是史蒂夫的前女友，交通广播的主持人。她总是犯迷糊，无论是在平时生活还是在工作中。因此，在交通广播中她随意改变路名、胡乱指挥，导致多人出了车祸。她有性感的身材和姣好的面容，同时她十分擅用自己的性感作为武器去吸引异性，这招曾一度挽留了史蒂夫。

苏珊 (Susan)：是史蒂夫的继任女友，也是杰夫的同事。在她的计划下，犹豫不决的史蒂夫向她求婚。她曾与三名男主角都相处过，但是和史蒂夫在一起后却没做过任何出格的事情。她美丽聪慧，是个人见人爱的女孩。

萨利 (Sally)：是苏珊的莫逆之交，但她却由于外表不及苏珊而一直嫉妒着她。作为一名美容师，她对衰老和肥胖极度敏感，因此导致她十分"恨嫁"，她曾说自己的每一次笑容都只能留给单身男士。她的虚荣心比较强，曾和一名屠夫相处，却告诉大家他是个外科医生，最后闹出很多笑话来。

🔊 Passage 1 🎥

剧情介绍：

（选自第1季第1集）一开始，史蒂夫就和好友杰夫讨论着该如何把简甩掉，但是发现并无帮助之后便独自去了常去的酒吧。苏珊和萨利是好朋友，区别在于一个身边男性不断，而另一个却十分"恨嫁"，时刻担心自己的衰老，她们也去了那个酒吧，而简和正与苏珊交往的派崔克也去了酒吧，就这样，故事开始了。

Scene: In the bar, Jane and Steve were dating. Jane spouted, but not a word entered Steve's ears. In fact, Steve was thinking how to break up with Jane.

在酒吧里，简和史蒂夫在约会。简在滔滔不绝地说话，可史蒂夫并没听她说什么，实际上，史蒂夫想的是如何跟简分手。

🔊 **Jane:**	And my sister said no, so I said yes. Then she said no again, so I just said yes. But then she said no, so I said yes, yes, yes.	**简：**	我姐姐一个劲的说不是，而我一直说是，然后她又说不是，我还是坚持说是。但她还是说不是，我就说是，是，一定是。
Steve:	How does this story end exactly?	**史蒂夫：**	你到底要说到什么时候啊？
Jane:	She said I had an answer for everything.	**简：**	她说反正我怎么说都有理。
Steve:	Right.	**史蒂夫：**	的确。

Jane:	And I just said "yes"!		简：	然后我就跟她说"就是"。
Steve:	Jane, okay, listen to me, okay? I know I've tried to say this before, and I know I never seem to get anywhere, but this time, Jane, I am going to put it very, very simply. It's over between us.		史蒂夫：	简，够了，听我说，行吗？我知道我以前也这么说过，我也知道每次都不了了之。但是这次，简，我打算直接跟你说，非常直接地，我们之间完了。
Jane:	You want us to **slit**[1] up?		简：	你是想和我分手？
Steve:	Yes, oh, yes, I do.		史蒂夫：	对对，我就是这么想的。
Jane:	I don't accept.		简：	我才不接受呢。
Steve:	What?		史蒂夫：	什么？
Jane:	I don't accept it.		简：	我不接受。
Steve:	No, no, you can't not accept it. I'm **breaking up with**[2] you.		史蒂夫：	不行，你不能不接受，我就是要跟你分手。
Jane:	Don't I get a say in it?		简：	我难道没有发言权吗？
Steve:	Of course you don't.		史蒂夫：	你当然没有。
Jane:	If I don't get a say, then I don't accept it. Anyway, then my sister just looked at me, and she said no, no, no.		简：	连发言权都没有，那我肯定不会接受。不说这个了，我姐姐看着我，然后她说不不不……
Sally:	Mary Kelly does not **fancy**[3] you.		萨利：	玛丽·凯莉才不可能喜欢你呢。
Patrick:	I can *tell*[1] from the way she acts around me, she finds me attractive.		派崔克：	从她的举止，我就能看出来，她觉得我很有吸引力。
Sally:	Is there any form of female behavior, you don't interpret as finding you attractive?		萨利：	女人的什么行为才不会让你误以为你有魅力呢？
Patrick:	It's never really come up.		派崔克：	好像还真的没有。
Susan:	If you two are finished, I thought you wanted to speak to me.		苏珊：	如果你们俩说完了的话，我想你该跟我好好谈谈了吧？
Patrick:	Yeah, yeah, I do. Could you give us a minute?		派崔克：	对，正是。能让我们单独待会儿吗？
Sally:	Mary Kelly thinks you're a complete idiot.		萨利：	玛丽·凯莉肯定认为你是个大傻蛋。
Patrick:	Why does she keep looking at my arse when we're talking?		派崔克：	那为什么我们说话的时候，她老盯着我的屁股呢？
Sally:	She's **lip-reading**[4].		萨利：	因为她只会读唇语。
Patrick:	We need to talk.		派崔克：	我们得好好谈谈。
Susan:	Sure.		苏珊：	当然。
Patrick:	About our relationship. I'm just starting to think it's all getting a bit hot and heavy, and we both need to back off and cool down. You know, maybe we should just both		派崔克：	关于我们的爱情，我在想我们的感情是不是过于激烈和沉重了点儿？我们需要退一步，先冷静一阵吧。或许我们都该好好想想以

	think about where everything's going and whether we're starting to commit more than we intend to or…or want to?		后发展的方向，或是我们做出承诺的速度是否超过我们预期的发展，或原想要的发展。
Susan:	What relationship?	苏珊：	什么爱情啊？
Jane:	And then my sister said "absolutely not". So I said "absolutely yes".	简：	后来我姐姐又说"当然不是"，于是我反驳"一定是"。
Steve:	It doesn't matter whether you accept it or not. It's over, you're **dumped**[5]. Look, um, it's not you, okay? It's me.	史蒂夫：	不管你愿不愿意接受，我们结束了，你被甩了。问题不在于你，懂吗？是我的问题。
Jane:	Then why am I the one that's getting dumped? You should be the one that gets dumped.	简：	那为什么是我被甩？被甩的应该是你。
Steve:	Exactly, it's all my fault. So dump me.	史蒂夫：	正是，这都是我的错，你甩了我吧。
Jane:	No.	简：	不要。
Steve:	What?	史蒂夫：	什么？
Jane:	We can work on your problems.	简：	我们可以解决你的问题。
Patrick:	I can't believe you!	派崔克：	我真不敢相信!
Susan:	Well, I didn't mean to hurt your feelings. I just never saw it as a relationship as such. I just thought we were having a bit of fun, a bit of sex.	苏珊：	我不是想伤害你，只不过我不认为我们是在谈恋爱，我觉得我们在一起是挺开心的，然后再一起上个床什么的。
Patrick:	Well, yeah, I mean, that's what I thought. I mean, that's pretty much the way I see it.	派崔克：	对，我也是这么想，我指的是，跟我想得差不多。
Susan:	Well, there you are, then.	苏珊：	那你没事吧。
Patrick:	Yeah.	派崔克：	当然。
Susan:	I mean, it's not as if we're being **faithful**[6] or anything.	苏珊：	我的意思就是我们用不着对彼此忠诚或什么的。

注释	
1. slit [slɪt] *n.* 割裂	**4. lip-reading** 唇语；信任
2. breaking up with 跟……分手，与……断绝联系	**5. dump** [dʌmp] *v.* 废弃；被甩
3. fancy ['fænsi] *v.* 想象；喜爱；设想；自负	**6. faithful** ['feɪθfl] *adj.* 忠实的，忠诚的；如实的；准确可靠的

📞 常用表达

tell 的用法

1. 做及物动词

    (1) tell 说

        inform 较 tell 郑重而正式

        relate 叙述自己所看到或经历的事

        report 将自己所调查的事报知他人

        a. 讲（故事、事实等），说，言，话，述

          tell the truth 说实话

          tell a lie 说谎

        b. 对（人）讲，告诉

          I will tell you. 我来告诉你。

          例：He asked where she lived and I told him.

              他问她的住处，我告诉了他。

        c. 告诉（人）……，对（人）讲……[to]

          例：He told us his adventures. = He told his adventures to us.

              他告诉我们他的冒险故事。

        d. 对（人）说（……事），传达，告诉 [of, about]

          例：He told me about his name.

               他把他名字的事讲给我听。

          例：I told him of her death.

               我把她的死讯告诉他。

        e. 告诉（人）（……事）

          例：He told me that he liked baseball.

               他告诉我他喜欢棒球。

          例：He told me that he had finished reading the book.

               他告诉我他已读完那本书。

          例：So she told me.

               所以她告诉了我。

          例：I told you so!

               你看，我早就说过的（你就是不听我的话）！

        f. 告诉（人）……，告知

          例：Tell me when you will leave London.

               告诉我你何时要离开伦敦。

          例：She will tell you what to do.

               她会教你怎么做。

(2) 吩咐（人）（做……），叫，命令，叮咛

    例：He told me not to drive too fast.

        他叫我（开车）不要开得太快。

    例：I was told to wear a suit.

        我被吩咐要穿成套的衣服。

    例：Do as you are told.

        叫你怎么做，你就怎么做。

(3) 知道

    a. 知道……，懂……

      例：He cannot tell (the) time yet.

        他还看不懂（钟表上的）时间。

      例：I can tell the time from the position of the sun.

        我可以从太阳的位置知道时间。

      例：You can tell him by his voice.

        你可以从他的声音听出是他。

    b. 看得出（……事）

      例：One can tell (that) she is intelligent.

        任何人都看得出她很聪明。

    c. 知道（如何……）

      例：He couldn't tell what to do.

        他不知道怎么办才好。

      例：There is no telling when he may come.

        他何时会来，不得而知。

      例：Nobody can tell what it is.

        谁也说不清它是什么。

(4) 分辨

    a.（在两者之间）辨别（差异等），识别，辨识 [between]

      例：You'll not be able to tell the difference between them.

        你（永远）无法辨别他们之间的差异。

    b. 辨别……[from]

      例：I can't tell one twin from the other.

        我无法辨别这对双胞胎哪个是哪个。

    c. 识别

      例：tell the twins apart

        识别双胞胎

    d. 辨别（……与否）

      例：I cannot tell whether it is true (or not).

        我无法辨别那是否真实。

(5) 显示，显露

    a.（物）表露，显示，表示

      例：Her face told her grief.

        她脸上流露着忧伤。

      例：This signpost tells the way to New York.

        这个路标指示前往纽约的路。

      例：The clock tells the time.

        时钟报时。

    b.（物）对（人）显示（……）

      例：A line of pink on the eastern horizon told me that daybreak was near.

        东边地平线上的一道淡红光线使我知道天快要亮了。

(6)（古）点数，计算

2. 做不及物动词

(1) 说

    a.（人）讲（……之事），叙述，说 [of, about]

      例：I'll tell about/of it.

        我来讲这件事。

    b.（物）显示（……），表露 [of]

      例：His hands tell of heavy labor.

        他的双手显示他干的是粗活。

(2) 密告（他人之事），告发；泄密；搬弄是非，打小报告 [on]

    例：Did he promise not to tell?

      他答应过不泄密吗？

    例：Helen told on her sister Mary.

      海伦打妹妹玛丽的小报告。

(3) 奏效，起作用

    a. 奏效；发生作用，影响；（炮弹等）命中

      例：His experience will tell in the end.

        他的经验终究会发挥作用。

      例：Money is bound to tell.

        钱一定不会白花的。/ 花了钱就一定有效果。

      例：Every shot told.

        百发百中。

    b.（对……）奏效；（对人、健康等）发生作用，给予影响 [on, upon]

      例：His age is beginning to tell on/upon him.

        他开始显得衰老了。

    c.（对……不利地）发生（作用影响）[against]

例：Everything told against him.

　　事事对他不利。

(4) 知道，辨别

　　例：You can never tell.

　　　　这可就不知道了。谁都拿不准。

　　例：Nobody can tell.=Who can tell?

　　　　谁晓得。

　　例：You never can tell.

　　　　（将来之事）谁也不知道（不能断定）。

　　例：You can't always tell from appearances.

　　　　你不能老是从外表来分辨。

all told 合计，总共

例：There were fifty of them, all told.

　　他们合计有五十人。

tell me another（口语）我不相信，我想你是在开玩笑吧

tell off

a. 申斥，责骂

　例：Betty was told off for being late.

　　　贝蒂因迟到而挨骂。

b. "军" 分派（人等）（工作）[for]；分派（人等）（去做……）

　例：Some of the soldiers were told off for guard duty.

　　　有些士兵被分派卫兵勤务。

　例：You're telling me!

　　　（不用你说）我清楚得很!

◁)) Passage 2 📷

剧情介绍：

（选自第 2 季第 1 集）杰夫每天上班都要坐一段地铁，最近他喜欢上了这种交通工具，因为每天都能看到一位美女的腿，他深信自己已经爱上了这位美女。而这天，他得到了与这位美女面对面的机会。

Scene:	The beauty that made Jeff admire in the heart the day in the subway coincidentally sat opposite to Jeff today, and she accidentally touched Jeff's leg when she sat down. What a good opportunity! However, it was a pity that Jeff was so nervous that he began to talk nonsense...

地铁里那位令杰夫心仪的美女这天很凑巧地坐到了杰夫的对面，而且在落座的时候还不小心碰到了杰夫的腿。好机会啊，可惜杰夫却紧张地开始胡说八道了……

◁)) **Chrissie:**	Oh, sorry.	克丽丝：	抱歉。
Jeff:	(Okay, this is it, Jeff; look at her. Just look at her, you can do it. Oh, I was right, she's gorgeous!) Sorry.	杰夫：	（杰夫，机会来了，看着她，快看，你能做到。我是对的，她漂亮极了！）对不起。
Chrissie:	Is something wrong?	克丽丝：	有什么不对劲吗？
Jeff:	No, no, nothing. Um...(Say something sensible, say something **sensible**[1].) You … you look just like the back of your head. No, I-I'm sorry. I mean, it's just, what I…	杰夫：	没有，什么都没有。（说点靠谱的话，说啊。）你……你看起来和你后面一样。不是，抱歉，我是说……
Chrissie:	Are you all right?	克丽丝：	你没事吧？
Jeff:	I'm fine, yeah, I'm great, thanks. It's just that I've always seen you sitting over there, and I could only see the back of your head.	杰夫：	我很好，好极了，谢谢。就是我总看见你坐在那边，我只能看到你的背。
Chrissie:	Oh, okay.	克丽丝：	好的。
Jeff:	But the front's just as good, better, in fact, because you've got a face, and I'm not just saying that.	杰夫：	你前面看起来也很好，实际上更好，因为你前面有脸。我不是随口说说的。
Chrissie:	Well, thanks.	克丽丝：	好吧，谢谢。
Jeff:	And—and you've got a leg. Uh, I mean…	杰夫：	你还有条腿，我是说，另一条腿。

another leg.

Chrissie: What?

Jeff: (Don't **panic**[2]. Keep it sensible. Concentrate.) I'm just saying it—it's great to see your legs together for once. Uh, no, no. What I meant was, normally, I enjoy your legs separately. Well, one of your legs anyway. It was sitting over there with the rest of you, so, obviously, you'd know that, but—but I could only see the left one.

Chrissie: Okay.

Jeff: But, you know, it's great to see them both here.

Chrissie: Well, that's good, huh?

Jeff: I'm not saying I *preferred*[1] them separately. You know, they're better together. I can see that. They're, well, they're like a leg team.

Chrissie: Good.

Jeff: Believe me, I'm not trying to part your legs. No, no, uh…not "part" in the sense of, you know, um—I mean, I don't want to—

Chrissie: What?

Jeff: **Amputate**[3] one.

Chrissie: I'm sorry?

Jeff: I'm not one of these amputators. (amputators?)

Chrissie: Amputators?

Jeff: Yeah, in case you were worrying, I'm not one.

Chrissie: What do you mean "amputators"? What are you talking about amputating for?

Jeff: I'm sorry, it's on my mind.

Chrissie: Why?

Jeff: (Explain—tell her you just got lost, tell her the truth.) Because…(The truth, for once, don't tell a stupid lie.) I got a wooden leg.

克丽丝： 什么？

杰夫： （别慌，说点人话，集中精力。）我是说，这很棒。总算有个机会能同时看到你两条腿。不不不，我是说通常情况下，我也喜欢单独一个的样子。你的一条腿，和你身体的其他部分在一起。当然这些你都知道，但是，但是我只能看到你的左腿。

克丽丝： 好的。

杰夫： 不过，看到两条腿在一起感觉真好。

克丽丝： 嗯，的确如此。

杰夫： 我不是说我喜欢它们单独的样子，我是说在一起最好，我能看出来，它们，这两条腿就像一个团队一样。

克丽丝： 好的。

杰夫： 相信我，我不是想要把你的腿分开，不不不，你知道不是那个"分开"的意思。我是说我不想……

克丽丝： 什么？

杰夫： 截断其中的一个。

克丽丝： 什么？

杰夫： 我不是截肢狂。（截肢狂？）

克丽丝： 截肢狂？

杰夫： 我怕你害怕，我真的不是。

克丽丝： 你说"截肢狂"是什么意思？你提到截肢是想说什么呢？

杰夫： 抱歉，我脑子里想到这个了。

克丽丝： 为什么？

杰夫： （快解释啊，告诉她你找不到北了，和她说实话。）因为……（快说次实话，别去编蹩脚的谎话了。）我装了义肢。

注释 **1. sensible** ['sensəbl] *adj.* 明智的；明显的；意识到的；通晓事理的 **2. panic** ['pænɪk] *n.* 十分惊慌 **3. amputate** ['æmpjuteɪt] *v.* 截肢；切断；删除

Chrissie:	Oh, oh, no, really?	克丽丝：	噢，是真的吗？
Jeff:	Yes, I had one of my legs amputated, but never mind, eh?	杰夫：	对，我有条腿被截肢了。不过别在意。
Chrissie:	I'm so sorry. Well, no wonder it's on your mind.	克丽丝：	我很遗憾，怪不得你脑袋里想到这些。
Jeff:	It's not a problem, really, easy come, easy go.	杰夫：	问题不大，没事，来得容易去得也容易。
Chrissie:	Which one?	克丽丝：	哪条腿？
Jeff:	I'm sorry?	杰夫：	什么？
Chrissie:	Which leg did you have amputated?	克丽丝：	哪条腿被截肢了？
Jeff:	(Think. Think. Why can't I think?) Sorry, it was such a long time ago.	杰夫：	（想啊，快想啊！怎么想不出来了。）抱歉，时间太久了。
Chrissie:	What?	克丽丝：	啊？
Jeff:	The left one, it was the left.	杰夫：	左腿！

常用表达

1. prefer 的用法：

(1) prefer A to B (A、B 皆为名词)

例：I prefer the blue ball to the black ball.

于黑色球相比，我更喜欢蓝色球。

(2) prefer doing A to doing B

=would rather do A than do B

=like doing A better than doing B

例：I prefer walking to running

我更喜欢走路而不喜欢跑步。

(3) prefer to do A(没有比较，只做一件事的就用这个）=would rather do A

例：I prefer to sing.

我更喜欢唱歌。

(4) 拓展内容 prefer to doing A rather than doing B

注意事项：prefer 有时态变化，过去式为 preferred，第三人称单数直接加 s。

would rather...than... 无时态变化。

🔊 **Passage 3** 📷

剧情介绍：

（选自第 3 季第 5 集）简在工作中结识了作为主持人的同事詹姆斯，并开始与他交往，令她郁闷的是詹姆斯坚持反对婚前同居的生活。苏珊和史蒂夫两人看上去像一对"老夫老妻"，两人相爱但是久处令他们缺乏激情。萨利和派崔克之间有一些尴尬，他们彼此充满爱意，但是又没有捅破那层窗户纸，两个人处在等待一个明确表白的朦胧阶段。杰夫与上司茉莉亚交往了，两个人在一起如胶似漆，特别是杰夫，好不容易有了一个女友，这令他十分珍惜。这天，这几位老友又在那个酒吧进行了小聚，简准备把新男友詹姆斯介绍给大家认识。

Scene: In the bar, Sally was chatting with a few friends. Basically, it was Sally who kept nagging, and the men were just listening…

在酒吧里，萨利在跟几个朋友聊天，实际上基本是她一个人说话，几个男人无奈地听她唠叨……

🔊 **Sally:** Hello, yourself.

James: And is this Patrick?

Sally: Yes, this is Patrick, here he is. You speak now, Patrick.

Patrick: Hi.

James: Good to meet you…at last.

Patrick: Likewise.

James: So I *gather*[1] you're not a couple?

Patrick: No, no, no, **definitely**[1] not. I mean, we go out, but we don't have sex.

James: Well, this is great. Jane's been telling me all about you guys. I feel like I know you all already.

Jeff: Guys, emergency! How long do **intestines**[2] take?

萨利： 你好。

詹姆斯： 这位是派崔克吗？

萨利： 对，他是派崔克。现在轮到你说话了，派崔克。

派崔克： 你好。

詹姆斯： 很高兴……终于……见到你了。

派崔克： 我也是。

詹姆斯： 我估计你们不是一对。

派崔克： 当然不是，我们出去约会，但是不上床。

詹姆斯： 这很好，简跟我提过你们，我感觉我早就认识你们了。

杰夫： 伙计们，十万火急！肠子有多长？

注释 1. definitely ['defɪnətlɪ] *adv.* 清楚地，当然；明确地，肯定地
2. intestine [ɪn'testɪn] *n.* 肠；内脏；下水

James:	Are you Jeff?		詹姆斯：	你是杰夫吗？
Jeff:	What?		杰夫：	什么？
James:	I think you're gonna fit right in.		詹姆斯：	我在把名字对号入座。
Steve:	This is Jane's new boyfriend, remember?		史蒂夫：	这是简的新男友，记得吗？
Jeff:	Please, I don't have much time. I've got to get back to Julia.		杰夫：	我没多少时间了，我得回到茱莉亚那儿去。
Susan:	Oh, so you're with Julia at the moment?		苏珊：	你现在跟茱莉亚在一起？
Jeff:	Yeah, well, we're sort of in the middle of something.		杰夫：	对，我们还有点事没做完。
Steve:	You have no idea the level to which we're getting that.		史蒂夫：	你不会知道我们怎么知道这点的。
Jeff:	Is he the one who doesn't...		杰夫：	他就是那个没有……
Steve:	We've covered that!		史蒂夫：	以后再讨论这个。
Jeff:	Okay, if you...if you swallowed something, something valuable, say, how long before it found its way...back to the light.		杰夫：	好的，如果你吞下了什么东西，比如说很贵重的东西，那东西多长时间才能……重见光明？
Steve:	Back to the light?		史蒂夫：	重见光明？
Jeff:	The light at the end of the...		杰夫：	就是那个……出来之后的光啊。
Steve:	Yes, Jeff, thank you, I have the image. Once again, a dark new place has opened in my mind.		史蒂夫：	谢谢，杰夫，你不用多讲，我已经能想象到了。又一个全新的黑暗角落在我脑海中展现。
Jeff:	I just need to know how long before it's ringside.		杰夫：	我想知道多长的距离才到边缘。
Steve:	Dark place number 3008.		史蒂夫：	黑暗角落 3008 号。
Jeff:	Why are you all staring at me?		杰夫：	为什么大家都盯着我？
Steve:	Jeff, do you maybe want to fill us in on what you and Julia have been up to?		史蒂夫：	杰夫，或许你可以告诉我们，你和茱莉亚刚才在干什么呢？
Jeff:	Well, we were...we were spending a quiet evening in front of the television. And in the course of events, I swallowed some of her **jewelry**[3].		杰夫：	我们……我们一晚上都……静静地坐在电视前。在这个过程中，我把她的首饰给吞了。
Steve:	You what?		史蒂夫：	什么？
Jeff:	There was a swallowage incident. I swallowed an item.		杰夫：	这只不过是一个吞咽事件，我吞了一件首饰。
Steve:	Right.		史蒂夫：	对。
Jeff:	Now, normally when I swallow Julia's jewelry, it doesn't really...		杰夫：	正常来讲，当我吞下茱莉亚的首饰时，它不是真的……

Steve:	Jeff, please! Normally has never been used in that sentence before.	史蒂夫：	杰夫，拜托。"正常来讲"这个词从来没有用在你说的这句话之前。
Jeff:	Well, you know what it's like when you've got your own actual, real-life girlfriend. It's like you've got a woman with a **nudity**[4] switch. And sometimes when she's lying there, and she's just so...so totally naked, I can't control myself. I just sort of...**hoover**[5].	杰夫：	你们知道这种感觉吧，当你有了你自己的、真正的现实生活中的女朋友时，就好像你手上有一个可以让女人脱光的按钮。有时候她躺在那儿，她看起来如此……彻底地裸着，我无法控制我自己，我就像吸尘器一样大口吸气。
Steve:	Okay.	史蒂夫：	好吧。
Jeff:	Obviously, now and then, in the course of any kind of nudity hoovering, you're gonna ingest items. It's just part of a relationship. But she doesn't usually notice, so normally I remain calm, let nature take its course. And, in due time, slip the relevant items, back into her jewelry box.	杰夫：	很明显，时不时的，在任何一种这样的吸气过程中，你总会吞下点什么，这是恋爱的一部分。不过她不常发现，正常情况下，我尽量保持平静，顺其自然，再在适当的时候，把吞下的东西偷偷放回她的珠宝盒里。
Steve:	I see.	史蒂夫：	明白了。
Jeff:	I don't mean directly.	杰夫：	我不是直接给她。
Steve:	I was **clinging to**[6] that hope.	史蒂夫：	我也希望你不要。

常用表达

1. gather 的用法：

(1) 集合，聚集，搜集；采集（摘）；收集（获，拾）；逐渐获得（加快）；渐增（强），恢复；推断（测）；揣想；了解；结论；得出想法；折皱；打皱；吸引，唤起注意；鼓起勇气；努力；使导弹进入制导波束内。

例：gather crops 收庄稼

gather flowers 采花

gather information/experience 逐渐获得消息 / 积累经验

gather strength 恢复体力

gather taxes 收税

gather one's brows 皱眉

注释 3. jewelry ['dʒuːəlrɪ] n. 珠宝；珠宝类   5. hoover ['huːvə(r)] v. 电动吸尘

4. nudity ['njuːdətɪ] n. 裸露；裸体像   6. clinging to 坚持；依靠；依附；紧握不放

例：The train gathered speed as it left the station.

火车离站时，速度逐渐加快。

例：What did you gather from his statement?

你推想他的声明是什么意思?

(2) 习惯用语

gather from 从……推测，从……获悉

gather in 收获；［口语］拾得（橄榄球）接住（球）

gather oneself up 鼓起勇气，打起精神，集中全力

gather oneself together 鼓起勇气，打起精神，集中全力

gather out 选出

gather round 围拢，聚拢；团结起来给予援助

gather together 集合，集聚，收集

gather up 收集；拾起；概括，总括；集中（精力等）；蜷缩（肢体等）；［口语］拘捕，抓起来

gather way（航海）出航；开始移动

(3) 近义词辨析

gather, collect, assemble, muster 都含"收集""聚集"的意思。

a. gather 系常用词，指"收集""聚集""集合在一起"。

例：The clouds are gathering.

云层在聚集。

b. collect 指"有计划、有选择地收集"。

例：He collects stamps.

他集邮。

c. assemble 指"为某一特定目的而收集"。

例：The dean assembled the students in the auditorium.

教务长把学生集合在礼堂里。

d. muster 系正式用语，特指"部队召集"或"为检阅、检查而召集"。

例：He mustered all his soldiers.

他把士兵召集在一起。

Chapter 2

科幻剧
Science Fiction

科幻剧源于科幻片，顾名思义科幻片即"科学幻想片"，H. 弗兰克给科幻片下的定义是：所描写的是发生在一个虚构的、但原则上是可能产生的模式世界中的戏剧性事件。其主题基本有如下四种：宗教与反叛主题、凡尔纳式科学享乐主义主题、权力与秩序主题、罪恶与拯救主题。尽管"科幻电影"一词出现于 1926 年左右，但是早在电影诞生之时，科幻片的雏形就已随之产生，如法国导演梅里爱的《月球旅行记》（1902 年）、《太空旅行记》（1904 年）和《海底两万里》（1907 年）。纵观科幻片的发展，除了早期的法国电影之外，美国科幻电影自诞生后，就以迅猛的势头成为主力，无论是资金、技术，还是经验和文学积累，其他国家都无法望其项背。此外，为了最大限度地迎合各种口味的观众，类型的拼贴和融合已经成为科幻片的一个重要特征，许多影片并非严格意义上的科幻片，但却具备一定的科幻元素。科学技术的发展为实现幻想提供了保证，也能成为新的科学幻想的源泉。

科幻剧在科幻片的基础上不断发展壮大。美剧中较为经典的科幻剧有《邪恶力量》《危机边缘》《超人前传》《X 档案》《星际之门》等，英剧中的《神秘博士》是经典科幻电视剧，同时也是英国最受欢迎的电视剧。

Supernatural 《邪恶力量》

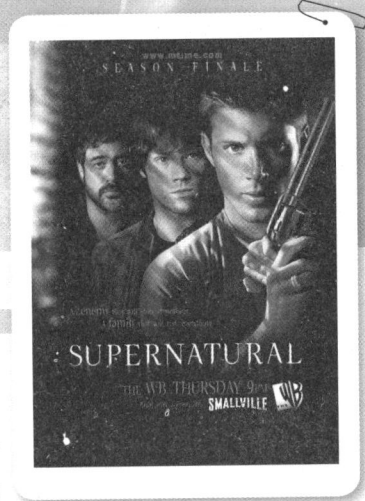

4

入选理由：

《邪恶力量》，又译《凶鬼恶灵》《狙魔人》《超自然档案》《神秘力量》，是由美国 WB 电视台（现更名为哥伦比亚及华纳兄弟联合电视网）播出的讲述灵异超自然现象的电视剧，在加拿大拍摄。该片的投资每集只有几十万，但在海外赚得盆满钵满，日均点击率 500 万，所以说是低投入、高收益的一档戏。除去可观的收入，该片也得到了影评界的一致肯定，迄今已获得青年艺术家奖（2010）、艾美奖（2008）、美国青少年观众票选大奖（2007）等诸多奖项，是一部值得欣赏的美剧。

Section 1 剧情特点：

该剧主要是围绕山姆·温彻斯特和迪恩·温彻斯特两兄弟开着 1967 年的黑色雪佛兰"羚羊"穿梭在美国各处，调查超自然或不可思议的事件并与之战斗的故事，那些邪恶的神鬼大多来自于美国的都市传说和民间故事。一切从他们 22 年前的童年开始，母亲被一股超自然力量所杀，父亲因此重操旧业，开始了捕猎之旅，即猎杀危害人类的超自然生物的旅程。父亲一边追查杀死妻子的恶魔的下落，一边教导两兄弟猎杀恶魔与超自然生物的知识。不过，山姆想过的是正常人的生活，于是他与父亲之间的裂痕越来越大，最终因为一次激烈的争吵而离家出走，独自去上大学。在大学里，山姆是个成绩优异的高材生，而且有了美丽的女友。哥哥迪恩却仍然坚定地留在父亲身边，继续追查。然而，父亲在追踪活动中失踪了，这下山姆勉为其难地和哥哥一起，抽出了一个周末来寻找失踪的父亲。本来想意思意思敷衍了事，却因一次可怕的悲剧事件而彻底改变想法的山姆，从此放弃了一切幸福快乐生活的想法，全心全意地投入了这一行动。

Section 2 对白特点：

虽然是一部科幻剧，也有惊悚成分，但是整个影片的对话还是比较诙谐幽默的，与影片的灰色基调形成较大的反差，极具看点。哥哥的话语将其小痞子的性格展现得淋漓尽致，弟弟的话语则时刻彰显了他细腻的特点。可是随着剧情深入，我们也可以通过对话发现哥哥对家庭的责任和对生命的执着让他有脆弱的一面，而弟弟则通过不断的成长展现出自己的毅力。剧集对话中涉及到了许多恶灵，这些大部分都是围绕圣经及流传于美国的民间故事展开的，因此我们可以通过该剧的对话和独白学习西方的传统文化。

Section 3　角色分析：

迪恩·温彻斯特 (Dean Winchester)：温彻斯特兄弟中的哥哥，嫉恶如仇、无所畏惧的血性男儿。珍爱自己的雪福来汽车，喜欢摇滚乐、电影，还有啤酒和火辣美女，表面玩世不恭，内心却孤独凄凉，背负着对父母的爱与怀念，背负着太多的重任与压力，怀着矛盾心情"监护"着弟弟，他决不轻弹的眼泪只留给自己的家人。迪恩最爱的人是山姆，最恨的是所有恶灵，即使其中一些恶灵救过他们多次，或者之前彼此间的关系很不错。

山姆·温彻斯特 (Sam Winchester)：迪恩的弟弟，即将进入法学院的高材生。高中之后就退出了父亲组织的"猎鬼"活动，和女友生活很愉快，职业前途一片大好。但是不久，女朋友被曾杀死母亲的黄眼恶魔阿兹赛尔（Azazel）杀害，从此，山姆全心全意地投入了捕猎行动，重新体会亲情。自女友死后最依赖的人就是哥哥。

🔊 Passage 1 🎥

剧情介绍：

（选自第1季第1集）深夜，温彻斯特夫人看见襁褓之中的小儿子旁边有个影子。被惊醒的温彻斯特先生闻声赶来，山姆安然无恙，但是，妻子被钉在了天花板上，身体熊熊燃烧。温彻斯特先生认为是山精鬼怪害死了妻子，决心复仇。他训练两个儿子搏斗，教他们制作银弹。22年过去了，山姆成了大学生，即将进入法学院，女友温柔漂亮。有一天，哥哥迪恩来了，告诉他父亲在追捕中失踪了，山姆很不情愿地答应帮忙。

Scene: One night, Sam was suddenly awakened because it seemed that someone came into the house. Sam softly approached the man, and was about to fight with him, only to find that the man was not some stranger but his brother Dean he had not seen for years.

一天夜里，山姆和女友已经入睡，突然山姆被惊醒了，房子里似乎来了不速之客。山姆轻手轻脚地来到那人身边，正要跟他搏斗，却发现来人不是别人，而是自己多年不见的哥哥迪恩。

Dean:	Whoa! Easy, tiger.	迪恩：	哇啊，放松，小老虎。
Sam:	Dean? You scared the crap out of me.	山姆：	迪恩？你吓死我了。
Dean:	That's cause you're out of practice. Or not. Get off of me.	迪恩：	那是因为你荒废了功夫。看来没有，放开我。
Sam:	Dean, what the hell are you doing here?	山姆：	迪恩，你来这里到底要干什么？
Dean:	I was looking for a beer.	迪恩：	我来找啤酒。
Sam:	*What the hell are you doing here?*[1]	山姆：	你到底要干什么？
Dean:	Ok, all right, we got to talk.	迪恩：	好吧，我们得谈谈。
Sam:	The phone?	山姆：	电话里不能说吗？
Dean:	If I'd called would you picked up?	迪恩：	我打你会接吗？
Jess:	Sam?	杰西：	山姆？
Sam:	Jess, hey. Dean, this is my girlfriend, Jessica.	山姆：	杰西。迪恩，这是我的女朋友杰西卡。
Jess:	Wait, your brother Dean?	杰西：	等等，他是你哥哥迪恩？
Dean:	I love the <u>Smurfs</u>[1]. You know, I got to tell you. You are completely *out of my brother's **league***[1].	迪恩：	我喜欢蓝精灵。知道吗，我得说，我弟弟真配不上你。
Jess:	Just let me put something on.	杰西：	我穿下衣服。
Dean:	No, no. No, I wouldn't dream of it, seriously. Anyway, I got to borrow your boyfriend here, talk about some **private**[2] family business, but nice meeting you.	迪恩：	别别，我不会胡思乱想的，真的。总之，我借你男朋友一用，谈点家里私事，很高兴见到你。
Sam:	No. No, whatever you want to say, you can say it in front of her.	山姆：	不不，无论你想说什么，她都可以听。
Dean:	Okay. Dad hasn't been home in a few days.	迪恩：	好吧，爸爸好几天不在家了。
Sam:	So? He's working overtime on a "Miller Time"[4] **shift**[3]. He'll stumble back in sooner or later.	山姆：	这怎么了？他在"米勒时间"加班呢？他迟早会回来的。
Dean:	Dad's on a hunting trip, and he hasn't been home in a few days.	迪恩：	他外出狩猎，几天过去迟迟未归。
Sam:	Jess, excuse us. We have to go outside. I mean, come on, you can't just break in the middle of the night, and expect me to hit the road with you.	山姆：	杰西，失陪一下，我们要出去说。我说，你不要半夜突然跑来，让我和你一起去。
Dean:	You're not hearing me, Sammy. Dad's missing. I need you to help me find him.	迪恩：	你没有听懂我的意思吗？山姆，爸爸失踪了。你需要帮我找他。
Sam:	You remember the **poltergeist**[4] in Amherst, or the devil's gates in Clifton? He was missing then, too. He's always missing, and he's always fine.	山姆：	你还记得阿穆赫斯特的捣蛋鬼，还有克利夫顿的魔鬼之门吗？那两次他不也是失踪了？他总是失踪，可又总是好好的。
Dean:	Not for this long. Now, are you gonna come with me or not?	迪恩：	但是从没这么久，现在你跟不跟我走？

Sam:	I'm not.	山姆：	不去。
Dean:	Why not?	迪恩：	为什么不去？
Sam:	I swore I was done hunting. For good.	山姆：	我发过誓再也不去抓鬼了，永远不去。
Dean:	Come on, it wasn't easy. But it wasn't that bad.	迪恩：	行了，我们实属不易，但也没那么糟糕。
Sam:	Yeah? When I told dad I was scared of the thing in my closet, he gave me a.45.	山姆：	是吗？小时候我告诉爸爸我害怕衣柜里有怪物，他却给我一支点45口径的手枪。
Dean:	What was he supposed to do?	迪恩：	那他应该怎么做？
Sam:	I was 9 years old. He was supposed to say:" Don't be afraid of the dark."	山姆：	我那时才9岁，他应该说"别怕黑"。
Dean:	"Don't be afraid of the dark" ? *Are you kidding me?*[3] Of course, you should be afraid. You know what's out there.	迪恩：	"别怕黑"？你逗我玩呢？你当然应当怕黑，你知道黑暗里有什么。
Sam:	Yeah, I know, but still...the way we grew up after mom was killed and dad's **obsession**[5] to find the thing that killed her. But we still haven't found the damn thing. So we kill everything we can find.	山姆：	我知道，但是妈妈被杀后我们那种成长方式，爸爸着魔似的寻找杀死妈妈的那个东西，但我们还没找到那个该死的东西。所以我们杀死能够找到的一切。
Dean:	Save a lot of people doing it, too.	迪恩：	这样做也救了很多人啊。
Sam:	You think mom would have wanted this for us? The weapon training and melting the silver into bullets? Man, Dean, we were raised like warriors.	山姆：	你觉得妈妈会希望我们这样吗？练习使用武器，给子弹里灌银，迪恩，我们的成长历程完全是战士的生活。
Dean:	So, what are you gonna do? Are you just gonna live some normal, apple-pie[2] life? Is that it?	迪恩：	那你想怎样？你想过那种正常的美国式生活？是吗？
Sam:	No, not normal, safe.	山姆：	不，不是正常的，是安全的。
Dean:	And that's why you ran away.	迪恩：	这就是你离家的原因。
Sam:	I was just going to college. It was dad who said if I was gonna go, I should stay gone. And that's what I'm doing,	山姆：	我原本只是想上大学，是爸爸说如果我要走，就永远别回去。我现在也一定不会回去。
Dean:	Dad's in real trouble right now, if he's not dead already. I can feel it. I can't do this alone.	迪恩：	爸爸现在一定遇到了大麻烦，如果不是已经死了的话，我能感觉到。我一个人不行。
Sam:	Yes, you can.	山姆：	你可以的。

注释

1. league [liːɡ] *n.* 联盟；社团；范畴
2. private ['praɪvət] *adj.* 私人的；私有的；私下的
3. shift [ʃɪft] *v.* 移动；变化；手段；轮班
4. poltergeist ['pɒltəɡaɪst] *n.* 敲击作响闹恶作剧的鬼
5. obsession [əb'seʃn] *n.* 痴迷；困扰；强迫观念

Dean: Yeah. Well, I don't want to.

Sam: What was he hunting?

Dean: All right. Let's see. Where the hell did I put that thing?

Sam: So when dad left, why didn't you go with him?

Dean: I was working my own gig…This voodoo thing down in New Orleans.

Sam: Dad let you go on a hunting trip by yourself?

Dean: I'm 26, dude. All right, here we go. So dad was checking out this two-lane blacktop just outside of Jericho, California. About a month ago, this guy…They found his car, but he'd vanished. Completely M.I.A.

Sam: So maybe he was **kidnapped**[6].

Dean: Yeah, well, here's another one in April, another one in December, 2004,2003,1998,1982…10 of them over the past 20 years…All men, all same 5-mile stretch of road. Started happening more and more, so dad went to go dig around. That was about three weeks ago. I hadn't heard from him since, which is bad enough. And then I get this voice mail yesterday.

(The voice: Dean, something is starting to happen, I think it's serious. I need to try to figure out what's going on. Be very careful, Dean. We're all in danger.)

Sam: You know there's EVP on that?

Dean: Not bad, Sammy. Kind of like riding a bike, isn't it? All right. I slowed the message down, and ran it through a **goldwave**[7], took out the hiss, and this is what I got.

(The voice: I can never go home.)

Sam: Never go home.

Dean: You know, in almost two years, I've never bothered you, never asked you for a thing.

Sam: All right, I'll go. I'll help you find him, but I have to get back first thing Monday, Just wait here.

Dean: What's first thing Monday?

Sam: I've this…I have an interview.

迪恩：对，但我不想那样。

山姆：他追捕的是什么？

迪恩：让我想想，我到底把它放哪儿了？

山姆：爸爸走的时候，你怎么不跟他去？

迪恩：我有自己的活，新奥尔良一桩巫毒事件。

山姆：爸爸让你独自抓鬼？

迪恩：我 26 岁了，伙计。好，找到了。爸爸在查加利福尼亚的耶利哥市郊外一段双车道柏油路。一个月前，这个人……有人发现了他的车，但他不见了，人间蒸发。

山姆：也许他被绑架了。

迪恩：有理，4 月份又一起，12 月一起，04 年、03 年、98 年、92 年，过去 20 年总共 10 起。所有人都是在同一段 5 英里道路上出事的，失踪事件越来越多，所以爸爸就去查了，大约是三周前，打那以后一直没有他的消息。这就够糟了，昨天我又收到了这封语音邮件。

（录音：迪恩，有事正在发生，我觉得很严重，我得搞清楚是怎么回事。千万小心，迪恩，我们都很危险。）

山姆：注意到里面的超自然电子异常现象了吗？

迪恩：不错嘛，小山姆，像骑单车这样的技能就是忘不掉哈。好吧，我把它放慢，通过音频编辑器软件进行处理，去掉嘶嘶声，得到了这个。

（录音：我永远也回不了家。）

山姆：永远也回不了家。

迪恩：知道吗？快两年了，我从未烦过你，从未要求你做任何事。

山姆：好，我去，我帮你找到他。但我周一大早就要回来，在这儿等我。

迪恩：周一大早你要干什么？

山姆：我有……有个面试。

Dean: What? A job interview? Skip it.

Sam: It's a law-school interview, and it's my whole future.

迪恩： 什么？工作面试？推了！

山姆： 是法学院的面试，我的未来就在眼前。

文化背景

1. Smurfs 蓝精灵

蓝精灵这一经典漫画形象是比利时漫画家沛优于 1958 年创作的，是一群活泼可爱的生活在大森林中的小精灵，它们戴着白色的小帽子，浑身的皮肤都是蓝色的。蓝精灵一问世就受到了大家的喜爱。该漫画和根据漫画改编的动画片被译为 25 种语言，在全世界广泛传播，近年来更被搬上了大银幕，成为历久不衰的卡通形象。山姆的女友衣服上印着的图案就是蓝精灵的形象。

2. apple-pie 意思是典型的美国式的生活，为了说明 apple-pie 是美国生活的一个特点，人们常说 "as American as apple-pie"。

常用表达

1. What the hell are you doing here?

the hell 是个语气用词，就是说，你究竟在做什么？带有责备的意味。

例： What the hell are you doing?

你究竟在做什么？

2. out of my brother's league 由于太好使别人配不上

3. Are you kidding me? 你开玩笑么？开什么玩笑！

例： A: Can you give me all your money? 你能把你所有的钱都给我吗？

B: Are you kidding me? 开什么玩笑！

🔊 Passage 2 📷

剧情介绍：

（选自第 1 季第 3 集）三个男孩去露营，结果神秘失踪。山姆和迪恩沿着父亲地图上的坐标，到达了一片森林的中部，开始调查这些失踪事件。两兄弟很快发现，他们遇到的对手是北美传说中著名的怪物——温迪戈雪怪。温迪戈雪怪原来也是人类，吃过人肉后变成了现在这种状态：有超人的力量和速度，靠食人为生。有着人的智慧，还有超人的力量，山姆要如何从温迪戈雪怪手中救出哥哥？温迪戈雪怪被击中了，化成了灰烬。山姆觉得自己好像开始爱上这种捕猎行动了。

Scene: Sam's girlfriend was killed by the evil spirit, which was almost the same as his mother. Hence, nothing could stop Sam from setting foot on the road of killing the devil with his brother Dean. One day, Sam and dean started their journey on a car, suddenly Sam was awakened by a nightmare.

山姆的女友被恶灵杀害了，与当年山姆的母亲遇害时的情景相同。这下，没有什么力量能阻止山姆与哥哥迪恩一起踏上降魔之路了。这天，山姆和迪恩一起开车上路，山姆被噩梦惊醒。

🔊 **Dean:** You okay?

Sam: Yeah, I'm fine.

Dean: Another **nightmare**[1]? Want to drive for a while?

Sam: In your whole life, you never once asked me that.

Dean: Just thought you might want to. *Never mind*[1].

Sam: Look, man. You're worried about me. I get it and...Thank you, but I'm perfectly okay. All right, where are we?

Dean: We are just outside of **Grand Junction**[2].

Sam: You know what? Maybe we shouldn't have left Stanford so soon.

迪恩： 你还好吧？

山姆： 我没事。

迪恩： 又做噩梦了吗？想开会儿车吗？

山姆： 你这辈子从没这么问过我。

迪恩： 只是觉得你可能想开，不开算了。

山姆： 伙计，你很担心我，我明白。谢谢你，但我很好。好了，我们到哪儿了？

迪恩： 我们在格兰姜欣附近。

山姆： 知道吗？也许我们不该那么早离开斯坦福。

Dean:	Sam, we dug around there for a week, we came up with nothing. If you want to find the thing that killed Jessica…	迪恩：	山姆，我们已经在那儿查了好几周了，却一无所获。如果你想找到杀害杰西卡的凶手……就要先找到老爸。
Sam:	Got to find dad first.	山姆：	
Dean:	Dad disappearing, and this thing showing up again after 20 years? It's no coincidence, Dad will have answers. He'll know what to do.	迪恩：	老爸消失，20 年后这东西又再次出现，这不是巧合，老爸肯定知道是怎么回事。他知道该怎么办。
Sam:	It's weird, man. These **coordinates**[3] he left us, this Black Water Ridge…	山姆：	真是奇怪。他留给我们的这些坐标，这个黑水山脉……
Dean:	What about it?	迪恩：	怎么了？
Sam:	There's nothing there. It's just woods. Why is he sending us to the middle of nowhere? So Black Water Ridge is pretty remote. It's cut off by these canyons here—rough terrain, dense forest. Abandoned silver and gold mines all over the place…	山姆：	那里什么都没有，只有一片森林。他为什么要我们去这种鬼地方？黑水山脉太偏远了，它被峡谷阻隔，地形复杂，丛林密布，附近都是废弃的金银矿山……
Dean:	**Dude**[4], check out the size of this friggin' bear.	迪恩：	老兄，快来看看这熊有多大。
Sam:	And a dozen or more grizzlies in the area. It's no nature hike, that's for sure.	山姆：	还有一群灰熊在那片区域栖息。可以肯定那里不是远足的好去处。
Wilkinson:	You boys aren't planning to go out near Black Water Ridge, by any chance?	威尔金森：	你们不会是碰巧要去黑水山脉吧？
Sam:	No, sir. We're environmental-study majors from U.C. Boulder—just working on a paper.	山姆：	不，先生，我们是博尔德大学环境系的学生，是为了论文来的。
Dean:	Recycle, man.	迪恩：	关于回收利用。
Wilkinson:	Bull. You're friends with that Hailey girl, right?	威尔金森：	屁话，你们是那个叫海莉的女孩的朋友吧？
Dean:	Yes. Yes, we are. Ranger…Wilkinson.	迪恩：	是，是的，我们是，威尔金森护林员。
Wilkinson:	Well, I will tell you exactly what I told her. Her brother filled out a **backcountry**[5] permit saying he wouldn't be back from Black Water until the 24th. So it's not exactly a missing person now, is it? Tell that girl to quit worrying. I'm sure her brother's just fine.	威尔金森：	我把跟她说的话再跟你们说一次，她弟弟出示了露营许可证，说他一直要在黑水山脉待到24号，所以他现在还不算是失踪人口，不是吗？告诉那女孩不要再担心了，我保证他弟弟没事儿。

注释

1. nightmare ['naɪtmeə(r)] *n.* 恶梦；梦魇般的经历

2. Grand Junction 格兰姜欣，美国地名，位于科罗拉多州

3. coordinate [kəʊ'ɔːdɪneɪt] *n.* 坐标；相配之衣物

4. dude 花花公子、纨绔子弟，这里相当于"哥们儿""老兄"

5. backcountry ['bækkʌntri] *n.* 偏僻地区

Dean: We will. Well, that Hailey girl's quite a pistol, huh?

Wilkinson: That is putting it mildly.

Dean: Actually, you know what would help is if I could show her a copy of that <u>backcountry permit</u>[1]. You know, so she could see her brother's return date.

Sam: What, are you cruising for a **hookup**[6] or something?

Dean: What do you mean?

Sam: The coordinates point to Black Water Ridge. So what are we waiting for? Let's just go to find dad. Why even talk to this girl?

Dean: I don't know, maybe we should know what we're walking into before we actually walk into it.

Sam: What?

Dean: Since when are you all "Shoot first, ask questions later" Anyway?

Sam: Since now.

Dean: Oh, really?

迪恩：	我们会的，是海莉太急了。
威尔金森：	有过之而无不及。
迪恩：	如果我们能拿那份证明的复印件给她看看，那就更好了。这样她就知道她弟弟什么时候回去了。
山姆：	你是跑来泡妞的吗？
迪恩：	你什么意思？
山姆：	我们已经有了坐标，还在等什么？我们直接去找老爸，去找这个女孩干什么？
迪恩：	我不知道，也许去之前我们应该调查好情况。
山姆：	什么？
迪恩：	你什么时候变得这么冲动？
山姆：	现在。
迪恩：	哦，真的吗？

文化背景

1. backcountry permit 边远地区许可证

本片故事发生地格兰姜欣位于美国落基山脉，这里地势险峻、环境复杂、人烟稀少，容易发生危险。按照相关规定，在此类地点露营、旅游，需要提前与当地的边远地区办公室（backcountry office，BCO）联系，确定旅行路线、人数、停留时间等，以保证旅行者的安全和当地生态环境的稳定。

常用表达

1. never mind

never mind=don't worry 不必担心

例：Did you miss the bus? Never mind, there'll be another one in five minutes.

你没赶上公共汽车吗？没关系，五分钟后就会又来一辆的。

注释 6. hookup ['hʊkʌp] *n.* 连接；接线图；联播

🔊 Passage 3 📷

剧情介绍：

（选自第 1 季第 3 集）一位游泳健将在湖里失踪了，尸体也没有被发现——这是 35 年来，湖里的又一名溺死者。迪安在报上看到了这起神秘的溺死事件，觉得很可疑。两人冒充野生动植物保护署的工作人员，向死者的父亲询问出事时的情景。死者父亲说当时好像湖里有什么东西在拉她，但是离得太远，没有看清楚。然而，当地的治安官对这一说法嗤之以鼻，他说湖水曾经被抽干过，也用声波探测器查过湖底淤泥，没有发现任何可疑现象。询问中，兄弟俩认识了治安官的女儿安吉拉和外孙卢卡斯。安吉拉的丈夫，也就是卢卡斯的父亲也是在同一个湖里溺死的，事发时卢卡斯也在现场，亲眼目睹了父亲的死亡，从那之后便患上了失语症。顺着此事件调查下去，两人发现，死者遇害的同一个湖里，曾经神秘地淹死过不少人，然而这些溺水都被登记为"自杀"。卢卡斯一直在画画。迪恩惊奇地发现，画中的房屋和人预示了下一场溺水事件的发生。两兄弟推断，湖里可能居住着一个满怀报复之心的溺死鬼，后来发现的确如此，治安官少年时期曾和同伴比尔失手将另一个同伴男孩溺死在湖里。从那以后，当地就开始了湖中怨灵的传说。最后，男孩的鬼魂找上了治安官的外孙。治安官痛哭着对湖面忏悔："放过卢卡斯，把我收去吧！"卢卡斯回来了，治安官被拉下了湖。男孩的鬼魂得到了满足。

Scene 1: Another girl was killed mysteriously. In a cafe, Dean and Sam talked about relevant report on the newspaper.

又一个女孩神秘死去了，迪恩和山姆在一家咖啡馆里讨论近期报纸上的有关报道。

🔊 **Waiter:** Can I get you anything else?

(Dean smiled.)

Sam: Just the check, please.

Waiter: Okay.

Dean: You know, Sam, we are allowed to have fun once in a while. That's fun. Here, take a look at this. I think I got one. Lake Manitoc, **Wisconsin**[1]. Last week, Sophie Carlton, 18,

侍者： 还需要什么吗？

（迪恩笑了笑。）

山姆： 请结账。

侍者： 好吧。

迪恩： 山姆，我们可以偶尔找点乐子。那就是乐子。看这儿，我想我找到了一个，威斯康辛州，曼莱托克湖。上周，索菲·卡尔顿，18 岁，下水

walks into the lake, and doesn't walk out. Authorities dragged the water. Nothing. Sophie Carlton, is the third Lake Manitoc drowning this year. None of the other bodies were found, either. They had a funeral two days ago.

Sam: A **funeral**[2]?

Dean: Yes, they buried an empty coffin, for **closure**[3] or whatever.

Sam: Closure? What closure? People don't just disappear, Dean. Other people just stop looking for them.

Dean: Somenthing you want to say to me?

Sam: The trail for dad. It's getting colder every day.

Dean: What are we supposed to do?

Sam: I don't know. Something. Anything.

Dean: You know what. I'm sick of this attitude. You don't think I want to find dad as much as you do?

Sam: Yeah, I know you do it.

Dean: I'm the one that's been with him every single day for the past two years. While you've been off to college going to pep rallies. We will find dad, but until then, we're gonna kill everything bad, between here and there. Okay?

Sam: All right, Lake Manitoc. How far?

之后，就再也没出来。当局搜索了整片水域，什么也没找到。索菲·卡尔顿，是今年曼莱托克湖失踪的第三个人了，其他人的尸体也都没找到。前两天他们举行了葬礼。

山姆：葬礼？

迪恩：是的，他们埋了一具空棺材，做个了结之类的。

山姆：了结？什么样的了结？那些人不是简单的失踪，迪恩。人们却停止了寻找。

迪恩：你想跟我说什么？

山姆：爸爸，最近都没消息。

迪恩：那我们该怎么办？

山姆：不知道，总得做点事，任何事。

迪恩：你知道吗？我受够了你这种态度，你以为我不像你一样想找到爸爸吗？

山姆：嗯，我知道你想。

迪恩：在过去的两年里，是我每一天都陪在爸爸身边，那时你却在大学里开赛前动员会。我们会找到爸爸的，但在此之前，我们必须消灭这一路上所有的恶魔，明白吗？

山姆：好吧，曼莱托克湖。离这儿多远？

Scene 2: Finally they found the dead girl's father.

他们找到了去世女孩的父亲。

Dean: Will Carlton?

Will: Yeah, that's right.

Dean: I'm agent Ford. This is agent Hamill. We're with **U.S. Wild Life Service**[4].

迪恩：威尔·卡尔顿吗？

威尔：对，是我。

迪恩：我是探员福特，这是探员哈迈尔，我们是美国野生动物管理局的。

Will:	She was about 100 yards out. That's where she got dragged down.	威尔：	她大概游了 100 码远，那里就是她被拖下水的地方。
Dean:	And you're sure she didn't just drown?	迪恩：	你确定她不是溺水吗？
Will:	Yeah, she was a varsity swimmer. She practically grew up in that lake. She's as safe out there as in her own bathtub.	威尔：	是的，她是学校的游泳健将，她几乎是在这个湖里长大的，她在那里就像在自己的浴缸里一样安全。
Sam:	So no **splashing**[5], no signs of distress?	山姆：	那么没有水花？也没有因为痛苦自杀的迹象？
Will:	No, that's what I'm telling you.	威尔：	没有，就和我说的一样。
Sam:	Did you see any shadows in the water; maybe, some dark shape breach the surface?	山姆：	你看见水里的影子了吗？也许有个黑色的东西跃出水面？
Will:	No, again, she was really far out there.	威尔：	没有，再说一遍，她当时离得太远了。
Dean:	You ever see any strange tracks by the **shoreline**[6]?	迪恩：	你没在岸边看见什么奇怪的东西吗？
Will:	No, never. Why? What do you think is over there?	威尔：	没有，绝对没有，为什么这么问？会有什么东西在那儿？
Dean:	We'll let you know *as soon as*[1] we do.	迪恩：	我们一查清楚就告诉你。
Sam:	What about your father? Can we talk to him?	山姆：	你爸爸呢？我们能和他谈谈吗？
Will:	Look, if you don't mind, I mean, he didn't see anything, and he's kind of been through a lot.	威尔：	听着，如果你们不介意的话，他什么也没看到，而且他很痛苦。
Sam:	We understand.	山姆：	我们能理解。

常用表达

1. as soon as 一……就……，其中的从句通常用一般现在时表示将来时。

这个短语比较常用，口语和书面语都可以。它的特点是，在句子中的位置比较灵活，而且可以用于各种时态。

例：I'll write you as soon as I get there.

我一到那儿就给你来信。（一般现在时）

例：As soon as I went in, Jason cried out with pleasure.

我一进门，詹森就高兴得叫了起来。（一般过去时）

注释
2. funeral ['fjuːnərəl] *n.* 葬礼；[口] 麻烦事
3. closure ['kləʊʒə(r)] *n.* 关闭；终止，结束
4. U.S. Wild Life Service 美国野生动物管理局
5. splash [splæʃ] *v.* 泼洒，喷洒
6. shoreline ['ʃɔːlaɪn] *n.* 海岸线；海岸线地带

The X-Files

《X 档案》

入选理由：

《X 档案》是 20 世纪 90 年代走红于美国海内外的科幻电视系列剧，制作人是克里斯·卡特（Chris Carter）。1993 年 9 月 10 日于福克斯电视台首播第一季，2002 年 5 月 19 日播毕 9 季后结束。本剧在商业上十分成功，在评论界的口碑也很好，立刻吸引了庞大的影迷群体。两次荣获金球奖最佳戏剧奖，三次获得艾美奖最佳戏剧奖提名，三次金球奖最佳编剧奖，一次作家协会提名，两次导演协会提名，一次艾美奖提名。

Section 1 剧情特点：

美国 FBI 探员福克斯·穆德童年时曾经历一起离奇神秘的绑架案，他的妹妹萨曼莎在睡梦中被外星人劫持，至今下落不明。从此穆德便专注于神秘事件的研究，并专门负责 FBI 总部的 X 档案部门。因穆德行事乖张，难以驾驭，FBI 高层从联邦调查局学院调来女性法医黛娜·史考莉，表面上是协助穆德工作，实际上是希望这名崇尚科学的理性探员能够制约穆德的行为。两人最初的合作并不理想，完全不同的思维模式时刻导致争论的爆发。但随着各种离奇案件的出现及两人交往的加深，穆德和史考莉最终变成可以为对方出生入死的可靠伙伴。

Section 2 对白特点：

《X 档案》的许多独白和对白都涵盖了大量专业词汇。而且覆盖内容广，包括物种起源、宇宙进化、宗教神化、文化礼仪，等等。这不但归功于创造者，一位毕业于加州大学的高材生的丰富阅历，而且要归功于扮演男主角的大卫·杜楚尼，他本科毕业于普林斯顿大学，是耶鲁的研究生。女主角吉莲·安德森毕业于康奈尔。这样高学历背景的剧组阵容实属罕见，也使得《X 档案》在很多方面远远高于其他科幻片的水准，包括剧情所涵盖的知识范围、演员精辟的对白，以及人性刻画的深度。

Section 3 角色分析:

福克斯·威廉姆·穆德（Fox William Mulder）：穆德童年时对太空计划很感兴趣，并将太空人马可斯·贝尔特上校视为崇拜对象，他整夜不睡只为观看他登陆月球。穆德的妹妹萨曼莎在他 12 岁那一年离奇失踪，全家人用尽心力也无法找回。父母为了此事离婚，使穆德在青少年时就处于单亲家庭。妹妹的失踪使穆德对神秘现象及犯罪事件产生了兴趣，他坚信妹妹是被外星人绑架的。从牛津大学的心理系毕业以后，穆德就来到联邦调查局调查恶性案件，因为工作中的突出表现，他的前景一度非常光明。但却因过分的特立独行被调到位于地下的办公室调查关于超自然现象的"X 档案"。调查局为了监视他的工作特意委派史考莉来和他一起工作。调查的过程中他受到了各种各样的阻挠，但他从没放弃过，凭着自己的信念执着地追求。穆德代表了人类理性而不拘泥固守、探寻求索未知、渴求超越自身的优秀品质，在他身上充分诠释了身为人类的使命感与责任感。

黛娜·凯瑟琳·史考莉（Dana Katherine Scully）：史考莉毕业于马里兰大学，主修物理，同时具有法医资格，因此毕业后进入 FBI 的学院当教员。她注重客观理性的分析，后来也逐渐接受超自然现象，坚信每个案件背后都有合理的科学解释。史考莉被 FBI 高层委派去监视"怪人"穆德的工作。但在合作中她却被穆德的品格所感动，一些离奇的案件也给她的观念带来冲击，于是她不再为政府高层所左右，成为同穆德一起追寻真相的最可靠的朋友和搭档。

约翰·道格特（John Doggett）：约翰·道格特是一位无神论者，最初有些抵制超自然现象，直到他被各种灵异案件所震惊。他也有惨痛的经历——他的独生爱子不明不白的被人虐杀，并且导致了离异。值得欣慰的是他的心结最终得以解开。在莫妮卡·雷耶斯出现前，道格特几乎爱上了史考莉，这还一度成为他愿意留在 X 档案办公室的原因。像当初史考莉一样，道格特最初也是被派来监视史考莉的（穆德当时一度失踪），但也像史考莉一样，他更为迅速地成为了揭示真相的斗士之一。道格特忠诚可靠，因而有个"狗人"的外号，他和穆德的性格标志是狗和狐狸，但他们却是朋友。

莫妮卡·雷耶斯（Monica Reyes）：莫妮卡·雷耶斯是个正直坚强的女探员，被调入 X 档案部门后与道格特是搭档。于是她也加入了揭示真相的队伍。道格特的"狗人"外号就是她起的，最终她成为道格特的伴侣。雷耶斯与史考莉成为密友，同穆德、斯金纳、孤枪手等也是难得的团结。

辛迪加组织成员老烟鬼（Smoker/Cancerman Tribbiani）：老烟鬼代表着在隐秘之处操纵国家的那一小波人（即"辛迪加"组织，或称"影子政府"），许多改变历史的事情都与这群人有关。他是穆德的主要对头之一，此人神秘莫测，有关他的一切信息几乎都是秘密（其真实身份剧中曾有揭晓）。由于他手里永远夹着一支烟，所以代号为"老烟鬼"，而过多的吸烟使他得了肺癌，从此他又多了一个外号："癌人"。老烟鬼老谋深算，为人阴毒，但他内心也藏有许多悲伤的事。他有着很强的个人魅力——但并不是让人与之成为朋友的那种魅力。他虽然足智多谋，却也因为过分自大和特立独行而给"辛迪加"组织带来过许多麻烦甚至危机。因此在"辛迪加"中人缘较差，差到曾有过性命之忧。另外有一点不得不提，也是整个 X 档案室最避讳的一点，但却是不争的事实，即"癌人"的另一个身份：穆德的生身父亲。

局长助理沃尔特·斯金纳 (Walter Skinner)：身为前海军陆战队队员的调查局局长助理沃尔特·斯金纳，有很强的责任感，有时对穆德没完没了的古怪调查会失去一些耐心。他出于个人强烈的正义感曾多次帮助穆德等人，甚至同他们出生入死，因此他们的私交随着时间的推移越来越好。最初他不止一次警告穆德和史考莉，称他们调查的范围已到危险的程度。他也曾被迫关闭了 X 档案室，但是后来在自己的职权范围内又将其重开。

孤枪侠 (The Lone Gunmen)："孤枪侠"这个名字，来自于肯尼迪被刺的时候，凶手只有一个。肯尼迪被刺，一直是美国历史上不解的谜团，许多人相信凶手不只一个，而被捉的凶手奥斯华也被刺杀了，这种题材正是 X 档案阴谋论的最爱。孤枪侠第一次出现在《X 档案》中，是一个以监督政府、揭发阴谋为己任的团体之一，穆德称他们为 "an extreme goverment watchdog"（极端的政府看门狗）。他们的出现为剧情发展带来了更宽广的空间与角色互动的变化，也为许多历史悬案提供"不负责任评论"，适时弥补总是故弄玄虚、吊尽胃口的把戏。 至于三名成员拜尔斯 (Byers)、郎格利 (Langly)、弗洛黑克 (Frohike) 则是穆德的忠实密友，后来逐渐成为史考莉甚至是斯金纳、道格特的朋友。

🔊 Passage 1 🎥

剧情介绍：

（选自第 1 季第 1 集）史考莉从医学院毕业之后，来到美国联邦调查局成为其中一员。现在，她被上级部门调到了 X 档案部门，协助穆德的工作，并将调查活动写成报告，其实也是监视穆德的行动。一天，史考莉来到穆德的办公室，见到了这个外号"怪人"的穆德。这是他们 7 年合作的开始。他们接的第一个案子是发生在俄勒冈的高中生死亡事件，穆德相信这个案子和外星人有关。

Scene: FBI Headquarters; Washington, D.C. Agent Dana Scully walks up the stairs and around to a desk where a woman sits. After telling the woman what her name is, she continues through a group of offices and down a hallway. Reaching the door to Section Chief Blevins' office, she knocks.

华盛顿特区，FBI 总部。黛娜·史考莉探员走上楼梯，来到圆桌前对坐在那里的女人前报上姓名后，接着穿过办公区和走廊，来到科长布莱文斯的办公室门前，她敲了敲门。

Blevins: Come in. (Scully walks in and sees Blevins sitting at his desk.) Agent Scully, thank you for coming on such short notice. Please... We see you've been with us just over two years.

Scully: Yes, sir.

Blevins: You went to medical school but you chose not to practice. How'd you come to work for the F.B.I.?

Scully: Well, sir, I was **recruited**[1] out of medical school. Um, my parents still think it was an act of rebellion, but, uh... I saw the F.B.I. as a place where I could **distinguish**[2] myself.

Third man: *Are* you *familiar with*[1] an agent named Fox Mulder?

Scully: Yes, I am.

Third man: How so?

Scully: *By reputation*[2]. He's an Oxford educated Psychologist, who wrote a **monograph**[3] on serial killers and the **occult**[4], that helped to catch Monty Props in 1988. Generally thought of as the best analyst in the violent crimes section. He had a nickname at the academy... Spooky Mulder.

Blevins: What I'll also tell you is that Agent Mulder has developed a consuming devotion to an unassigned project outside the bureau mainstream. Are you familiar with the so-called "X-Files?"

Scully: I believe they have to do with unexplained phenomena.

Blevins: More or less. The reason you're here, Agent Scully, is we want you to assist Mulder on these X-Files. You will write field reports on your activites, along with your observations on the validity of the work.

布莱文斯： 请进。（史考莉走进办公室，布莱文斯正坐在桌前。）史考莉探员，谢谢你在这么短的时间赶来。请坐。你与我们一起工作两年了。

史考莉： 是的，长官。

布莱文斯： 你上了医学院却没有当医生，你怎么想到来 FBI 的？

史考莉： 我是从医学院被招揽过来的。我父母认为这是一种叛逆，但我认为 FBI 是个可以让我发挥的地方。

三号男士： 你知道福克斯·穆德探员吗？

史考莉： 是的。

三号男士： 怎么知道的？

史考莉： 我只听说过他。他是牛津毕业的心理学家，对连环杀手与邪教有所研究，在 1988 年协助捕获蒙特·波斯。被推崇为最佳暴力罪行分析家。另外，他有个绰号是"怪人穆德"。

布莱文斯： 我还要告诉你，穆德探员还从事另一项非主流的调查工作。你有没有听过"X 档案"？

史考莉： 我知道那是调查无法解释的现象。

布莱文斯： 差不多吧。史考莉探员，我们找你来是要你协助穆德。你将调查活动写成报告并加上你对工作的观察。

注释
1. recruit [rɪˈkruːt] *v.* 招聘，雇佣
2. distinguish [dɪˈstɪŋgwɪʃ] *v.* 区别，区分；辨别
3. monograph [ˈmɒnəgrɑːf] *n.* 专题著作，专题论文
4. occult [əˈkʌlt] *n.* 神秘学

Scully: Am I to understand that you want me to **debunk**[5] the X-Files project, sir?

Blevins: Agent Scully, we trust you'll make the proper scientific analysis. You'll want to contact Agent Mulder shortly. *We look forward to*[3] seeing your reports.

(The elevator rings and the door slides open. Scully steps out[4] into the basement and comes to an office secluded[6] in the back. She knocks on the door.)

Mulder: Sorry, nobody down here but the FBI's most unwanted.

(She opens the door to see Agent Fox Mulder sitting at his desk, going over some slides. Walking slowly to him, she sees various pictures of UFO's and a poster that reads "I Want to Believe" with a UFO on it. He looks at her.)

Scully: Agent Mulder? I'm Dana Scully, I've been assigned to work with you. (He shakes her hand.)

Mulder: Oh, isn't it nice to be suddenly so highly regarded? So, who did you tick off to get stuck with this detail, Scully?

Scully: Actually, I'm looking forward to working with you. I've heard a lot about you.

Mulder: Oh, really? I was under the impression... that you were sent to spy on me. (He smiles.)

Scully: If you have any doubt about my qualifications or **credentials**[7], th...

(He stands and takes out a paper from a pile with his telephone as a paperweight.)

Mulder: You're a medical doctor, you teach at the academy. You did your undergraduate degree in physics. (He takes off his glasses and looks at the paper.) "*Einstein's Twin Paradox*[1], *A New Interpretation*. Dana Scully Senior Thesis." Now that's a credential, rewriting Einstein.

Scully: Did you bother to read it?

Mulder: I did. I liked it. (He takes a slide **canister**[8]

史考莉：你们是要我去揭穿 X 档案？

布莱文斯：史考莉探员，我们相信，你会做出正确、科学的分析。请你去找穆德探员，我们期待你的报告。

（电梯声响了，电梯门打开了。史考莉走出电梯来到地下室，她走到隐藏在背后的办公室门前，敲了敲门。）

穆德：对不起，这里没有人，只有 FBI 最不想要的一个人。

（史考莉打开房门看到穆德坐在他的办公桌前，在看一些幻灯片。她慢慢地朝他走过去，看见各种各样的 UFO 照片和一张在不明飞行物上写着"我要相信"的海报。他抬头看向她。）

史考莉：穆德探员？我是黛娜·史考莉，被派来协助你的工作。（两人握了握手。）

穆德：很高兴突然受到抬举。你是得罪了谁才沦落到这里的，史考莉？

史考莉：事实上我很乐意与你合作。我听了很多关于你的事。

穆德：哦，是吗？我觉得你是派来监视我的。（他笑了笑。）

史考莉：如果你怀疑我的资历……

（他站了起来，并从压在电话机下的一沓纸中拿出一份文件。）

穆德：你是个医生，在学院教书。你大学主修物理。（他取下眼镜盯着论文。）"《爱因斯坦的双重矛盾全新解析》，史考莉毕业论文。"的确是很好的资历，改写了爱因斯坦。

史考莉：你读过？

穆德：是的。我很喜欢。（他拿起一

and puts it into the slide projector.) It's just that in most of my work, the laws of physics rarely seems to apply. (He walks past her and turns off the lights. She *glares at*[5] him **slightly**[9].) Maybe I can get your medical opinion on this, though. (He presses a button on the control and a slide comes up on the viewscreen of Karen Swenson, face-up.) Oregon female, age twenty-one, no explainable cause of death. Autopsy shows nothing. Zip. (He changes the slide to that of the two bumps on her back.) There are, however, these two distinct marks on her lower back. Doctor Scully, can you ID these marks?

Scully: Needle **punctures**[10], maybe. An animal bite. Electrocution of some kind.

(She walks up to the viewscreen. He changes the slide to that of a molecular diagram.)

Mulder: How's your chemistry? This is the **substance**[11] found in the surrounding tissue.

Scully: It's organic. I don't know, is it some kind of synthetic protein?

Mulder: Beats me, I've never seen it before either. But here it is again in Sturgis, South Dakota. And again in Shamrock, Texas.

Scully: Do you have a theory?

Mulder: I have plenty of theories. (He walks over to her.) Maybe what you can explain to me is why it's bureau policy to label these cases as "unexplained phenomenon" and ignore them. Do you believe in the existence of **extraterrestrials**[12]?

个幻灯片带子把它放进幻灯片放映机里。）只是在我的工作上，物理定律很少管用。（他走过她身边把灯关掉。她看着他。）也许这件案子，你可以用上你的医学观点。（他在操作台上按下按钮，屏幕上出现了凯伦·斯文森面部朝上的幻灯片。）俄勒冈女性，21岁，死因无法判别。验尸没查出任何问题。（他换了下一张幻灯片，幻灯片上凯伦·斯文森背部有两个斑点。）不过，下背部有两个斑点，史考莉医生，你能不能辨认这些斑点？

史考莉： 可能是针孔。或是被动物咬或电击？

（她走到屏幕前。穆德换了一张分子分析图的幻灯片。）

穆德： 你的化学好不好？这些物质是在伤口周围找到的。

史考莉： 是有机物质。我不知道。是一种合成蛋白吗？

穆德： 问倒我了，我也从未见过，不过再次发现于南达科他州。在得克萨斯州也有。

史考莉： 你有什么想法？

穆德： 我有许多想法。（他走到史考莉身边。）也许你可以解释一下，为何局里将这些案子列为不可解释现象并搁置。你相信外星人的存在吗？

注释
5. debunk [ˌdɪ'bʌŋk] v. 揭穿；拆穿……的假面具；暴露
6. secluded [sɪ'klu:dɪd] adj. 隐蔽的；隐退的，隐居的
7. credentials [krə'denʃlz] n. [管理] 证书；文凭；信任状 (credential 的复数)
8. canister ['kænɪstə(r)] n. 筒；（放咖啡，茶叶，烟等的）小罐；防毒面具的滤毒罐
9. slightly ['slaɪtlɪ] adv. 些微地，轻微地；纤细地
10. puncture ['pʌŋktʃə] n. 小孔；刺痕；穿刺术
11. substance ['sʌbstəns] n. 物质；实质；资产；主旨
12. extraterrestrial [ˌekstrətə'restrɪəl] n. 天外来客

Scully:	Logically, I would have to say "no." (He nods, having expected that answer.) Given the distances needed to travel from the far reaches of space, the energy requirements would exceed a **spacecraft's**[13] capabilties th...	史考莉：	逻辑上我不信。（他点了点头，接受了她的答案。）从外太空到地球需要的能量可能会超出常理的判断……
Mulder:	You know this Oregon female? She's the fourth person in her graduating class to die under mysterious circumstances. Now, when convention and science offer us no answers, might we not finally turn to the fantastic as a plausibility?	穆德：	这位俄勒冈女子，她是班上第四个死于这种情况的人。当科学无法解释的时候，我们只好寻求不可思议的解答。
Scully:	The girl obviously died of something. If it was natural causes, it's plausible that there was something missed in the post-mortem. If she was murdered, it's plausible there was a sloppy investigation. What I find fantastic is any notion that there are answers beyond the **realm**[14] of science. The answers are there. You just have to know where to look.	史考莉：	这女孩肯定是死于什么的。如果是自然死因，也许验尸漏查了什么。如果她是被谋杀了，可能是调查太轻率。我觉得不可思议的是任何凌驾于科学真理之上的看法，答案就在眼前。只是要知道方向。
Mulder:	That's why they put the "I" in "F.B.I." See you tomorrow morning, Scully, bright and early. (He walks back over to his desk and sits down.) We leave for the very **plausible**[15] state of Oregon at eight a.m.	穆德：	这是为何要加"调查"局的原因。明天一大早见，史考莉。（穆德走回桌前并坐了下来。）我们在八点钟前往不可思议的俄勒冈州。
(She smiles and walks out.)		（史考莉笑了笑离开了。）	

注释 **13. spacecraft** ['speɪskrɑːft] *n.* [航] 宇宙飞船，航天器
14. realm [relm] *n.* 领域，范围；王国
15. plausible ['plɔːzəbl] *adj.* 貌似可信的，花言巧语的；貌似真实的，貌似有理的

文化背景

1. Einstein's Twin Paradox 爱因斯坦的双胞胎悖论

爱因斯坦最初用两个时钟来描述他的狭义相对论的时间膨胀效应，即假设两个准确的时钟，其中一个静止，另一个钟以接近光速的速度运动。根据相对论，光速运动的钟会走得很慢，而静止的钟则正常。1911 年 4 月波隆哲学大会上，法国物理学家 P. 朗之万用双生子实验对狭义相对论提出了质疑，设想的实验是这样的：一对双胞胎，一个留在地球上，另一个乘坐火箭到太空旅行。飞行速度接近光速，在太空旅行的孩子会比他留在地球上的兄弟年轻。这就是著名的"双生子悖论"。

常用表达

1. be familiar with 熟悉

例：You should be familiar with how it works so you know what to expect.

您应当熟悉它是如何工作的，以了解会发生些什么。

As soon as I went in, Jason cried out with pleasure.

我一进门，杰森就高兴得叫起来。

2. by reputation 由（或通过）名声；由于知名度

例：She is a good lawyer by reputation.

她是名有声望的律师。

3. look forward to 盼望，期待

例：He was looking forward to working with the new manager.

他很期待和新经理一起工作。

4. glare at 怒视

例：People glare at me for cutting in. I beg to buy one of the pretend Monarchs.

我顶着排队人群的怒视，冲到队伍的最前面，请求买那个仿真的黑脉金斑蝶。

🔊 Passage 2 📷

剧情介绍：

精神病院前 FBI 探员杜恩声称被外星人劫持过，但人们认为他有精神病被送到精神病医院，由于别人的不信任，他绑架了精神病院医生想向其证明外星人是真实存在的，被 FBI 请来帮忙的穆德自愿成为人质解救其他人……

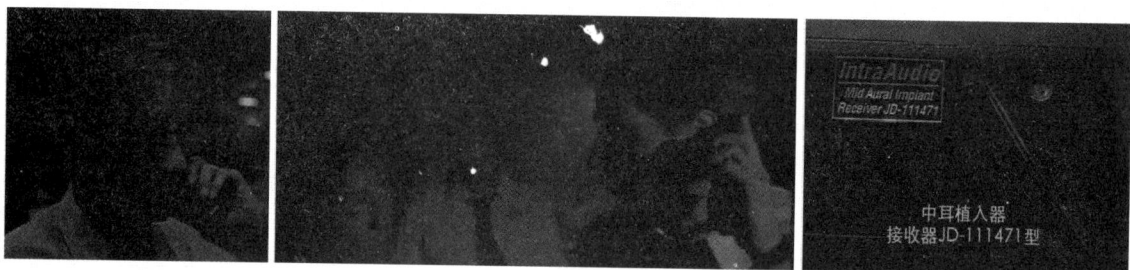

中耳植入器
接收器JD-111471型

Scene: FBI Headquarters; Washington, D.C. Scully is watching the news report. Reporter on TV: ...of the hostages[1]. As you can see, Carl, the SWAT team has taken positions on all the surrounding buildings... The phone rings and she picks up.

华盛顿特区，FBI 总部。黛娜·史考莉探员正在看新闻报道，电视上正在讲述：如你们所见，战术小组已经在四周建筑物定位……这时，电话响了起来，史考莉接起电话。

(Com: Commander)

🔊 **Scully:** Scully.

Mulder: It's me. I'm in Virginia.

Scully: Yeah, I know. I've been watching it on TV. What's going on out there?

Mulder: What's the media saying?

Scully: That an escaped mental patient is holding four people hostage in a travel agency.

(Cut to Mulder, who is talking on his cellular[2] phone away from the other agents.)

Mulder: Well, what they're not telling you is that he's former F.B.I. who also claims to be an alien **abductee**[3].

Scully: Seriously?

Mulder: Yeah, his name's Duane Barry. Look, Scully, I need your help. (Cut to Scully as she *boots up*[1] her computer.) I need you to find out what happened to him. Anything, transcripts from

史考莉： 史考莉。

穆德： 是我，我在维吉尼亚。

史考莉： 我知道，我正在看电视报道，怎么回事？

穆德： 媒体怎么说？

史考莉： 一个精神病患者在旅行社劫持了 4 个人质。

（画面转向穆德，他拿着移动电话，与其他探员保持了一定的距离。）

穆德： 他们有没有说他是个声称被外星人劫持过的前联邦探员？

史考莉： 真的吗？

穆德： 是的，他叫杜恩·巴里。听着，史考莉，我需要你的帮助。（画面转至史考莉，她正在启动电脑。）我需要你找到在他身上到

therapy sessions[4], hypnotic regressions[5]... (Cut back to Mulder.) Anything about his abduction experience.

(The lights suddenly go out and the agents murmur. Cut to Scully.)

Scully: Mulder?

(Cut back to Mulder. Men are screaming in back of him.)

Mulder: The lights just went out here.

(All the lights in the building go out. The snipers are watching.)

Man 1:   Stay back.

Man 2:   Come on, we're losing power!

Sniper: What the hell is going on?

(The fountain turns off. Duane, agitated[6], starts waving his gun around. Gwen screams. The only lights are from the police cars outside. The agents start looking through the windows.)

Man1:   Tactical unit, what are you guys up to?

Com: Nothing, absolutely nothing sir.

(A bright light builds outside, blinding the agents.)

Man 1:   Ah, what the? (The light fades and a gunshot goes off. The agents duck and cover.) Get down, everybody get down! Backup from command. Shots have been fired. Locate and report. I repeat, locate and report.

(More gunshots go off. Duane is shooting wildly. Gwen screams with each gunshot. Ambulances gather outside.)

Rich: We've lost our captured[7] line.

Man1:   We have either four or five shots fired!

(Mulder walks over to Rich.)

Mulder: What's the number there?

Rich: 555-2804.

底发生了什么。任何病例资料，催眠记录。（画面切换到穆德。）任何有关绑架的记录。

（灯忽然灭了，探员们窃窃私语。画面回到史考莉。）

史考莉：   穆德？

（画面回到穆德，人们在他身后叫喊。）

穆德：   灯忽然灭了。

（大楼里所有的灯都灭了。狙击手们盯着看。）

探员1：   保持原地不动！

探员2：   怎么回事？这里停电了！

狙击手：   发生了什么事情？

（大楼停电了。杜恩焦虑不安地持枪环顾着四周。格温尖叫一声。唯一的灯光是外面的警车发出的。探员们开始往窗外看。）

探员1：   战术小组，你们在搞什么？

指挥官：   什么也没有啊，长官。

（窗外闪现了一道亮光，使探员们感到一阵炫目。）

探员1：   额，那是？（亮光褪去，一声枪响。探员们都躲了起来。）蹲下，大家都蹲下。作战指挥，已经开火了。请确认位置并回报。重复，请确认位置并回报。

（更多枪声响起，杜恩野蛮地一顿乱射。格温随着枪声尖叫着。救护车聚集到外面。）

瑞斯：   话线断了。

探员1：   有4、5声枪响。

（穆德走到瑞斯旁边。）

穆德：   那边电话是多少。

瑞斯：   555-2804.

注释

1. **hostage** ['hɒstɪdʒ] *n.* 人质
2. **cellular** ['seljələ] *n.* 移动电话；单元
3. **abductee** [ˌæbdʌk'tiː] *n.* 被绑架者
4. **therapy sessions** 治疗法
5. **hypnotic regressions** 催眠记忆
6. **agitated** ['ædʒɪteɪtɪd] *adj.* 激动的；焦虑的；表现不安的
7. **capture** ['kæptʃə] *v.* 捕获；俘虏

(Mulder picks up the phone and dials.)

MAN 1: Repeat, we have either four or five shots fired!

Lucy: Our electrical substation blew. We've got no *power up*[2] and down the block.

(Duane picks up.)

Mulder: Duane?

(Cut to Duane.)

Duane: I told you.

Mulder: Is everybody all right, Duane?

Duane: You didn't believe me, did you?

(Cut back to Mulder.)

Mulder: No, I, I believe you. I just need to know if anybody gets shot.

(Cut to Duane, who's pacing....anybody's been shot. Duane looks down at Bob, who is bleeding heavily. Gwen is tending to him.

Gwen: I need towels. Kimberly? Kimberly? He's going to bleed to death. (She looks at Kimberly, who won't move.)

Duane: I guess we're going to need a doctor.

(Mulder moves the phone away from his ear, frowning[8]. A man turns on a small receiver and puts it in Mulder's ear while a man instructs him.)

Com: Now, you'll have almost full **ambient**[9] hearing loss in this ear. Your sense of balance might be affected slightly, particularly if you have to move quickly or get into a physical situation. If you get trapped or held in the building for some reason, we'll be able to warn you if there's a tactical assault. Now remember, he's either got four or five rounds left. Now, there's a wireless mic hidden in the top of this flak jacket. Speaking in a normal tone of voice, we should be able to hear anything you say up to a hundred yards. *Make* every *attempt to*[3] keep these devices **concealed**[10].

（穆德拿起电话拨了起来。）

探员1: 重复，有4、5声枪响。

露西: 一座电力站爆炸，我们没有电源了。

（杜恩接起电话。）

穆德: 杜恩？

（画面切到杜恩。）

杜恩: 我告诉过你的。

穆德: 大家都还好吧，杜恩？

杜恩: 你并不相信我，不是吗？

（画面回到穆德。）

穆德: 不，我相信你。我只是想知道有没有人受伤。

（画面回到杜恩，他踱来踱去……有人被击中了。他低头看了看鲍勃，鲍勃伤得很严重。格温正在照顾他。）

格温: 我需要毛巾。金柏丽，金柏丽，他会流血过多而死。（她看向已经吓到不敢动弹的金柏丽。）

杜恩: 我想我们需要一个医生。

（穆德皱着眉头把电话拿开。一名男子把一个接收器放进穆德的耳朵里并为他介绍。）

指挥官: 有时你会听不到四周的声音，平衡感也会受到影响。特别是你快速移动或是身体受到影响的话。假如你被劫持，发动攻击前我们会警告你，记住，他还有4到5发子弹。防弹衣内藏着一个无线麦克风，用正常音量我们都可以听到你说话。我们尽量隐藏这些装备，但若你让话筒靠近耳朵，它会使你的窃听器曝光。

You put a normal telephone handset to that ear, it'll cause feedback and reveal that you're wired.

(Lucy walks up to him.)

Lucy: You really want to do this?

Mulder: Yeah.

(They start walking, followed by the tactical commander and another man.)

Lucy: Your job will be to deliver medical help to the hostage. Anything else is just a bonus. You're to get in and get out. You are not to risk your own life. Whatever you believe...

Mulder: Don't jump into his **delusion**[11]. I can't *negotiate with*[4] him if he thinks I believe him.

Lucy: Right. (She points at the man standing next to her.) This is Agent Janus, he's a trained medic. He'll work on the hostage. You're to keep Duane Barry talking. Like I said, if he's talking, he's not going to shoot anybody including you.

(The tactical commander leads Mulder off to the side.)

Com: Now, I've got three snipers out there. Anything you can do to get him to the front door, all we need is one shot to the medulla **oblongata**[12].

(He touches the back of Mulder's neck where the medulla oblongata is located. Mulder nods. Mulder and Janus walk out, Janus carrying his orange case.)

Sniper: Tac. command, this is rooftop zero-two. I have them in sight. They're passing the fountain and approaching the front entrance now.

（露西走向穆德。）

露西： 你真的要这么做？

穆德： 是的。

（他们开始往出走，战术指挥官和另一个人跟着他们。）

露西： 你的任务是送药给人质，其他都是无所谓的。快去快回，你不必用性命冒险，不管你相信不相信……

穆德： 都不要受到他的迷惑，若他认为我信他就不能谈判。

露西： 对。（她指了指站在他身边的人。）这位是詹纳斯探员，是训练有素的医护，他会帮助伤者，你要保持跟杜恩对话，如果他一直讲话就不伤人，包括你。

（战术指挥官把穆德拉到别处。）

指挥官： 我安排了3位狙击手，你只要引他靠近前门，我们只需在他后脑开一枪就够了。

（他拍了拍穆德脖子的后面，也就是后脑所在处。穆德点了点头。穆德和詹走了出去，詹带着他橘黄色的医药箱。）

狙击手： 战术指挥官，我这里是屋顶2号。我看到他们了，他们正经过喷水池往前门走去。

注释

8. frown [fraʊn] *v.* 皱眉头

9. ambient ['æmbɪənt] *adj.* 周围的；外界的；环绕的

10. conceal [kən'si:l] *v.* 隐蔽，隐匿

11. delusion [dɪ'lu:ʒn] *n.* 迷惑，欺骗；错觉；幻想

12. medulla oblongata: ［解剖］延髓

📠 常用表达

1. boot up 启动

例：I pour myself some cereal and gulp it down in my home office while waiting for the computer to boot up.

在家中的办公室里等候电脑启动时，我给自己灌下一些谷类食物，狼吞虎咽地吃下去。

2. power up 上电，加电

例：It's certainly a positive sign that this market has some staying power up at these levels, and has the potential to go higher here.

这显然是一个正面讯号，市场有能力保持目前的水平，且有潜力上升。

3. make attempt to 试图

例：Make attempt to write the "han yu pin yin" of the characters being formed .

把汉语拼音拼出来的字，记录下来。

4. negotiate with 谈判

例：We tried to negotiate with them, but they refused.

我们试图与他们谈判，但被他们拒绝了。

Passage 3

剧情介绍：

（选自第 3 季第 19 集）有个人专门绑架小女孩。一名中学女孩被绑架。奇怪的是，一个小时候曾被同一个人绑架过的女子能感应到这个人的新罪行和被绑女孩的痛苦。通过她的感应，穆德找到了藏匿点，被绑小女孩最终获救，而这名女子却替她死去，得到解脱。

Scene1: University Medical Center Seattle, Washington. 10:31AM. Mulder told Scully about a girl being kidnapped from her bedroom.

华盛顿大学医学中心。上午 10：31。穆德告诉史考莉关于一个女孩在她的卧室被绑架的事情。

Mulder:	Thought you missed your flight.	穆德：	我还以为你错过了飞机。
Scully:	We were delayed in D.C. I tried you on your cell phone.	史考莉：	机场遇到点麻烦，我打了你手机。
Mulder:	Oh, I forgot it. I left in kind of a hurry.	穆德：	太急，我忘带了。
Scully:	Your message said something about a kidnapping?	史考莉：	你留言上说是关于绑架的？
Mulder:	Yeah. Fifteen-year-old girl...named Amy Jacobs was taken from her bedroom last night. 10:00.	穆德：	一个 15 岁的叫艾米的女孩昨晚从床上绑走了，10 点。
Scully:	Is she here?	史考莉：	她在这儿吗？
Mulder:	No, they haven't found her.	穆德：	他们没找到她。
Scully:	Well, what are we doing here?	史考莉：	我们来这干什么？
Mulder:	A 30-year-old woman named Lucy Householder...was admitted here shortly after 10:00. She collapsed at work, suffering from some kind of **seizure**[1]...and what her doctors are calling "**glossolalia**[2]."	穆德：	一个叫露西·斯霍尔德的 30 岁女人，在 10 点后不久进了医院。她突然从工作中倒下，像发了羊癫疯一样。医生说她胡言乱语。
Scully:	**Incoherent**[3] speech.	史考莉：	语无伦次。

注释
1. seizure [ˈsiːʒə] *n.* （疾病的）突然发作
2. glossolalia [ˌɡlɔsəuˈleiliə] *n.* 语意不清；言语不清
3. incoherent [ˌinkəuˈhiərənt] *adj.* 语无伦次的；不连贯的

Mulder:	Technically, but whether she knew it or not, she was repeating the exact words spoken by Amy's abductor...at the exact same time, 20 miles across town.	穆德:	差不多，但不管她知不知道，她重复的是绑架艾米的人说的话。在相同的时间，在离小镇 20 英里的地方。
Scully:	That's **spooky**[4].	史考莉:	太奇怪了！
Mulder:	That's my name, isn't it? Turns out Lucy Householder knows a little something about kidnapping herself. When she was eight years old, she was taken from her bedroom while her parents were asleep. She was missing for five years until she escaped and someone found her by the side of a road. Apparently, her **abductor**[5] had kept her locked in a basement the entire time. They never caught him.	穆德:	这不就是我办案的类型吗？露西·豪斯霍尔德小时候也被绑架过。她八岁时在父母睡觉时被带走，直到 5 年后逃脱，有人在路边发现她，绑架者把她关在地下室里 5 年，他们一直没有抓到他。

> **Scene2:** FBI Regional Field Office, Seattle, Washington. 1:53 PM.
> 华盛顿州西雅图FBI分部，下午1:53。

Eubanks:	Agent Mulder. Lucy Householder. You get anywhere on that?	尤本:	穆德探员，露西·豪斯霍尔德，她那里怎么样？
Mulder:	I'm workin' on it.	穆德:	我正处理。
Eubanks:	Got one of my guys on the line. Says she's got a criminal record. Prostitution, **narcotics**[6] convictions. She's done some time.	尤本:	我的人说她有犯罪记录，卖淫、吸毒，经常犯些事。
Mulder:	That doesn't surprise me, given her history.	穆德:	根据她的经历，我并不感到惊奇。
Eubanks:	She's also got a boyfriend doing time for assault and child endangerment. Used to live with him up in the hills. Pretty sketchy characters.	尤本:	她男朋友是个危险人物，有过侵犯儿童的记录。过去他们住在山上，两个真是天生一对啊。
Mulder:	I don't think she's involved.	穆德:	我想不是她干的。
Eubanks:	Closest thing I got to a lead. I can tell him to shift some men...	尤本:	这是得到的最接近的线索。我敢说他一定绑架过一些人。

Mulder:	No, let me follow up on that, okay? Thanks.	穆德：	不，让我跟进好吗？ 谢谢。
Scully:	Mulder. Got something. Something weird.	史考莉：	穆德，找到了一些奇怪的东西。
Mulder:	What?	穆德：	什么？
Scully:	I was going over Lucy Householder's medical workup, and something hit me. Her blood type is "O" positive.	史考莉：	我看了露西的就医记录，有些东西让我吃惊。她的血型是 O 型阳性，是吗？
Mulder:	Yeah?	穆德：	是啊，怎么了？
Scully:	**Forensics**[7] lifted two blood types off of her work clothes, "O" positive and "B" positive. Two guesses as to what Amy Jacobs' blood type is.	史考莉：	但她的工作衣服上有两种血型，O 型阳性和 B 型阳性。另外一个可能是艾米的血。
Mulder:	How could it be Amy Jacobs' blood? Lucy was all the way across town.	穆德：	怎么是艾米的血？露西离小镇远着呢！
Scully:	I don't know, Mulder, but it *begs the question*[1].	史考莉：	我不知道，但这是个问题。
Mulder:	Because it matches the victim's blood type? How many have "B" positive blood, Scully? One in five? That's hundreds of thousands of people in the local population alone.	穆德：	就因为和受害者血型相符？有多少人血型是 B 型阳性，史考莉？五分之一？本地数百上千的人是这个血型。
Scully:	We're not talking about the local population. We're talking about a woman who's tied to this case, who had somebody else's blood on her.	史考莉：	我说的不是当地人，而是说和这个案子有关的那个女人。她认识多少个是 B 型血的。
Mulder:	Lucy is a victim, Scully, just like Amy Jacobs. If she's got any connection to this case, that's the extent of it.	穆德：	露西也是受害人，史考莉，和艾米一样。如果她和此案有关，那也是同一个绑匪。
Scully:	Well, we'll know soon enough.	史考莉：	我们很快就会知道了。
Mulder:	What are you talking about?	穆德：	你什么意思？
Scully:	I'm running a **P.C.R.**[8] on her blood to see if there's a D.N.A. match.	史考莉：	我正在做聚合酶链式反应看看 DNA 是否相符。
Mulder:	Will you keep that under your hat2?	穆德：	你能暂时不公布吗？
Scully:	Why?	史考莉：	为什么？
Mulder:	Because I don't want Lucy Householder treated like a suspect in this case...until it's absolutely certain that she is one, okay?	穆德：	因为我不想露西被当成嫌疑犯，除非确定她真的是。

注释

4. spooky [ˈspuːki] *adj.* 幽灵般的；有鬼般的
5. abductor [æbˈdʌktə] *n.* 诱拐者
6. narcotic [nɑːˈkɒtɪk] *n.* 麻醉毒品

7. forensics [fəˈrensɪks] *n.* 辩论术；取证
8. P.C.R. *abbr.*【生物工艺学】polymerase chain reaction
聚合酶系列（或连锁）反应

Scene3: Amy's blood was found on Lucy and she was suspected by the Agents except Mulder.

露西被怀疑为嫌疑犯，只有穆德认为她是无辜的。

Mulder:	You're gonna drive her away with this.	穆德：	发通缉令，她会逃的。
Eubanks:	She's been driven away, Mulder.	尤本：	她已经逃了，穆德。
Mulder:	A half-dozen witnesses placed her across town at the time of the kidnapping.	穆德：	很多证人看见她在绑架发生时，在小镇的另一端。
Eubanks:	I'm well aware of the facts.	尤本：	我知道。
Mulder:	Then trust me on this. She's not working with Wade.	穆德：	相信我，她没有为韦德工作。
Eubanks:	How'd she get the blood on her?	尤本：	那她身上的血迹怎么解释？
Mulder:	She may have bled it.	穆德：	是她流的。
Eubanks:	She bled Amy Jacobs' blood?	尤本：	她流的是艾米的血？
Mulder:	Yes, it may explain why there was so little of it on the carpet in Amy's bedroom.	穆德：	是，这就是为什么它和艾米卧室的地毯上的血是一致的。
Agent:	Agent Eubanks? Line three.	探员：	尤班克斯探员，3号线。
Eubanks:	I don't have time for this nonsense, Agent Mulder. We've got a young girl's life *at stake*[3].	尤本：	我没时间听这些废话，穆德探员。一个小女孩的生命正处于危险中。
Scully:	I hate to say this, Mulder, but I think you just ran out of credibility.	史考莉：	我不想说这些，穆德，他们不相信你说的。
Mulder:	He's wrong, Scully.	穆德：	他错了，史考莉。
Scully:	You're protecting her beyond the point of reason.	史考莉：	你没有理由保护她。
Mulder:	I'm protecting her because I think she's connected to Amy Jacobs, just not the way everybody else thinks she is.	穆德：	我保护她是因为她和艾米有联系。别人可能不会这么想。
Scully:	Did you consider for one minute that the person she's connected to is Carl Wade?	史考莉：	你有想过和她有联系的人吗？
Mulder:	Carl Wade. Why would she be connected with Carl Wade?	穆德：	是卡尔·韦德吗？为什么她要和卡尔·韦德联系？
Scully:	For the same twisted reason that abused	史考莉：	一个扭曲的原因，被虐待的儿童

children crave their parents' love...or hostages develop sympathy for their **captors**[9]. I mean, maybe Lucy developed some kind of emotional dependency.

Mulder: After five years in a dark pit, I'm sure she developed some kind of connection with Wade, just not the kind that you're suggesting.

Scully: It makes more sense than the notion that she's bleeding Amy Jacobs' blood.

Mulder: I don't know how to explain it, but I think that Wade's abduction of Amy...triggered some kind of physical response in Lucy. Some kind of **empathic**[10] transference.

Scully: Mulder, you can't...

Mulder: That's how I account for what Lucy's going through. That's how I account for the identical words that corresponded to Amy...and the spontaneous wounds and blood as well.

Scully: Then why did she run? If she's innocent, what was she running from?

Mulder: Because she's afraid.

Scully: You don't see what you're doing, do you, Mulder? You are so close to this that you just don't see it.

Mulder: What don't I see?

Scully: The extreme rationalization that's going on your personal identification with the victim--or, in this case, the suspect.You're becoming some kind of an **empath**[11] yourself, Mulder. You are so sympathetic to Lucy as a victim--like your sister--that you can't see her as a person who's capable of committing this crime.

缺少父母的爱，或者人质逐渐同情绑架他们的人，也许露西对他产生了依赖的心理，由于被关进地下室里5年。

穆德： 5年被关在黑暗的地下室，我相信她和韦德产生了某种联系，但也不是你说的这种依赖。

史考莉： 她身上有艾米的血更能说明问题。

穆德： 我不知道怎么解释，但韦德对艾米的绑架引发了露西的身体感应，是一种感情转移。

史考莉： 穆德，你不能……

穆德： 那就是我为什么明白露西发生的事，明白她什么会说和艾米类似的话，莫名其妙的受伤和流血。

史考莉： 如果是无辜，她为什么要逃跑？

穆德： 因为她害怕。

史考莉： 你知道自己在干什么吗，穆德？你太投入了，让你看不到真相。

穆德： 看不到什么？

史考莉： 极端合理化。你对这个案子里的受害者，或对嫌疑人的个人判断能力受到了影响。某种程度上你是同情你自己，穆德，你把露西当成了你的妹妹，以至于你不认为她有能力犯罪。

注释
9. captor [ˈkæptə] *n.* 捕获者；俘房者
10. empathic [ɪmˈpæθɪk] *adj.* 移情作用的；神入的
11. empath [emˈpɑːθ] *n.* 同理心，移情

Mulder: You don't think I've thought of that? I have. Not everything I do and say and think or feel goes back to my sister.You, of all people, should realize that sometimes...motivations for behavior can be more complex and mysterious than *tracing them back to*[4] one single childhood experience.

穆德： 你以为我没这样想过吗？我又不是每件事、每句话、每个想法或者感受都会和我妹妹有联系。你们所有人应该意识到，比起追溯他们个人的童年经历，行为动机有时是复杂而神秘的。

常用表达

1. beg the question 提出问题，产生疑问

例： Nonetheless, setting such a target does beg the question—just what should the United Nations do to help realize this change?

然而，如果制定这样一个目标就必须提出如下问题：联合国应当做什么才能帮助实现这一转变？

2. keep sth. under one's hat 隐瞒，保密

例： It's not wise to keep information like that under your hat.

将那样的事情隐瞒起来是不明智的。

3. at stake 危险，利害攸关

例： At stake is not only the health of humans but that of the earth.

处于紧要关头的不仅是人类的健康，还有地球的健康。

4. trace back to 追溯到

例： He said that these tomatoes trace back to the southern Ukraine during the early 19th century.

他说，这些西红柿的起源之地是 19 世纪初的南部乌克兰。

Doctor Who
《神秘博士》

入选理由：

　　《神秘博士》是由英国广播公司制作的英国科幻电视剧，被《吉尼斯世界纪录大全》列为世界上最长的科幻电视剧，也被列入有史以来"最成功"的科幻电视系列剧。此片开播之初，其充满想像力的剧情、低成本却有创意的特效及前卫的电音配乐等都让它获得各界肯定。这部电视剧在英国流行文化中占有相当重要的地位，许多影评人认为这是英国电视史上最好的电视剧之一。这部电视剧赢得了英国影艺学院电影电视奖，也获得了 5 次英国戏剧类国家电视奖。

Section 1　剧情特点：

　　《神秘博士》是一部由英国广播公司出品的科幻电视剧。此片描述了一名神奇的名为"神秘博士"（Doctor Who）的时间领主，他用伪装成 50 年代英国警亭的时间机器塔迪斯（Time and Relative Dimension（s）in Space，时间和空间相对维度）在时间、空间中旅行冒险。他与其搭档在时间、空间中探索未知，打击邪恶力量，拯救文明，帮助人们纠正错误。

Section 2　对白特点：

　　《神秘博士》中的神秘博士操着英国北部的口音。他和他的同伴有时回到过去，在那里人们说着中世纪英语；有时他们回到二战时期，在那里我们又能听到美式英语；有时在现代伦敦，在那里人们说着纯正伦敦音英语……所以，我们能从中领略不同时期不同风格的英语。

Section 3　角色分析：

神秘博士 (Doctor Who)： 忧郁的战争幸存者，经历了他的种族和敌人戴立克（Dalek）的战争，是他的种族中唯一活下来的人。他的第一个同伴是来自地球的罗斯·泰勒。神秘博士会在细胞遭到损害后重生，重生后的神秘博士由不同演员扮演。他是一个英雄人物，鼓励他的同伴和其他人勇于面对困难。机智、豪爽的个性和外表掩盖了他的孤独和内疚。

罗斯·泰勒 (Rose Tyler)： 她是第九任和第十任神秘博士的灵魂伴侣，当第九任来到地球的时候，罗斯·泰勒协助神秘博士击败了外星人，并受邀一同前往世界末日。为了拯救地球，她被父亲带到了一个平行世界。后来两个宇宙之间的缝隙打破了，罗斯·泰勒重新回到地球并协同第十任神秘博士一起击败了戴立克。

玛莎·琼斯 (Martha Jones)： 玛莎·琼斯开始时是一个医学生，在她工作的医院发生了特殊事件，之后遇到了第十任神秘博士，并成为他的同伴一起周游宇宙。最后为了拯救神秘博士，她环游世界寻找对付神秘博士的宿敌——法师的方法。击败了法师之后，玛莎·琼斯发现自己不能忍受自己单恋神秘博士而神秘博士始终深爱着罗斯·泰勒的事实。她离开了神秘博士，曾短暂回归协助神秘博士击败戴立克，后来加入了火炬木小组，喜欢上神秘博士的另一个同伴米奇·史密斯。

唐娜·诺布尔 (Donna Noble)： 之前在唐娜·诺布尔的婚礼上，第十任神秘博士破坏了一切，唐娜·诺布尔失去了她的工作和未婚夫，因此拒绝了神秘博士成为她的同伴的提议。之后苦心寻找神秘博士行踪的时候她再次与第十任相见，两人一拍即合，成为了神秘博士的同伴。唐娜·诺布尔直言不讳，富有爱心，非常幽默，和神秘博士有深厚的友谊。她永不满足于小小的世界，最后拥有半个时间领主的力量。但是这股力量过于庞大，神秘博士只好抹去她的记忆和力量，后来神秘博士在唐娜·诺布尔的婚礼上露面，并祝福她。

艾米·庞德 (Amy Pond)： 作为一个七岁的女孩，在生活中，艾米·庞德只有她的姑姑，当第十一任神秘博士到她家后院的那个晚上，一切都改变了。艾米请求他调查一个在她墙上不寻常的裂纹。第十一任神秘博士承诺艾米·庞德在五分钟内将返回，但是无意中第十一任神秘博士迟到了十二年，最后艾米·庞德还是在结婚前夕跟着神秘博士旅行了。在她的身上能看到各种优秀的品质，独立有主见，勇敢坚定。

🔊 Passage 1 🎥

剧情介绍：

（选自第 1 季第 8 集）罗斯·泰勒让神秘博士带她回到父母的婚礼上，并回忆她小时候妈妈对她说的话。之后，罗斯·泰勒和神秘博士回到了 1987 年，又回到了皮特·泰勒出车祸的那一刻……

Scene 1: Little Rose Tyler and her mum, Jackie Tyler, at home.

小罗斯·泰勒和她妈妈杰姬·泰勒，家中。

(Peter Alan Tyler, my dad. The most wonderful man in the world. Born 15th September 1954.)

Jackie: Come here, Rose. Come here.

Little Rose: Who's that?

Jackie: It's your daddy. You weren't old enough to remember when he died in 1987, 7th of November. D' you remember what I told you? The day that Stuart Hoskins and Sarah Clark got married. He was always having adventures. Ah, he would have loved to have seen you now.

(Rose Tyler and Doctor Who are in Tardis.)

Rose: That's what Mum always says. So I was thinking could we... Could we go and see my dad, when he was still alive?

Doctor: Where's this come from all of a sudden?

Rose: All right. If we can't, if it goes against the laws of time or something, never mind, just leave it.

Doctor: No, I can do anything. I'm just more worried about you.

Rose: I wanna see him.

Doctor: Your wish is my command. But be careful what you wish for...

(Rose Tyler and Doctor Who go back to the wedding ceremony of Rose Tyler's parents.)

The priest: I, Peter Alan Tyler, take you, Jacqueline Andrea Suzette Prentice...

（皮特·艾伦·泰勒，我的父亲，这个世界上最好的人，生于 1954 年 9 月 15 日。）

杰姬： 过来，罗斯，过来。

小罗斯： 他是谁？

杰姬： 你的父亲。在他死的时候你还太小，所以没印象。1987 年 11 月 7 日。你还记得我跟你说了什么吗？那天是斯图亚特·霍金斯和莎拉·克拉克结婚的日子。他总是去冒险。啊，他一定会很想见你。

（罗斯·泰勒和神秘博士在塔迪斯里。）

罗斯： 妈妈一直都这样说。所以我在想……我们可不可以？我们可不可以去父亲还活着的时候？

博士： 你怎么忽然有了这个念头？

罗斯： 如果我们不能，如果那是会和时间规定或者别的什么冲突，没关系，忘了就是了。

博士： 不，我可以做任何事，我担心你更多。

罗斯： 我想见他。

博士： 你的愿望就是我的命令，不过要注意你的愿望……

（罗斯·泰勒和神秘博士回到了罗斯·泰勒父母的婚礼上。）

牧师： 我，皮特·艾伦·泰勒，愿意娶你，杰奎林·安德里亚·苏泽特·普伦蒂斯……

Pete Tyler: I, Peter Alan Tyler, take you, Jacqueline Susanne... Suzette...Anita?

Jackie Oh, just carry on. If it's good enough for Lady Di...

Rose: (to Doctor Who) I thought he'd be taller.

Pete: To be my lawful wedded wife. To love and behold till death us do part...

(Rose Tyler recalls what her mother said to her when she was little.)

Jackie: He died so close to home. I wasn't there, nobody was. It was a **hit-and-run**[1] driver. Never found out who. He was dead when the ambulance got there. I only wish there'd been someone there for him.

Little Rose: I want to be that someone. So he doesn't die alone.

(Rose Tyler and Doctor Who in Tardis.)

Doctor: November the 7th?

Rose: 1987.

(Rose Tyler and Doctor Who go back to 1987.)

Rose: That's so weird. The day my father died. I thought it would be all sort of **grim**[2] and stormy. It's just an ordinary day.

Doctor: The past is another country. 1987 is just the Isle of Wight. You sure about this?

Rose: Yeah. This is it, Jordan Road. He was late... He'd been to get a wedding present, the **vase**[3]. Mum always said, "That stupid vase." He got out of his car. And crossed the road...Oh, God. This is it.

(A car comes over and hits Pete Tyler.)

Doctor: Go to him. Quick!

Rose: It's too late now. By the time the ambulance got there, he was dead. He can't die on his own. Can I try again?

(Rose Tyler and Doctor Who go back to the moment of Pete Tyler's car accident again.)

Doctor: Right, that's the first you and me. It's a

皮特：我，皮特·艾伦·泰勒，愿意娶你杰奎林·苏珊娜……苏泽特……安妮塔？

杰姬：噢，继续。这对"……夫人"是值得的。

罗斯：（对神秘博士说）我以为他会高点。

皮特：作为我合法的妻子，相爱永远，此志不渝……

（罗斯·泰勒回忆她小时候妈妈对她说的话。）

杰姬：他死的时候离家很近，我不在场，也没有人在。那司机撞人了就逃离了现场，所以永远都找不出谁是凶手。救护车到场时他已经死了，我只希望那时能有人在他身边。

小罗斯：我希望我能是他身边的那个人，那样他就不会孤独地死去。

（罗斯·泰勒和神秘博士在塔迪斯里。）

博士：11月7日？

罗斯：1987年。

（罗斯·泰勒和神秘博士回到了1987年。）

罗斯：太意外了，我父亲在这天去世，我以为是狂风暴雨、电闪雷鸣的一天，原来只是这么平常的一天。

博士：过去好比另外一个国家，在1987年仅仅是怀特岛。你肯定是今天？

罗斯：是。是这里，约旦路，他迟到了……他去拿婚礼礼物，一个花瓶，妈总是说"这该死的花瓶"。他下了车，然后过马路……噢，老天，就是他。

（一辆汽车开了过来撞到了皮特·泰勒。）

博士：过去看看他，快！

罗斯：现在太迟了，救护车来的时候他已经死了，他不能孤单的死掉，我能再来一次吗？

（罗斯·泰勒和神秘博士又回到了皮特·泰勒出车祸的那一刻。）

博士：那是第一次的我和你，这主意真

| | very bad idea, two sets of us being here at the same time. Just be careful they don't see us, wait till she runs off and he follows, then go to your dad. | 糟糕，我们两队人同时在这里出现。要注意点儿,他们看不到我们。等到她走开，他跟上去了，你就去你爸爸那儿。 |

Rose : Oh, God. This is it. I can't do this.

Doctor: You don't have to do anything you don't want to. But this is the last time we can be here.

(Rose Tyler runs to Pete Tyler's car to stop him.)

Doctor: Rose! No!

Rose: I did it. (to Pete Tyler)I saved your life!

Pete: **Blimey**[4], see the speed of it? D' you get his number?

Rose: I really did it! Oh, my God, look at you, you're alive! That car was gonna kill ya!

Pete: Give me some credit. I did see it coming. I wasn't gonna walk under it.

Rose: I'm Rose.

Pete: Oh, that's a **coincidence**[5], that's my daughter's name.

Rose: That's a great name. Good choice. Well done.

Pete: Right. I better **shift**[6]. I've got a wedding to go to.

Rose: Is that Sarah Clark's wedding?

Pete: Yeah. Are you going?

Rose: Yeah!

Pete: Do you and your boyfriend need a lift?

(Screeching.)

(Rose Tyler and Doctor Who in Pete Tyler's home.)

罗斯：噢，老天，就是他。我做不到。

博士：不要做自己不想做的事情，但这是我们最后一次在这里。

（罗斯·泰勒跑去皮特·泰勒的车跟前阻止他。）

博士：罗斯！不要！

罗斯：我成功了！（对皮特·泰勒说）我救了你！

皮特：天呀，注意车速没？你看到车牌号吗？

罗斯：我真的成功了！噢，老天，看看你自己，你还活着！那车差点要了你的命！

皮特：给我点奖励，我确实看到车撞过来，我还不想死在车轮下。

罗斯：我叫罗斯。

皮特：噢，太巧了，我女儿和你的名字一样。

罗斯：那是个很好的名字,不错的选择，不错。

皮特：我要走了，我要去参加婚礼。

罗斯：是莎拉·克拉克的婚礼吗？

皮特：是的，你也要去吗？

罗斯：是的。

皮特：你和男朋友需要搭车吗？

（尖叫声。）

（罗斯·泰勒和神秘博士在皮特·泰勒的家里。）

注释
1. hit-and-run 肇事后逃逸的
2. grim [grɪm] adj. 冷酷的，残忍的
3. vase [vɑːz] n. 装饰瓶，花瓶
4. Blimey ['blaɪmɪ] interj. 啊呀
5. coincidence [kəʊ'ɪnsɪdəns] n. 巧合；一致
6. shift [ʃɪft] v. 移动，转变　move quickly 迅速移动

Pete: Right, there we go. Sorry about the mess. If you want a cup of tea, kitchen's down there, milk's in the fridge. Well it would be, wouldn't it? Where else would you put the milk? Mind you, there's always the **windowsill**[7] outside. If someone invented a windowsill with special **compartments**[8] —one for milk, one for **yoghurt**[9], you could make a lot of money out of that, sell it to students and things. I should write that down. Anyway, excuse me a minute, gotta go and change.

(Pete Tyler goes away and leaves Rose Tyler and Doctor Who alone.)

Rose: All the stuff Mum kept. His stuff. She kept it all packed away in boxes. She used to show me when she'd had a bit to drink. Here it is...on display. Where it should be. Third prize at the bowling. First two got to go to Didcot. Health drinks! **Tonics**[10], mum used to call them. He made his money selling this Vitex stuff. He had all sorts of jobs, he was so clever. **Solar**[11] power! Mum said he was going to do this - now he can! OK, I'll tell him you're not my boyfriend.

Doctor: When we met, I said, "travel with me in space." You said no. Then I said, "Time machine".

Rose: It wasn't some big plan. I just saw it happening, and I thought I can stop it.

Doctor: I did it again. I picked another stupid ape. I should've known. It's not about showing you the universe. It never is. It's about the universe doing something for you.

Rose: So it's OK, when you go to other times, and You save people's lives, but not when it's me saving my dad?

Doctor: I know what I'm doing. You don't! Two sets of us being there made that a vulnerable

皮特： 不好意思，这里太乱了。如果想喝茶，一直走就会看到厨房，牛奶在冰箱里。一切都会很好的，不是吗？你想把牛奶放哪呢？麻烦你了，那些一直在窗台外面。如果有人发明了窗台有特殊功能，一是为了牛奶，另一个是为了酸乳酪，你就可以因此赚一大笔钱，把这卖给学生或其他人。我要把那给写下来。总之，等我一下。

（皮特·泰勒走开了，只有罗斯·泰勒和神秘博士在。）

罗斯： 所有的一切妈妈都保存着，他的一切。她把这儿所有的东西都收藏在箱子里，她在酩酊大醉后会给我看这些。这是……陈列品，保龄球比赛第三名,前两球全中。健康饮料，滋补品，妈妈经常这样叫，他的钱是靠卖这些赚回来的，他什么工作都干，是个很聪明的人。太阳能卫星! 妈妈说他要做这研究，现在他能做了。好吧，我告诉他你不是我的男朋友。

博士： 当我们见面时，我说"和我一起空间旅行"，你说不肯。然后我说"时间机器"。

罗斯： 那些都不是预谋，我看到这事发生。然后我想我能阻止。

博士： 我又犯了个错。我选了另外一个笨蛋，我应该会知道，这并不是仅仅给你看看宇宙，永远都不会是,这个宇宙因为你所做的事情。

罗斯： 当你去另外一个时空救了别人的生命时,难道我不应该救爸爸吗？

博士： 我知道自己在做什么，但你不知道。那里我们两组人使时空上出

point.

Rose : But he's alive.

Doctor: My entire planet died, my whole family. Do you think it never occurred to me to go back and save them?

Rose: But it's not like I've changed history. Not much. I mean, he's never gonna be a world leader. He's not gonna start World War Three or anything.

Doctor: Rose. There's a man alive in the world who wasn't alive before. An ordinary man. That's the most important thing in creation. The whole world's different because he's alive.

Rose: Well. Would you rather him dead?

Doctor: I'm not saying that.

Rose: No. I get it. For once, you're not the most important man in my life!

Docto: Let's see how you get on without me. Give me the key. The tardis key. If I'm so insignificant, give it me back!

Rose: All right then, I will!

Doctor: You've got what you wanted, so that's goodbye then.

Rose: You don't scare me! I know how sad you are! You'll be back in a minute! Or will you hang around outside the TARDIS waiting for me. And I'll make you wait a long time!

现脆弱点。

罗斯： 但他活着。

博士： 我的整个星球灭亡了，还有我整个家庭，你以为我没想过要回到过去挽救这一切？

罗斯： 但这并不能改变历史，一点也不，我意思是说，他绝不会是个世界领导人，也不会发动第三次世界大战或别的什么。

博士： 罗斯，现在有个之前不曾活着的人活着，一个普通人，那是创物主创造的最重要的生物，整个世界都因他的存在而改变了。

罗斯： 你宁愿他死？

博士： 我没这样说。

罗斯： 但我这样想。只有这一次，你不是我生命中最重要的人。

博士： 那我们来看看没有我你怎么过吧，把钥匙给我，塔迪斯钥匙，如果我是那么不重要，把它还我。

罗斯： 好吧，我现在就给你！

博士： 你已经得到你想要的，那么就再见吧！

罗斯： 你吓不了我，我知道你有多伤心，你马上就会回来，或者你会拿着钥匙在外面等着我，我会让你等很久的！

注释
7. **windowsill** ['wɪndəʊsɪl] *n.* 窗沿，窗台
8. **compartment** [kəm'pɑːtmənt] *n.* 隔间（尤指火车车厢中的）
9. **yoghurt** ['jɒgət] *n.* 酸奶
10. **Tonic** ['tɒnɪk] *n.* 滋补剂
11. **solar** ['səʊlə] *adj.* 太阳的，利用太阳能的

🔊 Passage 2 📷

剧情介绍：

（选自第1季第8集）罗斯·泰勒让神秘博士带她回到她父亲皮特·泰勒去世的那天，罗斯和皮特谈论着过去和未来，结果因为扰乱时间而引来了一群像蝙蝠一样的吞噬怪兽，神秘博士也因保护大家被吞噬。最终皮特·泰勒自我牺牲修正了时间线，才挽救了所有人……

Scene: In the church, bat monsters were flying back and forth, and screaming and bumping sound could be heard everywhere.

教堂里，蝙蝠怪物飞来飞去，到处都是尖叫声和撞击声。

🔊 **Pete:** You, um, you never said why you came here in the first place. If I had a time machine, I wouldn't have thought 1987 was anything special. Not round here, anyway!

Rose: We just *ended up*[1] 'ere.

Pete: Lucky for me, eh? If you hadn't been there to save me.

Rose: That was just a coincidence. That was just really good luck. It's amazing.

Pete: So, in the future, um, are me and her indoors still together?

Rose: Yeah.

Pete: You still living with us?

Rose: Yep.

Pete: Am I a good dad?

Rose: You...You told me a bedtime story every night, when I was small. You were always there, you never missed one. And...umm...you took us for picnics in the country every Saturday. You

皮特：你，嗯，你从没告诉我为何首先来这里，如果我有时间机器，我不会认为1987年会有什么特别，总之不会到这附近。

罗斯：我们刚好停在这里罢了。

皮特：对我来说很幸运，嗯？如果你不曾到这里来救我。

罗斯：那只是个巧合，那确实是很幸运。太让人惊讶了。

皮特：那么，在未来，恩，我和她仍然在一起生活吗？

罗斯：是的。

皮特：你仍然和我们一起住？

罗斯：是的。

皮特：我是个好爸爸吗？

罗斯：你……每晚临睡前会给我讲故事，那时我还小，你总会在那里，从不缺席。然后……嗯……每个周六你都会带我们到郊外野餐，你从不让

never **let us down**[1].You were there for us all the time. Someone I could really rely on.

Pete: That's not me.

Doctor: Right, no-one touches that key! Have you got that? Don't touch it. Anyone touches that key, it'll be...well, **zap**[2]! Leave it be, and everything will be fine. We'll get out of here. All of us. Stuart. Sarah! You're gonna get married, just like I said!

Rose: (to Doctor) When time gets **sorted**[3]...

Doctor: Everybody here forgets what happened. (to Pete) And don't worry, the thing that you changed will...stay changed.

Pete: You mean, I'll still be alive. Though I'm meant to be dead. That's why I haven't done anything with my life. Why it meant nothing.

Doctor: Doesn't work like that.

Pete: Rubbish. I was so useless, I couldn't even die properly! Now it's my fault all this has happened.

Rose: This is my fault.

Pete: No, love. I'm your dad. It's my job for it to be my fault.

(Jackie appears.)

Jackie: Her dad? How are you her dad? How old were you, 12? Oh, that's disgusting!

Pete: Jacks, listen. This is Rose.

Jackie: Rose? How sick is that! Did you give my daughter a second-hand name? How many are there? Do you call them all Rose?

Pete: Oh, for God's sake, look! It's the same Rose.

(Pete passes little Rose to Rose.)

Doctor: Rose! No!

(One bat-like **monster**[4] flies into the church. People scream.)

我们失望，你总是一直守侯着我们，是一个我真正能依靠的人。

皮特：那不是我了。

博士：对了，谁也不能碰到钥匙，听明白没？不要碰那钥匙，谁碰了那钥匙，就会完蛋。就放那儿，一切都会好起来，我们会逃出这里，我们都能。斯图亚特，莎拉，你们会结婚的，就如我所说的。

罗斯：（对博士说）当时间在整顿时……

博士：在坐的各位会忘记发生的一切，（对皮特·泰勒说）不要担心，你所导致的变化会……停止改变。

皮特：你是说，我仍然活着？尽管我打算去死？那是为何我没能塑造好人生，为何一无所有。

博士：不是这样的。

皮特：废话! 我很没用，我甚至不能正常死去! 现在发生这些都是我的错。

罗斯：是我的错。

皮特：不是，我亲爱的，我是你爸爸，我犯的错误我会弥补的。

（杰姬出现了。）

杰姬：她的爸爸？你怎么会是她的爸爸？你那时几岁了，12 岁？噢，那多恶心。

皮特：杰姬，听着，这是罗斯。

杰姬：罗斯？！你有病啊？你给我的女儿一样的名字？还有多少个罗斯？你叫她们都叫罗斯？

皮特：噢，看在上帝的份上，请务必看，是同一个罗斯呀。

（皮特把小罗斯·泰勒递给了罗斯·泰勒。）

博士：罗斯，不要!

（一只像蝙蝠一样的怪物飞进了教堂。人们尖叫起来。）

注释
1. let down 使失望
2. zap [zæp] *v.* 杀死
3. sort [sɔːt] *vt.* 挑选；把……分类
4. monster ['mɒnstə] *n.* 怪物

🔊 **Doctor:** Everyone, behind me! (to the bat-like monster) I'm the oldest thing in here!

(Doctor confronts the bat-like monster.)

Rose: Doctor!

(The bat-like monster flies away. Rose goes to pick up the key.)

Rose: Cold...He's cold. Oh, my God, he's dead. It's all my fault. Both of you! All of you! The whole world!

Pete: Ah, come on!

(Screeching resumes.)

woman: This is it. There's nothing we can do. It's the end.

(Pete observes the cars outside the church. Then he goes to have a talk with Rose.)

Pete: The Doctor really cared about you. He didn't want you to go through it again, not if there was another way. Now there isn't.

Rose: What are you talking about?

Pete: The car that should have killed me, love. It's here. The Doctor worked it out way back, but he, umm... he tried to protect me. Still...He's not in charge any more. I am.

Rose: But you can't. . .

Pete: Who am I, love?

Rose: My daddy.

Pete: Jackie, look at her. She's ours.

Jackie: Oh, God.

Pete: I'm meant to be dead, Jackie. You're gonna get rid of me at last.

Jackie: Don't say that.

Pete: For once in your life, trust me. It's gotta be done. You've got to **survive**[5], cos you've got to bring up our daughter. (to Rose)I never read those bedtime stories; I never took you on those picnics. I was never there for you.

Rose: You would've been.

博士： 各位，站在我后面。（对那只像蝙蝠一样的怪物说）在这里我是最老的东西。

（博士与那只像蝙蝠一样的怪物对抗。）

罗斯： 博士。

（那只像蝙蝠一样的怪物飞走了。罗斯·泰勒去拾钥匙。）

罗斯： 冷了……他变冷了。噢，老天，他死了。都是我的错，你们两个，你们全部，整个世界。

皮特： 啊，来吧。

（尖叫声重新开始了。）

女士： 是那怪物，我们无能为力，一切都要结束了。

（皮特观察教堂外的汽车，然后他走到罗斯·泰勒跟前和她进行了一次谈话。）

皮特： 博士确实很在意你，他不想你再次经历，即使是另外一种经历，现在不会了。

罗斯： 你在说什么呢？

皮特： 那车是要来撞死我的，亲爱的，在那里，博士能让它重新发生，但是他……他设法保护我，尽管如此，他现在已经无力支持了，由我来。

罗斯： 但你不能……

皮特： 我是谁，我的宝贝？

罗斯： 我的爸爸。

皮特： 杰姬，看着她，她是我们的罗斯。

杰姬： 噢，天呀。

皮特： 我要去结束生命了，杰姬，最后你还是会摆脱我了。

杰姬： 不要这样说。

皮特： 在你的一生里只有一次，相信我，这事必须要去做的，你要生活下去，因为你要把我们的女儿抚养成人。（对罗斯·泰勒说）我从未给你睡觉前读故事，也从未带你去野餐，我从未这样为你做。

罗斯： 但你想这样做过。

Pete:	But I can do this for you. I can be a proper dad to you now.	皮特:	但我可以为你做这事，我现在要做一个好爸爸。
Rose:	It's not fair.	罗斯:	这不公平。
Pete:	I've had all these extra hours. No-one else in the world has ever had that. And on top of that, I get to see you. And you're beautiful. How lucky am I, eh? So, come on, do as your dad says. You gonna be there for me, love? Thanks for saving me.	皮特:	我已经多活了几个小时，这个世界上从未有人这样，另外，我能看到你，而且你这么漂亮，我多幸运，嗯？所以，来，照爸爸说的去做，你会在那里陪着我，宝贝？谢谢救我一命。
(Bat-like monsters screech. Pete runs to a car.)		（像蝙蝠一样的怪物尖叫着。皮特·泰勒跑向汽车。）	
Pete:	Goodbye, love.	皮特:	再见了，宝贝。
Doctor:	(to Rose) Go to him. Quick.	博士:	（对罗斯·泰勒说）去他那儿，快！

常用表达

1. end up < 非正 >（以……）结束；最终成为（变得）；最后处于

例: She fled with her children, moving from neighbour to neighbour and ending up in a friend's cellar.

她带着孩子逃亡，从一个邻居家跑到另一个邻居家，最后逃到了一个朋友的地下室。

Passage 3

剧情介绍:

（选自第 2 季第 13 集）赛博人（Cyberman）宣称已统治地球，并要移除人类的恐惧、性、阶级、人种和信条，把所有人类都变成赛博人。而四个戴立克（Dalek）保护着同样从大球里出来的"创世方舟"，并扬言一个戴立克就能摧毁五百万赛博人。平行世界的罗斯的"父亲"皮特·泰勒也通过裂缝来到地球加入了战争。"创世方舟"是时间领主制造的监狱，里面关有数百万戴立克，一场恶战即将开始，人类面临灭绝。神秘博士逆转裂缝把赛博人和戴立克关进零空间，罗斯·泰勒被"父亲"接去平行世界无法回来，神秘博士引爆了一颗超新星以获得足够的能量穿越时空，向站在恶狼湾的罗斯·泰勒道别……

注释 **5. survive** [sə'vaɪv] *vi.* 幸存，活下来

Scene: Rose Tyler is taken to the parallel world.

罗斯·泰勒被带到了平行世界。

Voi: Voiceover（画外音）；**A man: A man's voice**（一个男人的声音）

Rose:	Take me back! Take me back! Take me back!	罗斯：	带我回去！带我回去！带我回去！
Pete:	It's stopped working. He did it. He closed the **breach**[1].	皮特：	不起作用了，他成功了，他关闭了裂口。
Rose:	No!	罗斯：	不！
(One Morning in the parallel world.)		（一天早上，在平行世界里。）	
Man:	Rose...	男声：	罗斯……
(Last night I had a dream.)		（昨夜我做了个梦。）	
Man:	Rose...	男声：	罗斯……
(I heard a voice, and it was calling my name.)		（我听见了一个声音在喊我的名字。）	
Man:	Rose... Rose...Rose...	男声：	罗斯……罗斯……罗斯……
(I had a dream, um... I told Mum and Dad and Mickey. Anyone else would think I was mad, but not those three. They believed it, because they've met the Doctor. So they listened to the dream... It was calling me... And that night, we packed up. Got into Dad's old Jeep and off we went. Just like the dream said. We followed the voice. Crossed the water, kept on driving, hundreds and hundreds of miles. Because he's calling.)		（我告诉了妈妈和爸爸，还有米奇，其他人都会觉得我疯了，但这三个人除外，他们相信了，因为他们见过博士，所以他们听了那个梦。他在呼唤我。那天晚上，我们整理行装，进了爸爸的老吉普，就出发了，就像梦中所述，跟着声音走，穿过海峡，继续开一百又一百英里，因为他在召唤着。）	
Man:	Rose...	男声：	罗斯……
(Here I am at last. And this is the story of how I died.)		（我来到了这里，最终，这就是我如何死去的故事。）	
(The blurred image of Doctor Who appears on the beach.)		（神秘博士的模糊影像出现了在沙滩上。）	
Rose:	Where are you?	罗斯：	你在哪里？
Doctor:	Inside the Tardis. There's one tiny little gap in the universe left, just about to close. And it	博士：	塔迪斯里面。宇宙里还有一个微小的缝隙留着，即将关闭，做此

takes a lot of power to send this projection. I'm in orbit around a <u>supernova</u>[2]. I'm burning up a sun, just to say goodbye.

Rose:	You look like a ghost.	罗斯:	你看起来像个鬼魂。
Doctor:	Hold on.	博士:	等一下。

(Doctor Who does something magic to make himself look real.)

（神秘博士施了一些魔法使自己看起来真实。）

Rose:	Can I ...	罗斯:	我能……
Doctor:	I'm still just an image. No touch.	博士:	我只是个图像，不能碰。
Rose:	Can't you come through properly?	罗斯:	你怎么才能完全过来?
Doctor:	The whole thing would **fracture**[3]. Two universes would collapse.	博士:	如果那样,所有的东西都会破碎,两个宇宙会崩溃。
Rose:	So?	罗斯:	那又怎样?
Doctor:	Where are we? Where did the gap come out?	博士:	我们在哪儿,这缝隙从哪露出来的?
Rose:	We're in Norway.	罗斯:	我们在挪威,
Doctor:	Norway! Right.	博士:	挪威,好吧。
Rose:	About 50 miles out of **Bergen**[4]. It's called Darlig Old Stranden.	罗斯:	大概在卡尔根北边 50 英里,这里叫作 Darlig Old Stranden。
Doctor:	Dalek?	博士:	Dalek?
Rose:	Darlig. It's Norwegian for bad. This translates as Bad Wolf Bay. How long have we got?	罗斯:	Darlig。挪威语意思是坏,翻译过来就是恶狼湾。我们还有多长时间?
Doctor:	About two minutes.	博士:	大约 2 分钟。
Rose:	I can't think of what to say!	罗斯:	我都不知道该说些什么。
Doctor:	You've still got Mr. Mickey, then.	博士:	那你还是跟着米奇先生?
Rose:	There's five of us now. Mum, Dad, Mickey and the baby.	罗斯:	这说来话长,妈妈、爸爸、米奇,还有婴儿。
Doctor:	You're not...?	博士:	不是你的吧?
Rose:	No! It's Mum. She's three months **gone**[5]. More Tylers on the way.	罗斯:	不……是妈妈,怀孕三个月了。
Doctor:	And what about you, what are you...?	博士:	那你怎么样,你去……
Rose:	Yeah, I'm back working in the shop.	罗斯:	是呀,我回商店工作了。
Doctor:	Oh, *good for you*[1].	博士:	哦,很适合你。

注释

1. breach [briːtʃ] *n.* 裂口
2. supernova [ˌsuːpəˈnəuvə] *n.* [天] 超新星
3. fracture [ˈfræktʃə] *v.* (使) 破碎, (使) 破裂
4. Bergen 卡尔根 [挪威西南部港市]
5. Gone [gɒn] *adj.* [俚语] 怀孕的

Rose:	Shut up! Nah, I'm not. The **Torchwood**[6] on this planet's still open for business. I think I know a thing or two about aliens.	罗斯：	闭嘴。不……不。这星球上的火炬木开始营业了，为了防止外星人攻击。
Doctor:	Rose Tyler. Defender of the Earth. You're dead, officially, back home. So many people died that day, and you've gone missing. You're on a list of the dead. Here you are, living a life, day after day. The one adventure I can never have.	博士：	罗斯·泰勒，地球的保卫者，那边你已经死亡了，那天很多人都死了，而你们失踪了，死亡名单上面有你们，你在这里，一天又一天地生活着，这一切我永远无法拥有。
Rose:	Am I ever going to see you again?	罗斯：	什么时候我能再次见到你？
Doctor:	You can't.	博士：	你不能。
Rose:	What are you going to do?	罗斯：	你要做什么呢？
Doctor:	I've got the Tardis. Same old life. Last of the Time Lords.	博士：	我有塔迪斯。老样子，时间领主的最后一人。
Rose:	On your own. I... I love you.	罗斯：	只有你自己。我……我爱你。
Doctor:	Quite right too. And I suppose... if it's my last chance to say it... Rose Tyler...	博士：	我也是。我猜……如果这是我说它的最后一次机会……罗斯·泰勒……

文化背景

1. supernova 超新星

超新星爆发就是一颗大质量恒星的"死亡"。质量大于 8 倍太阳质量的恒星，由于质量巨大，在它们演化到后期时，往往会发生大规模的爆发。nova 在拉丁语中是"新"的意思，这表示它在宇宙中看上去是一颗新出现的亮星（其实原本已存在，因亮度增加而被认为是新出现的）；前缀 super- 是为了将超新星和一般的新星相区分，也表示了超新星具有更高的亮度，以及更稀少的分布和不同的形成机制。

常用表达

1. Good for you. 很不错，很适合你。

例： A: I've decided to go back to school for some training in programming.

B: Good for you. When would you like to start?

A：我决定回学校进修程序设计。

B：不错啊！打算何时开始？

注释 **6. Torchwood** 火炬木（本剧中英国女王指定建立的研究外星人以保护地球的机构。）

Chapter 3

警探剧
Detective Drama

　　只要这世上还有人犯罪，就少不了抓罪犯的警察，也就有描写警察如何抓捕罪犯的警探剧。在美国所有的电视剧里，警探剧是常演不衰的一个大类。通常，这类电视剧都有一个固定的模式：主角一般都是那些铁面无私又心地善良的警察、FBI探员或是其他执法人员，有时也会是私家侦探或是扮演侦探调查人员角色的新闻记者和辩护律师，这些人物通常身手敏捷、枪法奇准，而且机智过人，能够冷静地、有条不紊地应对各种危险和挑战。除了塑造出一系列超人式的英雄主角外，警探剧在很大程度上依赖于故事情节的复杂多变和出其不意，重心在于展现警探们非凡的探案能力，他（她）们通过搜集各种线索和证据，盘问证人、展开推理，将犯罪事实拼凑在一起并最终破案。其中不乏动作性场面，特别是枪战、打斗和追逐，当然也少不了分析线索和证据，以及应用逻辑推理寻找犯罪嫌疑人的部分。总之，紧张、焦虑和悬念共同推动了激动人心的高潮，而最后的结局一定是犯罪分子被绳之以法，正义得到伸张。

　　近年来，美国也推出了不少反响不错的警探剧，在千篇一律的大框架没发生改变的情况下，编剧们开始在犯罪原因和犯罪心理的挖掘上下功夫，最新的刑侦手段、心理学成果都被应用到剧本中，《犯罪现场调查》《犯罪心理》《寻骨识踪》《别对我说谎》等都是其中的佼佼者。这些警探剧的情节设计更加曲折离奇，侦破过程更加惊心动魄，结局也更加匪夷所思，再加上演员不凡的表演功力，使观众即使知道结局也还是会被吸引着看下去。

Lie to Me
《别对我说谎》

入选理由：

　　《别对我说谎》是福克斯广播公司于2009年1月推出的一部题材新颖的探案心理剧。该剧讲述的是行为学家莱曼德博士领导的一家私人研究机构通过研究人的面部、身体、声音和语言表现来判定当事人是否在说谎。千万不要认为剧中人物识破谎言的招数是好莱坞编剧杜撰的，实际上，该剧是以面部解读专家保罗·埃克曼本人的经历和研究为蓝本整理改编而成的，因而剧中提到的所有识谎招数都有科学依据。其实，不仅是说谎的时候人有特殊的表情。人有43块面部肌肉，可以做出上万种表情，表达喜怒哀乐的细微情感。这种情感与人的生理反应、文化背景无关，非洲热带丛林中的原始部落居民面对野兽时的表情与衣冠楚楚的西方政客面对曝光自己丑闻的记者时是一样的恐惧。对人的细微表情加以仔细研究，可以知道人内心的很多秘密，这也是此剧着重所表现的。

　　《别对我说谎》曾备受福克斯广播公司的重视，在黄金时间强势推出，第一季的播出效果不错，但随后的剧集收视不甚理想，结果只播出了三季即被腰斩，看来人们对学习如何鉴定人的心理其实并不积极，对剧中莱特曼博士神奇的洞悉人心的观察术也不是很感兴趣。虽然如此，该剧毕竟是从一个全新的角度展现了罪案的侦破。在这部剧中，指纹、血液、DNA不再重要，男主角莱特曼博士带领的测谎四人组通过观察人们的一举一动、一颦一笑，就能揭开谎言迷雾，抵达案件的核心。这是一种大胆的尝试，开创了一种罪案类影视剧的新思路，也许后续的编导可以创作出更好的剧情，观众们可以耐心等待。

Section 1　剧情特点：

　　据说一个普通人在谈话的时候，平均每10分钟要说3个谎话，有时是为了逃避惩罚，有时是为了推卸责任，有时是为了讨好对方，有时是为了维护自己的尊严。总之，人类很善于撒谎，而莱特曼博士就是专门破解这些谎言的，他简直就是一个活的测谎仪，当你无意中抓挠下巴、扳动手掌、触摸鼻子或者拼命吞咽口水，他马上就知道你在撒谎——这可不是他瞎猜的，他有理论依据，据说他曾经花了3年的时间深入非洲原始部落研究那里的人们的眉毛，当然这么做的可能是面部解读专家保罗·埃克曼本人。但这个研究成果相当震撼，使得探案的过程成为解读面部表情的过程，而没

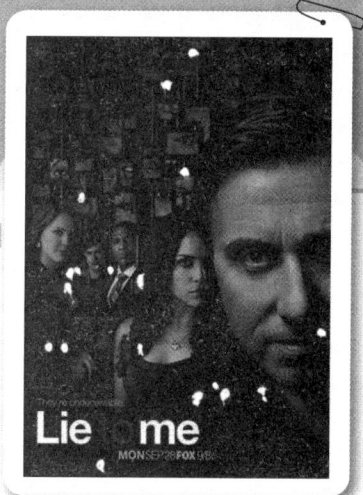

有通常警探剧中常用的警匪对射、飞车追逐等刺激火爆的场面。武戏改文戏可能也是这部连续剧最终没能走红的原因之一吧，毕竟坐着看嫌疑人动动眉毛撇撇嘴就定案听上去太悬了，能接受的人还是少数。这部系列剧算是为表情研究做了一个群众性的科普扫盲了。当然，《别对我说谎》是一部电视剧，它不是教科书，如果完全按照剧中介绍的谎话鉴别技巧来判定日常生活中周围人谁在说谎，其结果的可信度就值得怀疑了。

Section 2　对白特点：

《别对我说谎》适合有一定基础的英语学习者观看和学习，剧中人物的对话速度很快，特别是男主角莱特曼博士，说话又急又轻，而且语调平和，起伏很小，几乎听不清他在说什么，这对初学者来说算是个考验。

另外值得一提的是莱特曼博士的扮演者蒂姆·罗斯出生于英国伦敦，所以他说话带着一点淡淡的伦敦口音，跟正规的美式发音有明显区别，和我们能听到的英式标准发音也略有不同，很有特色。据说美国人崇拜英国的文化和历史，普遍觉得有英国口音的人很有品味，所以这种口音很吃香，有兴趣的话可以尝试模仿一下。

Section 3　角色分析：

卡尔·莱特曼 (Cal Lightman)：卡尔·莱特曼博士是一个怪人，虽然他是个世界顶尖的行为研究专家，能够从别人的面部表情中判断出这个人有没有说谎，虽然他所领导的莱特曼集团这样一家私营的研究机构能够为联邦政府、FBI、警察部门等找出背后的真相，但这些成就都不能改变一个事实，那就是莱特曼博士是个古怪的人物。首先是他本人没有一点大科学家的风度，七扭八歪的走路姿势看上去更像是街头的混混；复杂的经历让他跟一些身份复杂的人来往密切，给自己惹来不少麻烦；明明对部下很爱护，却总是一副挑剔、冰冷的样子；更重要的是他能洞悉人们的谎言，而人们又是这么地爱撒谎，所以他不相信别人，也经常看不起别人，这种不信任和高高在上的风格毁掉了他的婚姻，只给他留下了一个跟他一样古灵精怪的女儿。他倒真是个好爸爸，可惜女儿经常不领情。但莱特曼是个好人，在古怪的外表下隐藏着处处为别人着想的善良，是个外冷内热的家伙。

吉莉安·福斯特 (Gillian Foster)：中国有句老话叫"孤掌难鸣"，莱特曼集团这样大的一个私营机构，如果只有莱特曼一个人的话，一定难以为继，好在还有福斯特帮他。福斯特是个很有天赋的心理学家，她与莱特曼就像是左手与右手，即风格类似，又完全不同。同是心理学大家，面对工作同样的冷静、理性，但福斯特的理性里总带着女性的些许温柔，能够平衡莱特曼的生硬粗暴；她是行为学家，擅长通过肢体语言从整体上对人进行判断，是注重细节的莱特曼的必要补充。而且福斯特擅长与人打交道，可以帮助莱特曼联络外界，她独特的优雅魅力，可以轻松赢得别人的信任，这是莱特曼做不到的。

莉亚·托勒斯 (Ria Torres)：只有十万分之一的人在没接受过训练的情况下天生就有鉴别别人表情的能力，托勒斯小姐恰好就是这十万分之一。她本是交通局一名安检员，被莱特曼和福斯特招募到集团，成为机构最新的成员，在探案过程中屡次表现出色，深受老板器重。新工作给她带来的不仅是事业的成功，还帮她收获了美满的爱情，这个美丽的拉丁姑娘应该说是集团里最幸福的人了。

Passage 1

剧情介绍：

（选自第 1 季第 1 集）莱特曼是国际顶尖的谎言识别专家，曾帮联邦政府破获过多宗大案、要案。他总能在最后关头根据嫌疑犯的表情找出真相，他所创立的莱特曼集团跟政府许多部门都有联系，当政府部门遇到难题，就会来找莱特曼。这回是一个虔诚的教徒的儿子被指控谋杀了自己的老师，但是莱特曼根据审问时那个孩子的表现判定凶手另有其人，为此他开展了广泛的调查，最终战胜了人们的怀疑，锁定了真正的凶手并将其捉拿归案。

Scene 1: In the investigation room, Lightman was interrogating a suspect, trying to figure out the exact place of the buried bomb. The suspect was instructed to remain silent by his lawyer, and Lightman did not need him to speak anything because his facial expressions betrayed himself…

FBI 的审讯室里，莱特曼在询问一个嫌疑犯，想搞清楚该犯埋藏炸弹的准确地点。嫌犯的律师不让嫌犯说话，而莱特曼也不需要他说话，表情会告诉他一切……

attorney: I've instructed my client to remain silent. He's not gonna talk.

Lightman: That's okay. That's okay. I don't have much faith in words myself. Statistically speaking, the average person tells three lies per ten minutes' conversation. And granted, it's just regular people. We haven't studied people who are planning to **firebomb**[1] a black church. Could **skew**[2] differently.

Policeman: We don't have time for this scientist to talk to the guy. We *went at*[1] him for four hours, got nothing.

Lightman: Now, the FBI knows you want mass casualties. So right now <u>ATF</u>[1] is searching every inch of the two largest black

律师： 我已经让我的客户保持沉默了。他不会开口的。

莱特曼： 没关系，没关系。我自己也不怎么相信语言。根据统计，一般人每 10 分钟的对话里就会撒 3 次谎。当然，这还只是普通人，我们没有研究过那些计划炸黑人教堂的人，结果会有偏差。

侦探： 我们没时间让这个科学家盘问他了。我们查问了他 4 个小时，啥都没得到。

莱特曼： 现在，FBI 知道你想造成大规模伤亡，所以烟火局正在搜查州内最大的两所黑人教堂的每个角

churches in the state. The FBI got it wrong. Well, there's a **shocker**[3]. It's not one of those two churches. Maybe you want one of the smaller churches. One of the black suburbs.

Suspect:	You don't know what you're talking about.
Attorney:	Don't respond!
Lightman:	What do you say ATF starts with Southbridge? No, I'm only kidding. We'll skip that one. We're gonna focus on Lorton. You feel good about that? That's it! Lorton! Going after a church in Lorton.
attorney:	That accusation has no basis.
Lightman:	What do you mean?

落。FBI 弄错了。真令人震惊啊。不是这两所教堂。也许你是想炸个小点的教堂吧。一个在黑人社区的教堂。

嫌犯:	真不懂你在说什么。
律师:	不要回应!
莱特曼:	烟火局从南布里奇市开始搜如何？我开玩笑的啦，不要搜南布里奇。那我们就集中搜查洛顿市，你对那里的感觉好吗？就是这个！洛顿市！搜索洛顿市的教堂。
律师:	这一指控毫无根据。
莱特曼:	你什么意思?

Scene 2: Using the above-mentioned case, Lightman taught the FBI detectives how to recognize lies with facial expressions. The particular lecturing style and vivid cases aroused everyone's interest. And answered the students' questions with his own style…

莱特曼引用刚才的案例，在课堂上向 FBI 侦探们讲授如何通过表情识别谎言。如此特殊的讲课方式和生动形象的案例引起了大家的兴趣，他还用自己的方式回答了学员们的问题……

Detective:	When you accuse the suspect, and he acts surprised; is there a way to tell if it's real or if he's just trying to look **innocent**[4]?

(Lightman grabbed the cup on the desk and threw it onto the opposite wall.)

探员:	当你控告嫌疑犯时，他表现得很吃惊，如何判断他是真的吃惊还是装无辜呢?

（莱特曼拿起讲台上的杯子向对面墙上扔了过去。）

注释
1. firebomb ['faɪəbɒm] *v.* 用燃烧弹进攻
2. skew [skju:] *v.* 歪斜，偏离
3. shocker ['ʃɒkə(r)] *n.* 令人震惊的人或事
4. innocent ['ɪnəsnt] *adj.* 无辜的

Lightman: Now that's real surprise. Lasts for less than a second when it comes across your face, but if your suspect is surprised for more than a second, he's **faking**[5] it. He's lying. Now I *call out*[2] his target is actually Lorton, and watch it again. **Concealed**[6] **scorn**[7]. One personal **tip**[8]. You see this micro-expression in your **spouse's**[9] face, your marriage is coming to an end. Trust me. Yeah?

Detective: Don't these micro-expressions vary depending on the person?

Lightman: Let's *leave this up*[3]. And we'll go to the Kato Kaelin footage from the OJ trial[2].

(on the record: Mr. Kaelin, you got a lot of money for your appearance on Current Affair, didn't you?)

Lightman: Um, yeah.

Lightman: Scorn. Scorn. Huge scorn. Shame, shame, and shame. **Contempt**[10]. These expressions are universal. Emotion looks the same whether you're a suburban housewife or a suicide bomber. The truth is written on all our faces.

莱特曼： 这是真的吃惊，表情在你脸上持续不到一秒。如果嫌犯持续了超过一秒，那他就是装的，就是在撒谎。那么，当我说出了他的真正目标是在洛顿时，再看一次，掩饰的不屑。教你一个小窍门，如果你在你爱人的脸上也看到了这种微表情，那么你的婚姻就到头了。相信我。请说？

探员： 这些微表情不会因人而异吗？

莱特曼： 先把这个问题放着，我们来看看辛普森一案中卡托·柯林的作证录像。

（录像：柯林先生，你因为上"时事"节目而获得不少钱，是吗？）

莱特曼： 嗯，是的。

莱特曼： 不屑、不屑、很明显的不屑。羞愧、羞愧、还是羞愧。轻蔑，这些表情是一样的。不论你是郊区的主妇，还是炸弹杀手，表情看起来都是一样的。真相，就写在我们脸上。

Scene 3: Lightman came to the home of the high school student who was accused of killing a teacher. His father was a devout Christian, and homemade photos were hung here and there in the child's bedroom, but what can these bring to the case investigation?

莱特曼来到被控杀害老师的高中生的家里，他的父亲是位虔诚的基督教徒，孩子的卧室里挂满了自制的照片，这又能给案件带来什么转机呢？

Lightman:	James took these?	莱特曼:	这都是杰米拍的？
Foster:	Yes, he did.	福斯特:	没错，是他拍的。
James' father:	We let him **convert**[11] that bathroom to a **darkroom**[12] for his photography.	杰米父亲:	我们允许他把浴室改装成了曝光照片用的暗室。
Lightman:	Was that a problem?	莱特曼:	有什么问题吗？
James' father:	Well, it was taking too much time from his responsibilities as a witness doing God's work.	杰米父亲:	他花了太多时间做这些事情，都没有时间来完成上帝的旨意了。
Foster:	What did James tell you about Ms. McCartney?	福斯特:	关于麦卡特尼女士，杰米跟你们说过些什么你吗？
James' father:	He thought she was a good teacher.	杰米父亲:	他觉得她是个好老师。
Lightman:	And did you?	莱特曼:	那你认为呢？
James' mother:	James did not kill that woman. He would not take part in **wrestling**[13] practice, gym **class**[14], because he knows the Lord **condemns**[15] violence, even in sport.	杰米母亲:	杰米没杀那个女人。他都不会去参加那些摔跤训练、体育课，因为他明白上帝排斥暴力，即使是体育。
James' father:	If you **value**[16] something, you build a fence around it to protect it. And that's what we did with James. We **home-schooled**[17] him as long as we could to *shield* him *from*[4] drugs and sex and corruption.	杰米父亲:	如果你很珍惜什么东西，你就会围绕他建造一个保护壳来小心地呵护他。我们对杰米就是这样做的。我们尽可能让他在家接受教育，使他避免嗑药、滥交、腐败、堕落。
Foster:	Is that why you were angry about the material she was teaching him?	福斯特:	这就是为什么你如此生气的原因，你不喜欢她使用的教材？
James' father:	We are in the world, but not of the world. And we need to protect our children from **nonbelievers**[18].	杰米父亲:	我们生活在这个世界上，但不是为了这个世界而活着。我们要保护孩子免受无信仰者的污染。
Lightman:	Is there anything you wouldn't do to protect your son from a nonbeliever?	莱特曼:	为了保护你的孩子，你什么都愿意做吗？
James' father:	*Watch yourself*[5]. I'm a man of God.	杰米父亲:	你注意点儿，我可是上帝的子民。

注释

5. **fake** [feɪk] *adj.* 伪造的，假装的	13. **wrestling** ['reslɪŋ] *n.* 摔跤；格斗
6. **conceal** [kən'si:l] *v.* 掩藏，隐瞒	14. **gym class** 体育课
7. **scorn** [skɔːn] *v.* 轻蔑，鄙视	15. **condemn** [kən'dem] *v.* 谴责；定罪
8. **tip** [tɪp] *n.* 小窍门	16. **value** ['vælju:] *v.* 珍视，重视
9. **spouse** [spaʊz] *n.* 配偶	17. **home-school** 在家教育
10. **contempt** [kən'tempt] *n.* 蔑视，轻视	18. **nonbeliever** [nɒnbɪ'li:və] *n* 无信仰的人；（尤指）不信上
11. **convert** [kən'vɜːt] *v.* 使转变，改造	帝的人
12. **darkroom** ['dɑːkrʊm] *n.* 暗室，暗房	

📖 文化背景

1. ATF 烟酒、火器与爆炸物管理局（Bureau of Alcohol, Tabaco, Firearms and Explosives），是一个隶属于美国司法部（Dept. of Justice，DOJ），负责对烟酒枪炮征税、执法和释法的机构，其使命是保护公众免受暴力犯罪分子和犯罪组织的侵犯，打击非法使用和交易火器、非法使用和储存爆炸物品，打击纵火、爆炸行为和恐怖主义活动，打击非法转移烟酒产品。

2. OJ trial 著名的前美式橄榄球明星辛普森案（O．J．Simpson），1994 年被控杀妻，最终无罪获释，该案是美国历史上疑罪从无的最有名的案件。

Kato Kaelin 涉案人员之一，曾与被害的辛普森前妻有暧昧关系。

☎ 常用表达

1. go at 攻击；努力去做

例：The villagers went at building a dam with a will.

村民们劲头十足地着手修一座水坝。

2. call out 喊出

例：Being old and sly, I forbear to call out.

我上了年纪，人又机灵，所以并没声张。

3. leave up 放下不管

例：This is the task that seminars and speed reading books usually leave up to the reader.

研讨会或速读书籍，通常把这一步留给读者来完成。

4. shield from 屏蔽，使摆脱

例：She intended to shield the child from the bad information.

她打算不让这个孩子知道这个坏消息。

5.watch yourself 小心点

例：Watch yourself when you start to reach for that spoon, or you just might offend someone.

当您伸手拿那把勺子时可得注意，否则您有可能冒犯到别人。

🔊 Passage 2 📷

剧情介绍：

　　（选自第 1 季第 2 集）莱特曼相信自己对表情的研究和判断，而不信测谎仪，还拿研发、推广测谎仪的人开玩笑。但他不会拿案件开玩笑，不会被自己的感情左右，一切都要有证据，而这一点，新手托勒斯还差得远，她差点因为同情一个声称遭到强奸的女兵而犯错误。虽然有很好的天赋，可她需要学习的东西还很多……

Scene 1: Lightman was asked by Miller, chief of Department of Homeland Security, to evaluate the newly developed portable polygraph promoted by Whitmore, the commercial agent. However, Lightman gave them a special egg which had been taken by plane from West Africa. By this peculiar way, Lightman just wanted to tell them that even the so-called most advanced polygraph might make mistakes like the egg…

国土安全局部长米勒要莱特曼对代理商维德摩尔推销的最新研发的手提式测谎仪进行评估，而莱特曼却交给他们一枚从西非刚刚空运来的蛋。莱特曼以他独特的方式说明，所谓最先进的测谎仪其实和蛋一样会出错……

🔊 **Lightman:** The problem with all **polygraph**[1] tests is false positives.

Foster: Innocent people can fail if they feel an increase in any emotion: anger, fear, **sexual arousal**[2]. Not just guilt. Your polygraph is no better than the egg at telling us which emotion it's responding to.

Whitmore: No.

(Whitmore broke the egg.)

莱特曼： 所有测谎设备的缺陷都在于测试结果的假阳性上。

法特： 无辜的人们若是有任何情绪的增强，如愤怒、恐惧、或是性兴奋，都可能通不过测谎，而不仅仅是因为负罪感。你们的测谎仪比那个蛋好不到哪去，都没法识别被测者到底是何种情绪。

维德摩尔： 才不是呢。

（维德摩尔把蛋打破了。）

注释 **1. polygraph** ['pɒlɪɡrɑːf] *n.* 测谎仪
2. sexual arousal 性唤起

Lightman:	I've been wanting to try that for years. See, you would have been found guilty, but you were just angry. You should be, uh, spending your money studying the face. 43 muscles combine to produce a possibility of 10,000 expressions. Now, if you learn them all, you don't need a polygraph.	莱特曼：	这么多年来我一直都想试试。你看，你会被证明有罪，但实际上你只是生气。你应该把你的钱花在面部表情识别上。人脸有 43 块肌肉，大约能组合出一万种表情。现在，要是你掌握全部的表情，你就用不着测谎仪了。
Miller:	How much did we spend on this damn project anyway?	米勒：	这该死的项目到底花了我们多少钱？
Whitmore:	Uh, not much. I'm sure we can **recoup**[3] most of our costs.	维德摩尔：	呃，不是很多啦，我想大多数花销都可以收回的。
Lightman:	Now, that was lovely.	莱特曼：	现在，这可真有意思了。
Miller:	What?	米勒：	什么？
Lightman:	A gestural **retreat**[4].	莱特曼：	肢体阻抗。
Miller:	What's that?	米勒：	什么意思？
Lightman:	His step backwards, means he doesn't believe a word he just said. He's lying.	莱特曼：	他向后退缩，说明他自己也不相信他刚才说的话。他在说谎。

Scene 2: A female soldier accused a sergeant of rape. If it was true, the sergeant would not be permitted to go to the battlefield, and the U.S. army would lose a capable commander. So, Lightman was invited here, but this time the doctor pretended to be a gay to seduce the sergeant, and the conclusion was…

一个女兵指控一位马上要上战场的中士强奸了自己，如果这是真的，中士将不能上战场，而美军则少了一名有能力的指挥官。为此，军方请来了莱特曼，而博士这回是假装同性恋来试探中士，试探的结论是……

Foster: The **rape**[5] was unplanned, one time, with no additional violence. That suggests a power **assertive**[6] rapist, somebody who *is obsessed with*[1] **masculinity**[7], who needs others to see him as a man.

Lightman: If Sergeant Scott fit the profile, he would have reacted to my **overture**[8] with one emotion... **disgust**[9].

Torres: There was no disgust, just surprise.

Lightman: Correct... eyebrows up, jaw down.

Torres: Okay, but... the guy was totally amped up.

Lightman: Yeah, but he showed no deception, right? No sign of lying.

Torres: He looked like he wanted to throw me across the room.

Foster: A man charged with rape is even more likely to be angry if he's innocent.

Torres: Well, they can't both be telling the truth.

Lightman: They're not. Sheila Lake made two mouth **shrugs**[10] when she was describing the rape. That's a classic gestural **slip**[11]. It means she has no confidence in her words. The woman was lying.

福斯特: 强奸并无事先预谋，只发生过一次，而且没有附加暴力。这说明一个过分自信的强奸犯，是一种迷恋男子气概的人，他需要别人认同他是个男人。

莱特曼: 如果斯科特中士符合侧写，那么对我的提议，他只会有一种感觉——恶心。

托勒斯: 好吧，但他没表现出恶心，只有惊讶。

莱特曼: 正确，眉毛上扬，下颚下垂。

托勒斯: 好吧，但是……这个家伙在全神戒备。

莱特曼: 是的，但是他没有露出马脚，对吧，没有撒谎的迹象。

托勒斯: 他看上去简直就想把我从房间里扔出去。

福斯特: 无辜的人被控告强奸会感到更加愤怒。

托勒斯: 他俩不可能都说真话。

莱特曼: 他们是没有都说真话。沙拉·雷克在描述强奸过程时抿了两下嘴角。那是经典的犯错表情。表明她对自己的话没有信心，那个女人在撒谎。

Sence 3: The young assistant believed that the sergeant was a rapist, while Lightman insisted that the female soldier was a liar, so they argued heatedly. Lightman reminded Torres not to judge with personal feelings.

年轻的助手相信中士是强奸犯，而莱特曼则坚信女兵在说谎，他们之间展开了争论。莱特曼以他特有的方式提醒托勒斯不要让个人情感干扰了判断。

注释

3. **recoup** [rɪˈkuːp] *v.* 补偿，收回

4. **gestural retreat** 向后退

5. **rape** [reɪp] *v.* 强奸

6. **assertive** [əˈsɜːtɪv] *adj.* 坚决的，果断的

7. **masculinity** [ˌmæskjʊˈlɪnəti] *n.* 男子气概

8. **overture** [ˈəʊvətʃʊə(r)] *n.* 提议

9. **disgust** [dɪsˈɡʌst] *n.* 反感，厌恶

10. **mouth shrug** 抿嘴角，表示对自己说的话无信心

11. **slip** [slɪp] *v.* 失误，出错

12. **mortality** [mɔːˈtæləti] *n.* 必死性

Foster: You really think a woman would lie about rape?

Lightman: Unpleasant truths, human **mortality**[12], a moustache on a woman, three things we'd all prefer to ignore.

Foster: FBI crime reports have found that eight percent of rape **allegations**[13] are false.

Torres: Okay, but the army **vets**[14] I worked with at TSA[2] said that sexual assault was a big problem.

Lightman: It doesn't explain the gestural slip.

Foster: Lake's also not exhibiting any of the emotions a rape victim typically displays when **recounting**[15] her story.

Lightman: No shame, no fear. We should be seeing a lot of activity in the forehead, but there isn't any.

Torres: Maybe she's got post-traumatic stress.

Foster: Emotional **numbing**[16] might explain her inability to express her feelings.

Lightman: But not the mouth shrug.

Torres: Look, I'm telling you, there's something off about Sergeant Scott.

Lightman: You know, I once had actors *play out*[2] the **testimony**[17] from a rape case in front of 30 federal judges. And you know the biggest predictor of whether they believed the man or the woman? The gender of the judge.

Torres: You think I'm saying he's guilty because I'm a woman?

Lightman: Me, Darwin, and 2,000 years of evolutionary biology.

托勒斯： 你真觉得女人会撒谎说自己被强奸了？

莱特曼： 不中听的真话、人口死亡率、女人长胡子，这三种事情都是我们宁愿视而不见的。

福斯特： FBI 的犯罪报告证实，有 8% 的强奸案是假报的。

托勒斯： 好吧，但是我在（国防部）运输标准化局一起共事的老兵都说，性侵犯是个很严重问题。

莱特曼： 这无法解释这个犯错的表情。

福斯特： 雷克重述遭遇时也没有流露出强奸受害者的典型表情。

莱特曼： 没有感到耻辱，没有感到害怕，我们应该能在额头看见很多的表情，但是这里什么也没有。

托勒斯： 也许她有创伤后应激障碍。

福斯特： 情绪上的麻木也许可以解释她无法表达自己的感受。

莱特曼： 但是不能解释她抿嘴角。

托勒斯： 听着，我跟你说，斯科特中士有点不对劲。

莱特曼： 知道吗，我曾经叫一个演员在 30 个联邦法官面前表演一段强奸案的证词，你知道最影响法官判断相信男人还是女人的因素是什么吗？法官的性别。

托勒斯： 你觉得我认为他有罪，是因为我是女人？

莱特曼： 我、达尔文、2000 年来的生物进化论都这么认为。

Foster: Well, I think what Dr. Lightman is trying to say is that it's important not to let what you bring in the room affect what you see in the room.

福斯特：我想莱特曼博士想说的是不要让你的感受蒙蔽了你的眼睛，这很重要。

文化背景

1. TSA Transportation Standardization Agency，（国防部）运输标准化局。

常用表达

1. be obsessed with 痴迷于

例：He was obsessed with American gangster movies.
他迷上了美国黑帮片。

2. play out 演完；把（比赛等）坚持到底

例：The game was played out although the light was bad.
虽然光线不佳，比赛还是要坚持到底。

注释
13. allegation [ˌælə'geɪʃn] *n.* 指控
14. vet [vet] *n.* 老兵
15. recount [rɪ'kaʊnt] *v.* 详细叙述
16. numb [nʌm] *v.* 使麻木
17. testimony ['testɪmənɪ] *n.* 证词，证据

Passage 3

剧情介绍：

（选自第1季第3集）一个法官的独生女被杀了，谁会伤害这个品学兼优、活泼可爱的少女呢？莱特曼调查了死者的母亲、老师、同学，每个人都有说谎的表情，但都与凶杀无关，而最终凶手的落网也验证了福斯特之前的研究结论——在学校里，越是受欢迎的学生越会撒谎。

Scene 1: During the funeral, the classmates recollect in turn their stories about the diseased, and one of the stories drew Lightman's attention…

葬礼上，死者的同学们轮流上台追忆死者，其中一个女孩的讲话引起了莱特曼的注意……

Torres: Well, that girl seems very popular.

Lightman: Yeah. Foster did a study once— **popularity**[1] and lies in schools. You know what she found?

Torres: There's a connection?

Lightman: Yeah, the more popular the kid, the better the liar. Which makes me wonder why the queen **bee**[2] showed **unsymmetrical**[3] sadness when she was talking about her dead friend.

Torres: Uh, "when a person's facial expression" is not symmetrical on both sides of the face, "it is likely that they are pretending to feel the emotion". From your article in the journal for behavioral science, 2001.

Lightman: **Sucking up**[4] is really not your strong suit.

托勒斯： 那女孩看上去很受欢迎。

莱特曼： 没错。福斯特曾做过一个调查：学生在学校受欢迎的程度和说谎频率的关系。你知道她发现了什么吗？

托勒斯： 这两者之间有关系？

莱特曼： 是的，越受欢迎的孩子，就越会撒谎。这使我产生怀疑，为什么这个社交女王在提到她逝去的好友时表现出了不对称的悲伤表情。

托勒斯： 啊，"当一个人的两侧面部表情不对称时，他很可能是在伪装情感"。出自你2001年在行为科学期刊上发表的文章。

莱特曼： 拍马屁可不是你的强项啊。

Scene 2: through investigation, it was found out that the very school even turned a blind eye to drug abuse phenomenon among the students. Torres came to the school again and questioned the headmaster…

在调查中发现，被害女孩生前所在的学校为了让学生取得好成绩甚至默许学生吸毒、嗑药。为了查清真相，托勒斯又来到学校找到校长谈话……

(Head: Headmaster)

Head:	Ms. Torres, I thought we were clear about your involvement.	校长：	托勒斯小姐，我认为有关案件的事情我们已经说得够清楚的了。
Torres:	I'm not here to talk to any of your students. Uh, I came to congratulate you.	托勒斯：	我来这儿不是和你谈学生的。噢，我是来祝贺你的。
Head:	For what?	校长：	为了什么？
Torres:	Well, I was looking at your academic rankings for **strivers**[5] over the past decade. After you became **headmistress**[6] three years ago, test scores *shot up*[1], your national ranking went through the roof. I'm wondering how you *pulled that off*[2].	托勒斯：	我刚看了过去十年你们学校的学术排名。从你三年前担任校长后，学生的测试成绩一路飙升，你们学校的排名也名列前茅。我想知道你是怎么做到的。
Head:	Well, it wasn't hard. All I did was give our students the proper **motivation**[7].	校长：	噢，这其实并不困难，我所做的只是给了我们的学生足够的动力。
Torres:	What does that mean?	托勒斯：	那是什么意思？
Head:	Well, I restricted the number of ivy league[1] recommendations to the top kids in each graduating class.	校长：	我限定了每个毕业班向常春藤联盟学校推荐的人数。
Torres:	So you've created a reward system that feeds	托勒斯：	这么说你是建立了一个让他们担

注释
1. **popularity** [ˌpɒpjʊˈlærəti] *n.* 流行，受大众欢迎
2. **queen bee** 社交女王
3. **unsymmetrical** [ˌʌnsɪˈmetrɪkəl] *adj.* 不对称的
4. **sucking up** 拍马屁

5. **striver** [ˈstraɪvə(r)] *n.* 奋斗者
6. **headmistress** [ˈhedˌmɪstrɪs] *n.* 女校长
7. **motivation** [ˌməʊtɪˈveɪʃn] *n.* 动力

into their fears. If they're not *on track*[3] by the time they're 17, it's too late?

惊受怕的奖励系统。如果他们 17 岁时还没步入正轨，是不是就算太晚了？

Head:	Well, we give our best students the best chance at success.	校长：	我们给最好的学生以最大的成功可能。
Torres:	I need to see Danielle's academic records and transcripts of all the honor roll students.	托勒斯：	我要看看丹尼尔及其他所有优等生的学习成绩单。
Head:	You don't really think this had anything to do with her murder?	校长：	你不会真觉得这和谋杀案有关吧？
Torres:	Why not? You do.	托勒斯：	为什么不呢？你也是这么认为的吧。

Scene 3: Torres checked the transcript of the victim, and found that she even had the scores which should be got the day after her death. What happened?

托勒斯查看了死者的成绩单，发现死者居然有被害第二天后的考试成绩，究竟是怎么回事呢？

Torres:	Danielle's <u>GPA</u>[2] was excellent. But her <u>SAT</u>[3] scores were barely average. She took the test twice, scoring around the 65th **percentile**[8].	托勒斯：	丹尼尔的平均成绩很高，但她的学术能力评估测试成绩却是平平，她参加了两次考试，成绩只有 65 分。
Lightman:	So?	莱特曼：	那么？
Torres:	Well, she knew she wasn't going to make the top of her class, so she *signed up*[4] to take the SAT a third time. Score just got posted this week.	托勒斯：	她知道自己不可能挤进班级前列，所以又去考了一次。这周成绩刚出来。
Lightman:	94th percentile? That's quite an improvement. I wonder what she did differently.	莱特曼：	94 分？进步真不小啊，我想知道她怎么办到的。
Torres:	I can tell you one thing. She got murdered the day before she took that test.	托勒斯：	我得告诉你一件事，她在参加考试的前一天被杀了。

📖 文化背景

1. ivy league 常春藤联盟

指美国东北部八所大学，包括：成立于 1636 年的哈佛大学（Harvard University），成立于 1701 年的耶鲁大学（Yale University），成立于 1740 年的宾夕法尼亚大学（Penn University），成立于 1746 年的普林斯顿大学（Princeton University），成立于 1754 年的哥伦比亚大学（Columbia University），成立于 1764 年的布朗大学（Brown University），成立于 1769 年的达特茅斯大学（Dartmouth University），成立于 1865 年的康奈尔大学（Cornell University）。这八所大学都是美国一流大学，它们的历史悠久，治学严谨，教学水平高，学生质量好，因此常春藤大学有着优秀的声誉。

2. GPA 英语全称是 Grade Point Average，意思就是平均成绩点数（平均分数、平均绩点）。

美国的 GPA 满分是 4 分，即 A=4，B=3，C=2，D=1。GPA 的精确度往往达到小数点后 1 到 2 位，如：3.0，3.45。

3. SAT 全称 Scholastic Assessment Test，中文名称为学术能力评估测试。

由美国大学委员会（College Board）主办，SAT 成绩是世界各国高中生申请美国名校学习及奖学金的重要参考。

🔊 常用表达

1. shoot up 向上发射；迅速成长

例：Sales shot up by 9% last month.

销售量上个月猛增了 9%。

2. pull off 胜利完成

例：It will be a very, very fine piece of mountaineering if they pull it off.

如果他们能成功，那将是一次非常了不起的登山壮举。

3. on track 在正道上；未离题

例：A UN spokesman insisted that the implementation of the peace plan is back on track.

联合国发言人坚持认为和平方案的执行已回到正轨。

4. sign up 报名；签合同

例：He was not the only one to sign up.

报名参加的不只是他一个人。

注释 **8. percentile** [pə'sentaɪl] *n.* 百分位（数）

Bones

《识骨寻踪》

8

👤 入选理由：

《识骨寻踪》是美国福克斯广播公司（FOX）2005年推出的罪案题材电视连续剧，目前已出8季。该剧部分内容改编自前刑侦检验官、现任该剧制作人凯丝·莱克斯出版的一系列侦探小说。这是一位不能小看的作者，她是美国北卡罗来纳州医事检查处的刑事人类学家、北卡罗来纳大学社会人类学教授、加拿大魁北克省犯罪暨法医研究所的法医，此外，她是全美刑事人类学协会十五名检定合格的法医之一，也是美国法医科学协会的成员，并担任刑事审判常任专家证人，写作小说只是她的业余爱好。虽然是利用业余时间写作，但这位法医专家在小说领域也是身手不凡的，她的第一本小说就登上了《纽约时报》的畅销排行榜，更荣获1997年的"阿瑟·埃利斯"最佳处女作小说奖，此后的12本布伦南系列，也是本本均登畅销排行榜，成为国际级畅销书，而根据这部畅销系列改编创作的电视剧《识骨寻踪》也大获成功。这部电视剧主要讲述的是女主人公布伦南博士所领导的杰斐逊协会法医学实验室协助警方侦破那些因尸体严重腐烂、烧毁或被破坏而使得普通的尸检方法无能为力的凶杀案件的故事。由于作者自己就是一名出色的法医专家，所以剧本对侦破过程有着更科学、更真实的描述，而且与一般好莱坞编剧的戏剧冲突设计角度不同，这部剧在情节中加入了大量关于人性的讨论，特别是对男、女同事之间由普通友谊逐渐上升到爱情的描写，可谓细致入微。换言之，除去那些可怕的、腐烂的身体，这部电视剧几乎可以看作是办公室"恋爱宝典"。总之，这是一部集言情、刑侦、恐怖于一体的系列剧，值得欣赏。

Section 1 剧情特点：

布伦南博士并不是FBI的警探，她是一名人类学家，擅长从骨骼残片中找出破案的线索。所以当联邦调查局发现高度腐烂的尸体，常规尸检无能为力时，他们会经常求助布伦南博士和她的团队，而布伦南博士所在的杰斐逊协会法医学实验室里人才济济，团队利用各种高科技的检测手段，常常使看起来毫无头绪的案子有迹可寻。

该剧的情节其实并不复杂，但是由于案件涉及的尸体经常处于高度腐烂的状态，腐烂的肌肉包裹着累累白骨，画面很恐怖，观众需要一段时间来适应这种"重口味"。该剧除视觉效果特殊外，剧中人物的塑造也与好莱坞传统的英雄美人的搭配不同。也许是由于作者本人就是一位杰出女性的缘故，整部剧呈现出一种"阴盛阳衰"的状态，作为 FBI 的男主人公明显是弱势的一方，无论是智商、学识，还是侦破能力、性格的果敢坚毅，与绰号"骨头"的女主角相比都低一头，经常因听不懂女主角过于专业的讲话而需要翻译，行动中这种男弱女强的设计很有喜剧效果。

剧中的一大特点就是科学仪器在侦破中的应用，例如剧中经常出现的三维激光人像模拟技术能够根据头骨的形状和上面残存的肌肉推断出死者的相貌特征，令人叹为观止。此外，侦破工作还涉及了大量昆虫学、生物学、地质学等相关方面的先进技术，样样都让人大开眼界。而整部剧最吸引人的地方还在于它对人与人之间感情的刻画，特别是将男女主演间的那种"比友谊近、比爱情远"的小暧昧刻画到了极致，所有人都知道他们彼此深爱着对方，而当事人就是死不承认，还坚决抵制将这种暧昧关系蔓延，始终保持同事关系而不突破同事与恋人的界限，这种状态居然持续了六季，这在爱情快餐化的好莱坞实属罕见。

Section 2　对白特点：

《识骨寻踪》适合对象和英语水平的关系不大，重要的是要有足够坚强的神经。剧中充斥着各种连皮带肉的骨头、没有嘴唇的牙床、探出眼眶的眼球、高度腐烂的肌肉和内脏，绝对挑战个人的忍耐极限，胆小的人看了恐怕连吃饭、睡觉都会成问题，所以观剧之前需要谨慎考虑自己的心理承受能力。当然，一旦习惯这些"重口味"，对白中所包含的大量医学、生物学等专业的词汇，对有一定英语学习基础的学生进一步提高听力的帮助还是很大的。对学习医学、生物学的学生而言尤其需要重视的是剧中的几位天才的对白都习惯用书面语言的表达法，与普通人日常生活的口语不同，仔细揣摩这些含有大量专业词汇的语句对完成理科论文会很有帮助。另外该剧中有很多同事间、特别是男女同事间有目的的互开玩笑和暗示性的对白，有助于年轻人学会如何与办公室的异性亲密交往的同时又保持距离的处理方法，对现实生活意义重大。

Section 3　角色分析：

坦普伦斯·布伦南博士 (Dr. Temperance Brennan)：布伦南博士是一位人类学家，她对人的了解绝对是名副其实的"入骨三分"。无论是腐尸上连着血肉的，还是被烈火烧过的，她都能一眼说出死者的性别、大概年龄、曾经受过的伤，而经过一系列检查研究，被害人的死因、生前的一些习惯、躯体的一些疾病、被埋的时间等都瞒不过她。也许是与骨头的交道打得太多了的缘故吧，这位被同事朋友们称为"骨头 (Bones)"的专家，其个性也像极了骨头，缺少女性的温柔，对一切情感类的东西完全没有感觉，一心痴迷于骨头研究，不问世俗金钱、不通人情世故，对待事物直截了当，心里怎么想，嘴上就怎么说，不知客套与婉转是什么意思，丝毫不顾及别人的感受。而且这位方下巴美女常常使用暴力，动不动就在审讯时给上嫌疑人一拳，很少向周围的人低头，也不知恐惧为何物，是真正意义上的女强人、铁娘子。不过在刚强的外表下，"骨头"是个善良、热心、慷慨大方的好人，时间长了周围人都是真心喜爱这块难啃的"骨头"的。

瑟雷·布斯 (Seeley Booth)：联邦探员布斯是个退役的狙击手，有着宽阔的胸膛、厚实的肩膀，健硕的身材，矫捷的身手，同时还特别擅长洞察人的心理，可谓是文武全才的优秀警探。可不知怎的，在这部剧里就是被"骨头"压着一头，处处显出差距，智商跟人家差了一大截就算了，学识比不上人家博士也不计较了，就连对待感情的态度上，也明显是"骨头"博士更刚毅坚强、果断干脆。而堂堂的 FBI 探员居然柔情似水，温婉缠绵，一反好莱坞传统意义上的FBI干警形象,如此性格错位的设计平添无数笑料,也是该剧吸引人的地方之一。不过，大侦探还是有两下子的，思维灵活，尤其擅长解决实际问题，也常常令这些精通理论的科学家们刮目相看。

杰斐逊协会法医学实验室的各位专家：当"骨头"博士协助 FBI 侦破那些因尸体严重腐烂、烧毁或被破坏而使得普通的尸检方法无能为力的凶杀案件时，杰斐逊协会法医学实验室里那些出色的同事们，就一一登场了。他们每一个都是智慧过人、学识渊博的专科专家，各有各的独门绝技，能让"骨头说话"，从而让狡猾的罪犯难逃法网。

安琪拉·马丁尼古 (Angela Montenegro)：安琪拉·马丁尼古其实是一个画家，这个中欧混血女子生性浪漫自由，想象力和情感一样丰富充沛。她的独门绝技是能用三维图象模拟复原尸骨体貌及再现原始犯罪现场。私下里她是"骨头"布伦南的闺蜜，常常替她解决感情上的烦恼，关心"骨头"的一切。她的活泼、开朗、热诚，与"骨头"的冷静、理智、内敛形成鲜明有趣的对比，但性格的差异并不影响二人的友谊，反而成就了彼此之间的信任与互补，成为工作和生活上的好搭档。

杰克·哈金斯 (Jack Hodgins)：超出所有人想象的是在这部借着探案讨论男女情感的系列剧中，个头不高、其貌不扬、性格怪异的胡须男哈金斯居然与高大热辣的安琪拉擦出爱情的火花。杰克·哈金斯出自杰斐逊协会的董事家族，身价过亿，而且对别人总是一脸的不屑，自称"实验室之王"，但他的骄傲自大完全来自对自己才华和能力的自信而不是对家族财富、权势的依赖，而当他面对集智慧、美貌、才华于一身的"骨头"时，会发出由衷的感叹：在她面前，自己像个白痴。其实杰克·哈金斯本人是一名卓有成就的昆虫、孢子和矿石方面的专家，拥有 3 个博士学位，是个不容小觑的人物。

兰斯·斯维特 (Lance Sweets)：据说是 FBI 怀疑研究所的 BB 组合（布伦南和布思）都有问题，所以特意给这个团队配备了一个心理咨询师。这位姓斯维特的咨询师被大家称为"小甜甜"，个性也确实温和可人。只有 22 岁的他虽然已经有了 3 个博士学位，但并不像一般的心理咨询师那样阴郁、神秘，长着一张娃娃脸的斯维特喜怒哀乐全在脸上，虽然精通业务，侧写百发百中，对别人的谎言能一眼识破，被称为会走路的测谎仪，但他本人完全不会说谎，他不说真话的时候连"骨头"博士都能看出来。但他总是不遗余力地帮助小组的成员解决心理问题，还促使布伦南和布思正视彼此间的关系，是二人最终走到一起的催化剂。

凯姆·萨拉杨 (Camille Saroyan)：做领导是件好事，但如果是做一帮天才的领导可就不一定了，水平不够的领导可统帅不了杰斐逊协会法医学实验室这些智慧过人又个性鲜明的专家们。凯姆的领导能力是无可置疑的，她是个聪明的普通人，作为新来的老板，知道调整自己来适应这个以"骨头"为中心的集体，多次容忍"骨头"的顶撞，也对哈金斯那些稀奇古怪的实验睁一只眼闭一只眼，而当手下遇到麻烦也一如既往的支持和信任，最终她赢得了众天才的信任，成为受人尊敬的老大。

Passage 1

剧情介绍：

（选自第 1 季第 16 集）很少有人知道，美国首都华盛顿的地下还有一座迷宫一样的地下城，那是由各种地铁线、下水道、矿井和隧道组成的地下王国。一天，在一处地下管道的竖井口底部发现尸体，经调查发现死者是一位记录片制作人，女性，死于谋杀，而谋杀与一批美国南北战争时期保存在地下城中的宝藏有关，最终凶手被抓获，宝藏也得以重见天日。

Scene 1: The female body was sent to the experiment table. It would be better to be called some bone fragments rather than a female body. The team members stood around the table, discussing death causes and looking for some clues…

地下发现的女尸已经送到研究所的实验台上，说是尸体，其实就是一些粘着血肉的碎骨残片，小组成员都围在实验台旁边工作，讨论着死亡原因，寻找破案线索……

Hodgins: I'd set time of death at about ten days, when the Missing Persons Report was filed.

Booth: You sure?

Hodgins: See the ratio of fly **larvae**[1] to **Silphidae**[2] beetles?

(Hodgins showed Booth the beaker filling sample of fly larvae, Booth fended it off with a notebook in his hand.)

Booth: Yeah. Ten days. I believe you.

Brennan: She fell approximately 40 feet and landed feet first, which explained the crushed **tibias**[3].

Booth: That's what killed her?

Brennan: Not necessarily. Her skull sustained **traumatic**[4] injuries that are **inconsistent**[5] with a feet-first fall.

哈金斯：我确定的死亡时间大概 10 天左右，就是失踪人口报告建立的时候。

布斯：你确定？

哈金斯：看到这苍蝇蛆与葬甲科虫的比率了吗？

（哈金斯把装有尸体上蛆蝇样品的烧杯拿给布斯看，布斯忙用手中的笔记本挡开。）

布斯：嗯，10 天，我相信你。

布伦南：她从大概 40 英尺的地方摔下来，脚先着地，这就解释了为什么她的胫骨粉碎了。

布斯：这是她的死因？

布伦南：不一定，她头骨的外伤和脚先着地的情况不符。

注释
1. **larvae** ['lɑ:vi:] *n.* 幼虫（larva 的复数形式）
2. **silphidae** ['sɪlfɪdi:] *n.* 葬甲科
3. **tibia** ['tɪbɪə] *n.* 胫骨
4. **traumatic** [trɔ:'mætɪk] *adj.* 外伤的
5. **inconsistent** [ˌɪnkən'sɪstənt] *adj.* 不一致的；前后矛盾的

Zark:	We found blood traces and bone chips on pieces of exposed pipe and **rebar**[6] **jutting**[7] from the side of the **ventilation**[8] shaft.	扎克：	我们已经在通风口侧面突出来的钢筋和管道上发现了血迹和尸骨的碎片。
Booth:	So that's what killed her?	布斯：	那就是她的死因？
Brennan:	No, not necessarily.	布伦南：	不，也不一定。
Zark:	The fingernails are totally clean.	扎克：	手指的指甲非常干净。
Brennan:	If she were falling, she would claw at the wall to slow her descent. It's an **instinctual**[9] response.	布伦南：	如果她是摔死的，她会用手抓墙来减慢自己下降的速度，这是本能反应。
Booth:	So she was dead before the fall.	布斯：	所以她摔下来之前就已经死了。
Brennan:	No. Not necessarily.	布伦南：	不，不一定。
Booth:	Bones. Please. Just tell me.	布斯：	骨头，拜托，你就直说吧。
Brennan:	She may have simply been unconscious.	布伦南：	她可能只是意识不清。

Scene 2: Brenan and Booth found a seal related to the victim when they returned to the underground city to investigate the case, then sent it to their lab. The seal attracted attention of Doctor Goodman, the lab director at that time. Angela did X-ray scanning on the seal in order to get its worn pattern, based on which the age of the seal could be determined.

布伦南和布斯在重返地下城调查谋杀案时得到一枚与死者有关的印章，并送回实验室检验。印章引起了时任实验室主任的古德曼博士的注意，安琪拉在给印章做 X 射线扫描以期获得磨损部分的图案。

Angela:	1778[1].	安琪拉：	1778 年。
Goodman:	It appears to be an official seal of some kind. Oh, my God!	古德曼：	好像是某种官方的标志。噢，我的天啊！
Angela:	Aren't you going to go after him?	安琪拉：	你不打算去追他？
Hodgins:	No.	哈金斯：	不。
Angela:	Why not?	安琪拉：	为什么不？
Hodgins:	Because he is now officially in charge of that medallion.	哈金斯：	因为现在他正式掌管那块金属了。

(Doctor Goodman showed the seal to Brennan and Booth.)

Brennan: Treasure[10]?

Goodman: It's an official **vault**[11] seal, manufactured by the War Office. It was established in 1778. The Latin "sigal" and the "saur" tie it to the treasury.

Booth: A bank vault kind of vault?

Goodman: Much better. The War Office established several vaults under the city to safe keep cultural treasures.

Brennan: They must all be empty by now.

Goodman: No, no. Several were unaccounted for after a series of **cave-ins**[12] and **mudslides**[13] in the early 1900s.

Booth: So you're saying this seal came off a vault full of treasure buried beneath the city?

Goodman: It could contain currency, **gold ingots**[14], paintings and engravings. The original draft of Lincoln's **inaugural**[15] address was never recovered. This could be an extraordinary find. We have to find these artifacts before they're stolen or *sold off*[1].

Booth: What's the monetary value of this thing?

Goodman: Priceless. You can't put a value on our cultural **heritage**[16].

Booth: I think someone did. That's why Marni's dead.

（古德曼博士将印章拿给布伦南和布斯看。）

布伦南： 财宝?

古德曼： 那是官方保险库的封印，战争委员会生产的，1778 年造的。拉丁文的 "sigal" 和 "saur" 放在一起是财富的意思。

布斯： 一个类似于银行保险库之类的保险库?

古德曼： 比那个好很多。战争委员会建造了几个地下保险库以妥善保管文化财富。

布伦南： 现在它们肯定都清空了。

古德曼： 不，不是的。有几个在 19 世纪早期由于一系列的塌陷和泥石流已经没有记录了。

布斯： 这么说你觉得这个印章是属于城市地底某个满是宝藏的保险库里的?

古德曼： 这里面可能包括货币、金块、油画和雕塑。 林肯的就职演说的原稿就从未被找到过。这可能是个惊人的发现。我们必须在这些艺术品被偷走和卖掉之前找到它们。

布斯： 这些东西大概值多少钱?

古德曼： 无价，你无法给文化遗产定价。

布斯： 我觉得有人那么做了，这就是为什么玛尼会死。

注释

6. rebar [rɪ'bɑː] *n.* 钢筋	**13. mudslide** ['mʌdslaɪd] *n.* 泥石流
7. jut [dʒʌt] *v.* 突出；伸出	**14. ingot** ['ɪŋɡət] *n.* 铸块，锭
8. ventilation [ˌventɪ'leɪʃn] *n.* 通风 **ventilation shaft** 通风井	**15. inaugural** [ɪ'nɔːɡjərəl] *adj.* 开始的；开幕的；就职的，就职的
9. instinctual [ɪn'stɪŋktʃuəl] *adj.* 本能的	
10. treasure ['treʒə(r)] *n.* 财宝	**16. heritage** ['herɪtɪdʒ] *n.* 遗产；传统
11. vault [vɔːlt] *n.* 地下室，保险库	
12. cave-in 塌方	

Scene 3: There maybe were treasure vaults underground buried by the government during Civil War period. The team members were going to search for the vaults, but they need a map because the whole underground network was just like a huge labyrinth.

地下可能埋藏着南北战争时期政府埋藏的宝藏，布斯他们要去寻找，可地下网络像迷宫，他们需要一张地图。

Booth:	Wow. All that exists under the city?	布斯：	哇噢! 这全部都真实存在于城市下?
Goodman:	Yes. What we can **corroborate**[17].	古德曼：	是啊，我们可以证明的。
Booth:	Good point, Bones, you know, not *rushing off*[2] to find those guys.	布斯：	想法不错，骨头，你知道，就是没急着冲下去找那些人。
Brennan:	How accurate is this?	布伦南：	这个有多精确?
Angela:	Blue is modern, near 100% accurate. Yellow is historical.	安琪拉：	蓝色的是现代的，可以说几乎是100% 准确。黄色的是有历史记载的。
Goodman:	**Estimate**[18] 80%.	古德曼：	估计有 80% 的把握。
Angela:	Red represents less exact **renderings**[19] from stories, memoirs, accounts from city workers…	安琪拉：	红色代表不十分确切的传说、回忆，市政建设人员的描述……
Goodman:	Unfortunately, if this treasure exists, it probably exists in one of the red tunnels.	古德曼：	不幸的是,如果这些宝藏存在的话,很有可能是在一个红色隧道里。
Booth:	Well, we found that Civil War victim near a cave-in. Maybe the treasure's on the other side?	布斯：	我们是在一处塌方地附近找到南北战争时的受害者的，那宝藏可能就在另一边?
Goodman:	**Inductive**[20], **reductive**[21] or **deductive**[22]?	古德曼：	归纳、还原还是推理?
Brennan:	Deductive.	布伦南：	推理吧。
Goodman:	As you wish. Ms. Montenegro, please remove all tunnels containing power, cable or utility lines.	古德曼：	如你所愿。马丁尼古小姐，请把隧道里面所有包含电力线、电缆线及其他实用线路的隧道都去掉。
Brennan:	And fiber **optics**[23].	布伦南：	还有光缆线。
Angela:	Yes… also steam tunnels and transit access?	安琪拉：	好的。还有蒸汽管道和运输管道?

Booth: Oh, what about diamond dust? You said that there was diamond dust in the old tunnels. There was also diamond dust on the Civil War guy…So…what? I'm not allowed to help now?	**布斯:** 那金刚石灰沙呢？你说过是在旧的隧道里面有金刚石灰，那个南北战争的家伙身上也有金刚石灰。哦……怎么了？现在我都不能帮忙了吗？
Goodman: That's inductive logic.	**古德曼:** 那是归纳逻辑。
Brennan: We agreed on deductive.	**布伦南:** 我们选择了推理法。
Booth: I'm sorry, I'm just, you know, trying to think outside your box.	**布斯:** 对不起。我只是……想尝试跳出你们的框架之外。
Brennan: Can you indicate where we found Marni Hunter's body and the Civil War victim?	**布伦南:** 你能指出我们在哪发现的玛尼·亨特和那个南北战争受害者的吗？
Booth: Because, you know, if Marni was killed near the treasure and moved, and the Civil War guy was murdered by his **accomplice**[24]…	**布斯:** 因为你知道的，如果玛尼在宝藏附近被杀害然后被移走，那个南北战争的受害者被他的同伙杀害……
Angela: Mm, *gotcha*[3].	**安琪拉:** 嗯，明白了。
Brennan: Can you connect the two bodies?	**布伦南:** 能把这两个尸体连接起来么？
Booth: This one's the closest.	**布斯:** 这个是最近的。
Goodman: There's no way to get there.	**古德曼:** 但是没法互通啊
Booth: Wait, can you put some more blue lines back in that area?	**布斯:** 等一下，你能把那里的蓝线放回去吗？
(Noticing the atmosphere change caused by his unusual thinking mode, Booth explained for himself.)	（布斯不同寻常的思维模式引来在场其他人的关注，布斯察觉到气氛的改变，忙替自己解释。）
Booth: It's just a guess. Throwing it out there. **Sue**[25] me.	**布斯:** 猜猜而已，试试看嘛，还起诉我不成？
Brennan: And connect where Marni Hunter's body was found. Somewhere along that line is where the treasure is.	**布伦南:** 然后连接玛尼·亨特的尸体被找到的地方，沿着线就可以找到宝藏。
Booth: What's that blue line?	**布斯:** 那些蓝线是什么？

注释
17. corroborate [kəˈrɒbəreɪt] *v.* 证实
18. estimate [ˈestɪmət] *v.* 预测、估计
19. rendering [ˈrendərɪŋ] *n.* 描写；打底；（建筑物等）透视图
20. inductive [ɪnˈdʌktɪv] *adj.* 归纳的
21. reductive [rɪˈdʌktɪv] *adj.* 还原的
22. deductive [dɪˈdʌktɪv] *adj.* 演绎的
23. fiber optics 光纤
24. accomplice [əˈkʌmplɪs] *n.* 同谋，同伙
25. sue [suː] *n.* 控告

📖 文化背景

1. 1778 年前后正是美国独立战争期间，北美 13 州的殖民地民兵在与当时世界最强大的英军的作战过程中设法埋藏财产是完全可能的。文物古董的价值不仅仅在年代的长短，而且要考虑其在本国历史文化上所处的地位。而对于仅有二百多年历史的美国来说，1778 是其历史的开端，这个时期保存下来的历史文物当然是无价之宝。

☎ 常用表达

1. sell off 廉价销售，卖掉

例：We had to sell things off to pay the brewery bill.

我们不得不变卖东西以偿付啤酒厂的账单。

2. rush off 仓促跑掉

例：I'm sorry to have to rush off like this.

我就这样匆忙走掉了，很抱歉。

3. gotcha 答对了；好了；明白啦

例："He gotcha, Helen. Give the boy credit."

"他答对了，海伦。该表扬这个男孩。"

Passage 2

剧情介绍：

（第 6 季第 1 集）为挽救凯姆的名誉和事业前途，所有人从世界各地赶回来帮助她办理一宗无名尸体的案子。之前大家各奔前程，造成整个法医团队人手稀缺，凯姆不堪重负。重归实验室揭开全新线索的同时，大家伙儿也有各自的发现。他们都悟到原来他们真正的归属就是在华盛顿一起协同工作的地方。"骨头"出高价将失去奖学金的温德尔雇了回来。安琪拉怀孕了，哈金斯满心狂喜。

Scene : The team helps Cam solve the case of an unidentified boy; after making personal discoveries, the members of the team realize they belong in Washington, D.C. Brennan is checking the X ray while Angela is sitting aside, eager to tell her something.

小组帮助凯姆解决了一个身份不明的男孩的案件。在各自有所发现后，小组成员意识到他们在华盛顿。布伦南正在检查 X 射线，而安吉拉坐在一边，急于告诉她一些事情。

Wendell:	If you don't mind me asking, Dr. Brennan, why do you keep staring at the X ray?	温德尔：	要是你不介意我问一下，布伦南博士，你为什么老是盯着这张 X 光图？
Brennan:	Because I'm suffering the nagging certainty that my eyes are seeing something which my brain refuses to process.	布伦南：	因为我感到困扰。我的眼睛肯定看到了一些东西，但我的脑袋拒绝处理这些信息。
Wendell:	Isn't your brain *supposed to*[1] be the smart one? Hey! Angela! You want something to eat?	温德尔：	你的脑袋不是应该非常聪明的吗？安琪拉，想吃些什么吗？
Angela:	I do. Yes. But I want it in Paris.	安琪拉：	是的，但我想在巴黎吃。
Angela:	Are her eyeballs and brainpan arguing again?	安琪拉：	她的眼睛和脑袋又在吵架了吗？
Wendell:	Yeah. Clash of the Titans[1].	温德尔：	是啊，诸神之战。

Brennan:	I've got it. There's nearly **imperceptible**[1] damage to the **hyoid**[2].	布伦南：	我知道了。这里有个很细微的伤痕，在舌骨处。
Wendell:	The little boy got **strangled**[3].	温德尔：	这小男孩被勒过。
Brennan:	Well, it's not cracked or crushed. It's more like there's a hole or a **puncture**[4].	布伦南：	这不是破裂或者压碎的，这更像是一个洞或者刺孔。
Wendell:	I'll check it out on the actual bone.	温德尔：	我去骨头上检查一下。
Angela:	Sweetie...Sweetie, can I get some attention over here?	安琪拉：	亲爱的……亲爱的，能关注一下这里吗？
Brennan:	Yeah, uh, yes, it's very good to see you. Because you are my best friend and I love you like a sister. I assume, not having an actual sister to use as a control.	布伦南：	对了，是的，很高兴见到你。因为你是我最好的朋友，我就像亲姐妹一样爱你。我这样假定，因为我没有亲姐姐，无法对比验证。
Angela:	Right. Yes, yes, I know. So, um...what is the deal with Booth? Is it weird seeing him again?	安琪拉：	是的，我知道。那你跟布斯什么情况？再一次见到他感觉怪吗？
Brennan:	Not at all weird. Very nice.	布伦南：	一点都不怪，挺好的。
Angela:	Are there any old **surges**[5] of feelings? Anything like that?	安琪拉：	还会感觉到之前的那种激情吗？或者类似的感觉？
Brennan:	Booth fell in love in Afghanistan.	布伦南：	布斯在阿富汗时找了女友。
Angela:	Oh. Oh sweetie, I'm so sorry.	布伦南：	天啊！亲爱的，我很遗憾。
Brennan:	Why? Are you in love with Booth?	布伦南：	为什么？难道你爱上布斯了？
Brennan:	A little bit, but that's not what I mean. Don't tell me that you're happy about him finding somebody else?	安琪拉：	有点儿，但我不是这个意思。别告诉我你为他爱上了别人而感到高兴。
Brennan:	I'm very pleased for him. A committed romantic **dyad**[6] is exactly the kind of relationship Booth seems to require to be happy.	布伦南：	我为他感到十分高兴。专一浪漫的二人关系正是布斯需要的，他会感到十分幸福。
Angela:	Did you think about Booth at all when you were away?	安琪拉：	你走了之后想念布斯吗？
Brennan:	Yes, I did. A few times I actually dreamed about him.	布伦南：	想呀。有几次做梦还梦到他。
Angela:	Oh, well, there you go. Dreams are very meaningful.	安琪拉：	噢，这就对了。梦境里的事情是很有意义的。
Brennan:	I dreamed about the work we do. I dreamed about catching murderers and getting justice for people who were killed. What does that mean?	布伦南：	我梦到我们一起工作，梦到我们一块抓杀人凶手，替那些不幸的受害者伸张正义。这样的梦意味着什么？
Angela:	It means you're going to die loveless and alone.	安琪拉：	意味着你会一辈子孤身一人。

Brennan:	I don't follow your reasoning.	布伦南:	我无法理解你的推理逻辑。
Angela:	Sweetie, can you ask me how I am, please?	安琪拉:	亲爱的，你就不想问问我怎么样了?
Brennan:	Well, I already know how you are. You love living in Paris, and you don't miss murderers and violence.	布伦南:	我已经知道你怎么样了。你喜欢生活在巴黎，你一点都不想念这些谋杀犯、暴力犯罪。
Angela:	What I did miss is my period.I hope you're hugging me because you're excited about being an aunt.	安琪拉:	我倒是很怀念我的例假。我希望你拥抱我，因为你即将成为阿姨而感到激动。
Brennan:	No, I'd have to be your sister to do that. Oh, which I am—**metaphorically**[7].	布伦南:	我又不是你亲姐姐，怎么成阿姨了? 不好意思，姐姐只是个比喻的说法。
Angela:	Yes, you better be, because I haven't even told Hodges yet.	安琪拉:	是啊。我连孩子他爸都还没告诉呢。
Brennan:	**Anthropologically**[8] speaking, women often *confide in*[2] other women before broaching9 sensitive subjects with their mates.	布伦南:	从人类学角度讲，女人在向配偶透露某些敏感消息之前往往先跟她们的同性朋友分享。
Brennan:	Okay.	安琪拉:	知道了。
Wendell:	Dr. Brennan was right. I found a very small puncture in the boy's hyoid.	温德尔:	布伦南博士说得对，我在小孩的舌骨处发现了一个小孔。
Camille:	A puncture? Like he was stabbed?	凯姆:	一个孔? 难道他被刺伤过?
Hodgins:	Well, that's what I thought, so I took a close look, and I found...	哈金斯:	我之前也是这样认为的，于是就仔细地检查了一下，结果发现这个。
Brennan:	Cellulose?	布伦南:	纤维素?
Hodgins:	Wood. My best estimate is hardwood. Maple, alder or ash.	哈金斯:	木头。我估计是硬木的可能比较大，枫树、桤树或者岑树。
Brennan:	I don't believe a stabbing would cause this kind of damage.	布伦南:	我不认为刺伤会导致类似的伤害。
Camille:	How else would a sharp piece of wood *come into contact with*[3] the hyoid?	凯姆:	如果不是刺伤，一根尖锐的硬木如何跟舌骨发生接触?
Wendell:	Maybe a toothpick.	温德尔:	也许是牙签。
Brennan:	Combined with **concomitant**[10] damage to the **sternum**[11], I propose the following	布伦南:	考虑到我们同时在胸骨上找到的伤痕，我提出以下情景以供参考:

注释

1. imperceptible [ˌɪmpə'septəbl] *adj.* 感觉不到的; 极细微的	7. metaphorically [ˌmetə'fɔrikli] *adv.* 隐喻地; 用比喻
2. hyoid [ˈhaiɔid] *n.* 舌骨	8. anthropologically [ˌænθrəpə'lɑdʒikli] *adv.* 人类学上
3. strangle [ˈstræŋgl] *v.* 把……勒死; 使……窒息	9. broach [brəutʃ] *vt.* 提出; 钻孔; 开始讨论; 给……开口
4. puncture [ˈpʌŋktʃə] *n.* 穿刺; 刺痕	10. concomitant [kən'kɔmitənt] *adj.* 相伴的; 共存的
5. surge [sɜːdʒ] *n.* 汹涌; 大浪, 波涛	11. sternum [ˈstɜːnəm] *n.* [解剖] 胸骨
6. dyad [ˈdaiæd] *n.* [生物] 二分体; 一对	

scenario[12]: A child swallows something, perhaps a toothpick. He chokes. He stops breathing. Someone tries to save him.

Wendell: The damage to the sternum was from the Heimlich **maneuver**[13]?

Camille: What about him being tied up like this?

Hodgins: Yeah, that mostly looks bad.

Brennan: There are cultures where the binding of hands and feet is part of the burial ritual. Ancient Jews, some Asian cultures, including the subcontinent.

Hodgins: Angie says the boy was Asian.

Camille: So we're not looking at a murder? We're looking at **negligence**[14] or maybe even an accident?

Brennan: Logically, I'd say yes.

孩子把某种异物吃到嘴里，也许是根牙签，他呛着了，无法呼吸，某人想救他。

温德尔： 胸骨上的伤痕是因为海姆利克急救法吗？

凯姆： 他手脚被绑在一起是怎么回事？

哈金斯： 看上去不像好事。

布伦南： 某些文化中，在举行葬礼仪式时会把尸体的手脚绑起来。古犹太人，某些亚洲文明，包括南亚次大陆。

哈金斯： 安琪说过这个男孩是亚洲人。

凯姆： 所以这不是谋杀案？而是过失或是意外？

布伦南： 从逻辑上讲，我认为是这样的。

📖 文化背景

1. Clash of the Titans 诸神之战

《诸神之战》是一部 2010 年的奇幻冒险电影，讲述了众神之首宙斯之子落入人间遭遇的种种事端，奥林匹亚山上的神仙都因此骚动起来，一场神与人、神与神之间的拯救与被拯救行动就此展开。本剧中指布伦南各种各样想法的争斗。

🖥 常用表达

1. be supposed to 应该，猜想会

例：Because the truth is, I'm not supposed to be here, standing here.

因为事实是，我本不应该在这里，不应该站在这里。

2. confide in 信任，信赖；向…吐露秘密

例：After ten years of friendship, he is the one I can confide in.

经过十年的交往，他是我可以充分信赖的人。

3. come into contact with 接触到；联系；开始做某事

例：Every day we come into contact with opportunities and information that can improve our life.

每天，我们都会接触到能改善我们生活的机遇或信息。

注释 12. scenario [sɪˈnɑːrɪəʊ] *n.* 方案；情节；剧本
13. **Heimlich** maneuver 海姆利克急救法，指挤压腹部，靠气流将卡在气管里的异物排出的方法。
14. negligence [ˈneɡlɪdʒəns] *n.* 疏忽；忽视；粗心大意

🔊 Passage 3 📹

剧情介绍：

（选自第 6 季第 20 集）这次的死者是一名成功的独立广告商，他加入了一个叫作"绝对诚实"的组织，从此只说真话，然而这种改变并没有给他带来幸福，反而引起了他与同业、客户及与妻子、儿子的矛盾，最终导致杀身之祸。那么诚实究竟是必要的吗？也许真如老板凯姆所说，绝对的诚实是人类礼貌、体谅的倒退，而善意的谎言则是人际关系的润滑剂，毕竟，世界上没有几个"骨头"一样的人。

Scene 1: Through investigation, it was discovered that the victim once joined in a gang named "Absolute Honesty". During the way back, Brennan, Booth, and Sweets discussed the necessity of being honest…

调查发现死者曾经参加一个名为"绝对诚实"的组织。在回来的路上，布伦南、布斯和斯维特对是否需要绝对诚实展开了讨论……

🔊 **Sweets:** Radical[1] honesty is a controversial notion[2], recently popularized[3] by an organization called "The Honesty Policy".

Booth: Yeah, well, I never heard of it.

Sweets: Well, their theory is that by speaking the absolute truth; we free ourselves of any pressure to make a good impression, and thus become truly free.

Booth: So they just say whatever they want and they *piss people off*[1].

Sweets: Yeah. It can be very aggressive.

Booth: Well, it explains why everyone in Dixon's life bailed in the last year.

斯维特： "绝对诚实"是一个很有争议的概念，最近由一个叫作"诚实方针"的组织推广开来。

布斯： 是吗，我从没听说过。

斯维特： 他们的理论就是说话要绝对诚实，这样我们就可以摆脱为了给别人留下好印象而造成的种种压力，从而得到真正的自由。

布斯： 所以他们就有什么说什么，惹大家生气。

斯维特： 是的，非常有攻击性。

布斯： 这样就解释了为什么去年以来所有狄克逊身边的人都跑开了。

注释
1. radical ['rædɪkl] adj. 激进的；彻底的
2. notion ['nəʊʃn] n. 概念
3. popularize ['pɒpjələraɪz] v. 使普及；使大众化；使通俗；推广

Brennan:	I see no reason why telling the truth would be considered **aggressive**[4].	布伦南：	我不明白为什么说实话会被视作有攻击性。
Sweets:	It is when you do it without exception. I mean, the small fictions that we call "white lies"[1] play a **crucial**[5] role in human interactions.	斯维特：	这是因为当你做这事的时候，无一例外。我的意思是，一点点我们所说的"善意的谎言"在人类彼此交流中起了巨大的作用。
Booth:	It's the glue that holds us together.	布斯：	是把我们联系在一起的强力胶。
Brennan:	How? A world without lies would be far more efficient.	布伦南：	怎么可能？没有谎言的世界的效率会更高。
Booth:	If…if no one had any feelings. But people do.	布斯：	如果，如果大家都是没有情感的，可能会。可惜人类有感情。
Brennan:	Do you lie to me?	布伦南：	那你跟我说过谎吗?
Booth:	No, Bones, I don't.	布斯：	没有，骨头，当然没有。
Sweets:	I would argue you're doing it right now.	斯维特：	我得说你现在就在说谎。
Booth:	Okay, fine, I am. It's not a big deal.	斯维特：	好吧，好，我是说过，可这也没什么大问题。
Brennan:	It is. Tell me a **significant**[6] **instance**[7] in which you have lied to me in the past.	布伦南：	问题很大。讲一个你过去欺骗我的典型例子。
Sweets:	Oh, this is a good discussion. Maybe you should try it, Agent Booth.	斯维特：	哇哦，真是个很好的探讨啊，你应该试试，布斯探员。
Booth:	I can't think of anything.	布斯：	想不起来了。
Brennan:	Again you are lying.	布伦南：	你又说谎。

Scene 2: Whatever other people's attitude, Miss Brennan was absolutely honest, even though her honesty may embarrass others. The new intern Bray managed to get a job opportunity from the director, but his excitement was punctured by Brennan…

不论别人如何，反正"骨头"小姐布伦南是绝对诚实的，虽然这种诚实会令别人很尴尬。这次新来的实习生柏瑞好容易才从主任那里要来了工作机会，本来很高兴，却被"骨头"刺到了……

Bray:	Dr. Saroyan gave me the job.	柏瑞：萨拉杨博士给了我那份工作。
Brennan:	Oh. What persuaded her?	布伦南：什么让她回心转意的？
Bray:	I did. I was honest with her about my…my need and my ability.	柏瑞：我啊，我对她坦承我的需要和能力。
Brennan:	Well, why wouldn't you have done that before?	布伦南：那你以前怎么不对她坦承呢。
Bray:	Because she's my boss, and I was nervous.	柏瑞：她是我老板，我紧张啊。
Brennan:	So you're a **coward**[8] *by nature*[2]?	布伦南：你原来是个胆小鬼。
Bray:	What? No.	柏瑞：什么？当然不是!
Brennan:	But you just said…	布伦南：你刚说的……
Bray:	Forget it. You know, Dr. Brennan, you may not realize it, but you can be extremely **abrasive**[9].	柏瑞：算了吧，你知道么，布伦南博士，或许你自己都没意识到，有时候你特别能伤人。
Brennan:	Oh, no. I'm well aware of that.	布伦南：没有，我很清楚。

Scene 3: Bray was over-excited because of getting the job for his honesty, so he began to be honest blindly to anybody in the lab regardless of the circumstances, even to the boss Cam. Finally, his absolute honesty frustrated Doctor Cam…

因诚实而得到工作的柏瑞非常地兴奋，开始在实验室里不分场合地说实话，甚至对老板凯姆也没例外，终于把凯姆博士惹急了……

Bray:	I have found that it's a real relief to say what's on your mind.	柏瑞：我发现想什么说什么实在是太爽了。
Camille:	I can see that.	凯姆：看得出来。
Bray:	I mean, I never would have gotten the job if I hadn't been honest. And even Hodgins pointing out my mistake has made me more careful.	柏瑞：如果不说实话，我根本得不到这份工作。哈金斯指出我的错误，只会令我更加谨慎。
Camille:	I suppose that's good.	凯姆：不错啊。
Bray:	It's liberating. For instance, a week ago, I never would have felt comfortable telling you how **acrid**[10] I find your **perfume**[11].	柏瑞：太轻松了，比方说，一周前我根本不会对你说我认为你的香水味刺鼻。
Camille:	It's not perfume. It's **lotion**[12], and I like it.	凯姆：这不是香水，是润肤霜，而且我很喜欢。

注释

4. **aggressive** [ə'gresɪv] *adj.* 好寻衅的；放肆的	9. **abrasive** [ə'breɪsɪv] *adj.* 伤人感情的
5. **crucial** ['kruːʃl] *adj.* 重要的；决定性的	10. **acrid** ['ækrɪd] *adj.* 辛辣的；苦的
6. **significant** [sɪɡ'nɪfɪkənt] *adj.* 重大的；有效的	11. **perfume** ['pɜːfjuːm] *n.* 香水
7. **instance** ['ɪnstəns] *n.* 实例	12. **lotion** ['ləʊʃn] *n.* 润肤霜
8. **coward** ['kaʊəd] *n.* 胆小鬼	

(Fortunately, Hodgins' video stopped timely this awkward dialogue.)

Hodgins:	Hello, all. Any more mistakes, Wendell?
Bray:	I was just telling Dr. Saroyan how much more careful I am now. You know, perhaps it's the monitor, but you look like a flying **squirrel**[13], Hodgins.
Camille:	Okay, that's it. I don't care what you do on your own time, but from now on, unless we are talking about the **evidence**[14], I do not want to hear one more honest word in this lab. Honesty is clearly the **downfall**[15] of civilization. **Civility**[16], **propriety**[17] and **manners**[18] are its **redeemers**[19]. Understood?
Hodgins:	Loud and clear.

（还好，哈金斯的视频及时终止了这段尴尬的对话。）

哈金斯：	大家好啊，又犯错了吧，温德尔？
柏瑞：	我正跟萨拉杨说我现在更仔细了呢。知道么，也许是显示器的原因，你看起来像只飞鼠，哈金斯。
凯姆：	够了，我不管你在私人时间里怎么样，但从现在起，除非是讨论证据，否则我不想在这实验室里再听到任何一句实话。显而易见，诚实是文明的倒退，礼貌、规矩和教养才是救赎，明白吗？
哈金斯：	非常清楚。

文化背景

1. white lie

不仅仅是美国人，中国人也会将黑颜色和白颜色视为两种对立的颜色。一般来说，黑代表黑夜和邪恶，而白象征着日光、善良或美德。"white lie"是指那种为了避免使对方感到难受而说的谎话，可翻译为"善意的谎言"。比如你的好友新交的男朋友是你见过的最丑的人，但是为了不要使她感到难受，当面你可能会说你认为对方很英俊。美国人单独把此类谎言提出来作为一个习惯用语使用，至少证明大多数人还是认为这些不怀恶意的小谎有时也是无可非议的，毕竟现实生活中恐怕很难找到像布伦南和柏瑞这样口无遮拦的人。

常用表达

1. piss off 惹怒，使厌烦

例：What did he say to piss you off?

他说什么惹恼了你？

2. by nature 就其本质而言，天生

例：Tigers are cruel by nature.

老虎生性残忍。

注释

13. squirrel ['skwɪrəl] *n.* 松鼠	**17. propriety** [prə'praɪəti] *n.* 礼节；规矩
14. evidence ['evɪdəns] *n.* 证据	**18. manner** ['mænə(r)] *n.* 举止；教养
15. downfall ['daʊnfɔːl] *n.* 没落，衰败	**19. redeemer** [rɪ'diːmə(r)] *n.* 救世主
16. civility [sə'vɪləti] *n.* 礼貌	

9

Sherlock
《神探夏洛克》

入选理由：

　　夏洛克·福尔摩斯，一个家喻户晓的名字，他曾经无数次被搬上银屏，而全世界一次又一次为这个聪明、倨傲、不可一世却又很寂寞的天才侦探所折服。来自福尔摩斯家乡的英国广播公司当然不会错过这个机会，推出了三集迷你电视剧《神探夏洛克》，虽然是翻拍，可这次的故事却完全不同，神探活跃的地方依旧是伦敦，但是时间却从 19 世纪转到了 21 世纪，福尔摩斯是属于这个时代的。《神探夏洛克》由本尼迪克特·康伯巴奇饰演大侦探夏洛克·福尔摩斯，马丁·弗里曼饰演他一生的好友兼伙伴约翰·华生医生。全世界因为他们的演绎，又掀起了疯狂的福尔摩斯热潮：剧情在下议院被讨论，全球都在上传相关信息，甚至连男装潮流都受到了影响。

　　看看这部英剧获得过多少奖项，你就会明白它有多精彩了：

　　2012 年英国学术电视奖：最佳剪辑；最佳音效；最佳编剧；观众选择奖。

　　2012 年伦敦南岸区天空艺术奖：最佳剧集。

　　2011 年英国学术电视奖：最佳剧集。

　　2010 年犯罪惊悚片奖：最佳电视剧集。

Section 1　剧情特点：

　　《神探夏洛克》是由英国广播公司推出的英国迷你电视剧，每季为三集，每集长达 90 分钟。主人公夏洛克·福尔摩斯是一个虚构的侦探人物，是由 19 世纪末的英国侦探小说家阿瑟·柯南·道尔所塑造的一个才华横溢的侦探形象改编而来。该剧将原作的时间背景从 19 世纪搬到了 21 世纪，讲述了在繁华热闹的伦敦大都市，时尚的大侦探夏洛克·福尔摩斯和他的得力助手约翰·华生经受的一系列危险的、不同寻常的历险。

Section 2 对白特点：

　　夏洛克·福尔摩斯自称是一名"咨询侦探"，也就是说当其他私人或官方侦探遇到困难时常常向他求救。该剧大部分故事都集中讲述一些比较困难、需要福尔摩斯出面调查的案子。福尔摩斯善于通过观察与演绎法来解决问题。柯南·道尔是从自己见习于爱丁堡皇家医院时一名善于观察的老师身上获得灵感，创造了福尔摩斯这一人物形象。福尔摩斯不但头脑冷静、观察力敏锐、推理能力极强，而且他的剑术、拳术和小提琴演奏水平也相当高超。 平常他悠闲地在贝克街221B公寓里抽着烟斗等待委托人上门或者做化学实验（他和好友华生的第一次相遇即是在福尔摩斯做化学实验的时候）。一旦接到案子，他立刻会变成一只追逐猎物的猎犬，开始锁定目标，将整个事件抽丝剥茧、层层过滤，直到真相大白。华生医生是他多年的室友、办案时的得力助手、他的传记作家，以及他一生的好朋友。福尔摩斯的相貌和外表，乍见之下就足以引人注意。他有六英尺高（合约183厘米），身体异常消瘦，因此显得格外颀长；细长的鹰钩鼻子使他显得格外机警、果断；下颚方正而突出，说明他是个非常有毅力的人；经常拿着烟斗与手杖，喜欢把情节弄得戏剧化，外出时头戴黑色礼帽。福尔摩斯的思考为众人所知，他那严谨的推理，丰富的想象力，令世界为之着迷。一个让全世界着迷的福尔摩斯和一个忠厚老实的室友形成了强烈的反差，这是该剧在独白上的一大特色。

Section 3 角色分析：

夏洛克·福尔摩斯 (Sherlock·Holmes)：第一主角，自称职业为"咨询侦探"，与华生医生合租贝克街221B公寓。平时待在公寓里等待警方的咨询或者关注报纸和网上的新闻案件，穿着随意，破案时行头通常为黑色西装，外面罩一件黑色长毛呢风衣，围深蓝色围巾。头脑反应迅速，洞察每个细节，知识丰富。在第一次见到华生时就看出了他的身世，令其大为惊讶。每当面对复杂悬疑的案件时就异常兴奋，视破案为实现人生价值的手段，破案时不许其他人干扰或者否定，靠贴尼古丁贴片保持思维兴奋。除了破案之外，几乎对任何事情都不感兴趣，一旦没有案子可破，就会焦躁不安。他擅长推理、小提琴和格斗术，使用演绎法来推断案情，个人网站名为"演绎法研究"，经常在上面发表一些断案的心得。性格坚强、自信、孤傲，厌恶权势，平时与人交往就像个孩子，跟现实格格不入，曾经只裹着一条床单就去了白金汉宫，破案时的我行我素更是得罪了很多警官。不过实际上还是相当关心周围的人，比起原作中的福尔摩斯，展现出了更多温情。视华生为"唯一的朋友"，另外也很重视女房东赫德森太太、莱斯特雷德警官和女法医茉莉·琥珀。与哥哥麦克罗夫特关系比较冷淡，跟莫里亚蒂是劲敌，欣赏的异性是艾琳·艾德勒。被莎莉·多诺万警官称作"怪胎"，她对夏洛克的能力抱有怀疑和不安，认为他早晚会从破案转移到犯案去证明自己的天才。这里的夏洛克就如同不谙世事却被世俗嫉恨的天才一样，后来被莫里亚蒂陷害时，世俗差点扼杀这个天才。因莫里亚蒂设下的圈套，夏洛克为保护华生和其他重视的人的生命，在华生面前坠楼，不过奇迹般的假死脱身。

约翰·H. 华生 (John H. Watson)：本作另一位主角，退伍军医，曾服役于前诺桑伯兰第五明火军团，夏洛克·福尔摩斯的室友、挚友和助手，与其合租贝克街 221B 公寓。左肩在战斗时中弹，留下了心理障碍以致跛足，但在"粉色的研究"一集中和夏洛克追踪凶手，穿越伦敦市区的过程中克服了心理上的伤残障碍而痊愈。有一个嗜酒的姐姐叫哈瑞（Harry）（华生的手机就是她送的，姐弟关系并不好），在"盲眼银行家"案中对女医生萨拉表现出好感。性格稳重、温和，对人友善，协助破案时果敢坚强。通常都是帮夏洛克跑腿调查或者一起抓犯人，枪法很准，曾经在夏洛克命悬一线时隔着两道窗户玻璃一枪打中凶手要害，非常欣赏、信任夏洛克，虽然对夏洛克的行事风格有所抱怨，却仍然愿意帮助他，每次夏洛克调查惹出麻烦，华生也总是帮他解释。麦克罗夫特曾想买通华生监视夏洛克，遭到拒绝。由于华生将他们办的很多案子都写成了博客发表，夏洛克名声大噪。当夏洛克被诬陷为骗子时，华生顶着巨大压力选择相信他，即使夏洛克在走投无路之际为了保护他亲口说自己骗了他时，华生依然坚信自己的看法，令孤傲的夏洛克感动地流下了眼泪。因亲眼目睹夏洛克坠楼身亡的惨状，华生大受打击，甚至不得不去看心理医生，暂时离开了贝克街，在夏洛克的墓碑前称其为"我见过的最好的人，最富有人情味的人"。

莱斯特雷德警官 (Lestrade)：教名格雷格，伦敦警局的警官，莎莉和安德森的上司。经常请夏洛克帮忙，算是夏洛克在警察中比较认同和相信的一个，每当需要警方的力量时，夏洛克总是第一个想到莱斯特雷德。后在部下和伦敦警长格莱森的巨大压力下违心地追捕夏洛克，但心里还是有所疑惑，后来被夏洛克和约翰逃脱。

麦克罗夫特·福尔摩斯 (Mycroft Holmes)：夏洛克的亲哥哥，英国政府的高级官员。他这个身份有时被夏洛克用来当做调查的通行证。跟夏洛克关系比较冷淡，但事实上还是相当关心这个聪明却叛逆的弟弟，一开始想通过收买华生来监视夏洛克但被拒绝，便在夏洛克和华生身边秘密安插保护人员。在无意向莫里亚蒂泄露了夏洛克的信息后，麦克罗夫特请求华生一定要保护好他。但在夏洛克做出一些出格的事时，麦克罗夫特还是有一种"恨铁不成钢"的意味，后因自己的疏忽间接导致了夏洛克的"死"，十分后悔。

吉姆·莫里亚蒂 (Jim Moriarty)：第一季和第二季的最终反派，自称是个"咨询罪犯"。聪明狡猾，行事低调谨慎，手下不计其数。视夏洛克·福尔摩斯为劲敌，所有的案子或多或少都与他有所关联。他制造出一连串案件，甚至拿华生和夏洛克身边的人相威胁，只为彻底打败他，抹杀掉夏洛克·福尔摩斯的存在。第二季最后与夏洛克在屋顶对决，为逼其自杀，饮弹自尽。

赫德森太太 (Mrs.Hudson)：贝克街 221B 的房东，有时也照顾夏洛克和约翰的生活。跟约翰一样，虽然对夏洛克抱怨不止，但跟他的感情很深。夏洛克曾经因为有个犯人伤害了她而愤怒地把那犯人扔出了窗户，她则在夏洛克的墓碑前像母亲数落孩子一样流着眼泪数落他以前住在公寓的种种"罪行"，把他当做自己的孩子一样看待。

茉莉·琥珀 (Molly Hooper): 法医，跟夏洛克关系比较好的人之一，对夏洛克抱有好感，在圣诞节时为他精心准备了一份礼物，夏洛克在被莫里亚蒂逼入绝境时曾请求她的帮助。

艾琳·艾德勒 (Irene Adler): 艾琳·艾德勒是福尔摩斯一生中最敬佩的女性，很多以福尔摩斯为题材的作品都将两人所谓的"爱情"当做噱头，如名侦探柯南剧场版《贝克街的亡灵》，但官方说法是，福尔摩斯并没有爱过她，只是把她当作一位可敬的对手。

◁)) Passage 1 ◉

剧情介绍：

（选自第 1 季第 1 集）伦敦警察局正为一系列自杀案件忙得不可开交，所有死者皆因服用了致命的有毒胶囊而死去。于是，走投无路的莱斯特雷德警官不得不向夏洛克·福尔摩斯——这位非官方的侦探顾问寻求帮助。夏洛克从案件的蛛丝马迹推断出，这一连串事件并非单纯的自杀，而是有一名杀人犯在幕后主使。与此同时，在寻找公寓舍友的华生和福尔摩斯经介绍相识，两人一拍即合，当即搬入贝克街 221B 的公寓。在推理与追击下，杀人凶手终于露出了真实面目——伦敦一名的士司机。福尔摩斯单枪匹马与凶手进入空无一人的大学，在那里，凶手透露了他的作案手法，那便是用手枪指着被害人，强迫他们参与一场俄式轮盘般的豪赌：两颗胶囊，一颗无害，一颗致命。当被害人做出了选择，凶手便拿起另外一枚胶囊，与之同时吞服。然而，连赢四局的凶手，果真是被命运眷顾吗？危险一触即发。紧要关头，尾随而至的华生举起手枪，射杀了出租车司机。在福尔摩斯的逼问下，快要气绝的凶手终于说出整个事件真正的幕后操控者——莫里亚蒂。本集改编自福尔摩斯与华生的首个案子：血字的研究（A Study in Scarlet）。在原著的基础上，编剧做出了许多巧妙有趣的改编。例如，受害人留下的死亡讯息：Rache，在原著中福尔摩斯解释为德语"复仇"。然而在本剧集中，夏洛克却否定了警官提出的"复仇"概念，继而指出 Rache 是女名：Rachel，被害人死去的女儿，同时也是她的手机密码。正是靠着这条死亡讯息，福尔摩斯开启了全球卫星定位系统，开始了对犯人的追击。除此之外，还有许多精心布置的细节，例如在全城禁烟的伦敦，大烟枪福尔摩斯没了经典的烟斗，只能靠尼古丁贴片保持思维兴奋。诸如此类的设计，无不在福尔摩斯与华生的冒险中，向原著致敬。

Scene:　In the lab

　　　　　在实验室

Sherlock:	How fresh?	夏洛克:	有多新鲜?
Molly:	Just in, 67, natural causes. *Used to*[1] work here. I knew him, he was nice.	莫丽:	刚刚送来, 67 岁, 自然死亡。以前在这儿工作, 我认识他, 他人很好。
Sherlock:	Fine. We'll start with the riding crop.	夏洛克:	好吧, 开始吧!
Molly:	So, bad day, was it?	莫丽:	今天不太顺哈?
Sherlock:	I need to know what **bruises**[1] from in the next 20 minutes. A man's alibi depends on it. Text me.	夏洛克:	20 分钟后告诉我尸体的瘀伤情况, 某人的不在场证明就靠"他"了, 发短信给我。
Molly:	Listen, I was wondering. Maybe later, when you're finished…	莫丽:	那个, 我想问一下, 等你工作完后……
Sherlock:	You've wearing **lipstick**[2]. You weren't wearing lipstick before.	夏洛克:	你涂了唇膏, 你以前从来不涂唇膏。
Molly:	I, er…I refreshed it a bit.	莫丽:	我……我想换换形象。
Sherlock:	Sorry, you were saying?	夏洛克:	不好意思, 你刚说什么?
Molly:	I was wondering if you'd like to have coffee.	莫丽:	我是想问, 你想来杯咖啡吗?
Sherlock:	Black, two sugars, please. I'll be upstairs.	夏洛克:	黑咖啡, 两块糖。麻烦了, 我就在楼上。
Molly:	Ok.	莫丽:	好吧。
John:	Bit different from my day.	约翰:	有点时过境迁的感觉。
Mike:	You've no idea!	麦克:	岂止如此。
Sherlock:	Mike, can I borrow your phone? There's no signal on mine.	夏洛克:	麦克, 能借你手机用下吗? 我的没信号。
Mike:	And what's wrong with the **landline**[3]?	麦克:	你不能用固话吗?
Sherlock:	I prefer to text.	夏洛克:	我喜欢发短信。
Mike:	Sorry, it's in my coat.	麦克:	不好意思, 在我大衣里。
John:	Er, here…use mine.	约翰:	给, 用我的吧。

注释　**1. bruise** [bruːz] *v.* 擦伤; 青肿; 击痕　　　**3. landline** ['lændlaɪn] *n.* 陆上运输; 地上通讯线; 輸送路线
　　　2. lipstick ['lɪpstɪk] *n.* 口红; 唇膏

🔊 **Sherlock:** Oh, thank you.

Mike: This is an old friend of mine, John Watson.

Sherlock: Afghanistan[4] or Iraq?

John: Sorry?

Sherlock: Which was it, in Afghanistan or Iraq?

John: Afghanistan. Sorry, how did you…?

Sherlock: Ah, Molly, coffee, thank you. What happened to the lipstick?

Molly: It wasn't working for me.

Sherlock: Really? I thought it was a big improvement. Your mouth's too small now.

Molly: Ok.

Sherlock: How do you feel about the violin[5]?

John: I'm sorry, what?

Sherlock: I play the violin when I'm thinking, and sometimes I don't talk for days on end. Would that bother you? Potential flat mates should know the worst about each other.

John: You told him about me?

Mike: Not a word.

John: Who said anything about flat mates?

Sherlock: I did. Told Mike this morning. I must be a difficult man to find a flat mates for. Now here he is, just after lunch, with an old friend clearly just home from military service in Afghanistan. Wasn't a difficult leap.

John: How did you know about Afghanistan?

Sherlock: Got my eye on a nice little place in central London. We ought to be able to afford it. We'll meet there tomorrow evening, seven o'clock. Sorry, got to dash. I think I left my riding crop in the mortuary[6].

John: Is that it?

Sherlock: Is that what?

John: We've only just met and we're going to go and look at a flat?

Sherlock: Problem?

John: We don't know a thing about each other. I don't even know your name.

夏洛克：　好，谢谢你。

麦克：　这是我的一个老朋友，约翰·华生。

夏洛克：　阿富汗还是伊拉克？

约翰：　你说什么？

夏洛克：　你是去过阿富汗还是伊拉克？

约翰：　阿富汗，不好意思，你怎么知道？

夏洛克：　莫丽，谢谢你的咖啡。你的唇膏怎么没了？

莫丽：　对我来说没什么作用。

夏洛克：　是吗？我倒觉得效果很好，不然你的嘴看起来太小。

莫丽：　好吧。

夏洛克：　你对小提琴有什么看法？

约翰：　不好意思，你说什么？

夏洛克：　我在思考问题时会拉小提琴，有时我会连续几天一言不发。你会介意吗？未来的室友应该彼此了结最坏的情况。

约翰：　你和他说起过我吗？

麦克：　提也没提过。

约翰：　谁说室友的事了？

夏洛克：　我提了，早上我告诉麦克。我这种人肯定很难找室友，而刚过午餐，他就带来自己的一个老友，还在阿富汗服过兵役，这不难推论。

约翰：　你怎么知道阿富汗的事？

夏洛克：　在伦敦市中心，我看中一处不错的房子。我们应该能付得起房租，明天晚上7点，在那里见。抱歉，赶时间。我大概把马鞭忘在停尸间了。

约翰：　就这样吗？

夏洛克：　怎么样？

约翰：　我们才刚见面，就要一起去看房子了吗？

夏洛克：　有问题吗？

约翰：　我们一点儿也不了解对方，甚至不知道你叫什么。

Sherlock: I know you're an Army doctor, and you've been invalided home from Afghanistan. You've got a brother worried about you, but you won't go to him for help, because you don't approve of him, possibly because he's an alcoholic, more likely because he recently walked out on his wife. And I know your therapist thinks your limp's psychosomatic[7], quite correctly, I'm afraid. That's enough to be going on with, don't you think? The name's Sherlock Holmes, and the address is 221B Baker Street. Afternoon.

Mike: He's always like that.

夏洛克：我知道你是个军医，刚从阿富汗因伤退役回来，你哥哥担心你，你却不肯向他求助，因为你看不惯他，可能因为对方是个酒鬼，更可能是因为他最近抛弃了自己的妻子。我也知道，你的咨询师认为你的瘸腿是由心理负担导致的，我倒觉得一点儿不错。这样应该差不多了吧，你觉得呢？我叫夏洛克·福尔摩斯，地址是贝克街 221B。午安。

麦克：好吧，他就这德行。

文化背景

1. psychosomatic 由心理负担导致的（心身疾病）

心身疾病是与心理社会因素密切相关，但以躯体症状表现为主的疾病，主要特点包括：①心理社会因素在疾病的发生与发展过程中起重要作用；②表现为躯体症状，有器质性病理改变或已知的病理生理过程；③不属于躯体形式障碍。心身疾病的流行病学目前尚缺乏大样本的调查资料，非精神科医生很少关注这些患者的心理因素，也很少把这些他们认为是内科的疾病而看成与精神科相关，因此患者往往接受的是躯体治疗，心理社会因素方面很少得到关注。

常用表达

1. used to 的肯定句结构：主语＋ used to ＋动词原形……

例：I used to go to the cinema, but I never have time now.

我过去经常去看电影，但现在没有时间了。

used to 的否定句结构

(1) 主语＋ did not use to ＋动词原形……

(2) 主语＋ used not to ＋动词原形……

注释
4. Afghanistan [æfˈɡænɪstæn] *n.* 阿富汗（国家名称，位于亚洲）　　**7. psychosomatic** [ˌsaɪkəʊsəˈmætɪk] *adj.* 心身的，心身失调的
5. violin [ˌvaɪəˈlɪn] *n.* 小提琴；小提琴手　　　　　　　　　　心身治疗的
6. mortuary [ˈmɔːtʃərɪ] *n.* 太平间；停尸间

第一种否定句型，就是把 used 当做实义动词来看，所以变否定句要用助动词 did；第二种否定句是把 used 当做情态动词，变否定句直接在 used 后面加 not 即可，used not 可以缩写成 usedn't。美式英语通常用 (1) 种形式，英式英语常用 (1) 种形式。

例：You didn't use to drink.
　　你过去不喝酒。

例：The shop usedn't to open on Sundays.
　　过去这家商店星期天不营业。

used to 的一般疑问句结构

(1) Did ＋主语＋ use to ＋动词原形……？

(2) Used ＋主语＋ to ＋动词原形……？

美式英语通常用（1）种形式，英式英语用（2）种形式。

例：Used he go to school by bike?
　　他过去骑车上学吗？

used to 用于省略句时，肯定式保留 to，否定式不保留 to。

例：—Used you play basketball?
　　—Yes, I used to.(No, I usedn't.)
　　—你过去常打篮球吗？
　　—是的，经常打。（不，不常打。）

🔊 Passage 2 🎥

剧情介绍：

　　（选自第 1 季第 2 集）某日夏洛克收到在银行任职的大学同学的一封电子邮件，偕同正手头拮据的华生前往银行。在头天午夜有人闯入为纪念前银行主席而保留的办公室，在一分钟之内用黄色涂料涂下一个符号（符号的一部分正好横在墙上银行主席画像的眼上，故为 Blind Banker）。夏洛克推理出那符号是给一个银行职员看的，前往那人的家中却发现他已经死在反锁的室内。在夏洛克进行调查的同时，华生也在一家诊所找了份临时工作。事件继续发展，在博物馆工作的姚素琳失踪，一名新闻记者同样死在自己反锁的家中。夏洛克沿线索找下去，再次发现黄色颜料的不明符号。原来两名死者都在一个组织内进行走私古董的活动，那些符号则是走私时使用的一种名为苏州码子的密码。夏洛克注意到姚素琳家的异常，从窗户翻入调查时遭人背面袭击。夏洛克和华生前往博物馆，又发现一尊雕像上的苏州码子。两人在涂鸦颜料专家的帮助下找到整面墙的苏州码子，又找到了躲在博物馆的姚素琳。姚素琳道出黑莲帮的走私活动和苏州码子其实代表的是一本书上的某页的某个单词。这时响起枪声，两人奔出追查，回来时姚素琳已死。华生约诊所的萨拉看中国马戏，夏洛克阴魂不散地跟来，两人在这个黑莲帮的马戏团里大闹了一场，警察来时黑莲帮的人已经逃走。夏洛克在门外的街道解出密码，是"寻找一支价值 900 万英镑的玉簪"的信息。门内萨拉和华生被绑至黑莲帮，夏洛克在千钧一发时赶至，混乱中黑莲帮杀手被误杀。原来是那银行职员走私时将玉簪偷走送给了情人。逃走的黑莲帮老大与莫里亚蒂在电脑上通信，惨遭射杀。本集中夏洛克穿梭在摩天高楼中，被现代的伦敦所包围，突出了"现代"这一被强调的元素。剧中夏洛克和华生两人更加熟络，对比也比第一集时更明显，譬如夏洛克对大学同学的支票持不屑态度，华生则在他出去后温言做好场面功夫顺便收下支票。萨拉的出现则为剧情加了许多可能性。

Scene:	At Lucky Cat
	在招财猫商店

🔊 **Sherlock:** It's an ancient number system—Su Zhou[1]. These days only street traders use it. Those were numbers written on the wall at the bank, and at the library. Numbers written in an ancient Chinese dialect. It's a 15.

夏洛克： 这是古老的记数法——苏州码子，如今只有街头商贩才会使用，这就是写在银行和图书馆墙上的数字，使用古汉语书写的数字，是十五。

John: What we thought was the artist's tag, it's a number 15.

Sherlock: And the **blindfold**[1], the horizontal line. That was a number as well. The Chinese number one, John.

John: We found it.

Sherlock: Two men travel back from China, both head straight for the Lucky Cat **emporium**[2].

John: What did they see?

Sherlock: It's not what they saw. It's what they both brought back in those suitcases.

John: And you don't mean duty free. Thank you.

Sherlock: Think about what Sebastian told us. About Van Coon, about how he stayed afloat in the market.

John: Lost 5 million.

Sherlock: Made it back in a week. That's how he made such easy money.

John: He was a **smuggler**[3]. Mm.

Sherlock: Cover would have been perfect. Businessman, making frequent trips to Asia. Lukis was the same. A journalist writing about China. *Both of them*[1] smuggled stuff about. The Lucky Cat[2] was their drop-off.

John: But why did they die? It doesn't make sense. If they both turn up at the shop and deliver the goods, why would someone threaten them and kill them after the event, after they'd finished the job?

Sherlock: *What if*[2] one of them was light-fingered?

John: How do you mean?

Sherlock: Stole something. Something from the hoard.

John: The killer doesn't know which of them took it, so threatens them both. Right.

Sherlock: Remind me. When was the last time that it rained? It's been here since Monday. No-one's been in that flat for at least three days.

约翰： 我们之前以为是涂鸦，其实是数字十五。

夏洛克： 画在眼睛上的横线，也是数字，汉字书写的数字一，约翰。

约翰： 我们解开了。

夏洛克： 两人均是从中国返回后，直接来了招财猫商店。

约翰： 他们看到了什么？

夏洛克： 这不是关键，关键是他们的行李里带回了什么。

约翰： 你不是在说免税品吧？谢谢。

夏洛克： 想想塞巴斯蒂安告诉我们范孔的事，他在股市上的大赚大赔。

约翰： 损失了五百万。

夏洛克： 一周就赚回来了，这就是他赚钱如此容易的秘密。

约翰： 他是个走私犯。

夏洛克： 他们的职业都是绝妙的掩护，商人频繁赴亚洲出差，路基斯也一样，他是报道中国新闻的记者。他们两人都参与走私，招财猫商店就是交货的地点。

约翰： 但他们为何被杀，这说不通啊。如果他们都是来店里交货，为何会遭到威胁，事成之后还被灭口呢？

夏洛克： 也许他们之中有人手脚不干净。

约翰： 什么？

夏洛克： 有人偷了东西，盗取了货物。

约翰： 杀手并不知道是谁，所以一并威胁他们，没错。

夏洛克： 帮我想想，上次下雨是什么时候？周一就放这了，公寓至少空了三天。

John:	Could have gone on holiday.	约翰:	房主也许度假去了。
Sherlock:	Do you leave your windows open when you go on holiday?	夏洛克:	你去度假时会不关家里的窗户吗？
John:	Sherlock!	约翰:	夏洛克！
Sherlock:	Someone else has been here. Somebody else broke into the flat and knocked over the vase, just like I did.	夏洛克:	有人已经来过，不光来过，还打翻了花瓶，就像我一样。
John:	Do you think maybe you could let me in this time? Can you not keep doing this, please?	约翰:	这次能放我进去了吗？你能不能别老这样？
Sherlock:	I'm not the first.	夏洛克:	之前还有人来过？
John:	What?	约翰:	什么？
Sherlock:	Somebody's been in here before me.	夏洛克:	有人比我先到。
John:	What are you saying?	约翰:	你说什么？
Sherlock:	Size eight feet. Small, but…athletic.	夏洛克:	穿八号的鞋，个子不大，但很健壮。
John:	I'm wasting my breath.	约翰:	我真是白费力气。

文化背景

1. ancient number system—Su Zhou 苏州码子

也叫草码，花码、番仔码、商码。是中国早期民间的"商业数字"。它源自中国文化历史上的算筹，也是唯一还在被使用的算筹系统，产生于中国的苏州。现在在港澳地区的街市、旧式茶餐厅及中药房偶而可见。

2. Lucky Cat 招财猫源于日本

自古以来被日本视为招财招福的吉祥物。在日本，招财猫的传说可以追溯到四百多年前的江户时代，可是真正出现陶器招财猫，却是一百五十年前。

常用表达

1. both of them 他们两个人

both of 是表示"两个"的意思，在这句话里边，them 肯定是两个人。

如果是三个人或者三个人以上，就不能用 both of 了，只能用 them, they。

注释
1. blindfold ['blaɪndfəʊld] n. 障眼物，眼罩
2. emporium [em'pɔːrɪəm] n. 商场，大百货商店；商业中心
3. smuggler ['smʌglə(r)] n. 走私者；走私犯；走私船

151

2. what if 要是……又怎样；如果……将会怎么样；如果……又怎样

例：What if it is true?

如果这是真的又该如何呢?

例：What if he doesn't agree?

如果他不同意该怎么办呢?

例：What if he comes back now?

如果他现在回来怎么办?

(1) 如果……该怎么办呢?

例：What if you should fail? 假如你失败了该怎么办呢?

可以把此句补充为：

What "would happen" if you should fail? 假如你失败了又有什么关系?

(2) 如果……又有什么关系? （=What though...?）

例：What if I fail? 即使我失败了又怎样!

可以把此句补充为：

What （does it matter）if I fail? 即使我失败了又怎样!

Passage 3

剧情介绍:

（选自第 1 季第 3 集）这一集里，夏洛克终于和前两集的幕后黑手见面了。一场爆炸后，夏洛克从莱斯特雷德那里收到了一个粉红色的手机，5 声滴声后从手机里通过短信传来了一张图片，夏洛克来到图片所示的地点，发现了一双鞋，同时一个可怜的女人打来了电话。如果在 12 小时里没有解决这个难题那么她就会被炸死。在成功解决了案子之后，手机发出了 4 声滴声，又一个可怜的人被安上了炸弹，而这一次只有 8 小时来破解神秘的泼上血的汽车事件。之后每解决一个案子，就又会出现新的难题和被绑架的无辜百姓。与此同时，警察也委托了夏洛克帮忙导弹计划的案件，可是夏洛克完全不理会，无法拒绝的华生只好自己来解决。在成功解决了著名主持人死亡案件和名画伪造案件后，再没有新的炸弹人出现了。夏洛克终于决定帮助华生来解决布鲁斯帕庭顿事件。成功找到失踪的 U 盘后，夏洛克向华生隐瞒了自己想要私会凶手的决定。当夏洛克来到约定的地方时，出现在面前的居然是说要去萨拉家的华生！原来华生也成了炸弹人质，而真正的凶手就是莫里亚蒂，那个在第一个案子时见到的茉莉的男友。

Scene: At home
在家里

John:	What the hell are you doing?	约翰:	你到底在抽什么风?
Sherlock:	Bored.	夏洛克:	本少爷无聊。
John:	What?	约翰:	什么?
Sherlock:	Bored.	夏洛克:	无聊死了。
John:	No...	约翰:	别……
Sherlock:	Bored! Don't know what's got into the criminal classes. Good job I'm not one of them.	夏洛克:	无聊无聊。犯罪阶层都蔫了吗? 还好我没去那边混。
John:	So you take it out on the wall?	约翰:	那你就拿墙壁撒气吗?
Sherlock:	The wall had it coming.	夏洛克:	不撒白不撒。
John:	What about that Russian case?	约翰:	俄罗斯的那个案子呢?
Sherlock:	Belarus? Open and shut **domestic**[1] murder. Not worth my time.	夏洛克:	白俄罗斯吗? 明摆着小两口情杀，没啥好查的。

注释 **1. domestic** [dəˈmestɪk] *adj.* 国内的；家庭的；驯养的；一心只管家务的

🔊 **John:**   Oh, shame. Anything in? I'm starving. Oh, …There's a head. A severed head!

Sherlock: Just tea for me, thanks.

John: No, there's a head in the fridge.

Sherlock: Yes?

John: A bloody head!

Sherlock: Well, where else was I supposed to put it? You don't mind, do you?

John: Well…

Sherlock: Got it from Bart's morgue. I'm measuring the coagulation of saliva after death. I see you've written up the taxi driver case.

John: Er…yes.

Sherlock: A study In Pink. Nice.

John: Well, you know. Pink lady, pink case, pink phone. There was a lot of pink. Did you like it?

Sherlock: Um…no.

John: Why not? I thought you'd be **flattered**[2].

Sherlock: Flattered? "Sherlock sees through everything and everyone in seconds…What's incredible, though, is how **spectacularly**[3] ignorant he is…About some things."

John: *Hang on*[1] a minute, I didn't mean that…

Sherlock: Oh, you meant "Spectacularly ignorant" in a nice way. Look, *it doesn't matter*[2] to me, who's Prime Minister or…

John: Yeah, I know.

Sherlock: …who's sleeping with who…

John: Whether the earth goes round the sun.

Sherlock: Not that again! It's not important!

John: Not impor…? It's primary school stuff. How can you not know that?

Sherlock: Well, if I ever did, I've deleted it.

John: Deleted it?

Sherlock: Listen. This is my hard drive, and it only

约翰：	可惜了呀，有吃的没，我饿死了。噢，……冰箱里面有颗人头，一颗刚割下来的人头。
夏洛克：	给我杯茶就好。
约翰：	不，冰箱里有颗人头。
夏洛克：	那又怎样？
约翰：	那可是人头!
夏洛克：	不然你让我放哪？你不介意的吧？
约翰：	真无语……
夏洛克：	从巴茨医院的停尸间拿来的，我在测量人死后唾液的凝固时间。你把血腥的哥那起案子写进了博客。
约翰：	写了。
夏洛克：	粉色研究。真想得出来。
约翰：	是嘛，粉衣女郎，粉色箱子，粉色手机，从头到尾都是粉色，你喜欢吗？
夏洛克：	不。
约翰：	为什么，我一个劲儿地夸你。
夏洛克：	夸我？"夏洛克能在瞬间看透世间万事万物，但令人难以置信的是，他对某些领域表现出的极端无知……"
约翰：	等下，我不是那意思……
夏洛克：	那你的极端无知也是在夸我咯？听着，我不关心首相是谁？
约翰：	好吧。
夏洛克：	或是谁和谁在一起……
约翰：	或是地球是围着太阳转。
夏洛克：	又来了，这无关紧要。
约翰：	什么？连小学生都知道，你怎么会不知道？
夏洛克：	就算我以前知道，后来也被我删除了。
约翰：	删除？
夏洛克：	听着，我的大脑就像一个硬盘，

makes sense to put things in there that are useful. Really useful. Ordinary people fill their heads with all kinds of rubbish. That makes it hard to get at the stuff that matters. Do you see?

John: But it's the solar system!

Sherlock: Oh, hell! What does that matter? So we go round the sun. If we went round the moon, or round and round the garden like a teddy bear, it wouldn't make any difference! All that matters to me is the work! Without that, my brain rots! Put that in your blog! Or, better still, stop **inflicting**[4] your opinions on the world! Where are you going?

John: Out! I need some air.

Hudson: Oh, sorry, love. Woo-hoo! Have you two had a little domestic? Oh, it's a bit nippy out there. He should have wrapped himself up a bit more.

Sherlock: Look at that, Mrs Hudson. Quiet, calm, peaceful. Isn't it hateful?

Hudson: Oh, I'm sure something will turn up, Sherlock. A nice murder. That'll cheer you up.

Sherlock: Can't come too soon.

Hudson: Hey, what have you done to my bloody wall? I'm putting this on your rent, young man!

只会存放有用的东西，真正有用的东西。普通人一般都是满脑子垃圾，关键时候起不了作用的，明白了吗？

约翰： 但这是太阳系啊!

夏洛克： 噢，这到底有什么关系，地球是绕着太阳转，就算是绕着月亮转，甚至是绕着公园转啊转，像只泰迪熊似的，也和我们没有半毛钱关系啊。我只在乎工作，不然大脑就要生锈了。都写进你的博客吧，要是你不添油加醋就更好了。你要去哪儿?

约翰： 出去透透气。

赫德森： 对不起，亲爱的。哎呀，你们闹别扭了吗? 外面有点冷，他应该多穿点儿。

夏洛克： 看啊，赫德森太太，安静，祥和，太平无事，不觉得讨厌吗?

赫德森： 放心吧，会有乐子的，一起错综复杂的谋杀案，让你兴奋起来。

夏洛克： 快点来吧，等死人了。

赫德森： 你怎么把墙弄成这副德行? 回头加在你的房租里，坏小子。

注释 2. flattered ['flætəd] *adj.* 高兴的，感到荣幸的；过分夸赞　　4. inflict [ɪn'flɪkt] *v.* 造成；使遭受（损伤、痛苦等）；给予（打
3. spectacularly [spek'tækjələlɪ] *adv.* 壮观地；引人注目地　　击等）

155

🕿 **常用表达**

1. hang on 等一下，别挂断

（1）电话用语（其后可接 a minute, a moment, a while 之类的词），意为：等一下，别放下话筒，别挂断。

例：Hang on! I'll call him.

等一下，我去叫他。

I'm afraid the (telephone) line is engaged. Would you like to hang on?

恐怕电话占线，请等一下好吗？

You say you want to speak to Mrs. Smith? If you hang on for a while, I'll go and see if I can find her.

你说你要找史密斯太太吗？请等一下，我去看看能否找到她。

（2）用作电话用语以外的其他情况，叫对方等一下（其后可接 a minute, a moment, a while 之类的词），意为：等一下。

例：—Got a match, Bob? 鲍勃，有火柴吗？

—Hang on. 等一下。

—We're going, Mary. 玛丽，我们走了。

—Hang on a minute. I'm not quite ready. 等一下，我还没准备好呢!

（3）表示抓紧，可译为：抓紧。

例：Don't let go. Hang on tightly. 不要放，抓紧。

Just hang on till I get help. 抓紧，等我找人来帮忙。

Hang on (to the strap); the bus is about to start. 抓好扶手，车要启动了。

2. it doesn't matter

例：It doesn't matter what I want. 不必在乎我需要什么。

It doesn't matter what I need. 不必在乎我渴望什么。

It doesn't matter if I cry. 如果我哭了，别担心。

It doesn't matter if I bleed. 即使伤心欲绝，别难过。

Chapter 4

律政剧
Legal Drama

    律政剧，主要讲述律师如何利用自己的才能与智慧为辩护人做辩护及协助警方破案的故事。一些美国法庭的辩论技巧和诉讼规则在这些剧目中得到了精彩的体现。律政剧一般围绕案件展开，其中的律师、罪犯、被告、原告等角色不一定是正义的一方，人物的个性迥异，每个案件的结局也往往发人深省。美国律政剧的另一大特点是紧随实事，大多数案件都可以在生活中找到原型。也许是今天才发生的案件，明天就会被搬上银幕。另外，律政剧的诉讼情节很少涉及最高法院，多是两个律师在一个老法官面前唇枪舌剑。两个律师常常能把歪理说直，走歪路子、插科打诨的成分居多，以博观众一笑。

    《波士顿法律》是美国律政剧的杰出代表作。此外，《白宫风云》也可以称得上是此类剧目的优秀代表作。

10

The West Wing
《白宫风云》

入选理由：

《白宫风云》是一部以政治为题材的美国电视连续剧，由华
纳兄弟电视制作公司制作，于 1999 年至 2006 年期间分七季放送
播映，曾经取得不少正面评价，其中包括来自政治学教授与前白
宫高级幕僚的肯定。《白宫风云》获奖无数，一共得过两项金球奖，26 项艾美奖，其中包括连续
四年的最佳电视连续剧奖（2000 年至 2003 年），此纪录与《希尔街的布鲁斯》并列为艾美奖电
视连续剧的最大赢家。本剧的知名度在后期逐年下降，但是节目与广告商的基本盘并未受到影响，
依然广受高收入族群的喜爱。

Section 1 剧情特点：

《白宫风云》的剧情大部分都是围绕巴特勒总统和他的幕僚如何面对各种法律事务或政治事件，
从台面下与国会议员的协商交涉到琐碎的私人领域，如感情生活及个人药物问题（前两季的主线）等，
都进行了深入的探讨。典型的剧集呈现先是随意介绍总统与幕僚团队的一天，其中通常会有一些观
念或主题连结每段剧情。而规模庞大、相互接合的白宫场景让制作单位能够拍摄出相当难得的长镜
头画面，像幕僚成员在白宫走廊上一边走一边谈论家国大事的连续主拍镜头。这些边走边谈的镜头
后来也成为本剧的重要特色。

Section 2 对白特点：

《白宫风云》有着大段的独白和长达数分钟的快速对话。《白宫风云》发展出一套"边走边谈"
的风格，摄影师以长镜头定轨摄影的方式，表现剧中角色一边在白宫长廊走动，一边谈论国家大事
的画面。典型的表现方式是摄影机从前方跟拍走在长廊上聊天的两个角色，其中一人通常会突然住
口，另一个角色加入，开始讨论另一个话题。"边走边谈"的风格能为讲述长对白的画面创造出一
种动感，因此后来电视系列剧有大量对白时，都会应用这项技巧。

约塞亚·巴特勒（Josaih Bartlet）： 曾两任新罕布什尔州州长，三届联邦众议院议员，两届州参议院议员，从政之前在大学任经济学教授。巴特勒以 1590 分通过了 SAT 考试，后来他再度参加 SAT 考试也是以同样的高分通过测试。他收到了威廉姆斯学院、哈佛大学和耶鲁大学的入学通知书，但是他最终却选择了圣母大学，因为他想当一个神父。他最终获得了圣母大学的神学学士学位，并在英国伦敦政治经济学院获得经济学硕士和博士学位。他在进入政界之前，是达特茅斯学院的终身教授，并且获得该学院的人道主义与文学荣誉博士学位。他能使用三种语言，包括英语、德语和拉丁语。他还获得过诺贝尔经济学奖，一般认为他的经济观点与凯恩斯主义相近。巴特勒最后选择了经济学家作为他的职业选择，原本他想当一名神父，但是在遇见他的妻子艾碧（一名胸外科医生）之后，他改变了主意。他跟他的妻子艾碧·巴特勒拥有三个女儿：伊丽莎白·巴特勒、伊莲娜·巴特勒和柔伊·巴特勒。他的两名外孙均是大女儿伊丽莎白·巴特勒的儿女。他通常在故事中被描写成一个严厉但是深爱家人的父亲。除了他的三个女儿之外，巴特勒也将他的私人助理查理·杨和白宫副幕僚长乔希·莱曼看成自己的儿子，同时他也将白宫新闻秘书（后来的白宫幕僚长）希捷·克莱格视为家人。

里奥·麦克加里（Leo McGarry）： 里奥是总统最好的朋友，也是副幕僚长乔希的导师，曾任美国劳工部长。他是伊利诺伊州芝加哥人，但是他还有部份家族成员是波士顿人。他拥有爱尔兰和苏格兰血统。2000 年年底，里奥·马加瑞与他结婚 20 多年的妻子离婚，原因是他的妻子再也无法忍受他的工作狂态度及遗忘结婚纪念日的习惯，并且里奥·马加瑞也承认他的工作比他的婚姻更重要。里奥是美国空军老兵，隶属于第 355 战术飞行大队，曾经在皇家空军基地驾驶过 F-105 "雷公" 战斗机。他能讲一口流利的西班牙语，并在穆勒－泰勒航空公司（一家美国国防部武器承包商）董事会供职 10 到 12 年，积累了大量个人财富。他还为一家化工及农药公司服务过，这家公司被指责在 20 世纪 80 年代造成印度哈里亚邦纳一次重大的化学污染事故。1997 年，他前往新罕布什尔州说服他的老朋友，新罕布什尔州州长约塞亚·巴特勒竞选民主党总统提名人。他担任约塞亚·巴特勒的总统竞选主管，并且是 "巴特勒为美国" 的主席兼秘书长。在竞选过程中，他先后聘任了乔什·莱曼、托比·齐格勒、山姆·希伯和希捷·克莱格为竞选团队成员。最后巴特勒击败了媒体热门人选约翰·霍因斯获得民主党提名，并最终赢得美国总统选举。在担任美国总统后，他任命里奥·马加瑞为白宫幕僚长。里奥·马加瑞在与其他白宫高级幕僚相处的时候，总是在专制与轻松的性格中转换。同时相对于其他幕僚，里奥·马加瑞也扮演了一个父亲的角色。

乔什·莱曼（Josh Lyman）： 乔什先后毕业于哈佛和耶鲁大学，获得法学硕士学位，他喜欢吹嘘自己 SAT 的口语测试拿到了 760 分一事。来自康涅狄克州，是一名犹太人，其祖父曾在二战中被监禁于纳粹集中营。他的姐姐在一次火灾中为保护乔什而丧生。他的父亲是一名律师，和白宫幕僚里奥是至交，在总统大选的伊利诺伊初选之夜，他的父亲去世。在为巴特勒竞选之前，他曾为当时民主党内呼声最高的霍因斯（后任副总统）工作，但是由于对霍因斯的政治价值不满，加之收到里奥的邀请，便加入了巴特勒阵营。尽管和总统的其他幕僚一样拥有一腔理想主义热火，但是乔什最能利用实际而现实的手段解决问题，有时甚至不惜动用谎言、政治威胁在内的各种手段，去达到他认为值得获取的结果。值得注意的一点是乔什与其助理唐娜的暧昧关系。尽管仅在第一季中和乔什发生过感情碰撞的就有前女友曼娣和那位金发碧眼、智慧过人的卢卡斯，但是乔什始终和唐娜有一种难以言说的化学反应，这也成为许多粉丝热议的话题。

托比·齐格勒 (Toby Ziegler)： 20 世纪 50 年代托比出生在纽约布鲁克林。工人阶层的家庭背景和离婚的经历让他显得沉闷而冷峻，平日不苟言笑。托比因此显得个性鲜明，为人稍显倔强。这也使他成为所有幕僚中最敢于挑战总统的人——理想主义的他总是希望总统能从更高更道德层面的角度处理问题。作为新闻主管，他对于语言和文字的把握出神入化，十分善于用语言攻击、讽刺任何他认为负面的东西，尤其对于有损于犹太人的说辞十分敏感，喜欢帮犹太人说话，比如选举哈里森为大法官等；他机智、敏锐，比如能看到退伍士兵尸体上的刺青；他也是个绝对的理想主义者；有些自傲，你很难获得他的道歉，因为他认为他总是对的。托比是一名犹太教徒，并且认为乔什的犹太血统没有他纯正；他的教育背景并没有其他幕僚那么夺目，不过他对于语言和遣词造句的兴趣和造诣都超过常人；托比也是一个忠实的纽约扬基球迷，他曾说过，截止 2002 年 5 月，他看过 441 场扬基球队的现场比赛。

萨姆·希伯 (Sam Seaborn)： 作为副主管的萨姆负责总统的讲稿写作，只不过大多时候都要受到新闻主管托比的吹毛求疵。在第一季中，萨姆的爱情故事可谓丰富，第一集开篇就是他和应召女郎罗拉的一夜风流，随后还出现了他和幕僚长的女儿恋爱的情节，有时候真的很难搞懂这些政治天才的情感生活。萨姆毕业于新泽西州的普林斯顿大学，而"Princeton"也成为了他在白宫中的代号。从普林斯顿毕业后，萨姆就读于杜克法学院，曾担任《杜克法律评论》的编辑。加入巴特勒竞选班子之前他就职于纽约一家大型法律公司，为石油巨头做包括漏油事件在内的多项指控的辩护。随后他收到好友乔什的邀请，出任巴特勒竞选班子的讲稿撰写人 (speechwriter)。

希捷·克莱格 (C.J. Cregg)： 作为白宫新闻发言人，这个被乔什评价为除总统和总统助理之外最忙碌的职位，希捷常常要面对各家媒体的刁难，也要负责围绕白宫所引发的公关危机。讲究效率，快语连珠，忠诚服务于总统，而这也和整个剧集的气氛、摄像方式相契合。希捷往往给人以严谨、严肃的感觉。不过这位中年女性也和《华盛顿邮报》驻白宫新闻记者丹尼产生过一段缠绵悱恻的感情。此外，当白宫庆祝节日的时候，希捷也乐于向所有人表演她最擅长的歌曲模仿节目，歌曲是一首名为"狙击杀手"的爵士音乐。希捷是天主教徒。加入白宫之前，曾供职于加州一所公关公司，年收入达 55 万美元。希捷毕业于加州大学伯克利分校，获得政治科学的硕士学位，并享受国家奖学金。

查理·杨 (Charlie Young)： 作为总统的私人助理，查理最初应聘的职位是白宫信使。但是却因为其稳重、真诚的个性，让乔什将其推荐至总统私人助理的职位。查理的父亲早逝，作为警察的母亲在一次执行任务中中弹身亡，他只能独立承担抚养妹妹的责任。在加入白宫之前，他曾做过高尔夫球童等工作。在第一季中，查理和总统的女儿柔伊约会，成为一大看点。很难说是柔伊主动约的查理还是查理主动约的柔伊，只是这种感情却是激怒了剧中所谓的"白人至上"主义者。

🔊 Passage 1 📷

剧情介绍：

（选自第1季第15集）希捷由于牙齿做了根管手术口齿不清，不得不找人帮她做下午的简报，乔什自告奋勇，结果由于他的说话方式把简报搞得一团糟，惹得大家众怒纷纷，受到了总统先生的批评……

Scene 1: Sam, Toby, and C.J. are in the empty press briefing[1] room, going over the next briefing.

萨姆、托比和希捷在没有别人的简报室里，为一会儿的简报做预演。

🔊 **Sam:**	Give me the bullet points.	**萨姆：**	告诉我重点。
C.J.:	I understand this stuff.	**希捷：**	萨姆，我已经了解。
Sam:	Excellent.	**萨姆：**	很好。
C.J.:	I really do.	**希捷：**	真的。
Sam:	I have complete confidence in you.	**萨姆：**	我对你完全有信心。
C.J.:	Thank you.	**希捷：**	谢谢你。
Toby:	Give him the bullet points.	**托比：**	告诉他重点。
C.J.:	I feel bathed in your confidence as well, Toby.	**希捷：**	托比，我也可以感觉到你对我的信心。
Toby:	C. J.?	**托比：**	希捷。
C.J.:	Forgive student **loans**[1] to people who become teachers —and spend at least three years teaching in a rural or inner-city school. Give cash bonuses to people who leave other careers to become teachers and provide **federal**[2] money for grants to individual school districts to use older, more experienced teachers to train younger, less experienced teachers.	**希捷：**	免除一些学生的贷款，这些学生毕业后要在乡下或城市贫困区教学三年。现金补助给其他行业转行当老师的人，并为各学区提供联邦经费，雇佣年长而有经验的老师来训练年轻无经验的老师。

注释 1. **loans** 贷款（loan 的复数形式）；借贷
2. **federal** ['fedərəl] *adj.* 联邦的；同盟的

🔊 **Toby:**	Should note that half of all new teachers quit in the first three years.	托比：	你应该说明有半数新老师工作未满三年就离职了。
C.J.:	It's right here on my index card, Toby.	希捷：	托比，我都记在卡片上了。
Toby:	Very good done.	托比：	做得非常好。
Josh:	(comes in the door) Toby.	乔什：	托比？
Toby:	Yeah.	托比：	是。（走了进来）
Josh:	Got a minute?	乔什：	你有时间吗？
Toby:	Yeah.	托比：	好。

(Josh and Toby head out one door, as C. J. and Sam get ready to leave by the other.)

（乔什和托比先走了出去，希捷和萨姆准备从另一个门离开。）

C.J.:	Thank you both.	希捷：	谢谢你们两位。
Sam:	Hey, you know what?	萨姆：	嘿，你知道吗？
C.J.:	What?	希捷：	什么？
Sam:	What time is your briefing?	萨姆：	你什么时候做简报？
C.J.:	Eleven o'clock.	希捷：	十一点。
Sam:	We should push it to one o'clock.	萨姆：	你应该延迟到下午一点。

(Sam and C. J. leave the briefing room into the HALLWAY. Carol follows them behind.)

（萨姆和希捷离开简报室走到走廊。卡萝加入了他们。）

C.J.:	I thought about that.	希捷：	我考虑过。
Sam:	Do it after the bill signing. Let this be the story. Let's control the news cycle.	萨姆：	等到法案签过后再做简报，让这件事成为新闻，让我们来控制新闻发生时间。
C.J.:	Carol, let's move the briefing to one.	希捷：	卡萝，把简报时间改到一点。
Carol:	You can't.	卡萝：	不行。
C.J.:	Why not?	希捷：	为什么不行？
Carol:	You have the thing.	卡萝：	一点钟你有事。
C.J.:	Yes, and this is a perfect excuse to **postpone**[3] the thing.	希捷：	对，这正好是大好理由来拖延这件事。
Carol:	You really don't wanna do that.	卡萝：	我不认为你该这么做。
Sam:	You have a thing?	萨姆：	你有事吗？
C.J.:	I have a dentist appointment at noon.	希捷：	我中午有牙医预约。
Sam:	What's wrong?	萨姆：	怎么了？
C.J.:	Nothing's wrong.	希捷：	没事。
Sam:	C. J.?	萨姆：	希捷。
C.J.:	I'm experiencing some pain.	希捷：	我最近牙齿有点痛。
Sam:	For how long?	萨姆：	多久了？
C.J.:	About a month now, but it'll go away by itself.	希捷：	大概一个月，但这痛会自己消失的。
Sam:	When?	萨姆：	何时？

C.J.: When I die, Sam. Carol, cancel the appointment. (walks into her office)

Sam: Carol, set the briefing for two o'clock. Keep the appointment.

C.J.: Sam!

(They enter C. J.'S OFFICE.)

Sam: Your teeth are the best friends you got, C.J.

C.J.: They are?

Sam: You take care of them, they'll take care of you.

C.J.: When'd you start talking like this?

Sam: I'm nuts for dental **hygiene**[4].

C.J.: Go away. Now.

Sam: Okay. (leaves)

希捷: 等我死时,萨姆。卡萝,取消预约。 (走进她的办公室)

萨姆: 卡萝,将简报改到两点,预约保留。

希捷: 萨姆。

(他们走进希捷办公室。)

萨姆: 希捷,牙齿是你最好的朋友。

希捷: 是吗?

萨姆: 只要你照顾好它们,它们也会照顾你的。

希捷: 你何时讲话像这样?

萨姆: 我非常注重牙齿卫生。

希捷: 请你马上离开。

萨姆: 好吧。(离开)

Scene 2: Bartlet comes in from the Mural Room. Senior staff are waiting for him.

巴特勒走进壁画房,高级职员们都在等着他。

Bartlet: I'm tired, I'm cranky, and my wife's in Argentina. Let's get this over with.

(They all follow him into THE OVAL OFFICE, where Bartlet stands in front of his desk and they form a semi-circle[5] around him.)

Bartlet: What?

Leo: Mr. President, we experienced a few public relations, what's the word...?

Toby: Catastrophes[6]?

巴特勒: 我现在很累,脾气也不好,妻子还在阿根廷,我们快点结束。

(大家跟着他走进椭圆形办公室,巴特勒站在他桌子前,大家围着他站成一圈。)

巴特勒: 什么事?

里奥: 总统先生,我们遇上了一些公共关系的……这怎么说呢?

托比: 悲剧?

---

3. postpone [pə'spəun] v. 使……延期;把……放在次要地位;把……放在后面

4. dental hygiene 牙齿卫生

5.semi-circle 半圆

6. catastrophe [kə'tæstrəfi] n. 戏剧(悲剧)的结局 [参较 catastasis, epitasis, protasis];悲惨的结局;毁灭,覆灭

Leo: ...incidents in the few hours you were away last night.

Bartlet: What kind of incidents?

(Everyone looks at Josh, who is looking at his feet.)

Leo: Josh.

Josh: Yeah? Oh. First, I'm happy to tell you that the incident involving Secretary O'Leary and Congressman Wooden has been *dispensed with*[1]. Though not really, and I'll get to that at the end. Sam asked C.J. to move the briefing to two o'clock so that we could fold in the teachers. C.J. had emergency root canal surgery at noon and so *was unable to*[2] brief.

Bartlet: Who did?

Josh: I did.

Bartlet: Oh God.

Josh: Yeah. A long story short, you're gonna be reading a bit today about your secret plan to fight inflation.

Bartlet: I have a secret plan to fight inflation?

Josh: No.

Bartlet: Why am I gonna be reading that I do?

Josh: It was suggested in the Press Room that you did.

Bartlet: By who?

Josh: By me.

Bartlet: You told the press I have a secret plan to fight inflation?

Josh: No, I did not. Let me be absolutely clear, I did not do that. Except, yes, I did that.

Bartlet: Josh, I'm a little confused.

Josh: Sir, there was this idiotic round robin. It was **sarcastic**[7]. There's no way they didn't know that. They were just mad at me for imposing discipline and calling them stupid!

Bartlet: Okay, before we go on. C.J., if blood is **gushing**[8] from the head wound you just received from a stampeding herd of bison, you'll do the press briefing.

里奥： ……你昨晚不在的那几个小时所发生的意外。

巴特勒： 什么样的意外？

（所有人盯着乔什，而他正盯着自己的脚。）

里奥： 乔什。

乔什： 是，首先，我很高兴的告诉你，奥莱瑞部长及伍登议员的事已经摆平了。虽然好像还没风平浪静，最后我会解决的。萨姆要求希捷把简报改到两点，所以可以把焦点集中在教师法案上，希捷中午动了紧急根管手术，所以无法简报。

巴特勒： 谁去做的？

乔什： 我。

巴特勒： 我的天啊。

乔什： 长话短说，你今天会看到一些新闻，有关你对抗通货膨胀的秘密计划。

巴特勒： 我有对抗通货膨胀的秘密计划？

乔什： 不。

巴特勒： 为什么媒体会报导这样的事？

乔什： 昨天在媒体室内有人这样暗示。

巴特勒： 是谁？

乔什： 我。

巴特勒： 你告诉媒体我有对抗通货膨胀的秘密计划？

乔什： 不是，我没有，让我说清楚，我没有这么做，好吧，我有。

巴特勒： 乔什，我不大懂。

乔什： 当时很奇怪，我是说反话，他们不可能听不出来。他们只是不高兴我对他们严厉并称他们愚蠢。

巴特勒： 好，在我说之前，希捷记住，就是你被一群乱窜的野牛撞到头破血流，也要由你来做简报。

C.J.: Yes sir.	**希捷：** 是，先生。
Josh: Mr. President...	**乔什：** 总统先生。
Bartlet: A secret plan to fight inflation?	**巴特勒：** 一个对抗通货膨胀的秘密计划？
Josh: There was no turning them back. I *denied it*[3] for half an hour. They wouldn't take no for an answer.	**乔什：** 他们全不听我的，我花了半个小时否认这件事，他们就是不信。
Bartlet: Were you clear?	**巴特勒：** 你说清楚了吗？
Josh: I was crystal clear. They said, "Do you think if the President has a plan to fight inflation, it's right that he keep it a secret?" I said, "Of course not!"	**乔什：** 非常清楚，他们说"你认为总统应该把他对抗通货膨胀的计划保密吗？"，我说"当然不"。
Bartlet: Are you telling me that not only did you invent a secret plan to fight inflation, but now you don't support it?	**巴特勒：** 你是说你不只是凭空捏造出通货膨胀的秘密计划，现在你还不支持这个计划？
Josh: When you put it like that, my president...	**乔什：** 总统先生，你这么说……

📖 文化背景

1. press briefing 新闻发布会 press secretary 新闻发言人

白宫的新闻发布会不是一开始就存在的。实际上，在美国建国后的一个多世纪里，白宫中并没有像今天这样需要面对大量媒体的质询，而新闻发言人制度是直到 1929 年才设立的。一般流程是每天下午新闻发言人在白宫的简报室将收集到和要发布的与美国总统及其政府行政部门有关的新闻和信息向公众公布，并回答记者的提问。发布会上所宣布的常见事项包括总统工作日程及其具体进程、动向等，也会对国内外的突发或关注度较高的事件做出回应。在美国政府中，新闻发言人是个相当重要的岗位。发言人负责各种新闻策划，是总统新闻班子的领导，可以列席很多重要会议，与总统商讨重大问题，如如何表态、与媒体保持良性互动等。新闻发言人的工作被公认为是除了总统外最繁重的工作。

⌨ 常用表达

1. dispense with 无需；免除

例：You can't dispense with a stove in winter here.

这里的冬天你不得不用炉子。

2. be unable to 不能做某事

例：Why should they be unable to reach, say, half of US productivity?

他们为何无法达到（比如说）美国一半的生产率水平？

3. I deny 我否认了

例：I do not deny but that it is difficult.

我不否认这是困难的。

注释
7. **sarcastic** [sɑːˈkæstɪk] *adj.* 挖苦的；尖刻的，辛辣的
8. **gush** [gʌʃ] *v.* 涌出；迸出

Passage 2

剧情介绍：

（第2季第3集）国会议员塞缪尔去世了，民主党国会竞选委员会急需一个新的人选加入，萨姆的老朋友汤姆被认为是合适的人选，但由于里奥的阻止，汤姆最终被民主党拒之门外。

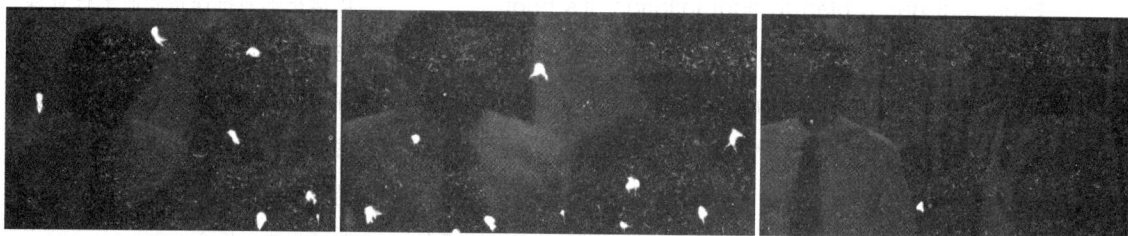

Scene 1: C. J. and Leo enter THE COMMUNICATIONS OFFICE and Leo leaves, only to be replaced by Sam. Sam *catches up*[1] as they *head for*[2] the Press Room.

希捷和里奥走进信息部，里奥离开了，萨姆追到希捷身边一起往新闻部走去。

Sam:	C. J.	萨姆：	希捷。
C.J.:	Oh, Holy Interrupt us, Batman!	希捷：	你好，抱歉打断了我们，蝙蝠侠。
Sam:	Grant Samuels died.	萨姆：	格兰特·塞缪尔死了。
C.J.:	Really?	希捷：	真的吗？
Sam:	Yes.	萨姆：	是的。
C.J.:	He's really dead this time?	希捷：	他这次真的死了吗？
Sam:	Yeah.	萨姆：	是的。
C.J.:	Cause last time you told me he was dead and he wasn't.	希捷：	你上次说他死了，但没有。
Sam:	He's dead this time.	萨姆：	这次死了。
C.J.:	Somebody **poked**[1] him a little to see...	希捷：	有人刨开他看了……
Sam:	He died, C. J.!	萨姆：	他死了，希捷。
C.J.:	Well, okay, then I shouldn't have made a joke.	希捷：	哦，好吧。那我不该开玩笑。
Sam:	I'm almost certain he's dead.	萨姆：	我几乎肯定他死了。
C.J.:	Sam!	希捷：	萨姆！
Sam:	I was making a joke, too! What, you work alone?	萨姆：	我也是开玩笑的，什么，你独自工作吗？
C.J.:	Give me some...	希捷：	给我一些……
Sam:	He's survived by his wife, Eileen, his son, Robert, his two daughters, Priscilla and Patty, and eight grandchildren.	萨姆：	他比妻子艾琳、儿子罗伯特、两个女儿普里西拉和帕蒂、八个孙子还长命。

| **C.J.**: | I'm not going to learn their names. | 希捷： | 我不想知道他们的名字。 |

Sam: Uh...that's fine.

萨姆： 额，好的。

C.J.: Eileen, Robert, Priscilla, Patty, and eight grandchildren. And I'm assuming it was complications due to...

希捷： 艾琳、罗伯特、普里西拉、帕蒂和八个孙子。我猜想是并发症因为……

(She gives Sam a knowing look.)

（她给了萨姆一个确信的表情。）

Sam: Uh... yeah.

萨姆： 是的。

C.J.: You know anything about **Theoretical Physics**[2]?

希捷： 你了解理论物理学吗？

Sam: Ah... The Grand Unified Theory.

萨姆： 哦，伟大的一元理论。

C.J.: You know anything about it?

希捷： 知道什么吗？

Sam: No.

萨姆： 不知道。

C.J.: Okay.

希捷： 好吧。

(Sam takes off. C. J. continues toward THE PRESS ROOM.)

（萨姆离开。希捷继续往新闻部走去。）

Scene 2: Sam is in his office, Ginger comes in.

萨姆坐在办公室，金捷走了进来。

(Sam walks out to the White House lobby[3] and sees a familiar person：Tom Jordan.)

（萨姆走到白宫大厅见到了他的熟人：汤姆·乔丹。）

Sam: Tom.

萨姆： 汤姆。

Tom: Sam, hello.

汤姆： 萨姆，你好!

Sam: I hope you weren't waiting too long.

萨姆： 希望你没有久等。

(They shake hands.)

（他们握了握手。）

Tom: No. I mean, I don't mind. Sam, this is my wife, Sarah.

汤姆： 没有，我不介意。萨姆，这位是我的妻子，萨拉。

注释
1. poke [pəuk] *v.* 拨　　　　　　　　　　知地物质构造、互相感化和物质活动地根本规律地学科。
2. Theoretical Physics 理论物理。是从理论上探究天然界未　　3. lobby ['lɒbi] *n.* 大厅；休息室；会客室；

Sarah： Hi.

Sam： It's nice to meet you. You got married.

Tom： Two years, with a baby on the way.

Sam： (to Sarah) Is it his?

(They all *chuckle*[4].)

Sarah： Yeah.

Sam： Okay, follow me.

(They all start walking.)

Sam： Tom and I had a contracts professor at Duke who couldn't stand me.

Tom： Those may be your thoughts, Mr. Seaborn, but that's not the law.

Sam： If he knew how many times I wanted to tell him to take the law and *shove it up*[3] his...Hey, have you guys been to the White House?

Tom： No.

Sarah： We were looking forward to a tour.

Sam： Ah...Well, that's my office over there. (points to his area.) And the President works in that round room over there. (points toward the Oval Office)And nobody else really matters. Come on in.

(They go inside the mural room.)

Sam： This is the **Mural**[5] Room.

Sarah： Hmm...can you tell us anything about it?

Sam： It's called the Mural room. Have a seat. Do you know why I wanted to talk to you?

(Tom and Sarah sit down, but Sam stays standing.)

Tom： I really don't.

Sam： Cause the Democratic Congressional **Campaign**[*1] **Committee**[6] asked me to. Grant Samuels died a few days ago.

Tom： Yeah, we saw it on the news.

Sam： He wasn't going to be running again anyways, cause he was pretty sick and the man who was going to be running in his place...

Tom： Seymour Worthen.

Sam： Right, isn't going to...

萨拉： 你好。

萨姆： 见到你很高兴。你结婚了。

汤姆： 两年前，买一送一。

萨姆： （对着萨拉）是他的吗？

（大家一起笑了。）

萨拉： 是的。

萨姆： 好，跟我来。

（他们一起往前走。）

萨姆： 汤姆和我在杜克是有一个共同教授，但这位教授不能忍受我。

汤姆： 那些可能是你的想法，但那不是法律，希伯先生。

萨姆： 如果他知道有多少次我想告诉他将法律扔掉……嗨，你们之前来过白宫吗？

汤姆： 没有。

萨拉： 我们期盼能有机会参观。

萨姆： 嗯，那边是我的办公室。（指了指他的区域。）总统在那个圆房子里工作，没有其他人打扰。进来吧。

（他们走进壁画房。）

萨姆： 这里是壁画房。

萨拉： 能介绍一下吗？

萨姆： 这里是壁画房。请坐。知道我为什么要跟你谈吗？

（汤姆和萨拉坐了下来，萨姆仍站着。）

汤姆： 真不知道。

萨姆： 是民主党国会竞选委员会叫我来的。萨缪尔几天前去世了。

汤姆： 我们在新闻上看到了。

萨姆： 他因病不能继续工作了，而那个代替他的人……

汤姆： 西蒙·沃森。

萨姆： 对，他不会干了。

Tom: Seymour Worthen isn't running?

Sam: Tom, you are a phenomenally attractive Democratic **candidate**[7] for that district. There are 162 games in major league baseball season and the players have a saying "Every team's going to win 54 games, every team's going to lose 54, it's what you do with the other 54 games that counts". In your district, you got **democrats**[8], you got republicans, and the other 54 games are women. Specifically young mothers, among who the number one issue is crime. You are a graduate of Oberlin and Duke Law School. You *passed up*[4] many **lucrative**[9] opportunities to work in the D.A's office. You are a **prosecutor**[10] with an exceptional conviction record and certainly nobody can hang "soft on crime" around your neck. You're active in local politics. You're personable. You are articulate and energetic. You are married and you're having a baby.

Sarah: I thought you didn't know that.

Sam: I'm sorry?

Sarah: When you were out in the lobby, it seemed as if you didn't know that Tom was married and that there was a baby on the way. And now it sounded like you already had that information.

Sam: Sarah, there's very little information about your husband that I don't have. And tell your mom happy birthday for me.

(Sarah blinks in dismay.)

Tom: Sam.

Sam: Tom, you'll have the full weight of the Democratic National Committee, the

---

汤姆： 他没在做？

萨姆： 汤姆，你是那个位子上最合适的人选。棒球赛季里有 162 场比赛，运动员们有个说法：每队胜负各 54 场，另外 54 场就是关键比赛。在你的区域，其他 54 场都是女性。具体来说是年轻的妈妈。妻子位居第一的是罪案，你是奥柏林和杜克的法学毕业生，你拒绝了优越的地方检察官的工作，你是个在定罪方面有非凡记录的检察官，没人敢说你对罪案手软，你在政治上很活跃，器宇不凡，发音清晰并且精力充沛。你结婚了，有孩子了。

萨拉： 我想你不知道。

萨姆： 什么？

萨拉： 在外面你好像不知道他是奉子成婚，而现在听起来你早就知道了。

萨姆： 萨拉，他只有一小点东西我不清楚。代我向你妈妈说生日快乐。

（萨拉惊慌地眨了下眼。）

汤姆： 萨姆。

萨姆： 汤姆，你将进入民主党全国委员会，国会竞选委员会；少数党领袖，我

注
释
5. **mural** ['mjʊərəl] *adj.* 墙壁的
6. **Democratic Congressional Campaign Committee** 民主党国会竞选委员会
7. **candidate** ['kændɪdeɪt] *n.* 候选人，候补者；应试者
8. **Democrats** ['deməkræts] *n.* 民主党员（democrat 的复数）；民主主义者
9. **lucrative** ['luːkrətɪv] *adj.* 有利可图的，赚钱的；合算的
10. **prosecutor** ['prɒsɪkjuːtə(r)] *n.* 检察官；公诉人；［法］起诉人；实行者

Congressional Campaign Committee; the Minority leader, whom we hope to make the majority leader, and the President of the United States. What do you say? You want to run for Congress?

Tom: There's a lot to consider, Sam. How much time do I have to think about it?

们希望他成为多数党领袖，总统。你怎么看？ 为国会工作吗？

汤姆：有很多东西要考虑，萨姆。我有多少时间考虑？

Scene 3: Charlie walks out of the Roosevelt room and passes Sam in the hallway.
查理从罗斯福厅走了出来，在走廊上碰到萨姆。

Sam: Hey, man.

Charlie: Hey.

(Sam walks towards Leo's office.)

Sam: Leo. (taps lightly on Leo's door frame)

Leo: Oh, Sam, come in. Close the door.

Sam: What's going on?

Leo: Josh is on the speaker.

Josh (VO): Hey, Sam.

Sam: What's going on?

Leo: A guy who went to college with Tom Jordan says he belonged to an association. The local papers are gonna carry it tomorrow.

Sam: Yeah. I checked that out weeks ago. It wasn't an exclusive association, they just didn't happen to have any black pledges.

Leo: Yeah, but you put this together with the **preemptive**[11] challenges in **voir dire**[12] and serious leaders in the African-American community have a problem.

Sam: I'll talk to him.

Leo: Nah.

萨姆：嗨，哥们。

查理：嗨。

（萨姆往里奥的办公室走去。）

萨姆：里奥。（轻轻地敲了敲里奥的门框。）

里奥：哦，是萨姆，进来，把门关上。

萨姆：什么事？

里奥：乔什在跟我们电话。

乔什（声音）：你好，萨姆。

萨姆：怎么回事？

里奥：汤姆的一个大学同学说他加入了一个协会。文件明天到。

萨姆：我几周前就检查过了。那不是个排外的组织。他们没有什么见不得人的誓言。经常有这样的协会。

里奥：是，但是当你把对证人的优先询问和非美会放在一起就有问题了。

萨姆：我会跟他们谈的。

里奥：不。

Sam: Leo.	萨姆: 里奥。
Leo: No, it's over, Sam. I'm going to...	里奥: 不，结束了，萨姆。我会……
Sam: No.	萨姆: 不。
Leo: I'm going to cancel....	里奥: 我会取消!……
Sam: No!	萨姆: 不!
Leo: The President's stop and shut down the money.	里奥: 总统的逗留并冻结资金。
Sam: You can't cut and run, Leo.	萨姆: 你不能这么做。
Josh (VO): We don't have any choice, Sam.	乔什（声音）: 别无选择，萨姆。
Sam: Of course we have a choice.	萨姆: 我们有选择。
CUT TO: INT. JOSH'S APARTMENT	（画面切转到乔什的公寓，乔什穿了件
(Josh is pacing around his apartment wearing a sweaty T-shirt.)	可爱的 T 恤在屋子里走来走去。）
Josh: We got a chance at the House. We've *only got* [3] weeks left. Leo's got to put the President and the money where the President and money can win.	乔什: 我们在白宫有机会，我们只剩下三周了。里奥必须把总统和资金放在最有可能取胜的地方。
Sam: Tom Jordan is running against the man...	萨姆: 汤姆正在对抗一个……
Leo: Well, you don't have to tell me.	里奥: 别告诉我。
Sam: You're going to hand it to him.	萨姆: 我们交给他。
Josh: Which will matter less if we get back the house.	乔什: 如果我们入主白宫就无关紧要。
Leo: Jordan is down by 7 and he's not going to come back from this.	里奥: 乔丹一比七走了，从此再也不会回来了。
Josh: Not only that, we stand by him, this is a national thing. It could drag down black turn out in districts where we're competitive.	乔什: 如果我们和他站在一起就是一件国家的事了。就会拉低黑人的支持率。
Sam: I told him....	萨姆: 我告诉他……
Leo: Yeah.	里奥: 是的。
Sam: I told him we would stand by him. I told him he would have our full support. I was the one who asked him to run. I was asked to ask him.	萨姆: 我告诉过他我们会支持他。我说过他会得到我们的全力支持。我是叫他参加的其中之一。我被选中叫他参加。
Leo: I know.	里奥: 我知道。
Sam: We walk away now, that's it. He's a **racist**[13]! The White House just said so!	萨姆: 我们现在走吧，他是个种族主义者。白宫刚刚这样说。

注释
11. **preemptive** [priˈemptɪv] *adj.* 优先购买的；先发制人的；有先买权的
12. **voir dire** 预备讯问；预先审查；陪审官资格审查
13. **racist** [ˈreɪsɪst] *n.* 种族主义者

171

Leo: We can't afford all the things we want, Sam. It's over.

(Leo puts on his glasses and the conversation is over. Sam leaves and slams the door on his way out.)

里奥： 我们负担不了所有的东西，就这样吧。

（里奥戴上眼镜，谈话结束了。萨姆狠狠地关了门走了出去。）

文化背景

1. Congressional Campaign 国会竞选

美国国会分众议院（representatives）和参议院（Senate）两院；参议员和众议员都是由各州选民经由直接选举产生。其中众议院议员有 435 人，每一名议员代表一个国会选区，任期为两年。众议院里议员的席次是以每一个州的人口依比例计算，如加利福尼亚州人口众多，选区也多，所以在众议院里就有 53 名众议员代表加利福尼亚州 而怀俄明州虽然面积广大，但是人口稀少，所以整个州就算一个国会选区，在众议院里只有一个席位。参议院议员有 100 人，不管州的面积和人口多少，每一个州都有两名参议员，每一名参议员的任期为六年。 每两年大约有三分之一的参议员需要改选。美国宪法规定，任何年龄满二十五岁，取得美国公民资格满七年，于某州当选并为该州居民者，都可以担任众议员；任何年龄满三十岁，取得美国公民资格满九年，或于某州当选并为该州居民者，都可以担任参议员。

常用表达

1 catch up 赶上；把……缠住

例： How, they ask, can India ever catch up with China?

他们不禁要问：印度怎能赶上中国？

2. head for 前往；出发；取向于

例： In the winter I head for the mall.

在冬日里，我前往这个购物商场。

3. shove up 推上

例： Yang Li is quite active and pull own agreeable friend Xiao Jing to shove up to this bread automobile.

杨丽倒是很主动，拉着自己的好朋友小静，挤上了这面包车。

4. pass up 拒绝；把……向上递

例： We could say that the offer was just too good to pass up.

我们会说这个提议太好，让人难以拒绝。

Passage 3

剧情介绍：

（第4季第7集）投票日来到了，巴特勒在辩论上出色的表现使幕僚们相信他们已经胜券在握，但是心神不定的托比打击着山姆。托比抽时间去医院看望做孕期检查的前妻安迪，沉浸在即将做父亲的喜悦中。山姆牵挂着选举结果。已经去世的霍顿出人意料的获胜了。乔希的助手唐娜填错了选票，她焦急地寻找一个愿意和她交换选票的人。这时，她遇到了海军上尉杰克·罗斯，而杰克即将到白宫工作。

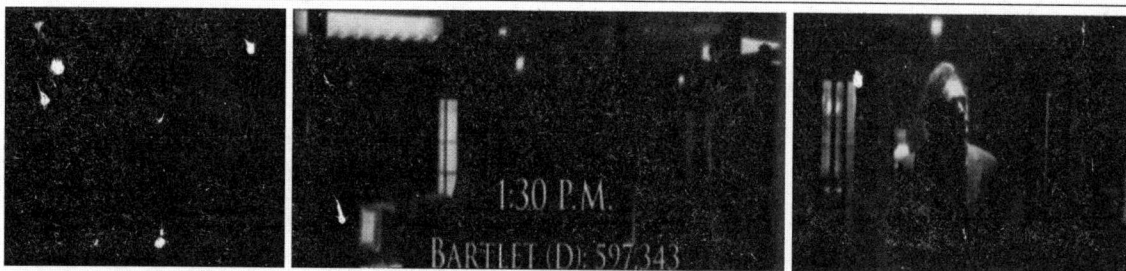

Scene1: Every one in the Whitehouse was excited about the election. Donna was greatly upset when Josh told her she had voted for the wrong person.

大选正在激烈进行，乔什告诉唐娜她并没有选总统，而是错选了别人，唐娜懊恼不已。

1:30 P.M. Bartlet: (D) 597, 343; Ritchie: (R) 551, 794; Wilde: (D) 16, 916; Webb: (R) 16, 864.

下午 1:30, 巴特勒（民）：597343 票；李奇（共）：551794 票；怀尔德（民）：16916 票；韦伯（共）：16864 票。

Josh: Nothing's happening right now. By the end of the night, 100 million votes will be *cast*. Polls have been open in the East for six and a half hours. You know how many *votes* have been *cast*[1]? One percent. Everybody votes after work. Not me, I vote first thing. The VNS exit polls are down in Michigan for a little while. And it's raining in Oregon. This is like the **ionization**[1] blackout period.

乔什： 现在还没有什么事，今晚将会开出约一亿张的选票，东岸的投票所已经开了六个半小时。你知道开多少票了？百分之一而已。每个人都在下班后投票，而我不是，我是先去投票。《选举人新闻》在密西根州做的出口民调，我们落后一点，奥勒冈州在下雨。这就像太空任务失去通讯的黑暗期一样。

Donna: Pumpkin Patch, anything I can do to get you to the movies for eight hours?

唐娜： 小可怜，我怎样才能让你去看八小时的影片？

Josh: Senior Staff.

乔什： 资深幕僚会议吗?

Donna: Yeah. But can you do me a favor?

唐娜： 是的，但你能帮我一个忙吗?

Josh: What do you need?

乔什： 你需要什么?

注释 **1. ionization** [ˌaɪənaɪ'zeɪʃn] *n.* 离子化, 电离; 电离化

Donna: This is a **photocopy**[2] of my **absentee**[3] **ballot**[4]. I was hoping the president could sign it and I'd have it framed.

Josh: Yeah.

Donna: You know the president's the first winner I voted for?

Josh: Is this a joke?

Donna: It's not hard to believe...

Josh: No, I mean this.

Donna: What are you talking about?

Josh: Toby already did the thing this morning with the **invalid**[5] ballots.

Donna: My ballot's invalid?

Josh: This isn't a joke?

Donna: It's invalid?

Josh: You voted for Ritchie.

Donna: Where?

Josh: Here.

Donna: Oh, my God.

Josh: Your picking-the-winner **streak**[6] is probably over.

Donna: No, no, no. It's an optical scan ballot. I drew a line through the **Democratic**[1] ticket.

Josh: Almost. You drew a line through the **Republican**[2] ticket. You didn't ticket-split. You voted for every Republican in Wisconsin. Check. You may have voted for McCarthy.

Donna: I'm gonna **rectify**[7] this.

Josh: How?

Donna: I don't know, but it'll be counted.

Josh: It will.

Donna: I don't want it counted.

Josh: I'm going in, you still want...?

Donna: Give me that.

唐娜：	这是我邮寄投票的影印本，我希望总统能在上面签名，我要把它裱起来。
乔什：	好的。
唐娜：	你知道总统是我投过的第一个胜利者吗？
乔什：	这是玩笑吗？
唐娜：	这并不难相信。
乔什：	不，我是指这个。
唐娜：	你在说什么？
乔什：	托比今天早上已经玩过废票的玩笑了。
唐娜：	我的选票是废票？
乔什：	不是开玩笑的？
唐娜：	是废票？
乔什：	你投给了李奇。
唐娜：	在哪里？
乔什：	这里。
唐娜：	喔，我的天啊！
乔什：	你选到胜利者的本能大概没指望了。
唐娜：	不，不，不，这是感光扫瞄的选票，我在民主党的票区划了条线。
乔什：	几乎是，你是在共和党的票区划线，你没有分开选票，你投给威斯康辛州每个共和党员。查查看，你搞不好还投给麦卡锡。
唐娜：	我要修改。
乔什：	怎么改？
唐娜：	我还不知道，但我的票会被算进去。
乔什：	会的。
唐娜：	我不希望这张被算进去。
乔什：	我要走了，你还想……？
唐娜：	那个给我。

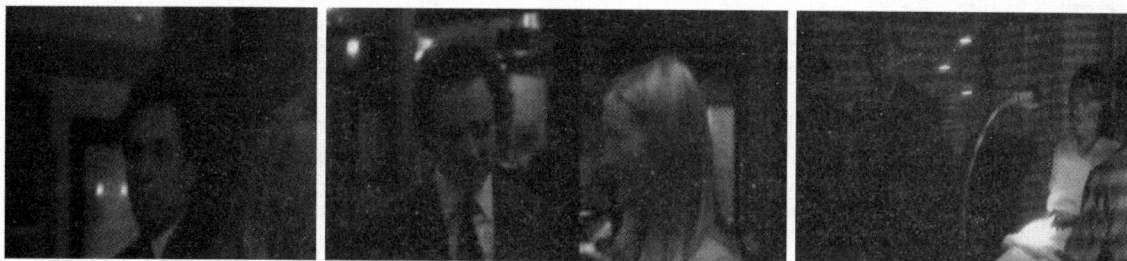

Scene2: Toby went to see his ex-wife for her pregnancy examination.

托比去医院看望前妻安迪，她正在接受孕期检查。

Toby: "Roll Call" has the pregnancy.

Andy: What?

Toby: "Roll Call" has the pregnancy. C. J. just told me.

Andy: When?

Toby: A little while ago.

Andy: Why are you telling me now?

Toby: I didn't wanna ruin the day for you.

Andy: Then why are you telling me now?

Toby: I couldn't help it.

Andy: "Roll Call" has it from where?

Toby: The Office of the Congressional.

Andy: Thanks.

Toby: What are you saying that to me for?

Andy: No, I was...I was saying it to them. I was asking it.

Toby: Just out of curiosity, how long did you think this was going to be **covert**[8]? These are twins, Andy. You think you're gonna go on *Meet the Press* and Russert won't notice you're the size of a school? Why not just come out and say: "I'm expecting twins, I couldn't be happier. The father's my ex-husband, Toby Ziegler, to whom I'll be remarried...on a date to be decided upon. I'm thinking Christmas."

Andy: I'm not marrying you again.

托比：《国会报》报道了怀孕的消息。

安迪：什么？

托比：《国会报》刊出怀孕的消息，希捷刚告诉我。

安迪：什么时候？

托比：稍早之前。

安迪：你为什么现在告诉我？

托比：我不想破坏你美好的一天。

安迪：那你为什么现在说？

托比：我不说受不了。

安迪：《国会报》从哪来的消息？

托比：国会办公室。

安迪：谢谢。

托比：你为什么那样问我？

安迪：不，我是对他们说的，我问了他们。

托比：我很好奇，你以为这件事能藏多久？他们是双胞胎，安迪。你就要上《会见新闻界》，你以为人家不会注意到你体形上的变化吗？何不走出来说，"我怀了双胞胎，我再快乐不过了。孩子的父亲是我前夫托比·齐格，我将要与他再婚，请期待我们的结婚日期。我想在圣诞节好了"。

安迪：我不会再嫁给你。

注
释
2. photocopy ['fəʊtəʊkɒpi] *n.* 复印件；影印本

3. absentee [ˌæbsən`tiː] *n.* 缺席者，缺勤者

4. ballot ['bælət] *n.* 投票；投票权

5. invalid [ɪn'vælɪd] *adj.* 无效的；不能成立的

6. streak [striːk] *n.*（与周围有所不同的）条纹；（通常指不好的）特征（倾向）

7. rectify ['rektɪfaɪ] *vt.* 改正，校正

8. covert ['kəʊvɜːt] *adj.* 隐蔽的，不公开的

Toby: Then say the first part at least.

Andy: I hadn't announced it because you don't... in the first 12 weeks because...that's when most of the things go wrong.

Toby: These bodies of yours, I don't know how you live with them.

Andy: They don't seem to mind.

Toby: I like the outsides.

Doctor: Hello, Andrea. Toby.

Andy: Hi. Honey, if you're gonna get **grossed out**[9]...and faint, you should sit.

Toby: She's kidding.

Doctor: How've you been feeling?

Andy: I feel great.

Doctor: Feel like you're getting enough **calcium**[10]?

Andy: What does that feel like?

Doctor: I don't know either. It's just something we ask. We don't even care about the answer. You should **draft**[11] a **release**[12].

Toby: Let that be my first act of fatherhood, drafting your release. Go back to my roots as we all must go. Now you're on offense, not defense.

Andy: I'm not gonna be on offense or defense.

Toby: The things we do in our lives...many of them are not voluntary.

Andy: You don't say. I think you've performed your first act of fatherhood already.

Toby: Yes, indeed. So let my second act be throwing you a little press conference.

Andy: Sounds fine. I, myself, can't make it, but you have a nice time, honey.

Toby: Do I need to tell you the first rule of damage control?

Andy: No, but the next time you refer to this pregnancy as damage...

Toby: Get the information out early, get it out yourself...do it *on your own terms*[2].

Andy: That's three rules.

🔊 **Toby:** Andy, look. I'm not kidding. You gotta...What was that?

Andy: That was...

Toby: Did you hear that?

Andy: Yeah, that was...

Toby: Andy, you can see their...heads. My kids have heads.

托比：安迪，我不是开玩笑，你要……那是什么？

安迪：那是……

托比：你听到了吗？

安迪：是的，那是……

托比：安迪，可以看到他们的……头。我的孩子有头了！

📖 文化背景

1. Democratic Party 美国民主党

是美国当代的两大主要政党之一，另一个是共和党。虽然"民主党"这个名称是在安德鲁·杰克逊（1829-1837）总统任期间所采用的，但它的起源最早可以追溯至托马斯·杰斐逊于1792 年创立的民主共和党。自从威廉·詹宁斯·布莱安在 1896 年掌控民主党以来，民主党在经济议题上的立场开始比共和党更左倾。自从 1932 年以来，富兰克林·德拉诺·罗斯福将他所提出的新政称为"自由主义"，成为了之后民主党的主要政策走向。

2. Republican Party 美国共和党

是美国轮流执政的两大政党之一，前身为 1792 年成立的民主共和党。1825 年，民主共和党发生分裂，其中一派组成国家共和党，1834 年改称辉格党。1854 年 7 月，辉格党与北部民主党和其他反对奴隶制的派别联合组建共和党，并且将党的价值奠基为"个人自由""国家团结"。而在当代政治中，共和党则被视为是社会保守主义（包括维护"家庭价值观"）、经济古典自由主义（包括支持"保守财政政策"），以及在外交、国防问题上采取强硬态度的右派政党。

📞 常用表达

1. cast a vote/ballot 投票

例：I cast a vote for the proposal.

对那项议案我投了赞成票。

例：In her late thirties, she cast a ballot for the first time in her life to back Obama.

三十好几的她人生第一次登记投票，支持奥巴马。

2. on one's own terms 根据自己的主张或条件

例：Either side wanted to end the war on its own terms.

双方都要求按自己的条件结束战争。

注释 9. **gross out**（使）呕吐
10. **calcium** [ˈkælsɪəm] *n.* 钙
11. **draft** [drɑːft] *vt.* 起草；制定

12. **release** [rɪˈliːs] *n.* 释放，排放；公映的新影片，发布的新闻 [消息]

Notes

Fairly Legal
《律政佳人》

11

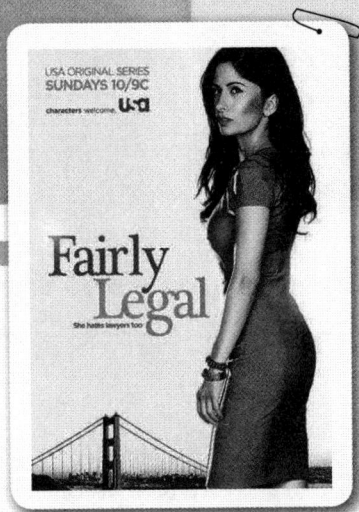

入选理由：

  该剧又名《律海佳人》，是由美国电视台拍摄，2011 年春天在美国首播的律政剧，第一季平均观众数为 320 万，共拍摄了两季。主角凯特·里德的扮演者由 2007 年热播警匪剧《重获新生》的女主角沙拉·沙黑担任。从剧名就可以看出该剧的两大特点：美女和律政。客观说，该剧在律政剧中不算很出色，但最大的亮点在于视角独特，打破律政剧的传统设定，不以常见的法官或律师为主角，而以法律调解人为主角，这个职业对于中国观众来说并不熟悉。美剧中关注这个职业的影视剧也比较少，所以人们可以通过观看此剧了解一些关于法律调解方面的常识。不做律师不打官司，致力于庭外调解，化干戈为玉帛，是不是符合和谐社会的潮流呢！

Section 1　剧情特点：

  该剧讲述顶级诉讼律师凯特·里德在工作中长期目睹官僚主义和不公正的判决结果，对律师这个职业产生了强烈反感。她决定改行当法律调解人，专门与律师为敌（当事双方如果同意调解，就没有官司，没有官司就不需要律师）。凯特用自己丰富的法律知识和女性特有的直觉，再加上天不怕地不怕的性格，成功介入了许多惹人注目的矛盾冲突，既有世界 500 强企业的大官司，也有因感情问题而闹离婚的小案子。父亲突然辞世后，凯特和"邪恶的继母"劳伦——也就是她的"新老板"一直格格不入，和担任助理检察官的前夫贾斯丁的关系也时好时坏。不过，有了得力助手里昂那多的帮助，凯特可以将所有的心思都花在工作上，而不用担心个人问题。即便如此，事情并非总是一帆风顺，每当她遇到疑难案件的时候，她的口才和灵机应变的能力都将接受新的考验。

Section 2　对白特点：

  该剧台词虽有不少法律术语，但是并不算生僻，只做了解即可，不是学习的重点。结合调解人的职业需要，独白的口语化程度很高，不少地道的日常口语，对汉语言环境中初学英语的观众来说，是很好的学习机会。特别是一些日常交往，例如如何与人打交道，如何关心安慰对方，如何讨价还

179

价等，用词简单表达形式却很丰富、生动，值得好好学习借鉴。女主角凯特口才很好，常用的一些讽刺用语都不算辛辣犀利，比较温柔，偏向可爱、幽默，不容易引起对方的反感，适合日常对话中应用。在日常交往中，我们可以尽量多用温和、商量的语气的表达，以利于在达到表达目的的同时维持良好的人际关系。

Section 3　角色分析：

凯特·里德 (Kate Reed)：该剧的第一主角凯特·里德是个典型的理想主义者，同时也是个感性又温暖的人，偶尔有些孩子气，可爱俏皮、脆弱敏感。她总认为司法能带来正义。然而作为一个律师，她却一次次在法庭上感到失望。她似乎没经过多少思考就做出了一个决定：退出她熟悉的律师行业，转行担任法律调解人。凭借与生俱来的对人性的理解，加上渊博的法律知识和一点点幽默感，凯特在与人争辩的时候总能占到上风。但她并不是个完美的职场女强人，工作中也会偶尔抓不住重点，在生活中更是常常迷糊，像个"傻大姐"，不太擅长处理自己的感情。当她在个人生活中遇到问题的时候总是搞得一团糟。

劳伦·米其林·里德 (Lauren McKinnon Reed)：凯特的继母，一个成熟美丽、精明能干、性格独立、自我意识很强、尖酸犀利的女强人，在凯特的父亲去世后掌管里德公司，与凯特关系紧张，却能够公私分明。继母一直是反面角色，劳伦饰演的继母也不例外。但她心肠并不算坏，和凯特争来斗去的过程也为该剧增添不少喜剧色彩。劳伦永远是理智、坚强的，工作努力上进，知道自己要什么。这样的女性在现代职业女性中占了大多数，与迷糊、八卦、感性的凯特形成对比。

🔊 Passage 1 📷

剧情介绍：

（选自第1季第1集）凯特·里德出身于律师世家，她刚刚去世的父亲是律师、她的哥哥是律师、她本人也曾经是一名律师，但是在目睹了太多的不公与罪恶后，凯特选择了离开，她成了一名法庭调解员，同时和她并不喜欢的继母劳伦一起维持着父亲遗留下来的公司。整天忙碌并穿梭于各色人中间的凯特依然保持着一颗善良的心，愿意帮助那些需要帮助的人。

Scene: In the morning, court mediator Kate went into a convenience store to buy a cup of coffee on the way to work, but encountered a gun robbery. The robber looked in a flurry, and it was obvious he was a green hand. At the crucial time, Kate, out of professional instincts, mediated between the robber and the store owner—she tried to soothe the angry store owner while admonishing the nervous robber...

法庭调解员凯特早上去上班的路上进便利店买咖啡，却碰到有人持枪抢劫便利店。这个劫匪慌慌张张一看就是个新手。正当剑拔弩张之际，凯特出于职业本能，大胆在劫匪和便利店店主中间周旋调解，一边安抚愤怒的店主，一边规劝慌张的劫匪……

(Sho: Shopkeeper   Rob: Robber   劫和店：劫匪和店主)

Rob: Give me the money! Come on!

Sho: OK. **Scram you**[1]!

Rob: Scram you!

Kate: **Hold on a second**[2]! Take it easy. Take it easy. First, put the gun down, 'cause you don't want to hurt anybody, all right? How's that coffee coming along? Um, you seem like the kind of guy who knows what he's doing. Yeah?

Rob: Yeah.

Kate: Yeah. Ok, so, we are not to have any problems here, right?

Rob: Yeah. No.

Kate: Right. OK. Good! So, just take the gun back on your shirt, because you don't want someone to **walk by**[3], and then see you, and right? How are we doing on that coffee? Good. Now. Educate me. What do you get when you rob a store?

劫匪： 把钱拿出来! 快!

店主： 好的。你滚吧!

劫匪： 滚你丫的!

凯特： 等会儿，别急，放松些。先把枪放下，你也不想伤人对吧? 我的咖啡好了吗? 你一看就是个有自知之明的人，对吧?

劫匪： 是的。

凯特： 好，所以不会闹出麻烦来，对吧?

劫匪： 是啊，不会。

凯特： 那就好，很好。你把枪放到 T 恤下面，以免有人路过看到你端着枪，明白? 我的咖啡呢? 很好。现在你可以告诉我你抢劫商店想要什么?

注释 **1. scram you** 粗话 "滚开你"；**scram** 本意迅速溜开，急刹车   **3. walk by** 经过路过
2. Hold on a second 等会儿

Rob:	You know, money.	劫匪：	你应该明白，因为钱。
Kate:	Right. How much? Give me your number.	凯特：	好，要多少，你说个数。
Rob:	500 bucks?	劫匪：	五百美元？
Sho:	Five? Forget it!	店主：	五百？你妄想!
Kate:	OK. Let's just say 100, alright? If you get shot, the emergency will cost you **grants**[4], so just give the guy 100 bucks.	凯特：	好，这样吧，一百块可以吗？要是他开枪打了你，叫急救车要花好几千块呢，所以就给他一百块吧。
Sho:	I won't give him a cent!	店主：	我一分钱都不会给他!
Kate:	Wait, wait, hold on a second! hold on, hold on. What will you buy with the money?	凯特：	等会儿，等会儿，冷静，冷静。你想拿钱买什么？
Rob:	Beer, and beef jerky.	劫匪：	啤酒和牛肉干。
Kate:	Beer and jerky. Nice, it's a **balance meal**[5]. So, how much does, let's say 50 bucks of beer and jerky cost you?	凯特：	啤酒和牛肉干？很好，有营养的食物。买这些需要多少钱？要不然给他五十块去买啤酒和牛肉干？
Sho:	Seventeen and fifty.	店主：	十七块五。
Kate:	Seventeen and fifty? *Are you kidding me*[2]? Who is robbing who?	凯特：	十七块五？开玩笑吧？到底是谁在抢谁？
Sho:	Hey , come on.	店主：	有没有搞错!
Kate:	All right, fine, fine. So, how does 50 bucks a beer and jurky sound you? I mean, as soon you gonna be running, right? So that's all you can carry.	凯特：	好吧好吧，来五十块钱的啤酒和牛肉干怎么样？我是说，你马上就要跑，多了也拿不动啊。
Rob:	OK.	劫匪：	好吧。
Kate:	OK. Good! So, seventeen and fifty whole sale, and we go on with our day.	凯特：	非常好，你花十七块五，我们各走各的，怎么样？
Sho& Rob:	Yeah.	劫和店：	好吧。
Kate:	And my coffee, right? You gonna get my coffee.	凯特：	还有我的咖啡，你给我倒咖啡吧。
Shor:	Yeah.	店主：	好。
Kate:	Ok, good. Black, okay? Here you go. And, uh How about this? Good. Ok? You are welcome.	凯特：	太棒了。黑啤，可以吧？拿着，还有这些东西给你，走吧，不客气。
Sho:	Hey! It's five seventy-five.	店主：	嘿，你的东西要付五块七毛五。
Kate:	For a coffee and a cookie?	凯特：	一杯咖啡一块饼干卖五块七毛五？
Sho:	Ha, it's **organic**[6].	店主：	嘿嘿，是有机食品嘛。

📖 文化背景

1. Organic Food 有机食品

有机食品也叫生态或生物食品,是国际上对无污染纯天然食品比较统一的提法。有机食品通常来自有机农业生产体系,这里所说的"有机"不是化学上的有机概念,而是指在生产过程中,不使用化学农药、化肥、化学防腐剂等合成物质,也不用基因工程生物及其产物。因此,有机食品是一类真正来自于自然、富有营养、高品质、安全环保的生态食品。但有机食品由于栽培工序复杂,各种成本偏高,产量也比不过普通蔬菜,使得有机农产品价格要比同类型的普通产品贵 30—50%。

📞 常用表达

1. seems like ... 看起来像……。常用句型 It seems like that。

例: It seems like that the price of petrol will rise.

好像石油要涨价了。

2. Are you kidding me? 开玩笑吧? 你耍我呢?

口语中常用来表示惊讶、置疑、嘲讽等多种语气。

例: —Are you kidding me?

—你开玩笑的吧?

注释 4. grant 作形容词表示很多,此处作可数名词表示一千美元   6. organic [ɔ:ˈgænɪk] *adj.* 有机的
5. balance meal 营养均衡的膳食

🔊 Passage 2 📷

剧情介绍：

（选自第2季第1集）在第一季的最后，凯特惹怒了劳伦，从里德公司被赶了出去，但是不放弃的凯特从哥哥那里拿到了里德公司的一半股份，又以合伙人的名义回来了。当里德公司面临财务窘境的时候，尽管凯特不喜欢劳伦，可还是选择了和劳伦并肩战斗，一起面对挑战……

Scene: Kate went to the Reed Company in the early morning, happened to meet Sam and Emma who came to ask for Lauren's help. Kate did not tell them she was no longer the company's employee, on the contrary received them, and started legal consultancy service about labor compensation....

凯特一大早到里德公司，恰巧碰到来找劳伦请求协助的祖孙俩：山姆和艾玛。凯特没有说明自己已经不是里德公司的员工，而是将计就计接待了他们，开始一场劳工赔偿案的法律咨询……

🔊 **Emma:** Excuse me, are you the **mediator**[1]?

Kate: Oh, yeah, *that's me*[1].

Emma: Reed & Reed came very highly recommended[2]. My grandfather and I just wanted to get here a little early, so someone could answer our questions.

Sam: You wanted to get here. I am doing this for her.

Kate: Sam, uh, you were saying that you were employed at Manwaring, they **knowingly**[3] exposed you to harmful chemicals—vinyl **chloride**[4], which then led you to getting sick. And now you are asking for 3 million dollars?

Sam: Ridiculous.

Emma: That company made you sick, and they know about it. They should pay.

Sam: They, they, they were my friends. Guys on

艾玛：借过一下，你就是法庭调解员吗？

凯特：呃，对，我就是。

艾玛：很多人推荐里德公司。我祖父和我想早点到，希望有人能回答我们的问题。

山姆：是你自己想来的，我只为她才来的。

凯特：山姆，呃，你是说你在为沃琳公司工作期间，他们蓄意将你暴露在有害的化学物质——氯乙烯之下，导致你生病了，你现在要索赔三百万？

山姆：开什么玩笑。

艾玛：他们在知情的情况下害你生病了，他们需要付出代价。

山姆：他们，他们，他们是我的朋友们，

the line, guys in the suits. We raised our kids together. George Alger came to my wedding; we had lunch together on the line once a week for 35 years.

Kate: Alger is?

Emma: His old boss runs the company now. I don't think they've even spoke in, what, ten years?

Sam: I got *the short end of the cancer stick*[2], all right? Doesn't mean you go to court.

Emma: He is from a different generation. You didn't **sue**[5] people. And I can appreciate his values, I really can. It's what makes him so great. But I also wanna help him to get what's fair.

Sam: The lawyers, they got one thing they always put first, that's themselves.

Kate: Yes!

Sam: Ask her about the character who *talked her into*[3] all this. If he's not a scumbag, I am a damn leprechaun.

Kate: Hey, Emma, I am just going to warn you now, this is not gonna go how you want it to go.

Emma: Why?

Kate: Because he and I agree about lawyers.

Sam: Ha.

Emma: I thought you were a lawyer.

Kate: If it's confusing to you, imagine how I feel.

Lauren: Hi, sorry to interrupt, Lauren McKinnon Reed, managing partner. You have a sec, Kate? What are you doing?

Kate: I came in early, saw that you had a **negotiation**[6]; one of the parties had arrived, so I just started answering their questions. Since when have you gone by Lauren McKinnon Reed?

车间里的员工,办公室里的员工。我们一起把孩子拉扯大,乔治·阿尔杰还参加了我的婚礼,我们曾经在生产线上一起吃过饭,每周一次,持续了三十五年。

凯特: 阿尔杰?

艾玛: 他以前的上司,现在是公司老总。我觉得他们都差不多十年没说话了?

山姆: 癌症耗尽了我的钱,也不代表我要告上法庭啊。

艾玛: 他那一代人和我们这一代不一样。你不能随便告人。我尊重他的价值观,我真的能。这也是他这个人的优点。但我也想他得到应得的。

山姆: 律师们,被他们放在第一位的事情那就是他们自己了。

凯特: 说得对。

山姆: 你问问她是谁怂恿她打官司的,这混球,当我是小矮人啊。

凯特: 嘿,艾玛,我先和你提个醒,这事情并不能像你想象的那样进行顺利。

艾玛: 为什么?

凯特: 因为我和他都觉得律师是自私的。

山姆: 哈。

艾玛: 你不就是个律师吗?

凯特: 如果你都搞不清楚了,那我的感受呢?

劳伦: 不好意思打搅一下,我叫劳伦·米其林·里德,是这家公司的经理合伙人。凯特,你有空吗?借一步说话。你在干什么,凯特?

凯特: 我来得早了点儿,看到你有个会谈,一方已经先到场了,所以我就开始回答他们的问题了。你什么时候开始管自己叫劳伦·米其林·里德的?

注释

1. **mediator** ['miːdɪeɪtə(r)] *n.* 法庭调解员、仲裁者。专职于庭外调解工作。

2. **recommend** [ˌrekə'mend] *v.* 推荐

3. **knowingly** ['nəʊɪŋlɪ] *adv.* 知情地、蓄意地

4. **vinyl chloride** 氯乙烯

5. **sue** [suː] *v.* 起诉、控告

6. **negotiation** [nɪˌgəʊʃi'eɪʃn] *n.* 会谈

Lauren: I fired you, Kate.

Kate: Yes, that was funny. I've had the keys to the building since I was 13.

Lauren: Kate, honey, while you've been sitting on your boat for the last month, being **impulsive**[7] and whimsical, I have being holding this firm together. You drove your father crazy, but I don't know, he tolerated it because I guess on some level he liked that his little girl never grew up.

Kate: I guess he liked having something sweet in his life.

Lauren: Oh, god! Kate, I am not your evil stepmother. God , I never was, get over it.

劳伦：凯特，我已经炒你鱿鱼了。

凯特：哈哈，真搞笑。十三岁开始我就有这栋楼的钥匙了。

劳伦：凯特，当你上个月坐在自己船上突发奇想、冲动行事的时候，我可是在运作整个公司。你父亲在世的时候都被你逼疯了。他忍受你，是不是因为某种程度上他享受女儿永远长不大的状态?

凯特：我想他希望自己的生活中有点甜蜜吧！

劳伦：天哪，凯特，我不是你的邪恶继母，我从来不是，你就别多想了。

📖 文化背景

1. mediator 法庭调解员

为了应对日益增加的诉讼案件，20 世纪 70 年代中期美国的三个法院启动了建立调解制度的程序。1978 年后这一程序转为义务调解程序，规定诉讼价值在 15000 美元以下的，由调解结案。凡符合法院调解管辖前提的申诉会被很快送往调解委员会。案件调解需一位调解员，可以由退休法官担任，也可由律师兼任，经过非正式的取证，最后做出裁决。如一方或双方当事人不服裁决，则启动正式的司法程序，之前的调解和裁决均归于无效。若当事方对调解结果没有正式提出任何异议，调解员做出的裁决具有法律拘束力。

📞 常用表达

1. that's me 就是我，也可以用 it's me。常用在打电话等场合。

例：A: May I speak to Tom? B: That's me, speaking, please.

A：你好，我找汤姆。B：说吧，我就是汤姆。

2. get the short end of the stick 受到不公平待遇；最后甩掉；耗尽了钱

例：Sometimes nice people get the short end of the stick.

有时候好人反而受到不公平的待遇。

3. talk somebody into something 怂恿某人卷入某事；说服某人做某事

例：The person might try to talk you into staying here.

那人可能会试图说服你待在原地。

注释 **7. impulsive** [ɪmˈpʌlsɪv] *adj.* 冲动

🔊 Passage 3 🎥

剧情介绍：

（选自第 2 季第 12 集）里德公司的经营终于步入正轨，而凯特和前夫的关系却还是起起伏伏、难以捉摸。两个人已经离婚了，却又重新开始了约会，只是这个约会却让贾斯丁陷入了麻烦。他们去听了一个巴西来的歌星的演唱会，还和这个歌星一起坐车出去，结果发生了车祸，而就在警察检查车祸现场时，在歌星的包里发现了毒品……

Scene 1: Reed received a significant client—Robin Archer, the president of an airline company. Everyone in the company, from top to bottom, was very excited for the arrival of the legendary figure, but Kate was excited because she received her ex-husband Justin's concert ticket...

里德公司迎来了个大客户——航空公司老总罗宾·阿彻，公司从上到下对这个传奇人物的到来都很激动，而凯特的激动却是因为收到前夫贾斯丁送的演唱会门票……

🔊 **Kate:** Robin Archer is in the conference room.

Lauren: Oh, my God. I'll just...

Kate: Archer is **hot**[1].

Leonardo: You wanna see some naked photos of him?

Kate: Oh, yeah! What's that?

Leonardo: It's autotrader.com. We need to find you a car. See how simple it is? So many to choose from. You can do side-by-side comparisons, find exactly what you need, oh, it would be ever so fun.

Kate: Oh, Leonardo, when you promise someone naked pictures of a cute boy, don't show them pictures of cars.

凯特： 罗宾·阿彻在会议室里。

劳伦： 哦，天哪，我只是……

凯特： 阿彻好性感！

里奥纳多： 想看他的裸照吗？

凯特： 好啊。这是什么？

里奥纳多： 是汽车拍卖网站。我们需要给你找辆车。看到有多简单吗？有好多选择，你可以并列比较，找到你真正需要的。这会非常有意思。

凯特： 里奥纳多，当你许诺某人帅哥的裸照时，你不能给人家看汽车照片。

注释 **1. hot** [hɒt] *adj.* 性感，身材惹火

Leonardo:	Cars are sexy when you are driving them yourself. They say, "Look at me, I'm not a 29-year-old **anomaly**[2] with some eccentric life skill deficit."	里奥纳多：	你自己开车的时候会很性感。他们说："看我，我不是29岁的没有生活能力的怪人。"
Kate:	Oh, come on, Leo. But you love driving me around. What is this?	凯特：	算了吧，里奥，你喜欢载着我兜风。这是什么？
Leonardo:	Oh, those were hand delivered from Justin, I believe that they are……	里奥纳多：	贾斯丁亲自送过来的，我想它们是……
Kate:	Tickets for **Claudia Alves**[3]?	凯特：	克劳迪娅·艾维斯的演唱会门票？
Leonardo:	Who is Claudia Alves?	里奥纳多：	克劳迪娅·艾维斯是谁？
Kate:	She is this amazing Brazilian singer songwriter. And she is performing at Opera House on Friday, but these tickets are for her private performance tonight at Hugo's!	凯特：	她是非常棒的巴西创作型歌手。她星期五会在歌剧院演出，但这门票是她今晚在希戈餐厅的私人演出，太棒了！
Leonardo:	So, you and Justin officially……	里奥纳多：	那么说，你跟贾斯丁正式的……
Kate:	No, not officially anything. We are simply just trying things out. But you know what, these are very spur of moment. They are not very Justin-like.	凯特：	不不不，没什么正式的。我们只是在试着考虑。但是你知道吗？这真是突发奇想，这不是贾斯丁的作风。
Benedict:	Perhaps he is *making a point*[3], "You'll like me better if I am not who I am".	本尼迪克特：	或许他在表达一种观点：如果我不是以前的我，你会更喜欢我。
Kate:	Thanks so much.	凯特：	非常感谢。

Scene 2: In the office, Lauren was negotiating vehemently with his client…

办公室里，劳伦在与客户进行你来我往地谈判……

Lauren:	It's been 50.	劳伦：	是 50。
Archer:	It was 50 when the market was 14,000 and you could check a bag for free. Where is your client?	阿彻的律师：	乘客的数量有一万四并可以免费托运一件行李时是 50 元。你的委托人在哪儿？
Lauren:	I don't think he need to here to be insulted. Is that why you are here? To insult him personally?	劳伦：	我觉得他不需要在这里被侮辱。或者这就是你在这里的原因？亲自侮辱他？
Archer:	Why is 35 an **insult**[4]?	阿彻：	为什么 35 元是一个侮辱？
Lauren:	My client's airline has made more money in the last ten years than all the regional airlines you have required put together. So, we could continue to play **footsie**[5] a little bit longer or we could lay our cards on the table and saw the thing up today before it gets even more expensive for you……	劳伦：	我委托人的航线在过去十年赚取的钱比你整个地区的航线加在一起还要多。我们可以继续再周旋，或者我们可以挑明了的话，在价格再度上涨前解决此事。
Archer:	What's your bottom line?	阿彻：	你的底线是多少？
Lauren:	52.	劳伦：	52 美元。
Lawyer:	52?	阿彻的律师：	52 美元？
Archer:	Why would I pay 52?	阿彻：	为什么我要付 52 美元？
Lauren:	Because Metro added four new routes and has three new landing spots at **S.F.O.**[6]	劳伦：	因为麦德龙集团新加了四条航线，并在旧金山国际机场有三个新的降落点。
Lawyer:	Since when?	阿彻的律师：	什么时候的事？
Lauren:	Since this morning.	劳伦：	今早。

注释
2. anomaly [ə'nɒməlɪ] *n.* 怪人
3. Claudia Alves 克劳迪娅·艾维斯，巴西创作型女歌手
4. insult [ɪn'sʌlt] *v.* 耻辱，羞辱
5. footsie 原意指用碰脚调情的动作。引申为耍花样。
6. S.F.O.=San Francisco 旧金山，美国的重要海港

Archer:	You secured those landing spots in the last two days.	阿彻:	你这两天一直封锁这个消息。
Lauren:	I don't like to *stay idle*[4].	劳伦:	我不想吃闲饭。
Archer:	I'll pay for the 52 bucks per share.	阿彻:	我会每股付 52 元。
Lawyer:	Robin!	阿彻的律师:	罗宾!
Archer:	I have a lunch at the Snapfish tomorrow at 1:00. Can you meet me there with the paper just before?	阿彻:	我明天一点会在喀嚓鱼餐厅吃午饭，你能不能在那之前拿文件到那里见我？
Lauren:	Of course. I will see if I can juggle my schedule.	劳伦:	当然，看看能不能调整一下我的时间安排。
Archer:	Yes, try. Nice tangoing[1] with you.	阿彻:	是的，尽量。很高兴和你跳探戈。
Lauren:	Did you say "**tangling**[7]"?	劳伦:	你是不是说了"纠缠"？
Archer:	Tangoing, it's a dance.	阿彻:	我说的是"探戈"，探戈舞。
Lauren:	Yes, yes.	劳伦:	哦，这样啊。

📖 文化背景

1. tangoing 探戈

探戈是一种双人舞蹈，起源于非洲中西部的民间舞蹈。16 世纪末到 17 世纪初，随着黑奴贩卖进入美洲，探戈舞融合了拉美民间舞蹈风格，形成了舞姿优雅洒脱、舞步豪放健美的特色。探戈舞步最显著的特点是"蟹行猫步"。当舞步需要前进时，舞者却做横行移动；当舞步需要后退时，舞者却作横向向前斜移。同时，探戈舞者的舞步常常随音乐节拍的变化而时快时慢，探戈也因此被称为"瞬间停顿的舞蹈"。

🎙 常用表达

1. show up 来到；出现；露面；显露。既可作及物动词组，也可作不及物动词组。

show somebody up 跨越；令某人难堪；带某人上来

show oneself up 献丑

例：You have to show up.
　　你也需要展示自我。

例：Please show her up.
　　把她带上来。

注释 **7. tangle** ['tæŋgl] *n.* 纠缠

2. make up 编造、虚构；化妆；组成；整理

例：Her beauty can't make up for her stupidity.

她的美貌并不能弥补她的愚蠢。

3. make a point 立论；表明一种观点；得一分

例：Lily knew not just how to make a point but also how to get it out.

莉莉不仅懂得如何找到关键点，而且知道怎么把它传播出去。

4. stay idle 吃闲饭

例：Now, I stay idle at home.

现在我赋闲在家。

例：Many students are hard working, but a few love to stay idle.

大多数学生都努力学习，只有少部分喜欢无所事事。

12

The House of Cards

《纸牌屋》

入选理由：

美剧《纸牌屋》是一部起用了奥斯卡班底，明星云集、投资上亿美元的豪华巨制，导演大卫·芬奇和奥斯卡影帝凯文·史派西的期待值出现了高度重合。《纸牌屋》的大热，不仅在于剧集制作精良，还在于有着深厚的观众基础。在广大民众的视野里，权力运行是神秘的"少数人游戏"，只能从政治剧集里窥视冰山一角。

普通民众追捧《纸牌屋》，大约是从中找到了职场奋斗的共鸣。谁没有亲历或目睹过人际关系纷争呢？而真正的掌权者如奥巴马，喜欢该剧则有另外的理由。奥巴马表示，自己非常羡慕《纸牌屋》里政府运转的高效："多希望可以有如此残酷无情的效率。"2014 年的情人节，《纸牌屋》第二季登上了中国主流视频门户的显赫版面。

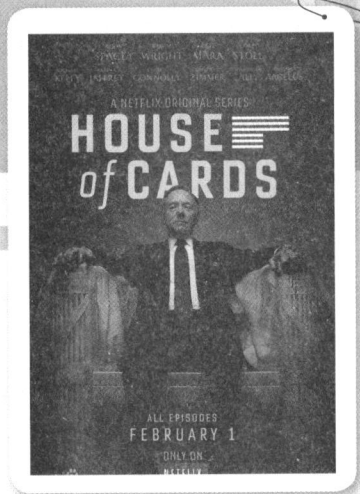

Section 1　剧情特点：

以往的好莱坞大片和美剧有个传统，即"精英治国"，白宫里是一群严格遵循法理和民主制度，为保障国民利益而勤勉工作的公仆。即使表现政治斗争题材的影视作品，也大致跳不出这个框架，所以好莱坞经常被视为宣扬"美式价值观"的机器。作为一部政治剧，通常情节晦涩，节奏缓慢。对于那些看惯了富有激情的剧集的人来说，如教育法案这种情节可能很难吸引他们。但是《纸牌屋》这部剧，却会越看越上瘾；不论是那些出色的场景还是凯文·史派西精湛的演技都足以吸引眼球。

《纸牌屋》主要描述一个冷血无情的美国国会议员及与他同样野心勃勃的妻子在华盛顿高层当中"运作权力"的故事，它以一个"反救猫咪"的设定为全剧开篇。由凯文·史派西出演的政客弗兰克在全剧第一场戏里，就以非常冷血的手段处死了一只重伤的小狗。这个片段也为全剧定下了基调：黑暗、冷血、权谋争逐的政客大战。这就是《纸牌屋》想要讲的故事，它是一出当代的权力游戏。

在全剧一开始，创作者就为主角设立了一个极具野心的复仇目标：干掉所有的障碍，爬上政治生涯的最高端，而随后的情节都围绕着这个复仇目标展开。某种程度上，《纸牌屋》的精彩来自弗兰克的个人魅力，他是一个被抽象之后的政客形象，冷血无情、工于心计，代表着普通民众对政客的种种假想，一切人都可成为好朋友并善加利用，而一切人又都是敌人随时可踩在脚下。他苦心经营又左右逢源，在纸牌屋里玩着一场高智商的政治游戏。

Section 2　对白特点：

《纸牌屋》是一部美国政治题材剧目，制作阵容堪称强大，本剧制片和剧本创作是曾经给多名华盛顿著名政客当过参谋并担任竞选文案执笔的鲍尔·威利蒙。《纸牌屋》被中国剧迷称为"美版《甄嬛传》"，它最有趣的地方在于各种内心独白。主人公弗兰克总会从剧情里跳出来，面对着摄影机喋喋不休说上一段。或是交代背景，或是对观众说说心里话，它打破了影片与观众的障碍，将两者紧紧联系在了一起。

《纸牌屋》里的台词非常经典，演员发音纯正地道。整部剧中，演员凯文·史派西总是直面镜头径直说出自己的计划——尽管许多电视剧都采用这一手法，但效果往往并不理想，可是凯文·史派西自然和纯熟的演技却让这一手法颇为奏效。该剧里有许多精彩的台词，其中包括一些谚语，例如，"Don't put the cart before the horse"，这句谚语很常用，字面直译为"别把车放到马前面"。马车当然都是马在前、车在后，把车放到马前面表示：doing things the wrong way round or with the wrong emphasis，意思是做事顺序错误或主次错误，形容做事不符合程序或本末倒置。字幕翻译为"为时过早"也算表达了意思。还有一些政治领域的精句也很典型，例如，"For those of us climbing to the top of the food chain, there can be no mercy. There is but one rule: hunt or be hunted"，"对于爬到食物链顶端的我们而言，绝不能心慈手软。我们的世界只有一条规则：弱肉强食"。第2季第1集的最后，无敌的安德伍德老师说出了政界生存真相，权力的法则：弱肉强食。这部被誉为白宫版《甄嬛传》的美剧尤其适合喜欢政治题材的学习者。

Section 3　角色分析：

弗兰西斯·安德伍德 (Francis Underwood)：凯文·史派西饰剧中男主角，美国国会众议院多数党督导，也就是大家口中的党鞭。他的任务是明确政党纪律，确保议员能按照党派意志行事。剧中的弗兰克正处于事业的巅峰期，从政多年经验丰富，刚刚带领全党成员帮助总统获取连任的胜利。而对他来说，更重要的事情是总统许诺给他的国务卿一职即将兑现，他从此将迎来自己政治生涯的新阶段。可惜天不遂人愿，总统临时变卦，将国务卿许给了别人。恼羞成怒之后，弗兰克决定开始自己的复仇计划。他在立法问题上多次与现任总统作对，并且命令自己一手扶持起来的年轻女记者佐伊利用新闻武器来帮助他。糟糕的是，当他与这名女记者陷入丑闻后，他自己的政治前途也蒙上了一层阴影。
弗兰克是个老奸巨猾的政客，第一季他从党鞭（国会多数党督导）爬到了副总统位置，第二季继续党同伐异，向权力巅峰冲刺。他的手段比较高明，看不出他在报复但却使总统身边的人一个个离开了总统或身败名裂，最后，才轮到总统本人。而他周围全是同类，为了获取权力，每个人都可以采取包括诽谤、贿赂、谋杀在内的一切手段。这里当然有为了增强戏剧效果的夸张，但做到了细节真实。

克莱尔·安德伍德 (Claire Underwood)：罗宾·怀特饰弗兰西斯之妻，负责运营一家非营利组织"净水计划"（Clean Initiative），旨在为不发达地区提供饮用水等援助。但是除了这种表述，克莱尔的事业似乎也是丈夫政治生涯中的重要筹码。克莱尔在商界和政界都吃得开，但她经营的"净水计划"却不怎么成功，为了获得资金支持，她违背了自己的一些原则，甚至不惜背叛丈夫。但她又总是默默支持丈夫。她很少笑，欺压员工和合作伙伴时也冷酷得不近人情，但她又会给乞丐钱，她是很矛盾的一个女人。克莱尔与丈夫因为流域法案吵翻而离家去亚当·嘉乐威那里时，歇斯底里地说她想变成举足轻重的人物。她想赢得人们的尊敬，所以她选择了弗兰克。究其原因，是因为弗兰克是权力的直接拥有者，而克莱尔则是权力的附庸。权势给她的净水计划带来了那么多好处，没有了权势也就没有了力量，没有了解决问题的能力。所以克莱尔爱上的是权势带来的安全感与无需畏惧艰难困苦的勇气。克莱尔曾经很坦诚地对自己的摄影家情人说，当面对众多追求者的时候，她深知只有弗兰克才能给她想要的，言下之意，当丈夫无法给与自己想要的东西时，婚姻便分崩离析。平心而论，这真的不怨她的丈夫。政治是一盘高深的棋盘，高手和普通玩家的区别就是在于能否透过迷雾看懂错综复杂的局势，懂得下一步如何落子。

佐伊·巴恩斯 (Zoe Barnes)：凯特·玛拉饰《华盛顿先驱报》记者，后因与老板产生矛盾而转职到"头条网（Slugline）"。在与安德伍德初次见面后迅速与其创建了互相利用的关系，二人发生性关系，同时安德伍德为她提供内幕新闻素材以打击政治对手。第二季中因试图调查彼得·罗素之死的内幕而被杀害。

佐伊·巴恩斯一出场时，一头长发乱糟糟地盘在头上，一条牛仔裤外加一件灰扑扑的短款夹克的打扮，怯生生地在报社办公大平台上左顾右盼。然而，一张照片，改变了佐伊·巴恩斯的人生。她是个工作狂，为了上头条什么都肯干，极富心机，她靠着安德伍德这棵大树出名，但背后却在调查船厂拆迁事件，使自己陷入极大的危险之中，讽刺的是她调查安德伍德并非是为了公理正义，而仅仅是为了搞到头条而已！按理说她跟安德伍德是有感情的（剧中她也说了一开始是欣赏他的），分手后落井下石的事情，一般观众难以接受，只能说她也很理性很冷酷。

🔊 Passage 1 📷

剧情介绍：

（第1季第1集）弗兰西斯·安德伍德做了一段漂亮的开场白，他是美国国会多数党领袖，一个老谋深算的职业政客，已经在国会待了很多年。他坚信新当选的美国总统及其幕僚背叛了他，于是发誓要将这一任总统赶下台。他在立法问题上多次与现任总统作对，并且命令自己一手扶持起来的年轻女记者利用新闻武器来帮助他。

Scene 1: In the evening, Frank and Claire were discussing about the dressing problem while Frank was declared to be appointed as Secretary of State during the way of driving home.

夜晚，弗兰克和克莱尔在坐车回家的途中讨论正式宣布其任命国务卿时的穿着问题。

Claire:	You need a haircut.		克莱尔：	你该理发了。
Frank:	You think?		弗兰克：	是吗？
Claire:	A little **trim**[1].What are you gonna wear?		克莱尔：	稍修剪一下。你准备穿什么？
Frank:	You mean for the meeting?		弗兰克：	开会的时候？
Claire:	For the announcement.		克莱尔：	正式宣布的时候。
Frank:	I'm wearing my navy blue, the one with the **pinstripes**[2].		弗兰克：	我准备穿海军蓝，带细条纹的那套。
Claire:	Good. You look handsome in that suit.		克莱尔：	很好，那套西服很衬你。
Frank:	I don't know if they will announce it before your board meeting.		弗兰克：	他们会不会在你的董事会前宣布还很难说。
Claire:	Well, as long as I can say the **donation**[3] is coming.		克莱尔：	只要这笔捐款保证能拿到就行。
Frank:	As soon as it's official, Sancorp will write you the check.		弗兰克：	一正式宣布，桑科公司就会给你支票。
Claire:	This is going to be a big year for us.		克莱尔：	今年对我们将会是重要的一年。

Scene 2: Mr. Hammerschmidt from the *Washington Herald* asked Lucas about the news information. News reporter Zoe ran into Mr. Hammerschmidt at Lucas's office. She said hello to him simply and then told Lucas she wanted to move to online post.

《华盛顿先驱报》报社里的汉默施密特先生询问卢卡斯相关新闻信息，新闻记者佐伊去找卢卡斯，碰巧遇到出来的汉默施密特先生，简单的打声招呼后，佐伊与卢卡斯谈论自己想做网络报道的想法。

(Ham: Hammerschmidt　　汉默：汉默施密特)

Ham:	Community of what?		汉默：	哪一个委员会？
Lucas:	I would say **immigration**[4], banking or education, but... None of my regular sources can confirm that. Because...		卢卡斯：	我猜是移民、银行或者教育。但是……但我常规的联络人都无法确认。因为……
Ham:	They don't know, or because they're not talking?		汉默：	他们是不知道，还是不愿说？

注释
1. trim [trɪm] *n.* 整理，修剪
2. pinstripe ['pɪnstraɪp] *n.* 细条纹，细条纹的布料
3. donation [dəʊ'neɪʃən] *n.* 捐款，捐赠
4. immigration [ˌɪmɪ'ɡreɪʃən] *n.* 移民，移民入境

Lucas:	Because they don't know.	卢卡斯：	他们不知道。
Ham:	Keep at it; get me something.	汉默：	继续查，挖点东西出来。
Zoe:	Sorry, I'm so sorry Mr. Hammerschmidt. Zoe... Barnes.	佐伊：	对不起，真抱歉，汉默施密特先生。我是佐伊·巴恩斯。
Ham:	Right.	汉默：	嗯。
Zoe:	Did it take him a year to remember your name?	佐伊：	他当年也过了一年才记住你是谁吗？
Lucas:	Longer.	卢卡斯：	不止。
Zoe:	Good morning, Lucas.	佐伊：	早上好，卢卡斯。
Lucas:	What can I do for you, Zoe?	卢卡斯：	有什么事吗，佐伊？
Zoe:	I am *sick of*[1] the Fairfax county **council**[5].	佐伊：	我受不了费尔法克斯的郡议会了。
Lucas:	You tell me everyday.	卢卡斯：	你每天都这么说。
Zoe:	Move me online. My own blog. First person, subjective, 500 words.	佐伊：	让我做网络报道。让我开博客，第一人称，主观视角，五百字篇幅。
Lucas:	Not gonna happen.	卢卡斯：	没门。
Zoe:	I'll go underground. **Backrooms**[6], the urinals! I'll *win over*[2] staff members on the Hill. They need a place to vent.	佐伊：	我去挖掘秘密，幕后消息。甚至去翻夜壶，去争取国会的人！他们也需要发泄。
Lucas:	A **gossip**[7] column?	卢卡斯：	八卦专栏？
Zoe:	No. We'll lift the **veil**[8].	佐伊：	不，是事实真相。
Lucas:	What's really going on. This is the *Washington Herald*[1], Zoe. It's not...TMZ[2].	卢卡斯：	现在到底怎么回事。这里是《华盛顿先驱报》，佐伊。不是……名人消息网。
Zoe:	Do you know how many people who watch TMZ?	佐伊：	你知道有多少人浏览名人消息网吗？
Lucas:	I couldn't care less.	卢卡斯：	我一点也不关心。
Zoe:	Which is why print journalism is dying.	佐伊：	所以报刊新闻业在衰落。
Lucas:	Then it will die with **dignity**[9]. At least with this paper.	卢卡斯：	那也不失体面，至少这份报纸是如此。
Zoe:	You are stuck in the 20th century, Lucas, you lack imagination.	佐伊：	你还活在 20 世纪吧，卢卡斯，缺乏想象力。
Lucas:	Maybe so, but right now I don't need imagination. I need copy. Your nights and weekends are	卢卡斯：	也许吧，但我现在不需要想象力。我需要报道。你自己的时间随意

yours, I applaud whatever you want to do, as long as it's not on my time.

Zoe: You're telling me to go back to work?

Lucas: I am.

Zoe: What you're really telling me is to fuck off.

Lucas: I'm telling you both.

支配，你想做什么我都没意见，但不能占用工作时间。

佐伊：你是让我去干活吗？

卢卡斯：没错。

佐伊：但你实际上是叫我滚蛋。

卢卡斯：两者都有。

Scene 3: Frank planned to brief the President about his views upon the Middle East policy, while he was told by Linda that the President-elect wouldn't come and the person selected as the Secretary of State was changed.

弗兰克准备向总统汇报自己关于中东政策的一些观点，却被琳达告知总统来不了，国务卿的人选情况有变。

Frank: The President-elect running late?

Linda: No, he couldn't make it. I'll brief him, though.

Frank: Okay. This is the memo, I've drafted on our Middle East policy we've been developing. Now, I want to borrow from Reagan. I'd like to coin the phrase "Trickle-down **diplomacy**[10]". That way...

Linda: Frank. I'm gonna stop you there. We are not **nominating**[11] you for the Secretary of State. I know, he made you a promise, but circumstances have changed.

Frank: The nature of promises, Linda, is that they remain immune to changing **circumstances**[12].

Linda: Garrett has thought long and hard about this. And he's decided we need you to stay in Congress.

弗兰克：当选的总统迟到了吗？

琳达：不，他来不了，我会跟他汇报的。

弗兰克：好的。这是我起草的备忘录，关于我们商讨的中东政策，我想借用里根的说法。造个新词，叫"滴入式外交"。这样……

琳达：弗兰克，我得打断你，我们不打算提名你为国务卿。我知道他向你承诺过，但现在情况有变。

弗兰克：所谓承诺，琳达，就是不论情况如何变化也不受影响。

琳达：加勒特已经深思熟虑过了，他认为我们需要你留在国会。

注释

5. council ['kaʊnsɪl] *n.* 参议会，理事会

6. backroom ['bækruːm] *n.* 密室

7. gossip ['gɒsɪp] *n.* 八卦，闲话

8. veil [veɪl] *n.* 面纱，掩饰物

9. dignity ['dɪgnɪtɪ] *n.* 尊严，高贵

10. diplomacy [dɪ'pləʊməsɪ] *n.* 外交

11. nominating [nɒmɪ'neɪʃən] *n.* 任命，提名

12. circumstance ['sɜːkəmstəns] *n.* 情况，环境

Frank: When was this decision made? And why wasn't I part of a conversation?

Linda: I'm sorry, Frank, if it been *up to*[3] me, I wouldn't have waited this long to tell you.

Frank: So you knew, you were going to do this.

Linda: It has been an **evolving**[13] discussion.

Frank: It's a **chicken-shit**[14] move.

Linda: Frank...

Frank: I was **vetted**[15]. Was that a **ruse**[16]?

Linda: No.

Frank: Let's be absolutely clear; you wouldn't have won without me.

Linda: You're right, but now we have to lead. And that means making tough choices. As you know, education is a top priority for us. A complete federal **overhaul**[17]. But it's not just the education, Frank, Congress has split. We need you there, more than we need you in the State Department.

Frank: I got you hired, Linda.

Linda: I know.

Frank: Donations, **endorsements**[18]. I wrote the campaign's entire foreign policy platform. I bring years of Foreign Affairs Committee...

Linda: Frank. Please.

Frank: I want to speak to Walker personally.

Linda: The decision is made. We need you, Frank. Will you stand beside us or not?

Frank: Of course, if that's what the President wants.

Linda: I'm very glad to hear that.

Frank: I'm curious. If not me then who?

Linda: Michael Kern.

Frank: Michael Kern? Well... that is an excellent choice.

弗兰克： 这是什么时候的决定？为什么我没参与商讨？

琳达： 我很抱歉，弗兰克，如果由我决定，我也不会等到现在才告诉你。

弗兰克： 那你早就知道要这么做？

琳达： 我们的确讨论了很久。

弗兰克： 这就是懦夫的做法。

琳达： 弗兰克……

弗兰克： 我都做过审查了，那都是骗我吗？

琳达： 不。

弗兰克： 我们打开天窗说亮话，没有我，你们赢不了。

琳达： 你说的没错，但我们现在执政了，所以得做出艰难的决定。你知道，教育是我们的重中之重，要进行彻底的改革，但不仅仅是教育，弗兰克，国会已经分裂了。我们更需要你待在国会，而不是国务。

弗兰克： 是我找你来的，琳达。

琳达： 我知道。

弗兰克： 捐款、博取公开支持，我为竞选写了整套外交纲领。我把外事委员会多年来……

琳达： 弗兰克，请别这样。

弗兰克： 我要单独和沃克谈。

琳达： 已经决定了，我们需要你，弗兰克。你会支持我们吗？

弗兰克： 当然了，如果这是总统所愿。

琳达： 很高兴听到这话。

弗兰克： 我很好奇，你们选了谁？

琳达： 迈克尔·科恩。

弗兰克： 迈克尔·科恩？嗯，真是绝妙的选择。

注释

10. **diplomacy** [dɪ'pləʊməsɪ] *n.* 外交

11. **nominating** [nɒmɪ'neɪʃən] *n.* 任命，提名

12. **circumstance** ['sɜːkəmstəns] *n.* 情况，环境

13. **evolving** [ɪ'vɒlvɪŋ] *adj.* 展开的，进化的

14. **chicken-shit** ['tʃɪkɪn 'ʃɪt] *adj.* 懦夫的

15. **vet** ['vet] *v.* 审查

16. **ruse** ['ruːz] *n.* 诡计

17. **overhaul** [.əʊvə'hɔːl] *n.* 检查，彻底检修

18. **endorsement** [[ɪn'dɔːsmənt] *n.* 担保，认可

文化背景

1. Washington Herald《华盛顿先驱报》

《华盛顿先驱报》为美国 20 世纪 30 年代的报社，后来被《华盛顿邮报》（Washington Post）兼并。

2. TMZ 美国名人消息网

TMZ 是 "Thirty Mile Zone" 英文的第一字母缩写，这区域主要是洛杉矶地区，汇集有很多名人，一些娱乐休闲网站经常从这里获取素材，专门搜集名人八卦和花边。美国名人消息网是一个走在最前沿的八卦网站，主要提供最新娱乐资讯、八卦、丑闻等内容。

常用表达

1. be sick of 讨厌，厌恶

例：I am sure you must be sick of all our noise.

我相信我们吵吵闹闹肯定会使您心烦。

2. win over 胜诉，赢得……的支持

例：He has won over a significant number of the left-wing deputies.

他争取到了相当数量的左翼代表的支持。

3. up to 由……决定

例：If it's up to me, I must have chosen you as the head.

如果这件事由我定的话，我一定选你为领导了。

Passage 2

剧情介绍：

（第 1 季第 3 集）发生新的事故，将会影响弗兰西斯新的教育法案，弗兰西斯只得亲自远行去和解。佐伊所代表的先锋报收到了采访，弗兰克也在所在的教堂进行发言，以抵消对其就位不利的因素。佐伊因对其上司汤姆表示不满被责令一个月不允许上电视报道。

Scene 1: Mrs. Tilden who owned the paper came to the newspaper office. She asked Tom to find Zoe and enquired about one report.

报社的东家蒂尔顿太太来到报社，让汤姆叫来佐伊，询问一则报道的相关情况。

Zoe:	You wanted to talk to me?	佐伊：	你找我吗?
Tom:	Come on in, Zoe. This is Mrs. Tilden, owner of…	汤姆：	进来，佐伊，这位是蒂尔顿太太，报社的……
Mrs. Tilden:	She knows who I am.	蒂尔顿太太：	她知道我是谁。
Tom:	Mrs. Tilden liked your **profile**[1] on Catherine Durant.	汤姆：	蒂尔顿太太很喜欢你对凯瑟琳·杜兰特的特写。
Mrs. Tilden:	No, I didn't. I loved it. In depth, **uncompromising**[2]. Normally I don't read things before they go to print, but Cathy's a friend. Tell me how you knew she'd be nominated before she did?	蒂尔顿太太：	不，不是喜欢，是非常喜欢。有深度，非常坚定。通常我不会在报道付印前阅读，但凯茜是我的朋友。说说你是怎么提前知道她会获提名的?
Zoe:	You want my source?	佐伊：	你想知道我的消息来源?
Mrs. Tilden:	Tom says you won't tell him.	蒂尔顿太太：	汤姆说你不肯告诉他。
Zoe:	I haven't told anyone.	佐伊：	我谁也没告诉。
Mrs. Tilden:	Well, I own the paper.	蒂尔顿太太：	我是报社的东家。
Zoe:	And I'm very grateful to be working here.	佐伊：	能在这里工作我深感荣幸。
Mrs. Tilden:	So you're not going to tell me either.	蒂尔顿太太：	那你也不准备告诉我了。
Zoe:	Which do you want, my source or my **integrity**[3]?	佐伊：	您想要什么，我的联络人还是我的尊严?
Mrs. Tilden:	Tom, move Zoe's piece to the front page of Sunday's edition.	蒂尔顿太太：	汤姆，把佐伊的报道挪到周日的头版。

Tom:	Let me *think that over*[1].	**汤姆：**	我会考虑的。
Mrs. Tilden:	You think it over as much as you want. Then put it on the front page.	**蒂尔顿太太：**	随你怎么考虑，然后把它放在头版。

> **Scene 2:** Gillian came to Claire's office to discuss about the cooperation between them.
> 吉莉安来到克莱尔办公的地方，讨论两人之间的合作问题。

Gillian:	I've worked really hard to gain a foothold with World Well. Six years ago it was just me and a macbook.	**吉莉安：**	为了让"世界之井"站稳脚跟，我付出了很多努力。六年前，只有我自己和一台笔记本。
Claire:	I understand.	**克莱尔：**	我明白。
Gillian:	And I had to **juggle**[4] two temp jobs just to pay the rent.	**吉莉安：**	打了两份临时工才付得起房租。
Claire:	It's your baby. You don't want to let it go.	**克莱尔：**	那是你的孩子，你不想放手。
Gillian:	Well, I just…	**吉莉安：**	我只是……
Claire:	And you wouldn't have to, Gillian. All I want is for you to grow what you've already built.	**克莱尔：**	你也不必放手，吉莉安，我只希望你把亲手建立的事业发展壮大。
Gillian:	I heard you fired half your staff.	**吉莉安：**	我听说你裁掉了一半员工。
Claire:	Yes, I did.	**克莱尔：**	是的。
Gillian:	That worries me.	**吉莉安：**	这让我很担心。
Claire:	I let them go to *make room*[2] for you.	**克莱尔：**	我让他们走是为给你腾位置。
Gillian:	I'm just not sure we're the right match.	**吉莉安：**	我只是不确定我们是否合适。
Claire:	To be honest, I'm a little uncomfortable working with someone who's **commissioning**[5] famous **photographers**[6],when I can't even buy my volunteers bus fair to the office.	**克莱尔：**	说实话，我不太愿意跟一个雇得起著名摄影师的人共事，我都付不起我志愿者的公车票。
Gillian:	Do you know who Nicky Hemler is?	**吉莉安：**	你认识妮姬·海姆勒吗?
Claire:	No.	**克莱尔：**	不认识。

注释
1. **profile** ['prəʊfaɪl] *n.* 特写，轮廓
2. **uncompromising** [ʌn'kɒmprəmaɪzɪŋ] *adj.* 不妥协的
3. **integrity** [ɪn'tegrɪtɪ] *n.* 正直，诚实
4. **juggle** ['dʒʌgl] *v.* 尽力同时应付，尽量兼顾
5. **commission** [kə'mɪʃən] *v.* 使服役
6. **photographer** [fə'tɒgrəfə] *n.* 摄影师

Gillian:	Nicky owns one of the biggest **galleries**[7] in Chelsea. She desperately wanted to represent Adam Galloway. I delivered on Adam, and *in return*[3], she contributes almost 40 grand a year to <u>CWI</u>[1]. That money goes to impact studies, lobbying efforts, research. World Well could benefit from that sort of money, Claire, and we can benefit from your **expertise**[8].	吉莉安：	妮姬拥有切尔西最大的画廊。她十分想做亚当·嘉乐威的代理人，我帮她牵了线，作为回报，她每年给"净水计划"捐赠近4万美元，这些钱用于影响研究、游说工作和调查。这种钱对"世界之井"益处良多，克莱尔。而你的专长对我们益处良多。
Claire:	Can I think about it?	克莱尔：	我能想想吗？
Gillian:	Of course. We don't have to jump into anything.	吉莉安：	当然。不必操之过急。

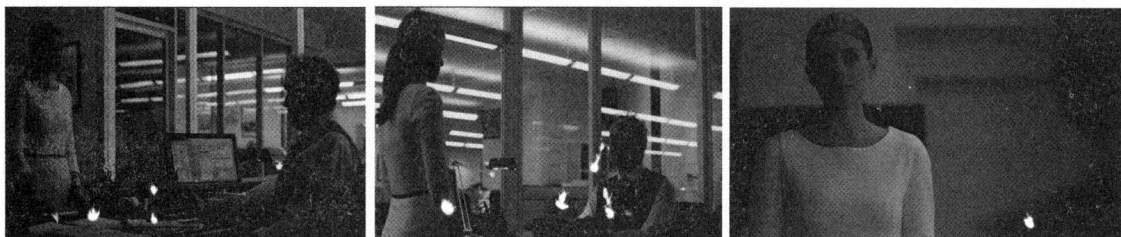

Scene 3: Tom was quite angry about Zoe's getting on the national television, so he asked her to have a talk at his office.

汤姆对于佐伊上国家电视台的行为感到很气愤，因此，将她叫到办公室训话。

Tom:	Your job is to report the news, not be the news.	汤姆：	你的工作是报道新闻，不是成为新闻。
Zoe:	I was promoting the paper.	佐伊：	我在推销我们的报纸。
Tom:	You were promoting Zoe Barnes.	汤姆：	你在推销佐伊·巴恩斯。
Zoe:	Is this about how I said we called you the **hammer**[9]? Because if that upset you, I apologize.	佐伊：	是因为我说我们叫你锤子吗？如果你是气这个，我道歉。
Tom:	you're missing the point. I don't want you talking about anything that happens here, not nicknames, not how **progressive**[10] we are, not whether we are adapting to the Internet. Any thoughts you have about this paper, you keep them to yourself, or you bring them to me. You don't get on national television and sp...	汤姆：	这不是重点，我不希望你讲这里的任何事情，别提昵称，别提我们有多进步，也别提我们是否适应网络时代。你有任何关于这份报纸的想法，要么藏在心里，要么告诉我。你不能上国家电视台，然后……
Zoe:	I'm sorry. I wasn't trying to...	佐伊：	抱歉，我没想要……

Tom: Don't **interrupt**[11] when I'm talking.

Zoe: You can speak to me like an adult, Tom. You don't have to lecture me like a little girl.

Tom: You haven't earned the right to be treated as an adult. You think a few front-page stories and some face time on TV makes you the next Judy Miller? You've got a long way to go. Don't be so **arrogant**[12].

Zoe: Okay, so you think when a woman asks to be treated with respect, that's arrogance?

Tom: Are you accusing me of sexism?

Zoe: Just making an **observation**[13].

Tom: No TV for a month.

Zoe: What?

Tom: You heard me. No interviews.

Zoe: That's completely unfair.

Tom: You want to make it no TV **indefinitely**[14]? We're done. You can go now.

汤姆: 我说话的时候别插嘴。

佐伊: 你可以像对大人那样跟我说话,汤姆。不用把我当成小女孩一样教训。

汤姆: 你还不配被当做大人,你以为几篇头版报道,在电视上露几次脸,你就是下一位朱迪·米勒了吗?你还有很长的路要走,别这么傲慢。

佐伊: 你认为一个女人要求受到尊重,是傲慢吗?

汤姆: 你是说我歧视女性吗?

佐伊: 只是说出我看到的而已。

汤姆: 一个月不准上电视。

佐伊: 什么?

汤姆: 你没听错。不准采访。

佐伊: 这不公平。

汤姆: 你想永远上不了电视吗?好了,你可以走了。

文化背景

1. CWI 净水计划

非政府组织(NGO)的一项慈善事业。

常用表达

1. think over 仔细考虑,重新考虑

例: Think over the matter and then make a decision. 这件事情斟酌斟酌再定。

2. make room 退让,腾出地方

例: Please step aside a little to make room for me. 请稍站过去一点,让我插个脚。

3. in return 作为报答

例: What did you give him in return? 你给他什么作为报答呢?

注释 **7. galleries** ['gæləriz] *pl.n.* 画廊

8. expertise [.ekspə'ti:z] *n.* 专业技术,专长

9. hammer ['hæmə] *n.* 锤子

10. progressive [prə'gresiv] *adj.* 前进的,进步的

11. interrupt [intə'rʌpt] *v.* 打断,插嘴

12. arrogant ['ærəgənt] *adj.* 傲慢的,自大的

13. observation [.əbzə'veiʃən] *n.* 观察

14. indefinitely [in'definitli] *adv.* 不确定地

🔊 Passage 3 🎥

剧情介绍：

（第1季第4集）汤姆的言辞没有通过公司老板玛格丽特那关，佐伊依然被留了下来，雷米找到克莱尔称桑科工业恢复捐款即将与其重新合作，但弗兰克并不赞成这样危险的做法。弗兰克勒令罗素来号召12个人参加选举，狠狠地"回报"了一下议员大卫。弗兰克告诉佐伊仍需要其辅助，佐伊自知不会接受白宫的工作，与上司发生争执被炒鱿鱼。另一方面弗兰克透露给鲍勃消息，挑起两派争端。

Scene 1: Tom asked Zoe to his office and told her that she was going to be the new White House correspondent.

汤姆将佐伊叫到办公室，告诉佐伊她将成为新一任驻白宫记者。

🔊 **Tom:** I know there's been some **tension**[1], and I'm probably more to **blame**[2] than you are. But I'd like to put that behind us. Zoe, you're going to be our new White House[1] **correspondent**[3].

Zoe: What about Janine?

Tom: I promoted her to Midwest Bureau chief.

Zoe: She's okay with that? She wants to *give up*[1] the White House?

Tom: It's the decision I've made.

Zoe: It's just that Janine has so much experience.

Tom: I thought you'd be more excited about this.

Zoe: I'm sorry. I... I just thought you brought me in here to... I don't know.

Tom: To fire you.

Zoe: Maybe.

Tom: Water under the bridge. We're starting over. So are you ready to take this on?

Zoe: Can I think about it?

Tom: People usually don't have to think about it when they're offered the White House, Zoe.

汤姆： 我知道最近我们有些紧张，而且我应该负主要责任，但过去的事就让它过去吧。佐伊，你将成为我们新一任驻白宫记者。

佐伊： 那简宁呢？

汤姆： 升任中西部总编辑。

佐伊： 她同意了吗？她舍得放弃白宫的工作？

汤姆： 这是我的决定。

佐伊： 可简宁毕竟经验丰富。

汤姆： 我还以为你会很兴奋呢。

佐伊： 抱歉，我还以为你叫我进来是要……我不知道。

汤姆： 解雇你。

佐伊： 也许吧。

汤姆： 都过去了，我们要重新开始。那么，你准备好了吗？

佐伊： 我能考虑一下吗？

汤姆： 有一份白宫的工作摆在面前，人们一般不用考虑的，佐伊。

Zoe: Just a day or two.

Tom: Janine is booked for a flight to Chicago on Friday.

Zoe: I'll let you know before then. I just need to... Thank you. Thank you, Tom.

佐伊： 只要一两天就好。

汤姆： 简宁将乘周五的航班飞往芝加哥。

佐伊： 我会在那之前回复你。我只是要…… 谢谢你，汤姆。

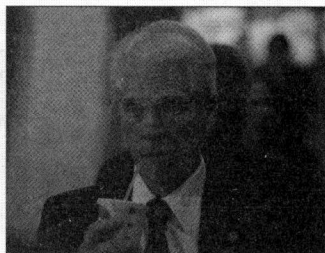

Scene 2: Frank was having dinner with David. Frank intended to make use of David with the post of Speaker.

弗兰克与大卫在一起就餐，弗兰克企图用议长的职位来利用大卫。

Frank: David. You mind if I join you?

David: Please. A salad, huh?

Frank: Yes. I'm trying to take better care of myself.

David: Good man. Diet?

Frank: Diet, exercise, everything. You ought to take better care of yourself too.

David: Well, they should stop serving such good pizza.

Frank: Oh, I'm not talking about the food. I'm talking about Birch. You are never going to be speaker unless you do something about it.

David: I'm very satisfied where I am.

Frank: Oh, come on.

David: For the time being², yeah.

Frank: Time being never. The only way you become Speaker is if Birch loses his **district**⁴ or retires, neither of which is going to happen before you and I have **dentures**⁵.

David: I'm not happy where this conversation is going, Frank.

弗兰克： 大卫，不介意我坐这儿吧。

大卫： 请坐，就吃沙拉啊。

弗兰克： 是啊，我想好好照顾自己。

大卫： 不错嘛，节食吗？

弗兰克： 节食，锻炼，各种方法，你也该 照顾好自己。

大卫： 他们这儿的披萨实在太美味了。

弗兰克： 我不是指饮食，我是指博奇。你 要想当上议长，就必须得有所行 动。

大卫： 我对自己的位置很满意。

弗兰克： 拜托。

大卫： 就目前来说，确实满意。

弗兰克： 一时就是永远，你想成为议长， 只有可能是博奇落选或退休，在 你我老到要装假牙之前，这两种 情况都不会发生。

大卫： 我不喜欢你这番话的势头，弗兰 克。

注释
1. **tension** ['tenʃən] *n.* 紧张
2. **blame** [bleɪm] *v.* 责备，谴责
3. **correspondent** [ˌkɒrɪsˈpɒndənt] *n.* 通讯记者，通信者
4. **district** ['dɪstrɪkt] *n.* 管区，（美国各州的）众议院选区
5. **dentures** ['dentʃəz] *n.* 假牙

Frank: If you want it, and I know you do, there's a way.

David: Okay. Right. I can't...

Frank: All you need is a simple majority... 218 votes. We're going to get at least 205 out of the G.O.P., and after that, all you need is 13 **Democrats**[6]. You and I make two.

David: Are you *out of your mind*[3]?

Frank: Just consider it for a moment.

David: You want to collude with the Republicans[2]?

Frank: I don't want to, but I would if you become Speaker in the process.

David: Never been done before.

Frank: There's a first time for everything.

David: This is **ridiculous**[7].

Frank: The Republicans would love a chance to knock Bob down a peg or two.

David: And you want to help them.

Frank: I want to help us. Bob will not play ball with the White House. Now, you're a **reasonable**[8] man, David, and he's not.

David: You know what I am? I'm a **discreet**[9] man. You're lucky for that. I'm not going to mention this to Bob, but if you ever bring it up again, I won't have a choice.

弗兰克：你想做议长，我知道你想，我有个办法。

大卫：好了，我不能……

弗兰克：票数过半就可以……也就是218票。我们在共和党能得到205票，这样，再有民主党13票就行。你我手里就有两票。

大卫：你疯了吗?

弗兰克：稍稍考虑一下吧?

大卫：你想和共和党串通?

弗兰克：我不想，但如果能让你当上议长，我会的。

大卫：这种事没有先例。

弗兰克：凡事都有第一次。

大卫：这太荒谬了。

弗兰克：共和党会很乐意杀杀鲍勃的威风。

大卫：而你想帮他们。

弗兰克：我想帮我们，鲍勃不会和白宫合作。你是个通情达理的人，大卫，他不是。

大卫：你知道我是什么人吗? 我是个谨慎的人，所以算你走运，我不会跟鲍勃说今天的事，你要是再提，我就没办法了。

Scene 3: Gillian came to Claire's office to discuss the budget of the South Sudan project.
吉莉安来到克莱尔的办公室跟她讨论南苏丹项目的预算问题。

Gillian: Claire, I'd like to put an order for the water **filters**[10] and the **well-digging**[11] equipment for the South Sudan project. Can we talk about the **budget**[12]?

Claire: How much?

Gillian: 200,000.

Claire: For one project?

Gillian: I know it's a lot, but it'll be our **flagship**[13] project in Africa, and we would be the first organization there to work on this scale.

吉莉安：克莱尔，我想为南苏丹项目的滤水器和钻井机械下订单，我们能讨论一下预算问题吗?

克莱尔：需要多少?

吉莉安：20万。

克莱尔：一个项目就要这么多?

吉莉安：我知道很多，但这是我们在非洲的旗舰项目，我们也是那里首家有如此规模的机构。

Claire:	I'd like to go over the **specifics**[14] first.	克莱尔：	我想先核对一下详情。
Gillian:	I have the budget right here.	吉莉安：	我已经做好了预算表。
Claire:	Let me just grab my messages, and then I'll come in to you.	克莱尔：	我先查一下留言，就来找你。
Gillian:	Okay. I'll be in my office.	吉莉安：	好，我在办公室等你。

文化背景

1. White House 白宫

白宫是美国总统的官邸和办公室。白宫是一幢白色的新古典风格砂岩建筑物，位于华盛顿哥伦比亚特区西北宾夕法尼亚大道 1600 号。因为白宫是美国总统的居住和办公的地点，"白宫"一词常代指美国政府，譬如"白宫宣布，英国首相访问美国"。

常用表达

1. give up 放弃，舍弃

例：She was not going to give up her hard-won freedom so easily.

她不会这么轻易地放弃得来不易的自由。

2. for the time being 暂且，暂时地

例：Don't breathe a word about this for the time being.

这事暂时不要嚷嚷出去。

3. out of one's mind 精神不正常，疯了

例：How can you beat this boy? You must be out of your mind.

你怎么能打这个小男孩？你一定是疯了。

注
释

6. **Democrats** ['deməkræts] n. 民主党人	11. **well-digging** ['wel'dɪgɪŋ] n. 钻井
7. **ridiculous** [rɪ'dɪkjuːləs] adj. 可笑的，荒谬的	12. **budget** ['bʌdʒɪt] n. 预算
8. **reasonable** ['riːznəbl] adj. 通情达理的，讲道理的	13. **flagship** ['flægʃɪp] n. 旗舰
9. **discreet** [dɪs'kriːt] adj. 谨慎的，小心的	14. **specifics** [spə'sɪfɪks] n. 细节，详情
10. **filters** ['fɪltəs] n. 过滤器	

13

Silk
《皇家律师》

入选理由：

《皇家律师》由皮特·莫法特担任制作人，英国广播公司剧情剧制作中心出品，于 2011 年播出，是一部关于生命、爱情及站在刑事法律最前线的、面对疑难案件的律师的故事。剧本由凭借迷你剧《司法正义》获得英国奥斯卡（BAFTA）最佳编剧的皮特·莫法特执笔。这部剧视角宏大，大胆且快节奏地带领观众洞察了刑事律师的世界，展现了这些法律工作者在工作和生活中的不同侧面。

Section 1　剧情特点：

剧情围绕着伦敦的几位大律师展开，两位主角——玛莎·科斯特洛和克莱夫·瑞德中只能有一位成为皇家律师（Queen's Counsel）。本剧向观众展现了律师界极端的压力、艰难的抉择、伦理的两难困境、个人与职业的重叠、原则的取舍等。但这样的环境依然折射了人性中美好温存的一面。

Section 2　对白特点：

《皇家律师》极具欣赏性，发音纯正，是英语学习者学习英音的好材料。其中有些法律术语，开阔了英语学习者的视野，扩充了词汇。

Section 3　角色分析：

玛莎·科斯特洛 (Martha Costello)：一个三十多岁、单身、富于激情的辩护律师，她的信念、她的偏见、她的良知及她的信仰的极限在刑事司法系统中被一系列的课程所检验。她让律师界充满了人情味。

克莱夫·瑞德 (Clive Reader)：他很风趣，有天赋但很危险。他和玛莎·科斯特洛同龄，同时都是律师，同时都申请了皇家律师资格。他和玛莎·科斯特洛是对手，也是曾经的情人。他是个花花公子，后来被玛莎·科斯特洛的正义和人情味感染，走上了"正道"。

比利·拉姆 (Billy Lamb)：议院的高级秘书。他是一名多面手，浑身上下都充斥着矛盾，他的生活及律师们的事业都在他的掌控之中。他很欣赏玛莎·科斯特洛，喜欢她的直白、单纯，尽管他暗暗相信她并没有机会成为一名皇室法律顾问。

尼克·斯雷德 (Nick Slade)：玛莎·科斯特洛手下的实习律师，他在工作中战战兢兢，但很善良。

🔊 Passage 1 🎥

剧情介绍：

（选自第 2 季第 4 集）玛莎·科斯特洛和委托人默西迪斯·科尔多瓦在一起贩毒案件中败诉，默西迪斯·科尔多瓦被判 14 年的有期徒刑，而克莱夫·瑞德的委托人即这个案件的共同被告获得较轻的判刑。玛莎·科斯特洛对此很自责，因为她觉得这个案件的判决冤枉了默西迪斯·科尔多瓦。在一次聚会上，玛莎·科斯特洛无意中见到在法庭上道貌岸然的克莱夫·瑞德竟然在楼梯间偷偷地吸毒……

Scene: Martha Costello and her student Nick Slade go to the prison where Martha Costello's client Gary Rush and Mercedes Cordoba are imprisoned.

玛莎·科斯特洛和她的学生尼克·斯雷德去了玛莎·科斯特洛的客户加里·拉什和默西迪斯·科尔多瓦所在的监狱里。

🔊 **Prison:** Who do you want first?

Martha: Can I do Gary Rush for two minutes and then Mercedes Cordoba?

Gary: I don't think you know what you're doing.

狱警：你想先见谁？

玛莎：先见加里·拉什，只需两分钟，然后是默西迪斯·科尔多瓦。

加里：我想你不知道你自己在做什么？

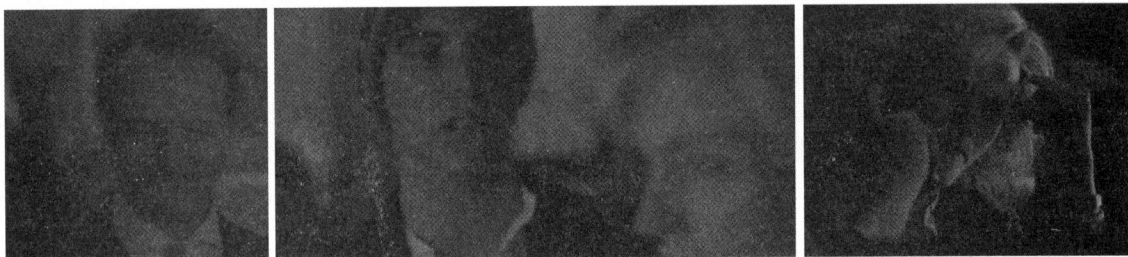

Martha:	I'm going to **get you off**[1].	玛莎： 我要把你弄出去。
Martha:	Mercedes Cordoba?	玛莎： 默西迪斯·科尔多瓦呢？
Prison:	Van's gone.	狱警： 车已经开走了。
Martha:	What? I told you I was going to be two minutes!	玛莎： 什么？我跟你说过只要等两分钟!
Prison:	There's no point shouting about it. She's gone. You've got 14 years to talk to her.	狱警： 没必要为了这个大喊大叫，她走了，你有 14 年可以和她说话。
Martha:	(to Nick Slade) Get the number for the prison and I'll call them.	玛莎： （对尼克·斯雷德说）找到监狱的号码，我要给他们打电话。

(Martha Costello and Nick Slade walk to a party.)

（玛莎·科斯特洛和尼克·斯雷德走向一个聚会。）

Martha:	**Touting**[2] party.	玛莎： 拉票派对。
Nick:	Touting?	尼克： 拉票?
Martha:	Billy invites lots of judges and all the <u>solicitors</u>[3] we're supposed to suck up to and we do lots of sucking up.	玛莎： 比利邀请了很多我们应该讨好的法官和律师，给了我们拍马屁的机会。
Nick:	Touting or tarting party?	尼克： 拉票派对还是拉风派对？
Martha:	First impressions, Nick. Make them like you.	玛莎： 注意第一印象，尼克。让他们喜欢你。

(Martha Costello goes to a room and has a call.)

（玛莎·科斯特洛走向一房间打电话。）

Martha:	Is there a **VO**[4] for a legal visit?	玛莎： 有合法探视的口头请求吗？
Martha:	Mercedes Cordoba.	玛莎： 默西迪斯·科尔多瓦。
Martha:	Why not? You should have received a request for one.	玛莎： 为什么没有？你们应该接到一个啊。
Martha:	She's pregnant, she's vulnerable and she's about to start a 14-year sentence tonight.	玛莎： 她怀孕了，很脆弱，而且今晚要开始 14 年的监禁。
Martha:	I need to see her.	玛莎： 我必须见见她。
Martha:	Hello?	玛莎： 喂？
Martha:	Hello?	玛莎： 喂？
Billy:	Excuse me.	比利： 抱歉，让一下。

Billy:	(to Martha Costello) Ah, Brian Frogett, Senior Partner from Cant Frogett rang to remind us he's too important to come to this kind of do, but he says he's making an exception because he heard about your performance today and he'd like to meet you.	比利：	（对玛莎·科斯特洛）哈，是布赖恩·弗劳盖特，勘特弗劳盖特律所高级合伙人提醒我们，以他的身份，他本不屑于这么做，但是他想破例，因为他听说了你今天在庭上的表现，想要见见你。
(Martha Costello walks to Brian Frogett.)			（玛莎·科斯特洛走向布赖恩·弗劳盖特。）
Brian:	What kind of question was that?	布赖恩：	那算什么问题？
Martha:	Sorry?	玛莎：	什么？
Brian:	Oh, what? You've forgotten? About the worst question asked of anyone in the witness **box**[5] ever? I know, let's see if the **burglar**[6] yawned, shall we? Tell me, did he yawn at all after beating the crap out of you?	布赖恩：	哦，什么？你已经忘了？关于证人席上问的最白痴的问题？我知道了，让我们看看入室行窃犯是不是打呵欠了，怎样？告诉我，他在把你暴打一顿之后到底打呵欠没有？
Martha:	You don't understand.	玛莎：	你不明白。
Brian:	**Aggravated**[7] doesn't **cover**[8] it, does it? We're going to have to invent a new term for this. How about **psychopath**[9] burglary? Will that do it?	布赖恩：	这个并不属于加重情节，不是吗？对此我们应该发明一个新术语，精神变态入室盗窃者？这个贴切吗？
Martha:	Who told you?	玛莎：	谁告诉你的？
Brian:	Another stupid question. Peter told me. Or was he wrong?	布赖恩：	又一个白痴问题。彼得告诉我的，他说错了吗？
Martha:	I told you, you don't understand. And I'm sorry, who's Peter?	玛莎：	我告诉过你，你不了解状况。另外，抱歉，彼得是谁？
Brian:	The outdoor clerk who's been with you all day.	布赖恩：	和你待了一整天的办事员。
Martha:	Hardly. He spent most of his day at a casting or on the phone to his agent. Maybe if you had an outdoor clerk who knew how to read a trial properly.	玛莎：	错了。他大部分时间在试镜或是和他的经纪人通电话，你要是有个知道怎么旁听审理的办事员就好了。

注释

1. **get off** 使获释或减轻处罚
2. **tout** [taut] v. 兜售；招徕；拉生意；
3. **solicitor** [sə'lɪsɪtə] n. 律师，法律顾问
4. **VO=Verbal Order** 口头命令
5. **box** [bɒks] n. 专席
6. **burglar** ['bɜːglə] n. 窃贼，夜盗
7. **aggravate** ['æɡrəveɪt] vt. 使（疾病、情况、罪过等）恶化，更坏，加重，加剧
8. **cover** ['kʌvə] v. 适用
9. **psychopath** ['saɪkəʊpɑːθ] n. 精神病患者

Brian: Was it him asking the suicidal questions or was that the brainless woman in the **wig**[10]?

Billy: I think you'd better leave.

Brian: What did you just say?

Billy: No-one ever talks to her like that.

Brian: Excuse me.

Brian: Excuse me.

(Brian Frogett leaves the party, breaking a vase in passing.)

Billy: Clear this up, clear this up. Get this cleared up, boys.

Billy: (to Clive Reader and Kate Brockman) It's called unconditional love. I'd do the same for any one of you.

Kate: It can be a **liability**[11] love.

Clive: What are you saying?

Kate: Brian Frogett is a big, big solicitor. He hates us; we lose work; we lose money. Where does love get you?

Billy: You all right, Miss?

Martha: Yes.

Billy: Sorry about that.

Martha: Thank you.

(Martha Costello calls her mother.)

Martha: Hello, Mum. It's me. You're not there so I...

(Martha Costello at this moment catches Clive Reader taking a drug on the stairs.)

Clive: How is she? Your Mum?

Martha: *How dare you?* [1]

Clive: Martha.

Martha: You **hypocrite**[12]. It should be you that goes to prison for 14 years, not her.

Clive: Why don't you just get off your... Jesus Christ,

布赖恩：　是他问了这些自杀性问题吗？还是那个没脑子的律师？

比利：　　我想你最好离开。

布赖恩：　你刚刚说什么？

比利：　　从来没有人和她那么说话。

布赖恩：　告辞。

布赖恩：　借过。

（布赖恩·弗劳盖特离开了聚会，顺道打碎了一个花瓶。）

比利：　　清理一下，清理一下这里。

比利：　　（对克莱夫·瑞德和凯特·布罗克曼说）这叫无私的爱护。我对你们每一个人都是这样的。

凯特：　　爱护可能是个坏事。

克莱夫：　你说什么？

凯特：　　布赖恩·弗劳盖特是个极其有身份的事务律师，他讨厌我们，我们丢掉工作，损失金钱。爱将你置于何种境地？

比利：　　你还好吗？

玛莎：　　还好。

比利：　　真是抱歉。

玛莎：　　谢谢。

（玛莎·科斯特洛跟她母亲打电话。）

玛莎：　　喂，妈妈，是我，你不在，所以我……

（玛莎·科斯特洛这时发现克莱夫·瑞德在楼梯间吸毒。）

克莱夫：　你妈妈好吗？

玛莎：　　你怎么敢？

克莱夫：　玛莎……

玛莎：　　你个伪君子！应该是你去坐14年牢，而不是她！

克莱夫：　你为什么不能使你的……耶稣基

Martha.

Martha: That's why people like Mercedes get screwed[13] by everybody so you can stick[14] coke[15] up your nose after a hard day in court.

Clive: Was it the wrong result?

Martha: You make me sick.

Clive: Was it the wrong result? Maybe you get in[16] too close sometimes, Martha. What are you doing? What the hell are you doing?

Martha: I'm calling the police. Give me the phone.

Clive: Just give me the phone. Give me the phone.

(Nick Slade goes upstairs now.)

Nick: *What's going on?*[2]

Clive: Who are you? Who the hell are you?

Nick: Give her the phone back.

(Nick Slade pushes Clive Reader downstairs.)

Martha: Nick, Nick, call an ambulance.

(Voice on the phone): Ambulance, please.

督啊，玛莎。

玛莎： 那就是为什么像默西迪斯那样的人受到不公，而你可以在法庭上遇挫之后吸大麻。

克莱夫： 这个判决有错吗？

玛莎： 你让我恶心。

克莱夫： 这判决有错吗？你有时候陷得太深了，玛莎。你干什么？你到底在干什么？

玛莎： 我要报警。把手机给我。

克莱夫： 把手机给我，把手机给我！

（这时尼克·斯雷德上楼了。）

尼克： 出什么事了？

克莱夫： 你是谁？你到底是谁？

尼克： 把电话还给她！

（尼克·斯雷德把克莱夫·瑞德推下了楼。）

玛莎： 尼克，尼克，叫救护车！

（打电话的声音）：救护车，快点儿。

注释

10. wig [wɪg] *n.* 假发（这里指律师所带的假发）

11. liability [ˌlaɪə'bɪlɪtɪ] *n.* 累赘

12. hypocrite ['hɪpəkrɪt] *n.* 伪君子

13. screw [skru:] *v.* <俚> 占便宜；诈骗

14. stick [stɪk] *v.* 插进

15. coke [kəuk] *n.* <俚> 可卡因

16. get in 陷入或使陷入

📚 文化背景

1. solicitor 事务律师

英国的律师制度分为两类：一种是讼务律师，也称大律师（barrister），一种是事务律师（solicitor）。两者资格的取得、训练、执业范围及所受到的管制都有所不同。传统上只有讼务律师可以代表当事人出庭，事务律师仅能向客户提供法律意见。但由于法律事务日趋复杂，两者处理的事务时常重叠，再加上此种区分方式造成对当事人的不便且费用较高，自 19 世纪 80 年代起，英国律师制度的改革呼声逐渐出现，目前事务律师也可以在某些法院代表当事人出庭。

📞 常用表达

1. How dare you? 你好大的胆子（有责问的意思）？

例：How dare you say such a thing!

你怎么竟敢说出这样的话来!

2. What's going on? 发生什么事了?

有时为了强调会说 **What's the hell going on?**

Passage 2

剧情介绍：

（选自第1季第1集）玛莎·科斯特洛是一个三十多岁，单身，但依旧富于激情的辩护律师，准备申请皇家律师资格。第一集她遇到两个案件，一个是私带毒品案，一个是入室抢劫殴打案。两个案子时间紧迫使她焦头烂额，但是两个案子背后的阴谋、内情、冤屈远远不止表面看到的这样。且看玛莎如何步步为营，站在正义的一边，以律师的角度让邪恶退步……

Scene: In the crown court, they're asking the witness...

刑事法庭上，案件审理进行到询问证人的环节……

(WJ: Woman judge　陪主席：陪审团主席)

Worker:	I come in three times a day. I help Mr. Dodd to get dressed in the morning, I give him his lunch and then I help him get to bed at night.	社工：	我一天来三次，早上我帮多德先生穿衣服，给他准备午饭，然后在晚上服侍他上床睡觉。
Kate:	And when you left him that evening he was in bed and everything was as it should be?	凯特：	你离开的那晚他已经睡了并且一切如常？
Worker:	Yes.	社工：	是的。
Martha:	No questions. Oh, actually, sorry, just one, sorry. Did you close the door behind you?	玛莎：	我没有问题。实际上，对不起，还有一个，对不起，你走时关上门了吗？
Worker:	Yes, of course.	社工：	是的，当然。
Martha:	Thank you.	玛莎：	谢谢。
Martha:	The **defendant**[1] lives a short distance away from the scene of the crime. And you arrested him because there is **CCTV**[2] **footage**[3] of a man on a **Vespa**[4] leaving from outside Mr Dodd's home address just after the burglary took place?	玛莎：	被告住得离犯罪现场很近，你逮捕了他，因为有一段监控录像的片段显示被告开着黄蜂牌小摩托离开了多德先生的家附近，就在入室盗窃发生后？

注释
1. defendant [dɪ'fendənt] *n.* 被告
2. CCTV *abbr.* **closed-circuit television** 闭路电视
3. footage ['fʊtɪdʒ] *n.* 连续镜头（一个特别性质或题目的一个镜头或一系列镜头）
4. Vespa ['vespə] *n.* 黄蜂牌小型摩托车（一种意大利制低座摩托车）

DS:	The defendant owns a Vespa. The footage isn't good enough for us to identify it 100%, but...	警官:	被告有台黄蜂牌小摩托录像片段不够清晰，所以不能百分百确定，但是……
Martha:	Grounds for suspicion? Grounds for arrest?	玛莎:	怀疑的理由充分吗？足够将他拘捕吗？
DS:	Yes.	警官:	是的。
Martha:	Was any of the stolen property **recovered**[5] from the defendant's flat?	玛莎:	从被告屋子里搜出来贼赃了吗？
DS:	No.	警官:	没有。
Martha:	Any **paraphernalia**[6] associated with burglary?	玛莎:	有作案工具吗？
DS :	These things are easily disposed of.	警官:	这些东西很容易被处理掉。
Martha :	Stick to the evidence officer, not supposition.	玛莎:	要依靠证据，而不是靠推测。
DS:	It's supposition based on 25 years of experience.	警官:	这推测建立在 25 年的经验上。
Martha:	Then came the ID **parade**[7]. Slam dunk. You haven't been in the court until now, so you won't know what Mr Dodd said in the witness box, but you will have heard about the...yawn moment?	玛莎:	接下来是列队指认，精彩的来了。你之前没有上庭，所以你不知道多德先生在证人席上说了什么，但是你应该听说过打呵欠吧？
DS:	It's...chilling. Torture an old man and then yawn. Was he bored? Tired?	警官:	恐怖……折磨一个老人，然后打呵欠。他无聊了？累了？
Martha:	And this is the kind of behaviour you'd expect from this defendant?	玛莎:	你认为这种事是被告会做的事情？
Judge:	Do you have any idea what you're doing, Miss Costello?	法官:	科斯特洛女士，你知道你自己到底在做什么吗？
Martha:	Is it right that this defendant has previous **convictions**[8]? Including three previous convictions for burglary?	玛莎:	被告有前科，对吗？包括三次入室盗窃？
DS:	Yes.	警官:	是。
Martha:	Can you tell us about the sentences Mr. Rush received for those **offences**[9]?	玛莎:	你能告诉我们拉什得到的判罚吗？
DS:	**Probation**[10] the first time, 80 hours community service the second time, followed by six months in prison.	警官:	第一次缓刑，第二次 80 小时社区服务，最后是 6 个月监禁。
Martha:	In 25 years of experience, how do you feel about those sentences?	玛莎:	以你 25 年的经验，你对这几次刑罚怎么看？
DS:	Too short.	警官:	太短。
Martha:	In 25 years of experience, if a man yawns	玛莎:	以你 25 年经验来看，如果一

and puts his gloved hand up to his mouth and then with the same hand opens the door using the handle, what will we find on the handle? DNA. Where is it?

Martha:	Who was the first officer to arrive on the scene of the crime?	
DS:	I was.	
Martha:	This was before the SOCOs, long before forensics had got to the flat. When the door handle was tested were any fingerprints found?	
DS:	No.	
Martha:	None? A door handle with nobody's prints on it? Not Mr Dodd's? Not the Social Worker from an hour before? Mr. Dodd couldn't have been clearer. The **intruder**[11] yawned. He put his gloved hand up to his face to cover his yawn. He opened the door with the same hand using the handle. Gather up all your experience, Officer, bring it to the front of your mind and park it next to your anger and tell this jury that someone didn't wipe the handle clean before it was tested. You've fitted up this defendant because you don't like him. He's got form and in your policeman's mind he hasn't been properly punished.	
DS:	So how did Mr. Dodd pick him out? Hey? If it wasn't him?	
Video:	One alligator, two alligator, three alligator, four alligator. One alligator, two alligator, three alligator, four alligator, five alligator, six...	

个人打呵欠，戴着手套的手放在嘴前，然后用同一只手握着门把手开门，我们可以在门把手上找到什么？是的，DNA。有吗？

玛莎： 第一个到达犯罪现场的警官是谁？

警官： 是我。

玛莎： 比犯罪现场调查组来得早，更早于法医到达现场，把手上检查出指纹了吗？

警官： 没有。

玛莎： 一个都没有？没有任何指纹的门把手？没有多德先生的指纹？也没有一小时前离开的社工的指纹？多德再清楚不过了，盗贼打呵欠了，他用戴手套的手挡住呵欠，用同一只手通过把手打开了门。警官，集合你所有的经验，用用脑子，不要让其被你的怒火掩盖，告诉陪审团，没有人在检验前把门把手擦干净。你设计陷害了被告，因为你讨厌他，以你警察的眼光看，他被惩罚得还不够。

警官： 多德先生怎么能把他指认出来？嗯？如果不是他的话？

录像： 一条短吻鳄，两条短吻鳄，三条短吻鳄，四条短吻鳄，一条短吻鳄，两条短吻鳄，三条短吻鳄，四条短吻鳄，五条短吻鳄，六条……

注释

5. recover [rɪ'kʌvə] *vt.* 找回（被盗、遗失等之物）

6. paraphernalia [ˌpærəfə'neɪlɪə] *n.* 随身用具

7. parade [pə'reɪd] *vt.* 展示

8. conviction [kən'vɪkʃən] *n.* 判罪

9. offence [ə'fens] *n.* 犯法

10. probation [prə'beɪʃən] *n.* 缓刑

11. intruder [ɪn'tru:də] *n.* 入侵者

Brian: That was something. That was really something.

布赖恩： 这招很厉害，真的很厉害。

Martha: You've seen the DVD of the ID procedure. You've heard the victim count in his very own, very particular, very precise way, the fact that Gary Rush is on that screen for two seconds, or alligators, longer than everyone else. You've seen the black screen either side of only one image on that video. The only evidence this **prosecution**[12] relies on is Mr. Dodd picking out the defendant on an ID parade. Not only is there no **forensic**[13] evidence, there is evidence of there being no forensic evidence, which, frankly, is impossible. If Gary Rush was in that flat and he yawned, then his DNA would be on that door handle. Is it safe to convict this man on this evidence? You as a jury have a sacred task. It is your job to apply the one basic principle on which everything in our justice system turns. The prosecution have to prove beyond all reasonable doubt that a defendant is guilty. Go back to your jury room and apply that principle to these facts and come back with the only proper **verdict**[14]. Gary Rush is not guilty.

玛莎： 你们看过列队指认的 DVD 了，你们听到了受害人用他非常独特且精确的方式计数，事实上加里·拉什在屏幕上，比其他人多停留了两秒，或者说多两条短吻鳄。你们看到视频里画像两边的黑色屏幕了吧，这起诉讼的唯一证据是多德先生在列队指认里面指认了被告，不仅仅是没有法医证据，而是有证据表明根本没有法医的证据，很明显，也不可能有法医证据。如果加里·拉什在那间屋子里打了呵欠，那他的 DNA 就会留在门把手上，这一证据足够将这个男人定罪吗？作为陪审团你们有神圣的任务，你们有义务将这基本法则应用到司法系统里的每一件事情上。诉讼中要排除一切合理怀疑，才能确定被告有罪。回到陪审团房间，将这一准则实际应用，带回来正确的裁决。加里·拉什无罪。

(Nick Slade and Martha Costello outside the CROWN COURT)

（玛莎·科斯特洛和尼克·斯雷德走到了法庭外面。）

Nick: Three convictions for burglary.

尼克： 三项入室盗窃指控。

Martha: We've had this conversation.

玛莎： 我们已经谈过这个了。

Nick: But obviously his **acquittal**[15] last year for another burglary isn't on the list of previous. But it is in the unused.

尼克： 但很明显，去年他的另一桩宣告无罪的入室盗窃指控不在前科的单子上，但是在未利用的卷宗里。

Martha: That's because it's an acquittal, Nick.

玛莎： 因为那是无罪释放，尼克。

Nick: Or because the victim was punched three times in the head and bottled out of giving evidence at the last minute. What does that tell you?

尼克： 或者是因为受害人脑袋上被重击了三下，没法在最后时刻给出证据，那能说明什么？

Martha: That DS Scarrow has a classic motive for

玛莎： 那名斯卡罗警官有动机陷害加

fitting up Gary Rush. That he walked into this crime and removed any possibility from his mind that Rush might not be the right man. It's about integrity of justice, Nick. It's about people getting a fair trial and that's all there is, and it matters so much.

Worker: Miss Costello?

Martha: Verdict?

(Martha Costello and Nick Slade go back to the courtroom.)

Man: Will the defendant please stand.

Wj: Will the **foreman**[16] please stand. Have you reached a verdict upon which all of you are agreed?

Foreman: Yes.

Wj: Do you find the defendant guilty, or not guilty of aggravated burglary?

Foreman: Not guilty.

Gary: Yes!

(The case is over. Martha Costello and Nick Slade go out of the courtroom.)

Martha: These two things are true. Gary Rush is a horrible man and it's right that he gets off. They are not mutually exclusive.

Martha: Let's go and see Mercedes Cordoba.

(In prison.)

the staff of the prison:(to Mercedes Cordoba) Come on.

Mercedes: They **raped**[17] me. Every time. Seven men. Always all of them so that when I was pregnant they wouldn't know who the father was. When my **belly**[18] grew bigger, they *made me*[1] swallow the drugs and I flew to London.

Martha: Where are your children?

里·拉什，他在查案时从脑子里清除了拉什不是罪犯的可能性，这关乎司法公正，尼克，这关乎被告能否得到公正的审判，那就是全部，非常重要。

工作人员：科斯特洛女士？

玛莎：陪审团有结果了？

(玛莎·科斯特洛和尼克·斯雷德回到了法庭。)

男声：被告请起立。

女法官：陪审团主席请起立，你们达成一致决定了吗？

陪主席：是的。

女法官：关于严重入室盗窃的指控，你们认为被告是否有罪？

陪主席：无罪。

加里：太棒了！

（案件审理结束了，玛莎·科斯特洛和尼克·斯雷德走出了法庭。）

玛莎：有两件事情千真万确，加里·拉什是个混蛋，还有他应该无罪释放，这两件事并不互斥。

玛莎：我们去见默西迪斯·科尔多瓦吧。

（在监狱里。）

监狱员工：（对默西迪斯·科尔多瓦说）出来吧。

默西迪斯：他们强奸了我。每一次，都是7个人，他们都是一起上，所以当我怀孕了，他们不知道谁是孩子的爸爸。当我的肚子变大，他们让我吞下毒品坐飞机去伦敦。

玛莎：你的孩子在哪儿？

注释
12. prosecution [ˌprɒsɪˈkjuːʃn] *n.* 起诉

13. forensic [fəˈrensɪk] *adj.* 法院的，适于法庭的

14. verdict [ˈvɜːdɪkt] *n.* （陪审团的）裁决，判决

15. acquittal [əˈkwɪtl] *n.* 宣判无罪

16. foreman [ˈfɔːmən] *n.* 陪审团主席

17. rape [reɪp] *v.* 强奸

18. belly [ˈbeli] *n.* 肚子

Mercedes: Every time the baby was born, they took the baby away. Three boys. Two girls. And then they raped me again. I don't know where my babies are.

Martha: Why didn't you tell me this? I could have used it.

Mercedes: I wanted a long **sentence**[19]. Here I am safe. I am away from them.

Martha: There is a **ground**[20] of **appeal**[21].

Mercedes: Why can't you hear me? I do not want an appeal. Thank you.

(Martha Costello and Nick Slade go out of the cell.)

Nick: What was the ground of appeal?

Martha: Me. Me being hopeless.

Nick: Gary Rush doesn't think you're hopeless.

默西迪斯： 每一次孩子出生，他们都把孩子带走，三个男孩，两个女孩。然后他们继续强奸我，我不知道我的孩子们在哪儿。

玛莎： 你为什么不告诉我这些？我本可以利用这些的。

默西迪斯： 我想要判得重一些，在监狱里我很安全，我可以远离他们。

玛莎： 我们有上诉的充分理由。

默西迪斯： 为什么你不能听我的？我不想上诉。谢谢你。

（玛莎·科斯特洛和尼克·斯雷德走出了监狱房间。）

尼克： 上诉的依据是什么？

玛莎： 我，我很绝望。

尼克： 加里·拉什不认为你会绝望。

📖 文化背景

1. Verdict 陪审团制度

陪审制起源于古代英国，并逐渐被美国等国家的司法制度所继承。现行制度是从一般市民中随机选出若干名陪审员，委派其参与刑事诉讼或民事诉讼的审理，并独立于法官做出事实认定及决定法律适用的司法制裁。陪审团在刑事案件中会就被告人有罪或无罪做出判断，而在民事诉讼中则会就被告有无责任或损害赔偿金额等做出判断。在英美法上称为 verdict，仅具事实认定之效果而非正式判决，法官会根据陪审团所认定的结果做出判决。

☎ 常用表达

1. make sb. do sth. 让某人做某事（有强迫的意思）

例： My mum made me do my housework.

妈妈让我做家庭作业。

注释 **19. sentence** ['sentəns] *n.* 判决　　　　　　**21. appeal** [ə'piːl] *n.* 上诉
20. ground [graund] *n.* 理由

Passage 3

剧情介绍：

（选自第1季第6集）凯特·布罗克曼在律师事务所里只是个初级律师，而这个律师事务所的负责人比利·拉姆把事务所的收入大部分都分给了像玛莎·科斯特洛这样的高级律师，所以凯特·布罗克曼对此一直很不满，她经常找机会怂恿同事出去单干并且采取了出去单干的行动，但这一行动被比利·拉姆发现了……

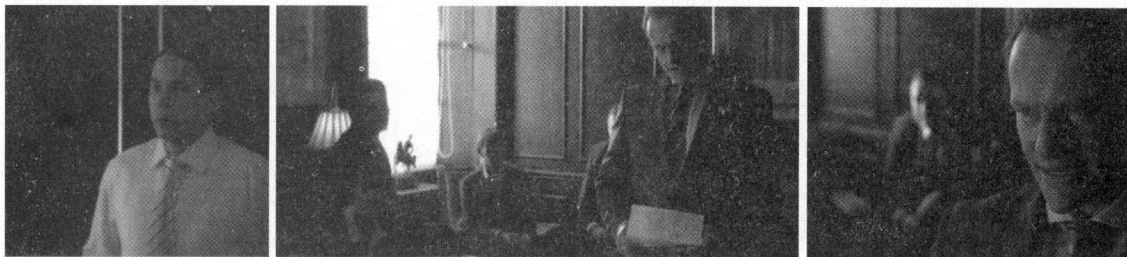

Scene: In the office, Martha and Billy were in quarrelling…

办公室里，玛莎和比利陷入了争吵中……

Jake:	What is it?	杰克：	什么？
Billy:	Ask Miss Brockman.	比利：	问布罗克曼女士吧。
Billy:	I want you all to hear what she has to say.	比利：	你们听她说吧。
Clive:	Billy.	克莱夫：	比利。
Kate :	I didn't want to do it like this.	凯特：	我不想这么做。
Billy:	Yes, you did.	比利：	不，你想。
Billy:	There's an empty building in Fountain Street. Tell them, Kate. All the bottom end led by her… and clerked by him. (pointing at John)	比利：	凯特，告诉他们，在喷泉街有一栋空的办公室，所以初级律师都是由她，还有出纳员（指着约翰·布莱特）领导的。
Kate:	I'm not leading this.	凯特：	我不是出头的那个。
Billy:	Oh, really, then who is?	比利：	噢，是吗，那是谁？
Kate:	Our new **Silk**[1].	凯特：	我们新的皇家律师。
Billy:	I did want to keep this a surprise. Martha Costello… Clive Reader…not this time. (to Kate) *Get out*[1].	比利：	我本来想把这个作为一个惊喜的。玛莎·科斯特洛，皇家律师。克莱夫·瑞德，这次不是。（对凯特说）出去。
Martha:	Billy, please. You don't know… This can't happen.	玛莎：	比利，别这样，你不知道的，不能这样。

注释 1. Silk: [sɪlk] *n.* (Brit 口) Queen's or King's Counsel, who wears a silk gown in court 御用律师

Billy: No, Martha.

Martha: It's what he's always saying. It's **sentimental**[2], it's stupid, but it's true. This is family.

Billy: Miss…

Martha: No, Billy, please. And what happens in families? They fight, and they hate each other and angry and jealous and foolish, but they stay together. This is the biggest moment of my career, it's everything I've **worked for**[3]… but having two letters after my name, it doesn't mean anything, if I don't have this… and all of you. Excuse me.

比利： 别，玛莎。

玛莎： 这是他经常说的，这很伤感情，很愚蠢，但是很现实。这是一个家。

比利： 女士……

玛莎： 不，比利，听我说。家里总是会出问题，他们会相互算计，讨厌彼此，生气、嫉妒、愚蠢，但是大家还是在一起。现在是我职业生涯中最重要的时刻，我一直在为之努力……但是冠上皇家律师这个称号其实并不能说明什么，如果我失去这里，还有你们大家。失陪了。

文化背景

1. Silk: 皇家律师（御用律师）（Queen's Counsel）

在英国，出庭律师从事律师业务 10 年以上，成绩突出者，经本人申请，由大法官批准，可以由英国女皇授予"皇家律师"称号。皇家律师是英国律师界的精英人物，相对于皇家律师而言，其他出庭律师被称为晚辈律师。

常用表达

1. get out 滚开！离开这里！（还可以说 get out of here）

例： I told him to leave and get out.

我叫他滚开。

注释 **2. sentimental** [ˌsentɪˈmentl] *adj.* 感伤性的，感情脆弱的
3. work for 为……尽力

Chapter 5

医务剧
Medical Drama

医务剧是指主要发生在医院中，以医生治病救人为主线展开故事的电视剧。在这些感人至深的故事中，还穿插着医生们自己的情感生活和喜怒哀乐。在医务剧中，医生可能扮演着多重角色：医生、丈夫、妻子、女儿、朋友等。这些角色的内在冲突使剧情在围绕治病救人的同时变得更为可信，相应人物的表现力也更为丰满。剧中的大部分情节都在医院中发生，有相对固定的主演阵容，角色人物的个性特征也基本完整、稳定。每集以不同医生救治不同病人为主，单集多在 40 分钟左右，每集可独立成章，上下集之间的情节彼此又有联系。与剧情片不同的是，医务剧以主人公的情感经历作为连接整个故事的主线，通过医生医术和心理的日趋成熟推动情节的发展。

《实习医生格蕾》是美国医务剧的优秀代表作。它以医学为主题，于 2005 年 3 月 27 日在美国广播公司首播并取得了很高的收视率。另外，优秀的医务剧还有《豪斯医生》《急诊室的故事》等，这些都称得上是此类剧目的经典之作。

14

ER
《急诊室的故事》

入选理由：

　　《急诊室的故事》是美剧史上首部严格意义上的医疗剧，自 1994 年 9 月开播到 2009 年 4 月大结局的播出，历时 15 年，共播出 15 季 246 集。该剧主要讲述了芝加哥市库克县综合医院急诊室里发生的故事，间或穿插一些在急诊室工作的医生们的故事。看似平淡的剧情却因其多线条的叙事方式、紧凑的故事情节和手持摄像机的使用变得如同电影一般精彩，深受观众欢迎，创造了超过 50% 的惊人收视率，获得 1 项金球奖、23 项艾美奖及 375 项各类提名。《急诊室的故事》的巨大成功不仅使医务剧成了美剧的主流，还对美国人的健康观念产生了不容忽视的促进作用，因而被政府部门誉为"增进公众健康知识的优质渠道"。有位评论家曾说过，有些剧集改变了电视荧屏，有些剧集改变了不少人的命运，还有极少数的剧集，以上两者都做到了。《急诊室的故事》就是这极少数之一。

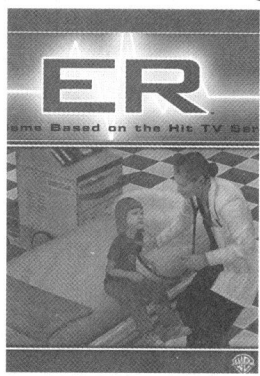

Section 1　剧情特点：

　　《急诊室的故事》讲述了发生在急诊室里真实而又感人的故事。在这里，没有疑难杂症，只有需要急救的病人；在这里，每天都会有人康复或者死亡；在这里，医德、人情和法律不断冲突。通过一个个相互独立的故事，讲述了人性的美与丑、善和恶，折射出一个有着诸多问题却很真实的现实世界。《急诊室的故事》开创了"P+P 模式"，将医疗专业知识和个人情感相结合，深深地触动了观众。因此，该剧始终弥漫着一股温暖感人的气息，表现出对人和生命的尊重和热爱。

Section 2　对白特点：

　　由于该剧中的很多场景都是在抢救病人，因此语言听上去简洁明了，给人一种紧张急促的感觉。严密的科学性和强烈的戏剧效果是克里顿作品的主要特色。由于对急诊室的生活比较了解，在制作电视剧时，克里顿对所有细节的真实性都有极高的要求，为此他还特地请了一批医学专家亲临指导。他们规范演员的每一个动作、表情，力求与真正的医生、护士一样。正是这种真实的效果，使该剧呈现出一种与死神赛跑的紧张气氛。加上高超的的摄影、剪辑技术，那种视觉冲击力比起惊险片来毫不逊色。该剧有趣、感人的情节和人物设计，使每一集都有奇巧、引人之处。而演员对角色的准确把握和生动表演，更加强了剧情的吸引力。

Section 3　角色分析：

马克·格雷尼医生 (Dr. Mark Greene)：急诊室的主力医生，对工作非常地投入。可是妻子不愿他在 36 小时倒班的急诊室工作，而马克坚持不离开医院的第一线，他因此付出了离婚的代价。

道格·罗斯医生 (Dr. Doug Ross)：英俊迷人的儿科医生，是马克的好友。虽然他医术出色，却是个爱喝酒的花花公子，前女友卡罗尔护士因此离开了他。

约翰·卡特医生 (Dr. John Carter)：急诊室新来的实习医生，只有书本知识的卡特在面对病人时手足无措，而在马克和本顿的指导下渐渐成为合格的医生，最终成为医院里广受尊敬的主治医生。

卡罗尔·海瑟威护士 (Carol Hathaway)：急诊室的护士之一，曾一度对生活失去希望的卡罗尔选择过自杀，从深度昏迷状态苏醒后又重回了急诊室。与道格之间牵扯不断的情愫也是令她烦恼的原因。

彼得·本顿医生 (Dr. Peter Benton)：勤奋的急诊室医生，卡特的老师。本顿想成为真正的住院医生，他抓住一切机会实践、提高自己的医术。

苏珊·路易斯 (Dr. Susan Lewis)：急诊室的医生，工作努力，业务能力出色。和卡罗尔、道格、马克关系都很好；尤其是和马克，两人暗生情愫，但由于马克总是羞于表达，最终苏珊选择离开。第三季退出本剧，第八季回归拍至第十二季彻底退出。

Passage 1

剧情介绍：

（选自第2季第1集）街头枪战，送来一堆伤员，还包括无辜孕妇。急诊室中和往常一样紧张忙碌。而刚放完暑假、直接从机场赶到医院的卡特完全没进入状况，对和本顿一起做手术的希克斯提的问题一问三不知。导师本顿对他的表现非常生气。马克第一次参加主任医师的会议，显得无所适从。其他医生却在那里谈天说地，无所事事，和楼下忙得不可开交的急诊室形成鲜明对比。杰里碰到一个病人，是位美丽的空姐，很义气地把这个病例给了道格·罗斯，道格很开心，因为可以施展一下自己的魅力。

Scene: Carter hurries from the airport back to the ER, where everybody is terribly busy.

卡特从机场匆匆赶回急诊室，每个人都在紧张的工作。

Carter:	What happened?	卡特：	怎么了？
Carol:	**Gang**[1] fight. Nice shirt.	卡罗尔：	团伙枪战。衬衫不错！
Carter:	**I'm a dead man.**[2]	卡特：	我死定了！
Carol:	Hey, welcome back, Carter.	卡罗尔：	欢迎回来，卡特。
Man 1:	Dr. Carter, I presume? **Great tan**[3].	男1：	卡特医生？皮肤晒得不错啊！
Carter:	Jerry, where's Dr. Benton, and has he been asking about me?	卡特：	杰里，本顿医生在哪儿？他提起过我吗？
Jerry:	Once or twice. He's doing a surgery crash section. Pregnant woman got shot. He just limped up.	杰里：	有几次。他正进行剖腹探查术，孕妇枪伤。他刚崴了脚。
Carter:	Hi, Dr. Greene.	卡特：	你好，格雷尼医生。
Neal:	Who was that?	尼尔：	那是谁？
Mark:	Carter, I think. Dr. Benton's student.	马克：	卡特，我想，本顿医生的学生。
Neal:	Tell him to slow down.	尼尔：	告诉他慢点儿。
Mark:	I phone Cardiology every day. They claim <u>CCU</u>[1]'s full. I go up and find empty beds. We had a rule-out MI here for two days.	马克：	我每天给心内科打电话，他们总说心脏监护室满员。我上去看过了，有空床，我们这里有个心肌梗塞的病人，在这儿已经两天了。
Neal:	Got a problem with another department you solve it. And you've got new third-years coming in today. Four of them, bright-eyed.	尼尔：	你已经是主治医师了，你能独立跟其他科室处理问题。今天有几个三年级学生来找你，共有四个，

	Staff[4] meeting at 4:00. Don't forget.	蓝眼睛。医生会议在四点。别忘了。
Doug:	Forget what?	道格： 别忘了什么？
Mark:	My first staff meeting's today.	马克： 我的第一次例会。
Doug:	Little boss, what did big boss want?	道格： 小老板，大老板想要什么？
Mark:	Something about me accepting the heavy mantel of my new position.	马克： 一些关于我接受主治医师聘任的事情。
Doug:	You set the **tone**[5], right?	道格： 你猜的吧，是吗？
Mark:	How're you set for cash?	马克： 猜对了，你手头宽裕吗？
Doug:	If you need the 200 bucks. I'm **strapped**[6] for cash right now.	道格： 你想要回 200 块？我现在急需钱。
Mark:	No, I'm making up a schedule for next week. I thought maybe you could pull a graveyard attending shift, get *extra*[1] cash.	马克： 不，我在准备下周的排班表。也许你能多值班，多拿点钱。
Doug:	Really?	马克： 真的吗？
Mark:	Consider it done.	道格： 考虑一下。
Jerry:	Dr. Greene? Three lost sheep claiming to be med students.	杰里： 格林医生，三只迷途羔羊，医学生。
Mark:	I thought there were four of them.	马克： 我听说的是四个。
Jerry:	One's doing a history of a bipolar. She'll be done by next Tuesday.	杰里： 那个学生在询问病史，估计要到下周二才能完成。
Mark:	This way, guys.	马克： 这边走，伙计们。
Doug:	Jerry? Anything of the pediatric persuasion up there?	道格： 杰里，有什么儿科病人等着吗？
Jerry:	I've got a Scandinavian flight attendant with a bum ankle and an earache.	杰里： 有个斯堪迪纳维亚航空的空姐脚踝疼，还有耳朵疼。
Doug:	And you **saved her all for**[7] me? I love you, big man. You know that.	道格： 专门为我留下来的吗？我爱你，大个子！你真了解我。
Hicks:	Nine months pregnant. Couldn't find the bullet?	希克斯： 九个月的孕妇，找不到子弹？
Benton:	Gotta be in the uterus somewhere.	本顿： 一定在子宫里的什么地方。
Hicks:	Pressure *barely*[2] holding. No time to waste.	希克斯： 血压很难维持，没时间了。
Carter:	Dr. Benton?	卡特： 本顿医生？
Benton:	Carter, don't *bother*[3] coming in here.	本顿： 卡特，别来添乱。
Carter:	I'm sorry. I came straight from the airport. Hurricane Phyllis in the Gulf.	卡特： 对不起，我是直接从机场的，遇上了菲利斯飓风。

注释
1. **gang** [gæŋ] *n.* 一群；一伙；（歹徒等的）一帮
2. **I'm a dead man** （口语）我完了，我死定了
3. **tan** [tæn] *n.* 棕褐色；黝黑
4. **staff** [stɑːf] *n.* 员工；全体人员；全体职员
5. **set the tone** 调子，定下基调
6. **strapped** [stræpt] *adj.* 身无分文的
7. **save for** 为……储蓄（储存，保存）

Hicks: Your student?

Benton: Don't remind me.

Hicks: Nice tan. Student, what is the most important anatomical structure to **identify**[8]?

Carter: Uh, the uterus?

Hicks: Ureter. You cut that and you're in big trouble. She can't pee. What's its name?

Benton: Carter.

Hicks: Cartery, basic anatomy. What muscle forms the floor of the pelvis?

Carter: Uh...

Hicks: Levator ani. The ovarian artery comes off the aorta just above the...

Carter: Comes off the aorta to...

Hicks: Inferior mesenteric artery. Doesn't the word "student" imply that you should be teaching him something?

Hulda: Hello.

Doug: I'm Dr. Ross, and you must be...

Hulda: Hulda.

Doug: Hulda... What a beautiful name, Hulda... What seems to be the problem?

Hulda: I hurt my ankle. It hurts very much.

Doug: Let's take a look at it.

Haleh: A man dropped his little vodka bottle in the aisle and she **slipped**[9].

Hulda: It tickles.

Doug: Haleh, lateral AP and oblique views, please. It doesn't seem to be broken. We're gonna get some X-rays and may consider a cast, just to be safe.

Hulda: Oh, and my ear is very **sore**[10]. For many months. All this going up and coming down, I think. Yes?

希克斯：	你的学生？

注释
8. identify [aɪˈdentɪfaɪ] vt. 识别，认出
9. slip [slɪp] vi. 滑脱
10. sore [sɔː] adj. 疼痛的

文化背景

1. CCU 心脏监护室

心脏监护室是重症加强护理病房 ICU(Intensive Care Unit) 中的一种，第一个 C 是冠心病（coronary heart disease）的缩写，是专门对重症冠心病设立的。

常用表达

1. extra 额外的

例： There were so many people that the company put on extra buses.

人数太多，公司加开了公共汽车。

Guests at this hotel can use the gym at no extra cost.

这家饭店的客人们可以使用健身房，不再额外收费。

2. barely 几乎不；刚刚；勉强；少量地

例： He is so weak that he can barely stand up.

他身体虚弱几乎站不起来。

I had barely started speaking when he interrupted me.

我刚刚开始讲话，他便打断了我。

We had barely enough money to last through the weekend.

我们的钱只能勉强维持到周末。

3. bother 烦扰；使恼怒；使不安；费心

例： I've no time to bother with such things.

我没时间为这种事烦恼。

Don't write anything that will bother the censor.

你可别写什么给检查员找麻烦的话。

It bothers me that he can be so insensitive.

他这样麻木不仁，我心里很不痛快。

The problem has been bothering me for weeks.

那问题已经困扰了我几个星期。

Don't bother about such trifles.

这丁点儿事不必放在心上。

Passage 2

剧情介绍：

（选自第2季第8集）为了避免任何诊断错误的可能，卡特把整间医院一半的仪器搬来急诊室，给一个病情轻微的病人做一系列的检查，居然检查出一个大问题来，医院的领导伍思里奇还因此让他参加一个手术。苏珊碰到一个超可爱的老太太，看病还带来了茶具一类的东西。为了给病房增加生气，她还热心地帮助病友照顾小宝宝。苏珊看到老太太想让她暂时带带自己的孩子苏斯，可是后来发觉她有严重的贫血症，必须要住院。可是老太太拒绝了，认为与其痛苦地延长生命，不如好好享受最后的人生。

Scene 1: Benton comes angrily to blame Carter for his ordering too many tests for the patient.
卡特给病人做的检查过多，本顿怒气冲冲地责怪卡特。

Benton:	Carter!	本顿：	卡特!
Carter:	What?	卡特：	怎么了？
Benton:	What the hell are you doing?	本顿：	你究竟在干什么？
Carter:	Nothing. She's got a history of lupus and renal failure and complained of **chest**[1] pain. I'm working her up.	卡特：	什么都没干，女病人主诉胸痛，有狼疮和肾衰竭病史，我正在看她。
Benton:	Carter, come.	本顿：	卡特，过来。
Carter:	Excuse me.	卡特：	对不起。
Benton:	Only an **idiot**[2] would order that many tests for chest pain.	本顿：	只有白痴才会让胸痛病人做那么多检查。
Carter:	I'm trying to be **thorough**[3]. She's Dr. Vucelich's patient.	卡特：	我只想全面点儿，她是伍思里奇医生的病人。
Benton:	You're kidding?	本顿：	别开玩笑
Carter:	No.	卡特：	没开玩笑。
Vucelich:	Dr. Benton.	伍思里奇：	本顿医生!
Benton:	Oh, God.	本顿：	我的天!
Vucelich:	Did you order these labs on my patient?	伍思里奇：	是你给我的病人开的检查吗？
Benton:	I apologize. I left my student unsupervised... I take full responsibility.	本顿：	抱歉，我没看住我的学生……我负全责。
Carter:	Dr. Benton had nothing to do with it.	卡特：	与本顿医生无关。

Vucelich:	Then you're the one I should thank.	伍思里奇:	那我就只感谢你一个人。
Carter:	Thank?	本顿:	感谢?
Vucelich:	Yes, the test for antiphospholipid antibodies was positive. Ms. Vucelich, she has a serious blood disease. We need to put her on heparin right away. So tell me, what was your thinking, son?	伍思里奇:	是的,抗磷脂抗体是阳性,病人有严重的血液病,我们要给她用肝素。告诉我,你是怎么想的,孩子?
Carter:	Actually, there was very little. Mrs.Briggs has a very complex history, so I took a **shotgun**[4] approach.	卡特:	其实没怎么想,她的病史很复杂,我想应该扩大检查范围。
Vucelich:	Don't underestimate yourself, Mr. Carter. *Given*[1] the circumstances, your approach was **valid**[5]. More than valid. Not that I *advocate*[2] indiscriminate testing. No need to order Chem-20s on everyone, right? But when someone has **a constellation of**[6] problems, you can't *hold back*[3]. Remember that, Benton. Good work.	伍思里奇:	别过分谦虚,卡特先生。在这种情况下,你的判断是对的。我并不是提倡天女散花式的检查,不是每个人都需要查生化20项的,是吗?但是如果某人有很多情况,那么你就不应该放过。记住我的话,本顿。干得好!
Benton:	Thank you.	本顿:	过奖。
Vucelich:	By the way, I'm doing a fem-pop bypass. You wanna assist?	伍思里奇:	顺便说一句,我要做一个股动脉—动脉人工血管旁路术,你想过来帮忙吗?
Benton:	Go, Carter.	本顿:	去吧,卡特。
Vucelich:	You know the procedure?	伍思里奇:	你知道手术步骤吗?
Carter:	Fem-pop bypass?	卡特:	股动脉旁路术?
Vucelich:	How many have you done?	伍思里奇:	你做过多少例?

Scene 2: Susan tells Mrs. Ransom about her illness and suggests that she should get treatment.

苏珊告知兰瑟夫人病情并建议她住院治疗,但她不肯接受苏珊的建议。

Susan:	Mrs. Ransom?	苏珊:	兰瑟夫人?
Ransom:	I must've **drifted off**[7]. Did you get my references?	兰瑟:	我一定是睡过去了,看过我的简历了吗?
Susan:	Oh, yes. Very, very impressive.	苏珊:	看过了,很出色。

注释

1. chest [tʃest] *n.* 胸部;胸腔
2. idiot [ˈɪdɪət] *n.* 白痴;傻瓜
3. thorough [ˈθʌrə] *adj.* 彻底的;完全的
4. shotgun [ˈʃɒtɡʌn] *adj.* 漫无目的的

5. valid [ˈvælɪd] *adj.* 有效的
6. a constellation of 一片,一群
7. drifted off 渐渐入睡

Ransom:	Thank you. I was thinking that I could drop **around**[8] tonight. Make it less **intrusive**[9] on the little one.	兰瑟：	谢谢你！我想我今晚就可以过去，对小家伙不会那么突然。
Susan:	Mrs. Ransom, we need to talk about your blood tests. Your red and white cells and platelet count are extremely low......which is suggestive of aplastic anemia, which is very serious.	苏珊：	兰瑟夫人，我们要谈谈你的血液化验结果，你的红细胞、白细胞、血小板计数都特别低……提示你可能患有再生障碍性贫血，很严重的一种疾病。
Ransom:	Perhaps you could give me a few pills. **Pep me up**[10].	兰瑟：	也许你能给我开点药，让细胞增多。
Susan:	Mrs. Ransom, your condition is most likely terminal. You need to be admitted for a bone marrow biopsy.	苏珊：	兰瑟夫人，你的病情基本上已经到了终末期，你要住院做骨髓活检。
Ransom:	Pish-posh! Not another one of those!	兰瑟：	不想又来一次。
Susan:	You've had one?	苏珊：	为什么要说"又"？
Ransom:	Yes, months ago. Most unpleasant.	兰瑟：	几个月前做过一次，太难受了。
Susan:	Have you been getting transfusions?	苏珊：	你输过血吗？
Ransom:	From their description, they're simply **ghastly**[11]. I would rather just carry on and hope for the best. I could come around about 7 tonight, if......that's convenient with you.	兰瑟：	他们让我输的，不过太恐怖了，还不如顺其自然。我可以晚上7点钟过去，如果……你方便的话。
Susan:	Mrs. Ransom, your disease has reached a **stage**[12] where you can't work anymore. You need to be admitted to the hospital.	苏珊：	兰瑟夫人，你的病情已经到了不适宜工作的阶段了，你必须住院治疗。
Ransom:	I think I'm the better judge of that. Don't you?	兰瑟：	我想我应该自己来决定，不是吗？

注释

8. drop around 串门
9. intrusive [ɪnˈtruːsɪv] *adj.* 闯入的，打扰的；侵入的
10. pep up 使振动；激励
11. ghastly [ˈɡɑːstlɪ] *adj.* 可怕的；恐怖的
12. stage [steɪdʒ] *n.* 阶段

📖 文化背景

1. ounce 盎司

盎司为英制计量单位，符号为 ounce 或 oz，作为重量单位时也称为英两。美国与英联邦国家使用英制单位，而欧洲大陆国家和我国则多使用公制单位，因此在读取数据时需要注意换算，如 16 盎司 =1 磅（pound）；1 盎司 =28.350 克。

常见的英制与公制换算还有长度方面的：1 英尺 =0.3048 米；温度方面的华氏温度与摄氏温度的换算：华氏度 = 32 + 摄氏度 × 1.8；等等。

☎ 常用表达

1. given 考虑到；如果

例：Given his age, he did it quite well.

考虑到他的年龄，他做得相当好。

Given their inexperience, they've done their best.

考虑到他们缺乏经验，他们已经尽力了。

2. advocate 提倡；主张

例：We don't advocate learning by rote.

死记硬背的学习方法，我们是不提倡的。

Many people advocate building more hospitals.

许多人主张增设医院。

We advocate higher salaries for teachers.

我们主张涨老师的工资。

3. hold back 隐瞒；退缩；抑制；阻止

例：She smiled and could not hold back tears of joy.

她笑了起来，禁不住流下喜悦的眼泪。

No one can hold back the wheel of history.

谁也无法阻止历史车轮的前进。

She just managed to hold back her anger.

她总算抑制住了自己的愤怒情绪。

🔊 Passage 3 🎦

剧情介绍：

（选自第 2 季第 8 集）苏珊找道格给她的孩子苏斯看病，道格告诉她孩子非常健康。这时送来一个婴儿患者，经急救无效后猝死。经过这样可怕的一幕，苏珊看着自己的宝宝健健康康，觉得自己无比幸福。

Scene: Susan asked Doug to have a look at her sick baby.

苏姗让道格看一下她生病的孩子。

🔊 **Susan:**	Doug? Doug?	苏珊：	道格？道格？
Doug:	He's not here.	道格：	他不在。
Susan:	I need you to take a look at Susie.	苏珊：	我想你看看苏斯。
Doug:	I'm not on yet, am I?	道格：	我还没上班呢。
Susan:	You're a **pediatrician**[1]. You're always on.	苏珊：	你是儿科医生，你总是上班的。
Doug:	Yes, but I'm not your pediatrician. What time is it?	道格：	是的，但我不是你的儿科医生。几点了？
Susan:	6:00 a.m. She was up half the night coughing.	苏珊：	早上 6 点，她半夜咳醒了。
Doug:	All right. There, there, little one. What's going on? Let's see. She's pretty **agreeable**[2].	道格：	好吧，小家伙，你怎么了？她很乖。
Susan:	That's because I **kept her company**[3] for the last five hours.	苏珊：	那是因为我抱了她 5 个钟头。
Doug:	What's the matter?	道格：	怎么回事？
Susan:	I got elbowed in the "Mommy and me" class yesterday.	苏珊：	昨天我带她上亲子课被人撞了一下。
Doug:	Sounds **vicious**[4].	道格：	很不舒服吧？
Susan:	Oh, yeah. It was. I had the blue end of the **parachute**[5], and little Susie was underneath... and this yuppie mother came by and yanked it and shoved me! I'm telling you, this mother thing is not easy.	苏珊：	当然。我带小苏斯坐降落伞，小苏斯在下面……有一个年轻妈妈走过来撞了我一下！我跟你说，当个妈妈可真不容易。
Doug:	You wouldn't know it by her. No temperature. Lungs are clear. No sore throat. This is the	道格：	当小苏斯的妈妈应该不会啊。没有发烧，肺部听诊正常，喉

	healthiest, happiest baby I have ever seen.		咙也不红，这孩子再健康、快乐不过了。
Susan:	I'm never gonna make Gymboree tonight.	苏珊：	今晚我不能再拼命抱她了。
Gloria:	Doug, paramedics are at the back door with an **infant**[6], unresponsive.	格劳丽亚：	道格，救护车在后门口，有个婴儿昏迷了。
Susan:	You need a hand?	苏珊：	要帮忙吗？
Doug:	Always.	道格：	再好不过了。
Susan:	Bye-bye. Can you hold her for a sec?	苏珊：	再见。你能帮我抱一会儿吗？
W1:	Hey, little Susie.	女1：	小苏斯。
Doug:	What do you got?	道格：	什么病人？
Lydia:	Two-month-old male...found **unconscious**[7] and cyanotic in his crib.	莉迪亚：	两个月大的男孩……被发现在摇篮里没有意识，紫绀。
Doug:	What is it? What's wrong?	道格：	出什么事了？
Father:	He was fine last night.	婴儿父亲：	昨天晚上还好好的。
Lydia:	Unresponsive at scene. Gave him two rounds of epi and atropine. Got nothing.	莉迪亚：	到达现场时没有意识，已经用过两次肾上腺素和阿托品，不起作用。
Father:	He just had a little bit of a cold.	父亲：	他只是小小的感冒。
Mother:	I just took him to a pediatrician yesterday.	婴儿母亲：	我昨天还带他看过医生。
Doug:	Tube him. Number four uncuffed. Hook up a compression, will you? Number one, straight laryngoscope.	道格：	插管，用4号接上压缩器，好吗？1号直接喉镜。
Susan:	I need tape on the tube.	苏珊：	我需要胶带固定导管。
Lydia:	Here you go.	莉迪亚：	给你。
Susan:	Temperature?	苏珊：	体温？
Lydia:	It's 93.	莉迪亚：	93度（华氏温度）。
Mother:	It wasn't a bad cold, not even a fever.	母亲：	感冒并不重，也没发烧。
Lydia:	Deep tendon reflexes absent.	莉迪亚：	深腱反射消失。
Doug:	He's unresponsive to pain. We should try a high dose epi. What does he weigh?	道格：	没有痛觉反射，试用大剂量肾上腺素。体重？
Father:	10 pounds?	父亲：	10磅？
Mother:	12.	母亲：	12磅。
Lydia:	Asystole.	莉迪亚：	心搏停止。
Doug:	Point five.	道格：	0.5毫克肾上腺素。
Father:	Did our doctor miss something?	父亲：	我们的医生有什么没注意的吗？

注释
1. **pediatrician** [ˌpiːdɪəˈtrɪʃn] *n.* 儿科医生
2. **agreeable** [əˈɡriːəbl] *adj.* 愉快的；和蔼可亲的
3. **keep...company** 陪伴……
4. **vicious** [ˈvɪʃəs] *adj.* 恶毒的；恶意的；剧烈的
5. **parachute** [ˈpærəʃuːt] *n.* 降落伞
6. **infant** [ˈɪnfənt] *n.* 婴儿
7. **unconscious** [ʌnˈkɒnʃəs] *adj.* 无意识的、失去知觉的

Doug:	What's your name?	道格：	你叫什么？
Father:	Kenway.	父亲：	肯威。
Doug:	We need you to wait outside.	道格：	你们要到外面去等。
Mother:	What's wrong with him?	母亲：	他怎么了？
Susan:	Gloria...	苏珊：	格劳丽亚……
Gloria:	Let the doctor do his work.	格劳丽亚：	让医生专心做事。
Mother:	I want to stay with my baby. Please.	母亲：	我要跟我的孩子在一起。
Doug:	Anterior fontanel is flat.	道格：	前囟平坦。
Susan:	Anything on the **monitor**[8] yet?	苏珊：	监护仪有什么显示？
Doug:	No petechiae or ecchymosis.	道格：	没有瘀点、瘀斑。
Susan:	Another dose of epi?	苏珊：	再来一次肾上腺素？
Doug:	What's his down **time**[9]?	道格：	昏迷时间？
Lydia:	45 minutes.	莉迪亚：	45 分钟了。
Susan:	Any **pulse**[10]?	苏珊：	有脉搏吗？
Lydia:	No.	莉迪亚：	没有。
Doug:	Pupils fixed and dilated. No rhythm. I'm gonna shock him.	道格：	瞳孔散大固定，没有心律，准备电击。
Susan:	Charging.	苏珊：	充电。
Doug:	Susan...Susan, it's over. Susan, it's over. It's over.	道格：	苏珊，苏珊，结束了……苏珊，结束了，结束了。
Lydia:	I'll mark the **chart**[11].	莉迪亚：	我整理病历。
Susan:	SIDS[1].	苏珊：	婴儿猝死综合征。
Doug:	Lydia, take him off the monitor. I'll get his parents back in here.	道格：	莉迪亚，去掉监护导线。我去找他父母。
Susan:	Will you stay with him?	苏珊：	你跟他在一起？
Connie:	You gotta look at that face. She was fast **asleep**[12]. Weren't you?	康妮：	看看她的小脸，她睡得很沉，是不是？
Susan:	Thank you, Conni.	苏珊：	谢谢你，康妮。
Connie:	You're welcome.	康妮：	不客气。
Susan:	My little girl. My little girl. Yeah. I love you. Yeah, I love you. Yeah, I love you.	苏珊：	我的小宝贝，小宝贝，我爱你，我爱你！

注释
8. monitor ['mɒnɪtə] n. 监视器；［计算机］显示器
9. down time 停机时间；故障时间；此处指婴儿的昏迷时间
10. pulse [pʌls] n. 脉搏
11. chart [tʃɑːt] n. 图表，此处指病历表
12. fast asleep 熟睡，沉睡

📚 文化背景

1. SIDS 婴儿猝死综合征

SIDS(Sudden Infant Death Syndrome)是指 1 岁以内的婴儿，平素健康，无明显病史突然死亡，且死后尸检找不到明显的致病因素。自 20 世纪 60 年代初期，各国学者就开始对其病因进行了广泛的研究，并提示了众多的病因学说，如睡眠窒息（睡眠姿势及包被过紧），胃—食道反流误吸，心传导组织发育缺陷，肺发育不良，低血糖、低血钙、尼古丁中毒、肾上腺异常等，但未发现特异性病因，一些规律还未被阐明。

📞 常用表达

1. company 公司；商号；陪伴；同伴；客人；［军］连；一群

例：The company has connections with a number of Japanese firms.

这家公司与几家日本商号有业务往来。

I've really enjoyed your company.

有你的陪伴我很开心。

I asked Benny to keep my son company while I went shopping.

我请本尼在我购物的时候陪伴我儿子。

His father asked him to avoid bad company.

他父亲要他不要交坏朋友。

He was appointed captain of a company of rifles.

他被任命为步枪连连长。

He came in company with a group of girls.

他是和一群女孩子来的。

2. charge

(1) 作名词。责任；电荷；指控；费用；照顾。

例：As group leader, you should take charge. 你身为组长，应当负起责任来。

He was arrested on a charge of armed robbery. 他被指控持械抢劫而遭逮捕。

Rub the leather and the rubber will produce the charge. 摩擦皮毛和橡胶会产生电荷。

The extra charge is for the water bed. 超额费用是因为有水床。

The nurse is in charge of the patients. 这位护士负责照顾这些病人。

(2) 作动词。要价；充电；控诉；委以重任。

例：How much do you charge per unit? 你们每件要价多少呢?

The suspect was charged with murdering his wife. 嫌疑犯因谋杀他的妻子被控诉。

Please charge these bills to my account. 请把这些帐单记在我的账上。

He forgot to charge the battery. 他忘记给电池充电了。

She was charged with an important mission. 她被委以重任。

Nurse Jackie
《护士当家》

👧 入选理由：

　　《护士当家》是 2009 年美国娱乐时间电视网推出的一部黑色医务剧，该剧特别邀请到荣获艾美奖和金球奖的埃迪·法可出演女主角，她将这个角色的特立独行、不拘小节表现得淋漓尽致。该剧于 2010 年获金球奖喜剧最佳女主角提名、2010 年美国艾美奖最佳喜剧提名、2010 年美国艾美奖最佳喜剧导演提名、2010 年美国艾美奖喜剧演员提名（全剧演员）等多项殊荣。《纽约客》曾对它赞誉不已：虽然它只展示出现实中护士的一面（甚至可以说是零面），但剧中用平述的方式描述复杂强烈又有些许诙谐的冲突，却让人倍感真实。《纽约时报》对这部剧也倍加赞扬：不冗长困乏的剧情片，不肤浅可笑的喜剧片，两者兼之，就是《护士当家》。

Section 1　剧情特点：

　　"医生只负责诊断，我们才负责治疗。"听起来荒谬的言论成为《护士当家》所要表达的中心。由于被他人忽略，从而加强自我肯定认知以证明自己的存在，这是人之常情，所以在医生唱绝对主角的医疗界，剧中的护士杰基试图用"主次颠倒"的方式来证明自己职业的非凡意义，甚至超过医生。但这"移位"肯定无法实现，因此《护士当家》呈现出不少无奈，医生库伯再怎么被杰基嘲笑吊儿郎当，也会凭着"经验"诊断出动脉瘤。与此同时，编剧也以巧妙的方式呈现出杰基周围所存在的黑暗：各取所需的性爱关系、唾手可得的违禁药物、因人性的缺陷而导致的生命垂危……杰基无法逃避，卷入其中，甚至成为制造者。明明有健康家庭的她，却每到医院就脱下无名指上的结婚戒指。她一面向患者解释药物成瘾的危害，一面又把违禁药物碾磨成粉状"一日三餐"定时服用。即便杰基是个病态的人，但你又无法把她同剧中的其他角色归为同类，因为杰基在冷眼旁观的同时，也很有自知之明，了解自己存在的问题。看到疼爱她的丈夫，活泼可爱的女儿，她会自己退到黑色的阴影下，因为家人在她的生活中显得太明亮了。作为一出医务剧，《护士当家》既没有《豪斯医生》里那么冷僻离奇的案例，也鲜见《实习医生格蕾》中错综纠结的情感关系，它只是以纽约全圣医院为主要背景，讲述着杰基·佩顿的工作和生活，较为生活化。然而，正是这些波澜不惊的情节，展现了杰基·佩顿独特的人格魅力。她摆脱了世俗道德观念的束缚，游走于光明与黑暗交接的灰色地带，但又时刻秉持着人性中那份可贵的善良。加之，剧中各具特色的配角围绕着主角杰基·佩顿轮番登场，用诙谐幽默的方式演绎着世间百态，一出黑色幽默剧跃然荧屏。

Section 2　对白特点：

该剧的语言非常精致考究，常有冷幽默，出现一些"言外之意"，使观众在观剧过程中充满意外的惊喜。只是些简单的小事情便能引人发笑，这是本剧的成功之处。随着剧情的展开，我们还会通过一些细枝末节的事件，了解美国本土的一些文化、社会制度、伦理、观念等，涉及的内容主要有：医疗救济体系、学校教育观念、家庭教育模式、上下级相处模式等，这无疑为观众了解西方人的文化和生活方式打开了一扇大门。

Section 3　角色分析：

杰基·佩顿 (Jackie Paton): 医术精湛的护士，慈祥和善的母亲，有夫可依的妻子，情感纠结的婚外恋者，不为人知的瘾君子，惩恶扬善的热心人……当把这一张张标签都贴在杰基·佩顿身上时，显而易见，她是一个异常尖锐的矛盾体。在依赖药物成瘾、和同事偷情、对老公满嘴谎言的表象下，她又时不时以其善良、温情、怜悯和敢作敢当带给你意外和感动。不管她对待药物、丈夫和感情如何，没有人能否认她是个好护士：善良、有正义感、有责任心、业务水平高！她挣扎于家庭与医院、婚姻与婚外恋之间，被认为自私或者道德沦陷，但是她对待病人的态度及对工作的热忱总是让人觉得她身上的光辉已经盖过了这些瑕疵。主角的高超演技更使得这一形象丰满真实。

歌莉娅·爱卡里塔斯 (Gloria Akalitus): 护士主管，作为上级主管的歌莉娅看起来很严肃但心地善良，这一角色也是本剧的一大笑点。

埃莉诺·奥哈拉医生 (Dr. Eleanor O'Hara): 医院的权威医生，拜金单身女郎，杰基的死党，与杰基截然不同的性格，却是她最好的朋友。她们有着共同的幽默感，都很能干，同样对感情看得很淡。奥哈拉操着一口浓重苏格兰口音的英文。

卓伊·巴尔考 (Zoey Barkow): 医院的实习生，护校毕业的学生。她以杰基为偶像，希望成为一名伟大的护士，可是总会粗心办错事，因此时常困惑，认为自己不能胜任护士工作。

埃迪·沃尔泽 (Eddie Walzer)：药剂师，杰基的情人，但并不知道杰基已婚。他知道杰基嗑药的秘密，并利用手中职权，向杰基·佩顿提供多种止痛药，后来因为医院引进自动售药机而离开医院。

凯文·佩顿 (Kevin Peyton)：杰基的老公，极力拯救家庭破裂的现状，酒吧小老板，个性不鲜明。

格蕾丝·佩顿 (Grace Peyton)：杰基的大女儿，虽然还是个小朋友，但是在缺乏母爱的情况下变得早熟，是个十足的问题儿童，需要杰基特别关注。

托尔·兰格伦 (Thor Lundgren)：护士，同时也是糖尿病患者，总和歌莉娅过不去。

Passage 1

剧情介绍：

（选自第 2 季第 1 集）在本集中，库伯向杰基献殷勤，邀请她一起看电影，但遭到无情拒绝。库伯在治疗时对患有糖尿病的护士托尔态度粗暴，被杰基严厉指责并被迫向托尔道歉。恼羞成怒的库伯向上司歌莉娅投诉杰基，说杰基对他呼来喝去，使他颜面无存。

Scene 1: Jackie criticizes Cooper for his offensive manner toward Thor, who suffers from diabetes.

杰基批评库伯对患有糖尿病的托尔态度蛮横。

Jackie: You are mad at me. Do not take it out on him.

Cooper: Who? Who am I taking it out on?

Jackie: Thor. He's **diabetic**[1]. You know that, right? The guy has a reaction, you go after him like a **bully**[2] on the playground. That's classy, Coop.

Cooper: I didn't. How am I supposed to know?

Jackie: He wears a big fucking bracelet that says "I am diabetic."

Cooper: I'm sorry.

Thor: Totally worth it.

Jackie: Come with me.

Thor: I am so sorry. I didn't time my **insulin**[3] right.

Jackie: You can't do that, Thor. Nurses **passing out**[4] on patients? Not good.

Thor: I know.

Jackie: It's a good thing it was Coop. The other doctors don't scare so easy.

Thor: He can't tell Akalitus that my blood sugar dropped in trauma. She'll move me to the chemo ward or, ugh, maternity. I love **trauma**[5].

Jackie: You just got to remember to eat. And you got to **lay off**[6] the fried shit and the cake. Jesus, Thor. what is with you and cake?

Thor: I don't drink. I don't smoke. I eat cake.

Jackie: Cake is good.

Thor: It's comfort food. Why do the things that are so bad for you make you feel the best?

Jackie: I hear ya.

(From Eddie: It's been 3 months and counting. Answer my calls!!)

杰基: 你有气冲我来，别拿他当出气筒。

库伯: 谁？我没拿谁撒气啊？

杰基: 托尔，你知道他有糖尿病，是吧？他一出岔子，你就像操场小霸王似的欺负他，真够绅士啊，库伯!

库伯: 我怎么知道他有病？

杰基: 他那手环大得直碍眼，上面写着"我有糖尿病"呢!

库伯: 对不起。

托尔: 值了!

杰基: 跟我来。

托尔: 实在对不起，我没按时注射胰岛素。

杰基: 你不能这样，托尔，护士在病人面前昏倒，这可不大好。

托尔: 我知道。

杰基: 幸亏在场的是库伯，其他医生没他那么容易恐吓。

托尔: 我在外科犯低血糖的事，但愿他不会告诉阿卡利特斯。她会把我调到化疗病区的，甚至妇产科，我爱外科。

杰基: 那你就别忘了吃饭。而且必须戒了油炸食品和蛋糕。天呐，托尔，你干嘛对蛋糕恋恋不舍的？

托尔: 我不抽烟不喝酒，就是爱吃蛋糕。

杰基: 蛋糕的确是好东西。

托尔: 它是安慰食品，为什么我的健康杀手恰恰最能让我开心？

杰基: 我理解。

（发信人埃迪: 这都三个月了，快回我电话! ）

注释
1. **diabetic** [ˌdaɪə'betɪk] *adj.* 糖尿病的
2. **bully** ['bʊlɪ] *n.* 仗势欺人者，横行霸道者
3. **insulin** ['ɪnsjəlɪn] *n.* 胰岛素
4. **pass out** <口> 昏厥
5. **trauma** ['trɔːmə] *n.* 创伤，此处指外科

Sam:	I get why I make you nervous.	山姆：	我知道你为什么见我就紧张了。
Jackie:	I'm sorry?	杰基：	什么？
Sam:	That time when I was fucked up and I told you it takes one to know one? I had no right to say that.	山姆：	当时我嗑药嗑得一塌糊涂，还跟你说，咱彼此彼此。我没权利说那话。
Jackie:	And I have no idea what you're talking about.	杰基：	我根本不知道你在说什么。
Sam:	But if you ever want to talk or go to a meeting.	山姆：	但如果你想谈谈或参加个交流会什么的。
Jackie:	Oh, I'm sorry. Can we get something straight right now? You and I are not **buddies**[7]. You got it?	杰基：	停，抱歉，打开天窗说亮话吧，咱不是好哥们，明白吗？
Sam:	If you say so.	山姆：	你说了算。
Jackie:	Good.	杰基：	那就好。

Scene 2: Gloria's office. She is phoning in her office and in a while Cooper comes.
歌莉娅在办公室里打电话，这时库伯走了进来要投诉杰基。

Gloria:	No, you listen to me. I spent my day off at a **pathetic**[8] medical equipment **auction**[9] in New Jersey **bidding**[10] on a refurbished med fusion syringe pump for the E.R. I won. I put it on my credit **card**[11]. You approved this. If I don't have a check on my desk in the morning, I'm gonna come down there and kick your ass! Thank you, monsignor. Have a good day. Come in.	歌莉娅：	不，你给我听着，我放弃休假去参加那破医学器械拍卖会，远赴新泽西给急诊室买了台翻新的台式输注泵。我竞拍到手了，还自掏腰包，你们也接受了。如果明早还不见收据，我就去狠狠教训你！谢谢您，阁下。祝您愉快！请进。
Cooper:	Got a minute?	库伯：	有空吗？
Gloria:	Certainly.	歌莉娅：	当然。
Cooper:	I need to **lodge a formal complaint against**[12] a nurse.	库伯：	我要投诉一名护士。

Gloria: Super.	歌莉娅: 好极了!
Cooper: It's nurse Jackie.	库伯: 是杰基护士。
Gloria: Really?	歌莉娅: 是吗?
Cooper: She constantly challenges my decisions, is bossy and rude and unpleasant. Bully. That's the word. She's a bully. There's *a chain of*[1] command here that she refuses to **acknowledge**[13]. I am at the top of that chain of command, okay? She is at the bottom and I am the top. If this were a food *pyramid*[14], I would be the **steak**[15].	库伯: 她总是质疑我的决断,颐指气使,粗暴无礼,横行霸道。对,就是这词,横行霸道。这里有上行下效的机制她却拒不遵守。她是下级,我是上级。这要是在食物金字塔里,我就是牛排。
Gloria: Well, technically, I think fats and oils are at the top of the food pyramid.	歌莉娅: 实际上,我记得食物金字塔顶端是脂肪和油。
Cooper: I am a good fucking doctor. And for a nurse, a nurse, to be messing with my head by constantly **undermining**[16] me? Am I going too fast? 'cause I can slow down if you need me to. What happens when a patient gets wheeled in here one day, and that poor guy sees Jackie *yelling at*[2] me like I'm the world's biggest **asshole**[17]? How do you think it makes the patient feel? I don't think it makes him feel any better.	库伯: 我是个妙手回春的医生。她一个小小的护士,就敢干扰我,鄙视我?我是不是说得太快了?需要的话,我可以慢点。如果有一天,来了一个病人,正好撞见杰基拿我当绝世大坏蛋那样呼来喝去怎么办?病人会怎么想?这对病人有弊无利。
Gloria: Thanks. I'll **get into**[18] this.	歌莉娅: 谢谢你。我会妥善处理的。
Cooper: That was good. I feel better. That was good.	库伯: 那就好。我感觉好多了。那就好。

注释
6. lay off 停止	**13. acknowledge** [ək'nɒlɪdʒ] *vt.* 承认
7. buddy ['bʌdɪ] *n.* 密友,好友;同伴	**14. pyramid** ['pɪrəmɪd] *n.* 金字塔
8. pathetic [pə'θetɪk] *adj.* 令人同情的,无价值的	**15. steak** [steɪk] *n.* 牛排
9. auction ['ɔːkʃn] *n.* 拍卖会	**16. undermine** [ˌʌndə'maɪn] *vt.* 逐渐削弱;暗中损害
10. bid [bɪd] *v.* 出价;投标	**17. asshole** ['æʃəʊl] *n.* <粗>讨厌的人
11. credit card 信用卡	**18. get into** 对……发生兴趣;卷入;进入
12. lodge a formal complaint against 对……进行正式投诉	

文化背景

1. food pyramid 食物金字塔

食物金字塔是一种为指导人们正确地选择饮食而设计的每日食物摄入量图表，为有助于人们理解各种营养物质的比例，结合人体生理特征做成了类似金字塔的形状。金字塔分为四层，居于底部的是人们每日不可缺少的谷物类食品，每天约要 300—500 克；第三层是水果类（100—200 克）和蔬菜类（400—500 克）；第二层是奶制品、豆制品以及鱼禽肉等蛋白类，每天需要 50 克左右；油脂类属于金字塔的最顶端，每天不超过 25 克。

常用表达

1. a chain of 一系列（一连串）

例： The traffic accident led to a chain of events.

交通事故引起了一连串的事件。

The enemy tank car caught fire and set off a chain of explosions.

敌人的油车着了火，引起了一连串的爆炸。

2. yell at 对……吼叫

例： Don't yell at me. It's not my fault.

别冲着我吼，那可不是我的错。

She yelled at the child to get down from the wall.

她喊着让小孩从墙上下来。

🔊 Passage 2 📷

剧情介绍：

（选自第 2 季第 3 集）本集中，库伯靠公关被评为曼哈顿 25 名最杰出的医生之一，并刊登在杂志上。得意洋洋的库伯拿着杂志到处炫耀。杰基的死党奥哈拉想用她母亲留下的财产给杰基的孩子们建立基金，但杰基告诉丈夫凯文时，却遭到他的坚决反对。

Scene: Cooper buys a lot of things in Eddie's shop and tells Eddie he is on the list of the top 25 docs of all Manhattan.

库伯到埃迪的药店里买了很多东西，并告诉埃迪他被评为曼哈顿 25 名杰出医生之一。

🔊 **Eddie:** So what are you shopping here for? This **stuff**[1] costs 10 times more than at a real **grocery**[2] store.	**埃迪:** 你为什么要来这里购物？这里的东西比真正的百货店要贵 10 倍。
Cooper: Okay, buddy, I'll be honest with you. I was worried about you. You took an **overdose**[3] and had to have your stomach pumped. Did you do it 'cause of, you know, this place?	**库伯:** 好吧，兄弟，实话和你说，我担心你。你服药过量，还洗了胃。是因为在这里给憋坏了吗？
Eddie: No, I didn't do it because of this place.	**埃迪:** 不，和这里没有关系。
Cooper: Whatever you say, bro. I'm just here to support, not judge. Hey, prepare for a mind explosion. I'm on the list of the top 25 docs of all Manhattan.	**库伯:** 随你怎么说。兄弟，我在这儿是表示支持的，不是来批评你的。嘿，准备好了，爆炸新闻！我被评为曼哈顿最杰出 25 名医生之一。
Eddie: I don't know what to say about that.	**埃迪:** 我不知道说什么好了。
Cooper: Yeah, I know. Right? I bought all this **crap**[4] so I wouldn't, you know, get you in any trouble with your boss.	**库伯:** 没关系，理解。我买了这么一堆废物，你老板不能找你茬了吧？
Eddie: I am my boss.	**埃迪:** 我的老板就是我自己。
Cooper: You are? They pay you **decent**[5]?	**库伯:** 是吗？薪水高吗？

注释
1. stuff [stʌf] *n.* 东西；原料；材料
2. grocery ['grəusəri] *n.* 杂货店
3. overdose ['əuvədəus] *n.* 配药量过多；过量
4. crap [kræp] *n.* <俚> 质量差的东西；垃圾
5. decent ['di:snt] *adj.* 相当好的；体面的

Eddie:	That's personal, Coop.	埃迪：	这是隐私，伙计。
Cooper:	Come on, seriously? With me, there's no such thing as too personal.	库伯：	得了吧，说真的，对于我来说没什么隐私。
Eddie:	I already knew that about you, Coop.	埃迪：	这点我了解，兄弟。
Cooper:	We kind of have a **shorthand**[6], right? Don't you think? A little bit, hmm? You and me.	库伯：	我们很有默契，是吧？你难道不觉得吗？有点儿？你和我？
Eddie:	Sending somebody a text?	埃迪：	在给别人发信息吗？
Cooper:	Nope. <u>Tweeting</u>[1]. Just letting people know where I am.	库伯：	不是，推特。让人们知道我在哪儿。
Eddie:	What people?	埃迪：	什么人？
Cooper:	My followers. I have 240. You should try it. A guy like you would probably have 100 at least.	库伯：	我的粉丝们，我有 240 个粉丝。你应该试试，像你这样的人至少能有 100 个。
Eddie:	No, thanks.	埃迪：	不用了，谢谢。
Cooper:	So, just so you know, if you need anything, if you just want to talk, you're on my way to work. I can *drop in* anytime you want.	库伯：	你要是有什么需要，你想找人说话，路过我的医院，我随传随到。
Eddie:	So anyway, who told you? Was it Jackie?	埃迪：	谁告诉你的？杰基吗？
Cooper:	It's all over the hospital that you tried to kill yourself.	库伯：	你要寻死的事整个医院都知道了。
Eddie:	Shit.	埃迪：	浑蛋！
Cooper:	No worries, man. I sent out a tweet saying you were totally alive.	库伯：	别担心，兄弟。我发推特说你活得很好。
Eddie:	Please don't do that.	埃迪：	请不要这么做。
Cooper:	All right. It's probably pretty much still an open wound for you.	库伯：	好，这可能对你是公然的伤害。
Eddie:	But Jackie told you, right?	埃迪：	但是杰基告诉你的，对吧？
Cooper:	No, I think it was Thor— the diabetic.	库伯：	不，我记得是托尔，我是说那个得糖尿病的。
Eddie:	So did she say anything, Jackie?	埃迪：	那她说什么了吗，我是说杰基？
Cooper:	Truth be told, we're not exactly talking at the moment. In fact, I had to file a **complaint**[7] against her with Akalitus for **insubordination**[8]. I will **crush**[9] her! Well, I should get to work. You sure you're okay?	库伯：	说实话，我们现在不太说话。事实上，我已经和阿卡利特斯就她不服从上级的事提出申诉了。我要把她打垮！我得回去工作了，你确定还好吗？
Eddie:	Yeah. Listen, sometimes I get **migraines**[10]. I mixed some **meds**[11], I drank a few beers. It	埃迪：	很好。有的时候我偏头痛，我弄点儿药，喝点儿酒。那是失误，

was mistake, no big deal. I'm good. In fact, I'm great. Tell everybody or not.

Cooper: Whatever you say, bro.

Eddie: All right, man.

(Jackie and O'Hara are chatting when Cooper walks by and throws the magazine to them.)

Jackie: So anyway, she left the house, I just **chucked**[12] the whole thing in the garbage. I know that if she **had her way**[13], she would be Mrs. Ginny Payton; I would be going home to some other **dude**[14].

O'Hara: Well, if you want to avoid people from your past, I recommend moving to another country. Worked for me.

Jackie: Another thing: I don't want Kaitlyn's **snottiness**[15] to **rub off on**[16] grace.

O'Hara: **Snot**[17] is **viral**[18]; snottiness is not.

Jackie: So anyway, I talked to Kevin about your idea of the gift for the girls and I—it just makes him uncomfortable.

O'Hara: Do you know what would make him really uncomfortable? A daughter who's a lap **dancer**[19]. Take the money. Get them an education.

(Cooper comes, throwing the magazine to them.)

Jackie: Okay.

O'Hara: 25 best doctors in Manhattan? Number 23, All Saints Hospital; Dr. Fitch Cooper?

Jackie: How did this happen?

O'Hara: It's a bloody **outrage**[20]. Where the fuck am I?

没什么大不了的，我挺好。事实上，我好极了！告诉大家吧。

库伯： 随你说什么，兄弟。

埃迪： 好的，伙计。

（杰基和奥哈拉在拉家常，这时库伯走过来把他获奖的那本杂志扔给她们。）

杰基： 她一离开我家，我就把整盘吃的都丢掉了。我知道如果当年让她得逞，她就会是吉尼·佩顿太太了，而我就和别人一起回家了。

奥哈拉： 你要是想逃避旧识建议你搬到别的地方去，反正这招对我管用。

杰基： 另外，我不想让凯特琳的自大影响格蕾丝。

奥哈拉： 流鼻涕是传染的，自大不是。

杰基： 还有，我和凯文提了你给孩子们设立基金的主意，我……就是这件事让他感觉不爽。

奥哈拉： 你知道什么会真正让他不爽吗？有一个跳脱衣舞的女儿。拿着钱，让她们接受教育。

（库伯走过来，把杂志扔给杰基后离开。）

杰基： 好的。

奥哈拉： "曼哈顿25名杰出医生"？第23名：圣慈医院费奇·库伯医生？

杰基： 这怎么可能？

奥哈拉： 这太过分了，我排多少位啊？

注释
6. **have (share) a shorthand** 有默契
7. **file a complaint** 投诉
8. **insubordination** n. 不服从，反抗
9. **crush** [krʌʃ] v. （常指通过武力）制服，镇压，彻底击败
10. **migraine** ['miːɡreɪn] n. <医>偏头痛
11. **meds abbr. medicaments** 医药制剂
12. **chuck** [tʃʌk] v. （口语）抛出，扔出
13. **have one's way** 得逞

14. **dude** [djuːd] n. <俚>男人，家伙
15. **snottiness** n. 自大
16. **rub off on** 因磨擦而沾上，因接触而对……产生影响
17. **snot** [snɒt] n. 流鼻涕
18. **viral** ['vaɪrəl] adj. 病毒的
19. **lap dance** 大腿舞，脱衣舞
20. **outrage** ['aʊtreɪdʒ] n. 暴行；骇人听闻的事件

📖 文化背景

1. Tweet 推特

推特是国外的一个社交网络及微博客服务的网站。它允许用户将自己的最新动态和想法以短信形式发送到手机和个性化网站群，而不仅仅是发送给个人。

🖋 常用表达

1. drop in 顺便拜访

例: By the way, why not drop in for a drink this evening?

顺便说一句，今晚到我家喝一杯怎么样？

She spent most of the day dropping in on friends in Edinburgh.

她一天的大部分时间都用来拜访在爱丁堡的朋友了。

Passage 3

剧情介绍:

（选自第 3 季第 1 集）上集中杰基的丈夫凯文无意中发现杰基的专用邮箱和信用卡，得知她不但瞒着他用了奥哈拉的钱，还是个嗑药的瘾君子。他约奥哈拉到家里告诉了她杰基嗑药上瘾的事，为此杰基和凯文发生了激烈争吵。杰基告诉歌莉娅奥哈拉已经知道她是瘾君子了。

Scene 1: Kevin discovers Jackie's P.O. Box and the credit card and feels cheated. A quarrel bursts out between them and Jackie defends for herself.

凯文发现杰基的专用邮箱和信用卡后感觉杰基骗了他，杰基和凯文发生了激烈争吵。

Jackie:	Kevin! Kevin! Where the fuck are you? Is she gone?	杰基:	凯文！凯文！你在哪里？她走了？
Kevin:	That's a nice way to treat **company**[1].	凯文:	你的待友之道还真可以！
Jackie:	O'hara, really? You couldn't handle this yourself?	杰基:	你居然找奥哈拉？这种事自己应付不来吗？
Kevin:	This isn't about me, Jackie.	凯文:	这不是我的问题，杰基。
Jackie:	Here, take a look at this stuff, Kevin. Well, we've got razors, fuckin' muscle relaxers. Half the shit on here is school supplies. Look, Gracie's ear-drops. A hundred and ten-Fuckin'-dollars unless you wanna buy the **generic crap**[2], which I don't. That's what this is.	杰基:	看看这些东西，凯文。有剃须刀，该死的肌肉松弛剂，这里面有一半的东西都是学校用品。看格蕾丝的滴耳剂，都是几百美元的东西。除非你肯买便宜货，我可不肯，就是这样。
Kevin:	I am not talking about ear-drops.	凯文:	我说的不是滴耳剂。
Jackie:	Okay, we got ambien, vicodin. I don't fuckin' sleep, Kevin. My body is falling **apart**[3]. What do you want for me? Call the cops. Why aren't the girls here?	杰基:	那好，还有安眠药、维柯丁、我晚上睡不着啊，凯文！整个身子都散架了，你想我怎么样？有本事叫警察啊！姑娘们去哪儿了？
Kevin:	They're fine. I don't keep secrets[1], Jackie.	凯文:	她们没事。我没有秘密的，杰基。
Jackie:	Kevin, neither do I.	杰基:	凯文，我也没有啊！
Kevin:	Bullshit! The credit card.	凯文:	胡说，你的信用卡呢？

注释
1. company ['kʌmpəni] *n.* 同伴，客人
2. generic crap 廉价货，不知名的产品
3. falling apart 散开，崩溃，破碎；散架

Jackie:	Separate, not secret. Separate. Since when do I have to run every little fuckin' thing by you? When have we ever done things like that? When was the last time you bought your own razors?
Kevin:	And you need a **P.O. Box**[4] to do all that?
Jackie:	You know what? Here. Here, take the fuckin' key.
Kevin:	Answer the question, Jackie. Why do you keep a P.O. Box? No, forget it. Not gonna believe a word. Doesn't matter.
Jackie:	No, it doesn't matter. You know why? Because I keep the house **stocked**[5]. That's my job because you can't manage money. And by the way, what message are we sending Fi? "I'm sorry, you're just not quite as important as Grace. We have money for her tuition, but not yours." It's tuition, Kevin! You find it! I should never have had to beg. For god's sake, I sure **as hell**[6] shouldn't have to sneak around. She is your daughter! You know what? From now on buy your own fucking razors! I'm getting my kids.

杰基：	是隐私，不是秘密，是隐私！我从什么时候开始需要样样事情都要经过你同意了？什么时候变成这样了？你最近是什么时候买的新剃须刀？
凯文：	那你还需要专门弄个邮箱？
杰基：	好，那这样，把这该死的钥匙拿去吧。
凯文：	回答我的问题，杰基，为什么要专门弄个邮箱？还是算了，反正你的话我一个字都不信，无所谓了。
杰基：	是无所谓，你知道为什么吗？因为家里的事都是我管，只有我能做，因为你管不好钱。还有，这样对菲儿会有什么影响？让她觉得"抱歉，你没有格蕾丝来得重要。我们付得起她的学费，但你的不行"。这可是教育啊，凯文！你自己掂量。我根本不该去乞求什么的，老天无眼，我就不该这么偷偷摸摸。她可是你的女儿！从现在开始你自己买剃须刀去吧，我去接孩子们了。

Scene 2: Jackie picks up her daughters.

杰基开车去接孩子们。

Jackie:	Hi, guys!
Fiona:	Mom!
Jackie:	Did you have fun?
Fiona:	Yes.
Jackie:	What did you have for dinner?
Fiona:	Bacon and snowballs.
Jackie:	Bacon and snowballs? Yippee!
Fiona:	And, oh my god, aunt Tunie has a boyfriend that's a **pilot**[7].

杰基：	嗨，孩子们！
菲奥娜：	妈妈！
杰基：	玩得开心吗？
菲奥娜：	嗯。
杰克：	晚饭吃了什么？
格蕾丝：	培根和冰激凌。
杰基：	培根和冰激凌啊，太棒了！
菲奥娜：	还有，图尼阿姨的男朋友是飞行员。

Scene 3: Jackie tells Gloria that O'hara learns her secret of taking painkillers.

杰基去找歌莉娅，告诉她奥哈拉已经知道她是个瘾君子。

Jackie: Can I steal you a minute? This is entirely **pree-mptive**[8]. There is nothing to be worried about.

杰基： 能占用你一分钟吗？我想预先给你说个事，没什么好担心的。

Gloria: Already worried.

歌莉娅： 但我已经开始担心了。

Jackie: Don't be. I've been doing this for 20 years, Gloria. Parts of my body are *giving out*[1].

杰基： 不用担心，我干这行 20 年了，歌莉娅，我身体的一部分扛不住啊！

Gloria: What are we preempting?

歌莉娅： 你想要预先说什么？

Jackie: I started *leaning on*[2] **painkillers**[9]. It was a couple months, totally **self-corrected**[10].

杰基： 我开始依赖止痛药了。有几个月了，完全属于自我调节。

Gloria: This doesn't have anything to do with the **Pill-O-Matix**[11], does it?

歌莉娅： 和那个取药机没关系吧？

Jackie: No, no, not at all. Nothing like that. My husband opened a credit card bill, but he called O'hara.

杰基： 没有没有，和那个无关。我丈夫查看了一张信用卡账单，他打电话叫了奥哈拉。

Gloria: Not good.

歌莉娅： 这不妙啊！

Jackie: No, no, no, not at all. Not for anybody. I'm fine, but he should not have called O'hara. Her family, like, drug **addicts**[12]. Like pump-your-stomach, die-in-your-sleep drug addicts. My husband feels like shit. He *had no clue*[3] what her deal was when he called her.

杰基： 太不妙了，对谁来说都不妙！我没事，但他不应该打电话找奥哈拉的。她家人一个个的都是瘾君子，动不动就送去洗胃，再不就是睡着睡着死了。所以她对此反应很大，我丈夫觉得很棘手，他打电话给她时完全不知道她的状况。

Gloria: I don't know what you want me to do.

歌莉娅： 我不知道你要我怎么做。

Jackie: I don't know. She might come in here. And if she does, I would just ask that you take whatever she says **with a grain of salt**[13],

杰基： 我不知道。她可能会来这儿，要是真来了，我只要你对她的话别太当真，仅此而已。

注释

4. P.O. Box 是 **Post Office Box** 的简写，邮政信箱

5. stock [stɒk] *vt.* 提供货物；备有

6. as hell 非常地，极端地

7. pilot ['paɪlət] *n.* 飞行员

8. preemptive [prɪ'emptɪv] *adj.* 先发制人的

9. painkiller ['peɪnkɪlə(r)] *n.* 止痛药

10. self-corrected *adj.* 自动调整的；自动修正的

11. Pill-O-Matix 自动售药机

12. drug addict 吸毒成瘾者；药瘾者

13. a grain of salt 有保留地

that's all.

Gloria: Respect your sister, but consider the source.

Jackie: I'm not sure what that means, but yes.

Gloria: Jackie, if a co-worker so much as raises I am required by law to inform H.R. That's just the way it is. Fix it.

Jackie: Got it.

歌莉娅： 态度尊重，但意见保留。

杰基： 我不确定是什么意思，但，好吧。

歌莉娅： 杰基，如果同事滥用药物，我应该依照法律通知人力资源部门。事情就该是这样子，搞定这事。

杰基： 明白。

📖 文化背景

1. secret 秘密

个人隐私是欧美文化中一个很重要的方面，更常用的单词是 privacy。对待隐私的不同态度更是体现了东西方文化在对待个人问题上的明显差异。在西方，凡当事人不愿他人知道或他人不便知道的个人信息，当事人不愿他人干涉或他人不便干涉的个人私事，以及当事人不愿他人侵入或他人不便侵入的个人领域都属于隐私范畴。具体的说，一个人的宗教信仰、年龄、工资、病历、性取向、服装的品牌、参加的俱乐部——几乎一切都是隐私，探听别人的隐私是一件非常无礼和冒犯别人的举动。这一点，对于习惯集体生活、习惯共享的中国人是要特别注意的。

🖲 常用表达

1. give out 用尽；出故障

例： Her patience finally gave out.

她终于失去了耐性。

After a month their food supplies gave out.

过了一个月，他们的食物已消耗殆尽。

One of the plane's engines gave out in mid-Atlantic.

飞机在大西洋中部飞行时，其中一个发动机出了故障。

2. lean on 依靠于……

例： We lean on our friends when we are in trouble.

我们遇到困难时依靠朋友帮助。

3. have no clue 无线索；全然不知

例： We have no clue as to where she went after she left home.

我们对她离家后去往何处毫无线索。

Mother said she had no clue what was inside.

母亲说她一点也不记得里面装的什么。

注释 **14. H.R.** abbr.(human resource) 人力资源部门

16

Call The Midwife
《呼叫助产士》

入选理由：

　　这是一部非常棒的电视剧，每天都在学习如何去爱，如何打开自己的思想，展现了非常细腻的情感，画面宁静美好。我们的一生要学习的就是如何感受爱，陪伴我们一生的也是我们的思想与感受，这需要每一天都坚持。富有人生哲理的旁白，以及每位人物透出的魅力，都能使我们学习到更多，感受到更多，并能引为己用。

　　英国广播公司的新剧《呼叫助产士》季终集最终俘获了 920 万观众，不仅创下全季收视新高，也帮助该剧轻松打破记录：凭借第一季平均收视 870 万（市场份额 29.6%）的好成绩，成为自 2001 年新收视测量系统采用后十年来英国广播公司 1 频道收视最高的新剧。

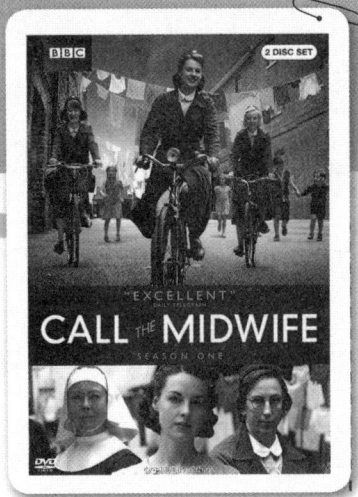

Section 1　剧情特点：

　　《呼叫助产士》根据珍妮弗·沃斯的同名回忆录改编，讲的是 20 世纪 50 年代伦敦东部贫民区一群助产士的故事。助产士作为一种特殊护士进行专门培训，在英国是从 20 世纪 50 年代开始的。作为社区助产士，沃斯和她的同事不仅要在医院帮助接生，还要到社区中走访孕妇和产妇，见到了人生百态。多年之后她将对这段回忆集结成书，大受好评，随后又出版了《贫民作坊的阴影》(*Shadows of Workhouse*)和《再见东区》(*Farewell to East End*)，这三部成为"助产士三部曲"。

　　她的回忆录给人最大的震撼是 20 世纪 50 年代伦敦东区的贫困，这与《唐顿庄园》完全是两个世界。当时英国虽然在二战中获胜，但整个国家却几乎破产，原来的"大英帝国"急剧萎缩，基本上要靠美国维持经济稳定，二战中实施的商品配给制度一直延续到战后。许多读者对书中所描述的当时的孕妇所面临的恶劣条件和社会压力感到震惊，电视剧并没有回避这些，但更多邻里互助及患难真情的场面，温馨催泪，吸引了大批观众。

Section 2 对白特点：

本剧是由珍妮弗·沃斯的同名回忆录改编的，所以与其他剧集单纯的对话相比，本剧的一大特色就是其中的内心独白。每次经历触动内心和灵魂的事情，主人公便会发表珍妮弗内心的想法和观点，这些话画龙点睛，往往为故事的发展和转折提供了重要线索。另外，"我是他的医院，他是我的血液""每一名母亲都是一位伟大的女英雄"，这样震撼人心的话在本剧中比比皆是，在享受纯正英语的同时，能感受到浓浓的爱。

Section 3 角色分析：

朱利安娜 (Julienne)：诺那塔斯修道院的修女，作为护士长她十分关心大家，识大体，顾大局，善于组织领导，能很好把大家团结在一起，大家对她都十分尊重。

伊万杰琳 (Evangelina)：诺那塔斯修道院的修女，从小家境贫寒，所以对富人会有偏见。心胸狭隘，做事小气，爱刁难别人，但是心眼并不坏。

米勒 (Miller)：是一名年轻的护士，年龄较小，还是个小孩，也十分淳朴、可爱，是李的好同事、好朋友。

弗兰克林 (Franklin)：是一名年轻的护士，说话油嘴滑舌，年轻时尚，心眼较多。

查米 (Chummy)：第 2 集新来报到的实习生，家境殷实。长得人高马大，动作笨拙，但大大咧咧，心地十分善良。以实际行动证明了她可以把助产士做得很好，第 3 集中与当地一名警察开始恋爱。

珍妮·李 (Jenny Lee)：一位新获得助产士资格的女护士，年轻，家境优越，未经世事，让珍妮没有想到的是，她千里迢迢来到自己的工作地点，展现在她眼前的，竟然是一间修道院。在看到伦敦东区脏乱差的生活条件后，简直不敢相信自己的眼睛。本来可以去当空姐、模特，成为各种光鲜亮丽的角色。但她偏偏一负气，踩着高跟鞋，拎着小皮箱，走进了贫民窟。

Passage 1

剧情介绍：

（选自第1季第1集）年轻美丽的李只身一人来到伦敦东区的诺那塔斯修道院（Nonnatus House），成为了一名助产士，经过几次锻炼，终于成为一名合格的助产士。

Scene:	Outside the door. 在门外。

Lee: Hello, I'm Jennifer Lee. I was told to report the **matron**[1] in charge.

李： 你好，我是詹妮弗·李，他们让我来找护士长。

Joan: Venus and Saturn are now in **alignment**[2]. It is entirely appropriate that you should appear! Welcome to Nonnatus House. What do you suppose that is? One hears of visitors, from realms apart from ours.

琼： 上帝保佑，你来的正是时候。欢迎来到诺那塔斯修道院，你看，那是什么？有人说是远方来客。

Lee: I think it's an aeroplane.

李： 我觉得就是架飞机。

Joan: From the extreme height of your heels, I deduce that you are not a **nun**[3].

琼： 你鞋跟那么高，应该不是修女吧。

Lee: Are you a nun?

李： 你是修女吗？

Joan: We are the Sisters[1] of St. Raymond Nonnatus, midwives and district nurses, present at life's commencement and at its end. I assume you are possessed of the appropriate **credentials**[4]?

琼： 我们都是雷蒙·诺那塔斯的修女、助产士和地方护士，见证新生与死亡。你应该有资格证吧？

Lee: I'm a trained nurse. And I've just qualified as a midwife.

李： 我受过护士培训，刚拿到助产士资格证。

Joan: The blooms upon this table are my especial care. Dear St. Raymond Nonnatus, happy survivor of Caesarean **section**[5]. I feel we are prompted to go

琼： 桌上的这盆植物是我的宝贝，可敬的雷蒙·诺那塔斯，剖腹产出生的幸运儿。我们去吃蛋糕吧！他们以为他们藏得很

注释
1. **matron** ['meɪtrən] n. 主妇；保姆；妇女；女舍监
2. **alignment** [ə'laɪnmənt] n. 队列，成直线；校准；结盟
3. **nun** [nʌn] n. 修女，尼姑
4. **credential** [krə'denʃl] n. 证书；文凭；信任状
5. **Caesarean section** 剖腹产

	in search of cake. They think they can conceal things from me. But they are not sharp enough. I, you see, am attuned to feel vibrations. Only last week, I found a Batten burg hidden inside a Rinso box. You must have another slice.		好，但他们不够机灵。我天生敏锐。就上星期，我在肥皂粉盒里找到一块巴腾堡蛋糕。再来一块吧。
Lee:	I'm almost full.	李：	我已经吃饱了。
Joan:	You are young…you can never be filled. You have an appetite for life.	琼：	你很年轻，年轻人胃口好，多吃点。
Julienne:	Ah, hello. You must be Nurse Lee. I'm Sister[6] Julienne. This is Nurse Miller and Nurse Franklin, who will be your colleagues.	朱利安娜：	你好，是护士李吧？我是朱利安娜修女，这是护士米勒和弗兰克林，你们将会一起做事。
Miller:	Hello, *pleased to meet you*[1].	米勒：	你好，很高兴见到你。
Franklin:	Actually, pleased doesn't fully cover it. We're perfectly thrilled to have some **reinforcements**[6]!	弗兰克林：	说实话，"高兴"不足以表达我们的心情。你能过来支援，我们太激动了。
Julienne:	I'm sorry we're late, clinic was busy. I see you've already met Sister Monica Joan.	朱利安娜：	很抱歉我们来晚了，诊所很忙。你已经见过莫妮卡·琼修女了吧？
Lee:	Yes, I have.	李：	嗯，见过了。
Julienne:	We'll take care of the **formalities**[7] later. I'm sure that first you'd like some tea and cake.	朱利安娜：	一会再谈公事吧，咱们先喝喝茶，吃点蛋糕。
Evangelina:	I think you'll find, Sister Julienne, there is no cake.	伊万杰琳：	我以为你发现了，朱利安娜修女，没有蛋糕了。
Julienne:	Sister Evangelina, may I introduce Nurse Lee?	朱利安娜：	伊万杰琳修女，这位是护士李。
Evangelina:	There is nothing in this pot but crumbs.	伊万杰琳：	只剩下些渣。
Miller:	But Mrs. B made one this morning. I saw her when I came in from my delivery in Mitre Street.	米勒：	可是B夫人今早刚做了一个啊，我接生回来时在大街上看到她了。
Evangelina:	I know she did! It was coconut, which is a very insinuating ingredient, liable to smear itself all over the consumer's face.	伊万杰琳：	我知道，还是椰蓉的，一眼就能看出谁偷吃了，全黏在脸上了。
Joan:	Are you talking to me? You must calm yourself, my dear. You are turning quite scarlet. Our newcomer was hungry.	琼：	是在说我吗？别激动啊，亲爱的。脸都红了，新来的护士很饿。

Julienne: Nurse Franklin, go into the kitchen. You might seek out something else to eat. I seem to recall a packet of Gypsy creams.

Franklin: Let's hope Mrs. B has put a lock on the tin.

Evangelina: I bet the newcomer had one slice and you ate all the rest.

Joan: If I were a dog, she would not be satisfied until I had slunk beneath the table with my tail between my legs. How you all foam and fret. I shall retire to my chamber and see you all at **Compline**[8].

朱利安娜: 弗兰克林护士，你去厨房看看有什么吃的，我记得还有些奶油酥。

弗兰克林: 但愿 B 夫人给罐子上锁了。

伊万杰琳: 我敢说，新来的只吃了一块，你把剩下的全吃了。

琼: 如果我不做条夹着尾巴从桌下溜走的狗，她铁定不会满意的。你们太大惊小怪了，我先回房去了，晚祷时见。

文化背景

1. Sister 修女

修女是天主教中离家进修会的女教徒，通常须发三愿（即"绝财""绝色""绝意"），从事祈祷和协助神甫进行传教。天主教国家一般尊称修女为"Sister"。在中国，修女有时被称为"姆姆"。

常用表达

1. pleased to meet you.

sb. be pleased to meet you. 某人很高兴见到你。

例：I am pleased to meet you.

我很高兴见到你。

He is pleased to meet you.

他很高兴见到你。

注释 6. **reinforcement** [ˌriːɪnˈfɔːsmənt] *n.* 增援部队；救兵；加固物　7. **formality** [fɔːˈmæləti] *n.* 手续；礼节；拘谨　8. **compline** [ˈkɒmplɪn] *n.* 晚祷

🔊 Passage 2 🎥

剧情介绍：

（选自第 1 季第 1 集）诺那塔斯修道院的助产士们忙得不可开交，人人都闲不下来，这时，一个长得人高马大的实习生加入了她们，虽然成绩勉强过关，但是通过实习，她证明了自己可以成为一名合格的助产士，真正成为她们中的一员。

Scene:	In the Nonnatus House.
	在诺那塔斯修道院。

🔊 **Miller:** Oh, hello, Jenny. Up all night again? Mrs B kept you a **kipper**[1]. I'd be quick, *if I were you*[1], or Fred will have it.

Fred: I heard that, and I hate kippers. I tried somking'em once. It's a mug's game.

Miller: Flat type. Three advance delivery packs, one booking-in and two final home visits.

Julienne: Nurse Lee. How is Mrs Mason?

Lee: A little girl, Sister. No complications.

Julienne: Good, you'll have to see to Sister Bernadette's list later. She's been seconded to the hospital today.

Franklin: Nonnatus House. **Midwife**[2] speaking.

Evangelina: Short-staffed again.

Julienne: The new trainee is on her way. I can't deny I'm looking forward to an extra pair of hands.

Franklin: Doreen Riley. She's the twins case in Quebec Street.

Evangelina: We don't need an extra pair of hands. We need an octopus.

Julienne: When I get back from Mrs Riley, I'll contact the aquarium. In the meantime the new

米勒： 早啊，珍妮，又忙了一晚上吧？B 夫人给你留了腌鱼，赶紧去吃，不然法瑞德会抢。

法瑞德： 我听到了，不过，我不喜欢腌鱼。我尝过熏鱼，那味道，不如不吃。

米勒： 没劲。三个产前工具箱，一个预约，外加两个出诊。

朱利安： 护士李，梅森夫人怎么样了？

李： 是个女孩，没有并发症。

朱利安娜： 很好，你今天得照看下伯纳黛特修女的病人，她临时被调到医院帮忙了。

弗兰克林： 诺那塔斯修道院，我是助产士。

伊万杰琳： 人手又不够了。

朱利安娜： 实习生快到了，快点多双手来帮忙吧。

弗兰克林： 是多琳·赖利，在魁北克街，是双胞胎。

伊万杰琳： 一双手怕是不够用，得来一个万事通。

朱利安娜： 我先去莱利夫人那儿，回来联系护士站。还有，这是新护士

girl's details are on here.

Evangelina: Ah! Camilla Fortescue-Cholmeley-Browne?

Chummy: Yes.

Evangelina: Come in.

Chummy: I generally answer to Chummy. My pa used to say "Long dogs need short names".

Evangelina: Mm, follow me. And mind your head. I understand you qualified by a whisker, Nurse Fortescue-Cholmeley-Browne.

Chummy: I did pass. It was a bit of a scrape. Before that I was nursing for five years, and, well…

Evangelina: Come on , inside. Do you need me to go through this piece by piece?

Chummy: No, not **remotely**[3]. What's that?

Evangelina: It's an enema nozzle.

Chummy: It's made of glass.

Evangelina: Do you break things?

Chummy: No.

Evangelina: And are all your dresses pink?

Chummy: I do have another, in eau de nil.

Evangelina: I bet you look a picture in that too. Nurse Lee!

Lee: Uniforms. Standard pale blue. Two. I found some in the airing cupboard.

Chummy: All girls together. That's what we used to say at school. I could never bear all that fussing and flapping under dressing capes. Ha-ha. I've always been a long **shanks**[4]. Even as a child in India, I was always taller than my brothers. Poor old Mater, she used to be in tears, but my ayah just sewed flounces at the bottom of my frocks. It would look a bit rum round the hem of a nurse's outfit. Oh, I can't move my arms.

的个人资料。

伊万杰琳： 是弗特斯克·乔姆利·布朗恩吧？

查米： 是我。

伊万杰琳： 进来吧。

查米： 大家都叫我查米，我爸说大个子适合短名字。

伊万杰琳： 嗯，跟我来，小心头。劣等通过啊，弗特斯克·乔姆利·布朗恩护士。

查米： 我确实合格了，虽然有些勉强。在那之前我当了五年护士，还有……

伊万杰琳： 来吧，进来。需要我逐一介绍吗？

查米： 当然不用，那是什么？

伊万杰琳： 是灌肠喷嘴。

查米： 是玻璃做的。

伊万杰琳： 你常摔东西吗？

查米： 不是。

伊万杰琳： 你的衣服都是粉色的吗？

查米： 还有淡绿色的。

伊万杰琳： 没差多少，一样显眼，护士李。

李： 新制服来了，浅蓝色的两套，在衣橱里找到的。

查米： 女生喜欢扎堆，我上学那会儿总这么说，在那里大惊小怪的，让人受不了。我一直很高，小时候在印度，比哥哥们还高。我妈很担心，奶奶总会在我的裙底缝上荷叶边。护士服可不能缝荷叶边，太奇怪了，我胳膊动不了了。

注释

1. kipper ['kɪpə(r)] *n.* 腌鱼；家伙

2. midwife ['mɪdwaɪf] *n.* 助产士，是在正式助产学校学习或具有同等能力，能独立接生和护理产妇的中级医务人员。

3. remotely [rɪ'məʊtlɪ] *adv.* 遥远地；偏僻地

4. shank [ʃænk] *n.* 小腿；吸嘴杆；弓形垫；长腿的人

1. **if I were you** 虚拟语气

(1) 虚拟语气在 if 条件状语从句中的用法

与现在事实相反：

if + 主语 + were/did + 其他，主语 + should/would/could/might + 动词原形 + 其他

与过去事实相反：

if + 主语 + had done + 其他，主语 + should/would/could/might+have done + 其他

与将来事实相反：

if + 主语 + should + 动词原形 + 其他，主语 + should/would/could/might + 动词原形 + 其他

if + 主语 + did + 其他，主语 + should/would/could/might + 动词原形 + 其他

if + 主语 + were to do sth.，主语 + should/would/could/might + 动词原形 + 其他

(2) wish 引导的宾语从句

与现在事实相反：过去时（were）

与过去事实相反：had + 过去分词

与将来事实相反：would/could/might + 动词原形

例：I wish I were a bird.

我希望我是只鸟。

I wish he hadn't done that.

我希望他过去没有那么做。

I wish I would be rich in the future.

我希望我将来富有。

(3) 表示要求，命令，建议的虚拟语气

Keys: insist, order, command, advise, suggest, propose, demand, require, request, desire

这些动词后面的宾语从句要使用虚拟语气。即从句中的动词用 should+ 动词原形，或者省略 should，直接加动词原形。

例：The doctor suggested that he (should) try to lose his weight.

医生建议他应该尝试着减肥。

He insisted that we (should) tell him the news.

他坚持我们应该告诉他这条新闻。

(4) 表语从句、同位语从句中的虚拟语气

在 suggestion, proposal, order, plan, idea, advice, decision 等需要有内容的名词后面的表语从句、同位语从句中，要使用虚拟语气。其谓语动词应用：should + 原形动词，另外连接从句的 that 不能省略。

例：My suggestion is that we should go there at once.

我建议我们立即去那儿。

What do you think of his proposal that we should put on a play at the English evening?

他建议我们在英语之夜上演一出戏剧，你认为如何？

(5) It's necessary/strange/natural/ important/pity/no wonder/impossible+that 从句

从句中的动词要用虚拟语气，即 (should)+ 动词原形。

例：It is strange that he (should) say so.

他居然会这样说，真是奇怪。

It is a great pity that you (should) think so.

他居然会这样想，真是一件憾事。

It is natural that a bird (should) rest in trees.

鸟在树上安歇是很自然的。

(6) 在 It is/was suggested /ordered / demanded / proposed etc. 结构中要使用虚拟语气

例：It's requested that we（should）keep the stability of the society for the people's peaceful life.

我们应该维护社会稳定，给人们和平的生活。

It's suggested that the plan be carried out.

计划应该被执行。

It is ordered that all the troops (should) withdraw three miles away.

根据命令，所有部队撤至三英里以外。

It is arranged that he leave for Canada on Friday.

照安排，他星期五动身去加拿大。

It is suggested that the English evening be held on Saturday.

有人建议，英语晚会周六举行。

(7) would rather 后的宾语从句常用虚拟语气

例：I would rather you could teach me again.

我宁愿你再教我一遍。

The manager would rather that his secretary went to the meeting instead of him.

经理宁愿他的秘书代替他去开会。

(8) as if，as though 引导的从句

以 as if，as though（似乎，仿佛）引出的方式状语从句，如果表示真实情况应该用直陈语气；如果表示非真实情况则应该用虚拟语气，其谓语动词的虚拟式与 wish 后面宾语从句中谓语动词的虚拟式相同。

例：The little boy knows so many things as if he was a man.

这个小男孩知道这么多东西，好像他是个男子汉似的。

(9) 由 if only （要是……, 那该多好啊! ）引导的惊叹句。

例: If only I had passed the test !

我要是通过了测试多好啊!

比较 if only 与 only if:

only if 表示"只有"; if only 则表示"如果……就好了"。If only 也可用于陈述语气。

例: I wake up only if the alarm clock rings.

只有闹钟响了，我才会醒。

If only the alarm clock had rung.

当时闹钟响了，就好了。

If only he comes early.

但愿他早点回来。

(10) It is (high) time that

It is (high) time that 后面的从句谓语动词要用过去式或用 should 加动词原形，但 should 不可省略。

例: It is time that the children went to bed.

孩子们该去睡觉了。

It is high time that the children should go to bed.

孩子们该去睡觉了。

It is high time that we had our lunch.

该是我们吃午饭的时候了。

It is time that he made up his mind.

该是他做出决定的时候了。

Passage 3

剧情介绍:

（选自第1季第1集）爱的故事在继续。本集穿插介绍了李与一名叫科利特的老人的关于爱的故事。临终前不久，科利特告诉李："我很想念我的家人，没有他们的陪伴，每天醒来都是痛苦的。可是只有敞开心扉爱过，才能懂得那种心痛。只有了解如何去爱，才能懂得生活的真谛。"

| **Scene:** | At home |
| | 在家 |

Lee:	Mr. Collett, I'm Nurse Lee. I'm here to see about your ulcers.	李：	科利特先生，我是护士李，来检查您的溃疡。
Collett:	Ah, yeah, well, *it's my pleasure to*[1] have you here. I'm sure we're going to get along famous. Follow me. I've, er...I've got the boiling water ready.	科利特：	很高兴见到你，我们一定能很快热络起来。跟我来。我……哦……已经烧好热水了。
Lee:	Um...Where can I lay out my **instruments**[1]?	李：	嗯……器具该放哪儿？
Collett:	Oh, just move that out the way.	科利特：	把那些踢一边去就行。
Lee:	I'm going to clean the wounds now. It may sting, Mr Collett.	李：	要清理伤口了，会有些疼，科利特先生。
Collett:	Joe. Joe will do fine. Yeah. Would you... Would you like a cup of tea?	科利特：	叫我乔就行了，你要喝茶吗？
Lee:	I'm fine, thank you.	李：	不用了，谢谢。
Collett:	Oh, It's no bother. It won't take but a minute. Oh,um...There. What...What's wrong?	科利特：	很方便的，马上就好，来，给你。怎……怎么了？
Lee:	I'd actually, er...prefer a cold drink, if you had one?	李：	其实，我想喝点冷饮，您有吗？
Collett:	Then that's what you shall have, my **maiden**[2].	科利特：	那来点儿这个吧，姑娘。
Lee:	Oh, no, I can't drink on duty. I meant orange squash or something.	李：	不不，上班时间不能喝酒，有没有橙汁之类的。

注释 1. instrument ['ɪnstrəmənt] *n.* 仪器；工具；乐器
2. maiden ['meɪdn] *n.* 少女；处女

Collett:	Oh. Well, I'm sorry. I…I don't have anything else.
Lee:	It doesn't matter.
Collett:	I got them from gun wounds during the war. The Boer War[1], this was.
Lee:	I thought you must be a soldier.
Collett:	A soldier. Hardly. I was 17. No older than you.
Lee:	You're **flattering**[3] me, Mr Collett.
Collett:	Yes. I…I am. Is it working?
Lee:	Absolutely.
Collett:	Over here. Beautiful bunch, eh?
Lee:	Lovely.
Collett:	Yeah. My two sons, they, er…joined the Great War and…they never came home. And my Sally…Yeah. A firebomb during the Blitz.
Lee:	I'm sorry.
Collett:	Don't be. I loved them. They loved me.
Lee:	There. All done.
Collett:	Now, are you sure I can't offer you a drink?
Lee:	I'm quite all right, really.
Collett:	Yes, of course, er…you have a great deal to do, no doubt.
Lee:	I have the evening off tonight. I could…come back then and share a glass with you? If…if you wanted that, I mean.
Collett:	Well, that would be a delight, my maiden. A thousand welcomes.

(at night)

Lee:	Thank you, Mr Collett.
Collett:	Joe. Joe. Joe. Yeah, well…I was afraid you wouldn't come. *Here you are.*[2] Mm.
Lee:	Well, of course I am. How are your legs?
Collett:	Oh, very comfortable, thanks to you. Do you mind?
Lee:	Not at all.
Collett:	This is luxury, isn't it? Ah, but it is. When I was young, I would…I'd never have

科利特：这样啊，抱歉，没有别的了。
李：没关系。
科利特：这是战争留下的枪伤，布尔战争。
李：我猜到了，您是名军人。
科利特：军人啊，倒也算不上。我当时17岁，和你没差多少。
李：您这是在夸我啊，科利特先生。
科利特：嗯。是……是啊，不错吧。
李：当然了。
科利特：看这个，看着幸福吧。
李：很幸福。
科利特：是啊，我的两个儿子，一战时上了战场，再也没有回来。还有我的萨利，那次空袭也把她带走了。
李：很抱歉。
科利特：没事的。我爱他们，他们也爱我。
李：好了，可以了。
科利特：你确定不来一杯吗？
李：真的不用了。
科利特：是啊，我懂，你还有事要忙。
李：我今天晚上有空，我可以……回来陪您喝一杯，如果您不介意的话。
科利特：那可真是太好了，姑娘。非常欢迎。

（晚上）

李：谢谢，科利特先生。
科利特：叫我乔。嗯……我还担心你不来了，终于来了。
李：我都答应您了，您的腿怎么样了？
科利特：挺好的，多亏了你。介意我吸烟吗？
李：不会。
科利特：这儿很豪华吧？确实如此，年轻的时候，我连做梦都没想过这些。

dreamed of such luxury. A warm bed at night. Enough food to eat. Huh! Oh. My Sally loved it here.

晚上能睡在温暖的床上，也能吃饱肚子。啊，我的萨拉也很喜欢这里。

📖 文化背景

1. The Boer War 布尔战争是英国人于 1899 年 8 月和布尔人之间为了争夺南非殖民地而展开的战争。

☎ 常用表达

1. it's my pleasure to 我很荣幸……

例：It's my pleasure.

我很高兴为你帮忙。

It's my pleasure to help you.

帮助你是我的荣幸。

It's my great pleasure to introduce tonight's speaker, Professor Lewis.

我很荣幸地介绍今晚的主讲人，路易斯教授。

Not at all. It's my pleasure.

不客气。这是我的荣幸。

It's my pleasure to know you.

认识阁下，深感荣幸。

It's my pleasure to be in the company of such a fine gentleman as yourself.

能和像你这样的绅士做伴，才是我的荣幸。

You're welcome.

不用客气。

2. Here you are.

(1) Here you are 的口语用法

  a. 表示要把某物递给某人，意为：给你，拿去吧；这就是你要的东西。

    例：—May I have a look at it? 我可以看看吗？

      —Here you are. 你看吧。

      —Pass me the keys, please. 请把钥匙递给我。

      —Here you are. 给你。

  b. 表示找到了要找的东西，意为：在这里；这不是！

    例：—Where's my pen? 我的钢笔在哪里？

注释 **3. flattering** ['flætərɪŋ] *adj.* 奉承的；谄媚的

265

——Here you are. 喏，这不是!

c. 表示找到了要找的地方，意为：（你，你们）到了。

例：Here you are! This is the way out.

　　到了，这就是出口。

d. 用来唤起某人对某情况或处境（尤指困境）的注意，意为：你看吧；你瞧吧。

例：You're always paying so little attention to your lessons, and here you are, you've failed in the examination again.

　　你总是那样不注意复习功课，你看吧，这次考试你又没及格。

e. 用来启发或引导某人发表看法，意为：你说呢；你说说看。

例：Here you are, what do you think of this idea?

　　说说看，这个意见你认为如何?

(2) 辨析"Here it is"和"Here you are"。

　　"Here it is"和"Here you are"都意为"给你，在这儿"，但其使用场合还是有些区别。当所给（递）的东西是对方要求的原物时，两者可通用。"Here it is"的复数形式为"Here they are"。

例：——May I borrow your bike? 我可以借你的自行车吗?

　　——Here it is./Here you are. 这就是。

　　——Where are my glasses? 我的眼镜哪儿去了?

　　——Here they are. / Here you are. 在这里。

当对方所给（递）的不是原物，而是替代物或同类物时，则只能用"Here you are"。

例：——I have left my pen at home. 我把我的钢笔丢家里了。

　　——Here you are. Use mine. 给你，用我的吧。

　　——Please pass me a glass of milk. 请递给我一杯牛奶。

　　——Here you are. 给你。

另外，购物时，售货员说"Here you are"表示"给你"；乘车到站时，司机说"Here it is"表示"到站了"；寻找东西时，自己发现时常用"Here it is"，别人发现时给你常说"Here you are"；乘车到站时，自己可以说"Here we are"。

Chapter 6

剧情剧
Story Drama

　　剧情剧是以一个或多个故事作为主线推动整个剧目的发展。在故事发展的同时，穿插角色之间的生活及情感纠葛。剧情剧的卖点主要是剧情。不同于动作片的打斗、爱情片的缠绵或喜剧片的搞笑，它往往节奏缓慢，通常是一种社会现象或一定人群的生活状态的写照，容易使观看者产生情感上的共鸣。剧情剧取材范围广泛，但多以现实生活为主。在剧情剧中，每个角色都有自己独特的个性，且个性基本完整、稳定，贯穿全剧。剧情剧每集之间联系较为紧密，单集在 40 分钟左右，季与季之间的衔接较其他剧目来说也较为紧凑，有始有终。只要不是因为演员合同到期，一般每个角色都会有相对合理的结局。外国剧情剧一般分为两类，一类是改编自优秀小说，另一类是由编剧边写边拍。

　　美剧中剧情剧较多，涉及犯罪、生活等。其中，《反恐 24 小时》和《越狱》是近期警匪剧的优秀代表。另外，《绝望的主妇》《广告狂人》也被喜欢剧情剧的观众奉为经典，并取得了很高的收视率。

Desperate Housewives
《绝望的主妇》

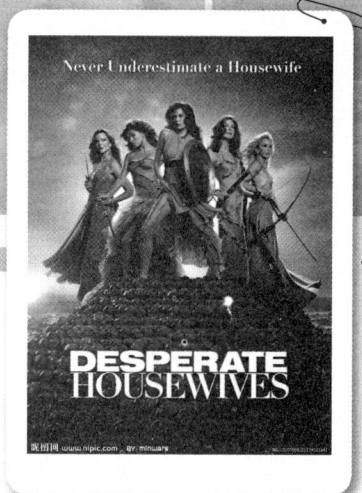

Never Underestimate a Housewife

DESPERATE
HOUSEWIVES

入选理由：

《绝望的主妇》是美国广播公司于 2004 年 10 月开始，在每周日晚九点播出的电视剧。故事背景设定在美国一个虚构的小镇——美景镇，它描绘了美景镇紫藤巷的四位家庭主妇的婚后生活，每季的剧情都有新的主线和主妇加入。该剧曾多次夺得美国单周收视排行榜冠军，并横扫美国各大颁奖典礼的多个奖项。其片名也很快形成席卷美国的文化现象，带动杂志报刊与脱口秀节目中的绝望、抓狂的主妇风潮，更在全球超过 130 个国家及地区播放。本剧揭示了一个生活的智慧：要想生活不绝望，主妇们就要学会不能太忠于自己的感受和想法。

Section 1　剧情特点：

《绝望的主妇》从主人公玛丽·爱丽丝·杨的视角，审视了富有的中产阶级聚居区的家庭主妇们鲜为人知的生活。大部分童话故事都以"公主和王子从此过着幸福生活"的圆满结局收尾，但很少有人知道王子和公主背后的婚姻生活会是怎样？《绝望的主妇》接替《老友记》《欲望都市》成为美国最热的都市喜剧，挖掘了"过着幸福生活"童话式女主角的生活真相。剧中四位女主角分别代表着四种截然不同的主妇形象：离婚主妇苏珊、完美主妇布瑞、强人主妇丽奈特和漂亮主妇加布里埃。这四个漂亮多金且无须为工作发愁的女性看似过着完美无缺的生活，但实际上都在用"幸福"粉饰着自己早已混乱不堪的生活，用自己的现实生活打破了"王子与公主"的婚姻童话。

Section 2　对白特点：

《绝望的主妇》是一部非常适合英语学习者观看和学习的影片。在剧中，主要演员的语速、语调和发音都带有地道美式英语的痕迹。经常模仿练习和反复观看收听，可以很好地锻炼和提高听力水平，纠正大家在断句和发音上存在的问题。另外，该剧完全以日常生活为主线，通过特定的人物和场景，将生活中零零碎碎的日常琐事刻画得活灵活现，大到婚姻死亡，小到鸡毛蒜皮。只要是生活中我们可能经历的情景，绝望的主妇们无时无刻不在动情演绎。

相信大家都注意到在每篇故事的开头、结尾和中间的过渡环节，都适时地插入了第三方的旁白。而且每篇故事旁白所用到的语句和词汇都值得我们细细品味和耐心琢磨，如果能很好地吸收并学以致用，相信会让大家今后的写作和演讲大放光彩。

值得肯定的是，这部电视剧的编剧绝对才高八斗，《绝望的主妇》里许多经典台词和犀利对白都相当出彩，引发了很多观众的共鸣和感触，得到了广泛的认可和引用。

《绝望的主妇》每集时长大约 43 分钟，与其他美剧不同的是，每一集都以一个大的主题为中心思想，再以多个场景相互辉映，使每篇故事都显得相对独立。大家在学英语的过程中可以逐步做到一个故事一篇总结，一个场景一种回味。另外，这部电视剧的语言通俗易懂、深入浅出，不像某些美剧，情节冗长、术语颇多，让人望而生畏。

Section 3　角色分析：

布瑞·范·德·坎普 (Bree Van De Kamp)：一提起布瑞，最贴切的描述词就是"力争完美"。她出生于一个传统富有的中产阶级家庭，有一个当大律师的父亲和严谨苛刻的后母。身为上流俱乐部的成员，又拥有职业是主治医生的丈夫，她永远保持着一丝不乱的红发，优雅知性的穿着，严谨安全的用词。布瑞的花园永远都是紫藤巷里最整齐美丽的，这曾导致隔壁老太太嫉妒地耍小手段破坏；她厨艺精湛得让孩子们渴望像普通家庭那样能吃到家常菜，而不是天天大餐。她对自己追求完美的要求近乎到了苛刻的程度。在布瑞的爱情和婚姻里，她始终以扮演完美妻子为目标，也渴望寻觅到一个正直虔诚、忠诚可信的丈夫。作为一个虔诚的天主教徒，布瑞最看重男人身上的品质是正直。

最精彩的"完美"计划：为了帮助年幼的女儿掩饰未婚先孕，自己装起了孕妇。孩子的外祖母做了外人眼里的母亲。

最尴尬的"完美"形象：极力隐瞒酗酒事实，却因为在商店贪杯到打烊也不肯走，最终醉醺醺地被卡在店门中间动弹不得，只能喊救命。

苏珊·梅尔 (Susan Mayer)：苏珊是一个儿童插画家（自由职业者）。前夫是一个风流不羁的律师，因为丈夫和秘书有私情而导致两人离婚。苏珊的厨艺糟糕透顶，能存活至今完全依靠早熟女儿的细心照顾，近乎神经质的敏感和好奇心让她和麦克的爱情故事发展得十分揪心。年近四十的女人却好像只有十四岁的心智，不成熟的思维逻辑和处理问题的方式一度让她的生活很混乱。和主治医生恋爱，却诚实地表达不想成为他开刀生涯的第一个实验病人，极伤对方的自尊心；在麦克昏迷中日日守候，却在他苏醒的关键时刻把持不住和别的男人约会，结果让情敌钻了空子。有机会做次灰姑娘，嫁给无比富有的英国男子，拥有无比豪华的婚礼，却还是选择忠实自己的内心嫁给管道修理工麦克，女儿为两人举办了月光下的婚礼，静谧浪漫、幸福安宁。

最精彩的"没脑子"：怀疑伊迪勾引麦克，偷偷闯入其家中，导致失火。

最尴尬的"没脑子"：为劝阻好友，却被误会勾引年轻男子而打成一团，被人踢到台前，曝光在聚光灯下，压轴礼服变成了褴褛衣衫，弄得自己狼狈不堪。

丽奈特·斯加沃 (Lynette Scavo)：很多人说，《绝望主妇》里最有代表性的、最接近现实的主妇是丽奈特，生活中大多数都市主妇都像丽奈特。丽奈特结婚以前是丈夫汤姆的上司，带领过一个人数不少的团队，可以说是职场的女强人，结婚之后，生了三个男孩一个女孩，其中有一对是双胞胎。屏幕里的丽奈特口才良好，精明干练，拥有积极的人生态度。

最精彩的"精明能干"：偷偷让女同事五岁的儿子戒掉母乳喂养，消除了办公室里男人们整天目睹女同事当众给孩子喂母乳的尴尬。

最尴尬的"精明能干"：由于癌症化疗导致头发脱落影响了夫妻之间的感情，丽奈特每晚改用不同的假发来打扮自己吸引汤姆的注意力，有一天丈夫最钟情的那款假发坏了，丽奈特坦诚的沟通最终赢得了丈夫的理解与爱，她光头上阵，做回了自己。

加布里埃·索利斯 (Gabrielle Solis)：加布里埃小聪明十足。她在善妒的丈夫和纯情的园丁之间游刃有余地平衡着婚姻和爱情的游戏，她为争夺丈夫的心，与漂亮修女明争暗斗，在教堂里上演了一场两个女人打架的戏，以及找女佣代孕的荒唐闹剧。一开始，她是一个退出时装舞台的美丽模特，一个渴望被爱、忍受不了无人问津的小女人，一个很爱自己、行为大胆、善于给自己找乐子的女人，她所做的一切都是在努力愉悦自己，填补空虚。随着剧情的深入，我们可以看到她细心地照料失明的丈夫，尽管她做得没有中国传统主妇那么尽善尽美，偶尔还会耍小性子、小脾气，但是这事发生在加布里埃德身上依旧让人难以置信。

最精彩的"小聪明"：影片中的加布里埃经常需要应付偷情出现的意外状况，每一次都化险为夷。她勇于捍卫自己的家庭，与漂亮修女斗智斗勇的那场戏最为精彩，特别是在教堂里穿着高跟鞋挺着娇小身躯的加布里埃与高大威猛的修女的打戏让人啼笑皆非。

Passage 1

剧情介绍：

（选自第1季第1集）故事发生在美国一个虚构的郊外住宅区紫藤巷，这里的住户们富足幸福，生活平静祥和，但是这一切被一声枪响彻底击碎了，社区居民中最美丽可人的主妇玛丽·爱丽丝·杨（布兰达·斯壮饰）突然在她完美的家中饮弹自尽。不过这并不是玛丽故事的结尾，死亡令她获得了从新的角度俯视生活的机会，玛丽的朋友们和她们的家庭是否如同表面上那么祥和完美，是否会如同她曾经的生活，也潜藏着令人绝望和疯狂的暗流？

本选段选自故事的最开始，玛丽·爱丽丝·杨用一种话外音讲述着她自杀的过程，在她的葬礼上，各个主妇悉数登场，她们所带来的食物也代表着她们目前的生活状态和性格：首先出场的是丽奈特·斯加沃，她被繁重的家务和淘气的孩子所拖累，没有时间做饭的她只能带来超市的炸鸡，炸鸡象征着她火爆的脾气和繁忙的状态；最后登场的是带着通心粉的苏珊·梅尔，家务活糟糕的苏珊唯一会做的就是通心粉，通心粉见证着苏珊的婚姻生活，如同做通心粉一样，她对生活中的每一件事情都处理不好，总是依靠家人和朋友。

Scene: In the off-screen of Mary Alice Young describing her perfect life, she triggered the gun to herself.

玛丽·爱丽丝·杨在描述自己所拥有的完美生活的画外音中，对准自己的太阳穴扣动了扳机。

Alice: My name is Mary Alice Young. When you read this morning's paper, you may **come across**[1] an article about the unusual day I had last week. **Normally**[2], there's never anything **newsworthy**[3] about my life. That all changed last Thursday. Of course everything seemed **as normal**[4] at first. I made my breakfast for my family.

Alice: Here we are. Waffles[1].

Alice: I **performed**[5] my **chores**[6]. I completed my projects. I ran my **errands**[7]. In **truth**[8] I spent the day as I spend every other day quietly **polishing**[9] until it **gleamed**[10] with perfection. That's why it was so astonishing when I decided to go to my hallway closet to **retrieve**[11] a **revolver**[12] that had never been used.

Alice: My body was discovered by my neighbor, Mrs. Martha Huber, who had been startled by a strange popping sound. Her curiosity aroused, Mrs. Huber tried to think of a reason for **dropping in on**[13] me unannounced. After

爱丽丝: 我是玛丽·爱丽丝·杨。阅读今天的晨报，你可能会看到一篇文章，关于上个星期我所度过的不平常的一天。通常，我的生活里是没什么新闻价值的。但是上周四，一切都改变了。当然，起初，一切看起来都很平常。我给一家人做好早餐。

爱丽丝: 华夫饼来了。

爱丽丝: 我做好了家务。完成我的家居作品。做了我该做的事，事实上，一切都和往常一样，直到一件不寻常的事情的发生。这就是我决定走向走廊的壁橱，拿起一把从没用过的左轮手枪。

爱丽丝: 我的尸体是被我的邻居玛萨·胡贝尔发现的，她被一声奇怪的声音吓了一跳。她觉得很好奇，胡贝尔太太想了一个不请自来的理由。在犹豫了一会儿

注释	
1. come across 偶然遇到	8. in truth 事实上
2. normally ['nɔːməlɪ] *adv.* 通常	9. polish ['pɒlɪʃ] *v.* 改进，上光
3. newsworthy ['njuːzwɜːðɪ] *adj.* 有新闻价值的	10. gleam [gliːm] *v.* （使）闪烁，（使）闪亮
4. as normal 通常	11. retrieve [rɪ'triːv] *v.* 找回
5. perform [pə'fɔːm] *v.* 完成	12. revolver *n.* 左轮手枪
6. chore [tʃɔː] *n.* （家庭或农庄的）杂务，杂活	13. drop in on sb. 顺便拜访某人
7. run errand 跑腿，办事	

some **initial**[14] hesitation, she decided to return the blender she had borrowed from me 6 months before.

Mrs H: It's my neighbor. I think she's been shot, there's blood everywhere. Yes, you've got to send an ambulance. You**'ve got to**[15] send one right now!

Alice: And for a moment, Mrs. Huber stood motionless in her kitchen **grief-stricken**[16] by this senseless tragedy. But, only for a moment. If there was one thing Mrs. Huber **was known for**[17], it was her ability to look on the bright side. I was **laid to rest**[18] on a Monday. After the funeral, all the residents of Wisteria Lane came to pay their respects. And as people do in this situation, they brought food. Lynette Scavo brought fried chicken. Lynette had a great family recipe for fried chicken. Of course, she didn't cook much as she was moving up the **corporate ladder**[19]. She didn't have the time.

Alice: But when her doctor announced Lynette was pregnant, her husband Tom had an idea. Why not quit your job? Kids do much better with **stay-at-home**[20] mums; it was so much less stressful. But this was not the case. In fact, Lynette's life had become so **hectic**[21] she was now forced to get her chicken from a fast food restaurant. Lynette would have appreciated the irony of it if she stopped to think about it, but she couldn't. She didn't have the time.

Lynette: Hey, hey, hey, hey! Stop it, stop it, stop it. Stop it.

Preston: But Mom!

Lynette: No, you are going to behave today. I am not going to be humiliated in front of the entire neighborhood. And, just so you know how serious I am...

之后，她决定来归还她 6 个月前从我这里借去的搅拌器。

胡夫人： （在电话中）我的邻居，我觉得她被枪击了，到处都是血。是的，赶紧派救护车，叫救护车。

爱丽丝： 过了一会儿之后，胡贝尔太太呆呆地站在厨房里，因为这件事情而感到极度悲伤。但是只有那么一会儿。 胡贝尔最大的特点，就是她总能把事情往好的方面想。星期一人们把我安葬了。葬礼之后，所有住在紫藤街的人都来表示他们对我的怀念和尊敬，就像人们在这种情况下都会做的，他们送来了点儿吃的。丽奈特·斯加沃带了炸鸡。斯加沃有一个大家庭，大家都喜欢炸鸡。当然，当她还是个职业女性的时候，她就很少做饭。她没有时间。

爱丽丝： 但是当她的医生告诉她怀孕了的时候，他的丈夫汤姆想了个办法。为什么不辞职呢？全职妈妈带出来的孩子会比较好，而且这样压力也比较小。但是事实并非如此。事实上，丽奈特的生活变得如此忙碌，以至于她不得不去快餐店买一只炸鸡。丽奈特如果仔细想想，可能会明白这是反话，但是她不能，她没有时间。

丽奈特： 嗨，嗨，嗨，嗨！住手！

普雷斯顿： 但是，妈妈！

丽奈特： 不，你们今天乖一点儿。我不想在大家面前丢脸。我是认真的……

Preston: What's that?

Lynette: Santa's cell-phone number.

Porter: How'd you get that?

Lynette: I know someone, who knows someone, who knows an **elf**[22]. And if anyone of you **acts up**[23], so help me, I will call Santa and tell him you want socks for Christmas. You willing to risk that?

Kids: Uh-uh! (all shake their heads vehemently)

Lynette: Okay.

Lynette: Let's **get this over with**[24].

普雷斯顿： 那是什么?

丽奈特： 圣诞老人的电话号码。

坡特： 你怎么知道的?

丽奈特： 我认识个朋友，她的朋友里有人认识一个小恶魔。所以，今天如果你们谁捣蛋，我马上打电话给圣诞老人，我会告诉他,你们圣诞节只要短袜就可以了。想试试吗?

孩子们： 唔! （他们都猛烈地摇头）

丽奈特： 好的。

丽奈特： 好，那么我们把这个收起来。

注释

14. **initial** [ɪˈnɪʃəl] *adj.* 开始的

15. **have got to** 必须

16. **grief-stricken** 极度悲伤的

17. **be known for** 因……而众所周知

18. **laid** [leɪd] *v.* （lay 的过去分词）使躺下，放置
    rest *v.* 使休息 **lay to rest** 安葬

19. **corporate ladder** 公司的官企业晋升制度；公司晋升度

move up the corporate ladder 升官；升迁

20. **stay-at-home** 驻家的；不工作，呆在家里的

21. **hectic** [ˈhektɪk] ［俗］*adj.* 兴奋的，紧张忙碌的

22. **elf** [elf] *n.* （双耳尖尖的）小精灵，恶人

23. **act up** 任性【这里指捣蛋，淘气】

24. **get over with** 〈口〉一劳永逸地做完，把……做完了事

📚 文化背景

1. waffle 华夫饼

又叫窝夫、格子饼、格仔饼、压花蛋饼，是一种烤饼，源于比利时，用配有专用烤盘（waffle iron）的烤炉制成。无论烤盘的形状如何，烤盘中的格子一般都是菱形或方形，这种格又称为华夫格。西方国家的人们吃华夫饼时往往搭配草莓酱、巧克力、糖、蜂蜜或者奶油等，既可以作为点心也可以当早餐。

📞 常用表达

1. be known for 因……而出名

例：be well-known for her beauty

她的美丽众所周知

2. make fun of 取笑某人或某事

例：Now, it's easy to make fun of Chambord, who was a pauvre type, a sad sack, in many ways.

取笑尚博尔伯爵很容易，在很多方面，他是一个可怜的家伙，是一个冒失鬼。

Passage 2

剧情介绍：

（选自第 2 季第 20 集）卡尔决定与伊迪分手，伊迪非常伤心，苏珊感到很内疚，陪伊迪去酒吧。伊迪认为酒吧的女招待勾引了卡尔，与其大打出手，苏珊帮忙，伊迪很感动，决定与其做姐妹，同时雇私家侦探调查卡尔的情人是谁。

布瑞继续和彼得交往，而且对其感情越来越深。但是彼得害怕重新陷入性瘾，拒绝接受她。布瑞想办法说服他。贝蒂决定把房子卖掉搬走，丹尼尔和马修设计让凯乐布攻击丹尼尔，布瑞很愤怒，决定报警。贝蒂很绝望，决定亲手结束凯乐布的生命。

埃德因为和妻子弗兰之间出了问题，总是安排丽奈特加班。丽奈特建议埃德与弗兰多沟通感情，但是埃德却让她替自己与弗兰网聊。弗兰发现后非常生气，埃德称是汤姆所为，决定解雇汤姆，丽奈特很无奈。

莉莉的生父决定要回孩子，加布用自己的手段让他签了放弃抚养权的文件。但是孩子的妈妈改变了主意，看着孩子被抱走，加布痛不欲生。

| **Scene:** | Susan and Edie are in the pub. |
| | 苏珊和埃德在酒吧中。 |

Edie: Ah, ah, ah, mm, mm. I asked for extra[1] spicy.

Waitress: I'm pretty[2] sure you said medium.

Edie: Are you? Well, maybe if you'd written it down, you could have spared[3] yourself the walk of shame back to the kitchen.

Susan: Edie, why are you torturing that girl?

Edie: That is her. That is the one that Karl is in love with. We have been here a million times and you should see the way that she flirts[4] with him. When she comes back

埃德：啊，哈，我刚刚要多放点儿辣酱。

服务员：我很肯定你刚才说的是中辣。

埃德：你肯定？要是你刚才记下来的话，现在就不用费力拿着东西走回厨房了。

苏珊：埃德，你干嘛折腾那女孩？

埃德：就是她，卡尔就是爱上她了。我们以前来过无数次了，你真该看看她是怎么和他卖弄风骚的。等她回来我要教训她，拿酒泼她，

注释
1. **extra** ['ekstrə] *adj.* 额外的
2. **pretty** ['prɪtɪ] *adv.* 相当的
3. **spare** [speə] *v.* 赦免
4. **flirt** [flɜːt] *v.* 调情

	here, I'm gonna shove this pitcher in her **perky**[5] little **mug**[6] and when she's...		然后等她……
Susan:	Let's not make a scene. It's not worth it. **For the sake of**[7] argument, let's, let's, let's say that it's someone else. You know, probably it would be a vulnerable lonely woman who Karl just **took advantage of**[8]. And what if this poor confused soul begged your forgiveness? What would you say?	**苏珊:**	好了，不要找麻烦，不值得。为了别吵起来，我们，我们就当是别人吧。可能，可能是个孤独无助的女人，恰好被卡尔占了便宜。而且要是……要是这个可怜、不知所措的女人，求你原谅呢？你会怎样？
Edie:	I'd say too little, too late, bitch, and then I'd kick her!	**埃德:**	我会说"太假了，太迟了，贱人"，然后揍她一顿。
Susan:	Oh.	**苏珊:**	噢。
Edie:	Yeah, but you don't have to worry about that cause I'm positive, it's her. I mean, who else could it be? Karl's office is all guys and the only women he sees are me, Julie, that, that lesbian who does his taxes and you.	**埃德:**	但是你不用担心，因为我肯定就是她。还能有谁？卡尔办公的地方都是男人，他能接触的女人，只有我、朱莉、那个收他税的女同性恋，还有你。
Susan:	You know what? It is her.	**苏珊:**	你知道我怎么想？就是她。
Edie:	Really? Why?	**埃德:**	真的？为什么？
Susan:	She just spit **in your wings**[9].	**苏珊:**	她……她刚刚朝你身边吐口水。
Edie:	You got my back?	**埃德:**	你看得见我后面吗？
Susan:	Uh, sure.	**苏珊:**	嗯……是的。
Waitress:	Here you go, extra spicy. You did that on purpose. You are going to pay! Fight! Fight!	**服务员:**	来了，重辣来了。你故意的。你要付出代价的，打。
Edie:	You! Hey, get off. Get off me, you **brats**[10]. Mayer! Four on one. Oh, a little help!	**埃德:**	你！你放开我。放开我，小屁孩。梅尔，她们四个打我一个。来帮我一下。
Matthew:	So, uh, when we leave who are you gonna miss the most?	**马修:**	我们离开的时候，你会最想谁？
Caleb:	I don't know.	**凯乐布:**	我不知道。
Matthew:	Yeah, you do. You say goodbye to her yet?	**马修:**	你当然知道。你和她告别过了吗？
Caleb:	No.	**凯乐布:**	没有。
Matthew:	Look man, it's, it's okay if you like her. You know, I think Danielle really likes you too.	**马修:**	听着，你可以喜欢她。我觉得丹尼尔也喜欢你。
Caleb:	Really?	**凯乐布:**	真的？
Matthew:	Yeah. She told me she'd be really sad if you left and didn't say goodbye. You know,	**马修:**	嗯，她告诉我，如果你不辞而别的话，她会很难过的。我觉得，

		I think that she might even want you to give her a little kiss.
		她可能还想让你亲吻她一下。

Caleb: But, Danielle doesn't even like me in her room. She gets mad.

凯乐布： 但是我在她房间里的时候，她都不喜欢我。她特别生气。

Matthew: Yeah. I talked to her about that. She feels really bad. But you know what? She told me if you come in her room again, she won't get mad. And Caleb, she's gonna act like she doesn't want you to kiss her, but she does.

马修： 嗯。我和她聊过了。她感觉很抱歉。如果你再去，她不会生气了。凯乐布，她可能会让你觉得，她不想让你吻她，其实她想。

Alice: Dale Helm, like all the students at Parson's Christian Academy, was taught that his future was safely in God's hands. What he didn't know was that Gabrielle Solis was about to force a **fumble**[11].

爱丽丝： 戴尔·赫尔姆和所有在帕尔森教会学校的学生一样，都被灌输这样的思想，你的未来尽由上帝掌握。但他不知道的是，加布里埃·索利斯就快要逼着她自己摸索未来了。

Coach: All right guys. We all know next week we're playing the **Falcons**[12]. We're gonna fry up those guys for dinner Cause we're the Huskies! Are you all the Huskies?

教练： 大家注意了，你们都知道下个星期，我们就要和老鹰队比赛了。我们要把那些小鹰们炸了当晚饭。因为我们是爱斯基摩队！爱斯基摩队怎么样？

Crowd: Huskies! Huskies! Huskies! Huskies! Huskies! Huskies!

人群： 上帝的球队！上帝的球队！上帝的球队！上帝的球队！上帝的球队！上帝的球队！

Dale: What are you doing? You can't be here.

戴尔： 你在这里干什么？你怎么能在这里？

Gabrielle: Let's talk **turkey**[13]. What is it gonna take for you to give up the baby?

加布里埃： 我们打开天窗说亮话。要怎么样你才放弃抚养权？

Dale: It's not gonna happen, okay? I gotta get back. I'm the **quarterback**[14]. It doesn't look right.

戴尔： 那是不可能的？我要回去了，我是四分位。这样不对。

Gabrielle: Okay, no, no. Wait! What about a car or college? Tuition's a killer these days. I could

加布里埃： 等等，一辆车怎么样？或者大学？现在的学费贵得要死。我

注释
5. perky ['pɔːkɪ] *adj.* 大胆的
6. mug [mʌg] *n.* 杯子；脸；苦读者
　vi. 扮鬼脸，做怪相；行凶抢劫
　vt. 给……拍照
6. for the sake of 为了；为了……的利益
7. take advantage of 利用
8. in your wings 在后方；在附近；在舞台两侧
9. brat [bræts] *n.* 乳臭未干的小孩
10. fumble ['fʌmbəl] *v.* 摸索
11. Falcons ['fɔːkənz] *n.* 猎鹰队
12. talk turkey （俚语）直率的说 turkey ['tɜːkɪ] *n.* 火鸡
13. quarterback 四分卫
14. dump [dʌmp] *v.* 倾倒，甩掉

	help you out.
Dale:	I don't need help. You hear those cheers? Those are for me. Last game, I threw two hundred forty-six yards. With stats like that, I could get into the college of my choice.
Gabrielle:	So why do you wanna be a dad? These are your glory days. A baby would ruin your life.
Dale:	Oh, I know. But Frank said once I get the baby, he's gonna take it off my hands.
Gabrielle:	But it's not even his!
Dale:	Libby **dumped**[14] him and he thinks that if he has the baby and she sees him acting all mature, she'll take him back.
Gabrielle:	No, no, no. I am not letting that idiot use my baby as a bargaining **chip**[15]!
Dale:	Hey, it's **outta**[16] my hands.
Gabrielle:	No, it doesn't have to be. Okay, just do the right thing and sign the release form.
Dale:	Look, I'm really sorry.
Coach:	Before we **adjourn**[17] today, let's take a moment to bow our heads.
Gabrielle:	Hello everyone! I'm Gaby Solis, class of ninety-four. Woo-hoo! I just wanted to give God a big shout out to this amazing season. The man **upstairs**[18] has definitely been on your side. You wanna know why? Because you boys live clean. You keep your noses up. You stay out of trouble. And you don't go **around**[19] getting strippers pregnant. And that's a good thing, 'cause if one of you caused a **scandal**[20] like that, ha, not only would that guy get kicked off the team and lose all of his scholarships, but God would drop your school colors so fast it'd make your head **spin**[21]! And then the football season would go to hell! No **pun**[22] intended. So my point is, do the right thing and no one gets hurt.

可以帮你付。

戴尔： 我不需要你帮。听到那些欢呼了？那都是给我的。上次比赛我扔出 246 码远，有这样的成绩，进哪所大学随便我挑。

加布里埃： 那你为什么还想当爸爸？你正当年呢。要个孩子会毁了你生活。

戴尔： 我知道，但是弗兰克说，只要我一拿回抚养权，他就会接手。

加布里埃： 这又不是他的孩子。

戴尔： 莉比把他甩了，他觉得，如果他得到孩子，她会觉得他成熟起来了，然后会回到他身边的。

加布里埃： 不，不，不。我绝对不会让他个白痴把我的孩子当筹码的。

戴尔： 喂，我又管不了这么多。

加布里埃： 不是这样的。你要做该做的事，签了这张放弃抚养权的表吧。

戴尔： 听着，我真得很抱歉。

教练： 在启程前，我们还是做一下祷告吧！

加布里埃： 大家好！我是加布里埃·索里斯，94 届学生。我想大声歌颂上帝，给我们如此精彩的一季比赛。上帝一定同你们站在一起。知道为什么吗？因为你们的生活很单纯。你们谨小慎微，你们不被麻烦缠身。不会和脱衣舞娘胡闹，让她们怀孕。这很好，因为如果你们中间的一个出了这样的丑事，不但会被踢出球队，丢了所有奖学金，而且上帝也会很快遗弃你，会让你极为头疼。那样的话，足球赛就见鬼去吧！就事论事，没有别的意思。我想说的是，把事情做对了，没人会受伤。

🔊 **Gabrielle:** Signed, sealed, delivered. Lily's ours.

加布里埃： 签了名，盖了章，都通过了。
莉莉是我们的了。

📞 常用表达

1. spare oneself 偷懒

sparing *adj.* 节约的；贫乏的；保守的

spare oneself 偷懒

spare time 消遣时间

not spare oneself 对自己的要求很严格

例： At this time, already 75-year-old Archimedes immediately did his best to help stroke enemy for the motherland.

这时，年已七十五岁的阿基米德，也立刻竭尽自己的所有才能，帮助祖国打击敌人。

2. for the sake of 为了；为了…的利益

例： Remove this little mark for the sake of your peace and my own.

为了你我的平安，请移走这小标记。

3. in the wings 在观众视线之外的舞台两侧；在幕后；准备着；在等待着，等待使用；在近旁，在眼前

例： wait in the wings 严阵以待

4. talk turkey （口语）坦率地说，打开天窗说亮话

talk cold turkey 直接地说

例： If you are willing to talk turkey, the dispute between us can be easily settled.

假如你愿意实实在在地说话，那么我们之间的争端就可以很轻易地解决。

注释	15. **bargaining chip** 谈判的筹码	20. **scandal** ['skændl] *n.* 丑闻；流言蜚语；诽谤；公愤
	16. **outta=out of** 超出	**Watergate scandal** 水门事件
	17. **adjourn** [ə'dʒɜːn] *v.* 延期，休会【这里指赛前休息】	21. **make one's head spin** 晕头转向
	18. **The man upstairs** （特指上帝）	22. **pun** [pʌn] *n.* 双关语
	19. **go around** 胡闹	

◁)) Passage 3 ◻

剧情介绍：

（选自第 3 季第 9 集）加布的离婚判决下来了，她非常忧伤。她的私人购物顾问维恩劝她和自己一起去培训那些参加"雪花小姐"选美大赛的选手，以此来散散心。面对那些资质平平的小女孩，加布用自己的减肥方法来教这些女孩，结果引来了家长的不满。苏珊问伊恩，为什么从不在他家过夜。两人终于去了伊恩家。苏珊对伊恩说，她感觉他仍然不想接受自己。伊恩承认了自己的感觉，答应接受苏珊进入自己的家，但感情上好像把珍妮赶出这个家。尽管如此，他仍然愿意尝试接受和苏珊的新关系。他亲自在珍妮的衣柜里腾空了一只抽屉，把苏珊的东西放了进去。丽奈特和汤姆到警察局说了自己对阿特的怀疑，他们认为阿特是个恋童癖，证据就是一地下室的玩具，还有满墙穿游泳短裤的男童照片。但警察说他们的证据不够充分，汤姆告诉丽奈特，他们无凭无据，不能指控阿特是恋童癖，建议她和一些专业人士，例如心理医生，去谈一谈。丽奈特没有接受这个中肯的建议，相反，她把自己的担心告诉了邻居太太麦克拉奇，麦克拉奇立刻把这件事告诉了自己的所有朋友。于是整个街区都知道了阿特有恋童嫌疑。

本段内容：布瑞婆婆的到来使布瑞的生活变得更加混乱，她嗜酒如命，把布瑞整洁干净的房间弄得一团乱，追求完美的布瑞忍无可忍，于是和丈夫奥森在伊迪的介绍下想为婆婆租一套房子，可是房子又难以使布瑞满意，她担心婆婆离开她和奥森的监督会更加肆无忌惮，只能让婆婆住在家中，于是矛盾还是继续存在。

Scene 1: Edie is showing Bree and Orson around.

伊迪带着布瑞和奥森参观房屋。

◁)) **Edie:**	Now this place is a real diamond in the **rough**[1]. **Cozy**[2] little two-bedroom plus **den**[3], with a highly **motivated**[4] seller.	伊迪：	这个地方可是未经雕琢的璞玉。舒适的两间卧室加上书房，卖主也急于转手。
Bree:	Oh, look, a highly motivated **cockroach**[5].	布瑞：	噢，看啊，还有一只焦急的蟑螂。
Edie:	Let's try to be positive, people. Fabulous location. Just walking distance to all sorts of fun shops.	伊迪：	让我们乐观一点。多好的位置啊。步行便可到各种商店。
Bree:	Right, from here I can see a bail **bondsman**[6] and an adult **bookshop**[7].	布瑞：	没错，从这儿就能看到一家保释担保行和一间成人书店。
Edie:	What do you expect in your price **range**[8]?	伊迪：	就你们出的那价钱还想怎样

Tara[9]?

啊？塔拉庄园？

Bree:	Let's go. Thank you.

布瑞：	我们走吧。谢谢你。

Gloria:	Wait. I'm not an impractical woman. I know that my son's resources are...like his achievements, rather limited. I want to see the rest of it.

格洛里亚：	等等，我不是一个不切实际的女人。我知道我儿子的财力，就像他的成就，相当有限。我想再看看这房子的其他地方。

Edie:	Okay. Now the lighting in the kitchen is a bit **harsh**[10]. The previous owner, well, let's just say he ran some sort of home-based medical business.

伊迪：	好的。厨房的照明有点刺眼。前房主，这么说吧，他经营一些家庭医疗生意。

Bree:	You cannot let your mother move into this neighborhood. It's filled with junkies and **whores**[11].

布瑞：	你不能让你妈妈搬来这种地方。到处都是瘾君子和妓女。

Orson:	And we'll owe them all an **apology**[12], but who cares? She likes it.

奥森：	是啊，我们还得给他们赔个不是，但谁在意啊？她自己喜欢。

Bree:	Of course she likes it. There's a twenty-four-hour liquor store across the street.

布瑞：	她当然会喜欢。对街就有家 24 小时营业的酒吧。

Orson:	She wants a house. This is the best we can afford without **bankrupting**[13] ourselves.

奥森：	她想要栋房子。这是我们在不破产的前提下能给她提供的最好的房子了。

Bree:	Orson, what if something should happen to her?

布瑞：	奥森，要是她在这出点儿意外怎么办？

Orson:	Stop worrying about her. Worry about us. Do you realize how much we've been fighting since she came? The woman's ruined every relationship that's **mattered to**[14] me, and she's doing it again.

奥森：	不要担心她了。担心一下我们吧。你意识到自从她来了后我们争吵了多少次了吗？那女人毁了所有我在乎的感情。她又在故伎重施了。

Edie:	Oh, my God!

伊迪：	噢，天啊!

Bree:	Are you all right?

布瑞：	你没事吧？

Orson:	Oh! Mother?

奥森：	噢，妈妈？

Edie:	It's just a little **spill**[15]. Her cane hit a loose tile.

伊迪：	只是滑了一下。她的拐杖杵到了一块松动的瓷砖。

注释

1. real diamond in the rough 未经雕琢的钻石
2. cozy ['kəʊzɪ] *adj.* 写意的
3. den [den] *n.* 书房
4. motivated ['məʊtɪveɪtɪd] *adj.* 积极性的
5. cockroach ['kɒkrəʊtʃ] *n.* 蟑螂
6. bail [beɪl] *v.* 保释　bondsman 保证人
7. adult bookshop 成人书店
8. price range 价格幅度

9. Tara 《乱世佳人》/《飘》（Gone with the Wind）里的斯嘉丽家的塔拉庄园
10. harsh [hɑːʃ] *adj.* 刺目的
11. junkie ['dʒʌŋkɪ] *n.* 有毒瘾者　whore [hɔː] 妓女
12. owe sb. an apology 要向某人表示歉意
13. bankrupt ['bæŋkrʌpt] *v.* 使破产
14. matter to 对某人很重要的，很在意的
15. spill [spɪl] *v.* 摔下，跌下

Bree:	Is anything broken?	布瑞：	有没有摔到哪里？
Gloria:	Well, obviously, the damn floor.	格洛里亚：	显然都怪这该死的地板。
Orson:	We'll need that fixed before she moves in.	奥森：	在她搬进来前我们得修好它。
Bree:	Are you insane? She obviously can't be *on her own*[16].	布瑞：	你疯了吗？她显然不能独自生活。
Orson:	Why, it's a loose tile.	奥森：	为什么，只是一块松动的瓷砖。
Gloria:	I'm **perfectly**[17] fine.	格洛里亚：	我完全没事。
Bree:	And *what if*[18] you weren't? What if she had broken something and she was lying here for hours? You are coming home with us.	布瑞：	如果你有事呢？如果她伤到了哪里躺在地上好几个小时呢？你和我们一起回去。
Orson:	Bree...	奥森：	布瑞……
Bree:	And I will not hear another word on the **subject**[19].	布瑞：	这个问题就不要再争论了。

Scene 2: Bree, Orson, Danielle, and Andrew are eating dinner.
布瑞、奥森、丹尼尔和安德鲁正在吃晚饭。

Bree:	It's just not right. Your mother skipped lunch, too.	布瑞：	这样不对，你妈连午饭也没吃。
Orson:	She said she wasn't hungry. Can't we just revel in her absence?	奥森：	她说了她不饿。我们不能尽情享受她的缺席吗？
Bree:	I know she's a **handful**[20], but she deserves some compassion. The woman watched a dream die yesterday.	布瑞：	我知道她是个难以控制的人，但是她应得到一些同情。这个女人昨天眼睁睁看着一个梦想破灭。
Danielle:	We all did.	丹妮拉：	我们都是。
Bree:	I'm taking her dinner up.	布瑞：	我把她的晚餐拿上去。
Andrew:	Oh, that's okay. I'll do it.	安德鲁：	哦，没关系，我来做吧。
Bree:	Oh, no, I'd **rather**[21] do it myself. I wanna talk to her.	布瑞：	不，我想自己来做，我想和她谈谈。
Andrew:	Oh, well, I'll let her know you're coming.	安德鲁：	哦，我会告诉她你要过来了。

Andrew:	Mom's coming. **Ditch**[22] the wine.	安德鲁:	妈妈要来了。把酒收起来。
Gloria:	Very well.	格洛里亚:	非常好。
Andrew:	You finished the whole bottle already?	安德鲁:	你已经把一瓶喝光了？
Gloria:	I was thirsty.	格洛里亚:	我很渴。
Bree:	Gloria, I've been thinking and...	布瑞:	格洛里亚，我一直在想……
Gloria:	Does no one in this house ever bother to knock?	格洛里亚:	住在这房子里的人都没有敲门的习惯吗？
Bree:	Is that alcohol? Where did you get that?	布瑞:	那是酒吗？你从哪儿弄来的？
Bree:	Andrew!	布瑞:	安德鲁！
Andrew:	When my grandma asks me a **favor**[23] with tears in her eyes, how...	安德鲁:	当奶奶含泪求我帮个忙的时候，我怎么能……
Gloria:	Oh, shut up, you little **extortionist**[24]. He charged me twenty bucks, plus five for the **corkscrew**[25].	格洛里亚:	哦，闭嘴吧，你这个小强盗。他管我要了20块，外加5块钱开瓶器。
Bree:	I'll deal with you later.	布瑞:	我一会儿再收拾你。
Andrew:	You can kiss that codeine good-bye.	安德鲁:	你可以跟那可卡因吻别了。
Bree:	Andrew brought her wine.	布瑞:	安德鲁给她买了酒。
Orson:	Oh, for God's sake. This is our house. If you expect to stay here, you're going to learn to obey a few rules.	奥森:	看在上帝的份上，这是我们的房子。如果你想住在这儿，你就得学着守点儿规矩。
Gloria:	I don't obey rules. I make them.	格洛里亚:	我不遵守规矩，我制定它们。
Orson:	Not anymore, mother.	奥森:	再也不会了，妈妈。
Gloria:	Just **watch yourself**[26], sonny boy.	格洛里亚:	管好你自己吧，乖宝贝。
Bree:	Okay, look, I know you're upset, but don't blame Orson. It's not his fault.	布瑞:	好吧，我知道你心烦意乱。但是不要指责奥森。这不是他的错。
Gloria:	It's all his fault. You think he's so wonderful. You don't know the half of what he's done.	格洛里亚:	这全都是他的错。你以为他很棒。你连他做过的一半事情都不了解。
Orson:	Let's go. I can't deal with her when she's like this.	奥森:	我们走。我管不了她，尤其当她变成这样的时候。
Gloria:	He doesn't want you to hear the truth, how he **cheated on**[27] Alma.	格洛里亚:	他不想让你听到实情，他是如何对阿尔玛不忠的。
Bree:	What?	布瑞:	什么？

注释
16. **on one's own** 独立地
17. **perfectly** ['pɜːfɪktlɪ] *adv.* 非常；十分
18. **what if** 如果……将会怎样
19. **on the subject** 关于这个问题
20. **handful** ['hændful] *n.* 文中意思是：难以控制的人
21. **I'd rather=I would rather** 我情愿
22. **ditch** [dɪtʃ] *v.* 收起，藏起
23. **ask a favor** 请人帮忙
24. **extortionist** [ɪkˈstɔːʃnɪst] *n.* 勒索者
25. **corkscrew** ['kɔːkskruː] *n.* 开瓶器
26. **watch yourself** 小心谨慎
27. **cheat on** 不忠于

Orson:	She's drunk!	奥森：	她喝醉了!
Gloria:	How he broke her heart and mine, all for his precious Monique.	格洛里亚：	他是怎样伤了她的心, 还有我的。都是为了他珍爱的莫妮可。
Orson:	You shut up, mother.	奥森：	你闭嘴, 妈妈!
Bree:	Monique Polier? I thought that was Harvey Bigsby's mistress.	布瑞：	莫妮可·波里尔? 我以为她是哈维·比格斯比的情妇。
Gloria:	Oh, she got around, that girl!	格洛里亚：	哦, 她无处不在。那个女孩!
Orson:	See, I told you. I told you she would do this.	奥森：	看吧, 我告诉你了, 我告诉你了她会这样做的。
Gloria:	There he was, cheating on Alma, not knowing all the time his whore was cheating on him.	格洛里亚：	他就是这样背叛了阿尔玛, 也从来不知道莫妮可其实骗了他。
Orson:	Stop it! You shut your evil mouth!	奥森：	把你邪恶的嘴闭上!
Gloria:	Or what? What are you gonna do to me that hasn't already been done?	格洛里亚：	否则怎样? 你打算怎么对付我? 你早就想做点什么了?
Orson:	Bree, no! Bree, wait! Bree!	奥森：	布瑞, 不! 布瑞, 等等! 布瑞!

常用表达

1. matter 对……重要

例: If it would facilitate matters, I would be happy to come to New York.

如果这有利于事态, 我将乐意来纽约。

2. what if 假使……将会怎样, 如果

例: A: We could tell him they wanted the couch to stay away from friends.

B: Okay, fine. What if we just flip it over?

A: 可以跟他说他们想让沙发离他们的朋友远点儿。

B: 这样吧, 干脆翻过来呢?

3. on one's own 独立地, 独自地

例: I can finish my homework on my own.

我不能独立完成作业。

4. would rather 情愿

例: I would rather give my kids up for adoption than end up like you.

我宁愿把自己的孩子送人领养, 也不想变成你这样的母亲。

Mad Men
《广告狂人》

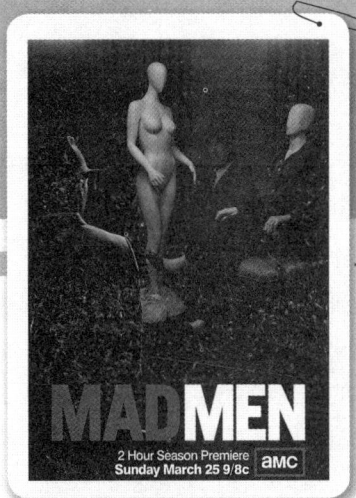

18

入选理由：

　　《广告狂人》由小众频道美国经典电影有线电视台推出，曾为美国有线电视台的"老大"家庭电影院执笔热门剧集《黑道家族》的编剧马修·威纳从创作到剧本一手打造了《广告狂人》。主演包括乔·汉姆，伊丽莎白·摩丝，詹瑞·琼斯，文森特·卡吉瑟等，都是有经验的实力派演员。最值得一提的是这部剧反映了 20 世纪 60 年代的故事，大胆地描述了美国广告业黄金时代残酷的商业竞争。剧中的色彩、灯光、演员装束都十分到位，剧情也很吸引人，真实有力地反映了当时广告业的辉煌，尤其是片中的精彩广告创意，连业内人士都认为能激发灵感。本剧在人物塑造方面也很成功，尤其是男主角唐·德雷柏。

　　此剧广受好评，赢得了不少电视奖项，包括 4 个金球奖及 15 个艾美奖。这也是首部获得艾美奖最佳剧情剧的基础有线台剧集。

　　与大部分美剧不同，《广告狂人》低调平静得出奇，而原本这样的题材完全可以被描绘得精彩至极。摒弃了情节上突出的大起大落，它以一种优雅的方式娓娓道来，精致迷人，一点点抓住你的心。《广告狂人》也还原了 60 年代的政治背景和社会大事件，比如肯尼迪与尼克松的总统大选，陷入受贿丑闻的尼克松不得不向广告公司寻求帮助，通过重新包装以挽救形象等。虽然这些并不是整部剧集的主线，但是穿插其中却令故事显得更真实。

Section 1　剧情特点：

　　《广告狂人》的时间背景是 20 世纪 60 年代，场景是在美国纽约市麦迪逊大道上一家名为斯特灵库柏的广告公司。纽约麦迪逊大道是广告公司的代名词，数百家广告公司及下游制作、代理、服务公司聚集在那里，形成了一个庞大的财富链——从小小的雪茄烟到总统候选人——广告无处不在。本剧主要讲述的是斯特灵库柏广告公司的创意总监唐·德雷柏的工作与生活，以及周边的人与事。同时也涉及到美国 60 年代的社会风貌及社会变迁。

　　这部剧描绘的美国社会文化，突出了吸烟、饮酒、性别歧视、女权主义等。比如吸烟，20 世纪 60 年代在美国比现在更常见，也是整部剧的特色。在首播集，"好彩"烟草公司的代表来到斯特灵库柏广告公司，希望能找到新的广告活动，因为《读者文摘》发布了吸烟会导致各种健康问题（包括肺癌）的报告。"好彩"烟草公司还注意到，广告是企业创意的主流，是中产阶级、年轻白人突破生存现状的出口。除了吸烟这个例子之外，剧中也有对未来的暗示和 60 年代的激进运动的描述：比如早期的女权运动等。

剧中的角色们也看到了广告业本身的变化，比如大众甲壳虫的"想想还是小的好（Think Small）"的广告被提及，但是被斯特灵库柏的很多人否决了。

多样化的主题，社会的流动和无情也是这部剧的元素。在这个社会动荡、风云变幻的时代，职业道德、无烟环境、反种族歧视等观念的诞生将对未来产生巨大影响。

Section 2　对白特点：

《广告狂人》让人迷恋的不仅仅是它独特的怀旧风，还有其中很打动人心的台词。这也再次证明剧中台词的经典及编剧的强大。《广告狂人》是一部"什么都懂（something of everything）"的作品，因广泛使用字字珠玑、表述内敛、寓意立体、指向多元的台词、表演和场景，在一定程度上摒弃了台词对白，用"结构叙事"等更多元的叙事手法，使其内容极为丰富复杂，值得反复捉摸玩味，以至于不同职业、不同性别的观众甚至是处于不同人生阶段的同一位观众在观看时都会有不同的感受和新的收获。观众在观赏本剧时，需要调动文化、语言知识、生活感知和对人的判断能力去揣摩剧情背景和背后的肌理，甚至是通过一个单词、一个语调暗示人物内心。

作为一部广告题材的美剧，片中出现了创意总监唐·德雷柏带领公司做出的不少引人注目的广告创意。一个很好的案例出现在第一季第一集，当时《读者文摘》杂志与联邦贸易署联手刊文，第一次将吸烟同癌症的联系公诸于世，令香烟公司陷入前所未有的负面漩涡。"好彩"烟草公司找到唐所在的斯特灵库柏广告公司，寻求市场推广策略，唐在最后关头给出了一个"It's toasted"（我们的烟是烤制过的）的广告语。该广告词既不回应、也不回避"吸烟危害健康"的说法，而是突出烤制香烟这道其实所有的香烟在制作过程中都存在的工序，利用 toasted 与手工制作、天然材料的某种健康联想及 It's toasted 本身在英语中的一语双关（"举杯庆贺"的意思），在消费者心中将"好彩"香烟与男性热衷的积极的、幸福的生活状态联系起来，成功将"好彩"香烟同"不健康"的其他品牌的香烟区分开，转嫁了舆论压力。类似精彩的广告语还有被提拔起来的女秘书佩奇为"妙龄佳人"唇膏设计的 "Mark Your Man"（用香吻标记你爱的男人）的广告词，意在传递出女性对男性的占有欲。

Section 3　角色分析：

唐·德雷柏 (Don Draper)：乔·汉姆饰。《广告狂人》中的男主角，斯特林库柏广告公司的创意总监兼初级合伙人，到了第四季，他成为斯特林库柏公司的合伙人。他喝酒成瘾、烟不离手，有着灰暗的过去，但在广告业有不错的成就。他娶了伊丽莎白·贝蒂·德雷柏，与她生了 3 个孩子。但唐自始至终笃信利益与道德不可调和，这令他和妻子之间产生了巨大的陌生感，"漠视道德"也令唐不断出轨，致使他与贝蒂的婚姻最终破裂。

唐·德雷柏堪称男人与女人梦想的化身——男人梦想成为他，女人梦想拥有他。这个角色魅力十足，也是剧集走红的关键因素。他的名字（Don Draper）取自美国地产大亨唐纳德·特朗普 (Donald Trump)。事实上，唐·德雷柏并不是一个完美的男人。他拥有最高领导层的办公室，却有着巨大的压力，每天要面对觊觎他职位的年轻的竞争对手。不过，你不得不承认他是一个广告奇才，他会在与服务生聊天的过程中，捕捉灵感，然后记录在纸巾上。工作之余，唐还要处理日益繁杂的私人事务，其中包括和蜜琪·丹尼尔的私情及对雷切尔·麦肯的爱恋。虽然与三个女人纠缠不清，但唐却处理得游刃有余。在第一季中，妻子贝蒂不得不去看心理医生；到了第二季中，知己麦肯将业务转投竞争对手；而在最新的第三季中，唐身边又有了新的女孩，但妻子有孕令他重新回归家庭。唐与几个女人关系的走向是《广告狂人》的一大看点。

佩奇·奥尔森 (Peggy Olson)： 伊丽莎白·莫斯饰。斯特灵库柏广告公司的新职员，被任命为唐·德雷柏的秘书。她是来自布鲁克林的乡下女孩，毕业于迪沃小姐的秘书学校。作为一名在第一季里刚刚进入斯特林库柏公司的秘书，佩奇的视角最初就是观众的视角，是她带领着观众在斯特林库柏的玻璃门后逡巡游弋，打开了一副生动的职场画卷。乡下出身的佩奇显然对自己的背景颇不满意，她一心想抹去自己身上的每一丝乡土印记，千方百计地想变成上流社会的"城里人"。

从个人奋斗的角度来说，佩奇与唐·德雷柏十分相似，她的崛起充满了偶然和变故，见证了女性时代曙光前的坎坷。在最初她以拙劣的技巧勾引上司唐未果后，她经过金西的点拨产生了做文案编写、进入男权社会的念头。她不再对洗手间里抽泣的女同事施予同情和关怀，戴上了代表男性审美的丝巾，抛弃了自己的私生子，像男人一样苛刻地对待广告配音员直至把配音员逼到崩溃痛哭。勤奋的佩奇很快也凭借自己的努力获得了升迁，她的女权思想甚至渗透进了她的广告创意中。在她为口红撰写了出色的广告文案之后，唐把她正式提升为初级文案，锦绣前程自此向佩奇敞开。

皮特·坎贝尔 (Pete Campbell)： 文森特·卡塞瑟饰。一个来自有背景的老派纽约家庭的年轻人，一个有雄心的客户主任。他曾尝试用他所知道的有关迪克的信息敲诈唐·德雷柏，但没成功。他和唐亦敌亦友。坎贝尔和他的妻子特鲁迪结婚后一直没有生儿育女，他一直到第二季的结尾才知道自己和奥尔森生有一个孩子。到了第三季，由于不满他在斯特林库柏的待遇，他私下决定离开公司。唐并没有意识到这些，仍邀请坎贝尔加入新的公司，只要坎贝尔能带去价值 800 万美元的客户。坎贝尔要求只有在他成为合伙人的情况下才会加入（尽管他的名字并没有出现在公司的名字中）。坎贝尔是仅有的几个不抽烟的角色之一。他在很多方面都很敬重唐。

贝蒂·德雷柏 (Betty Draper)： 詹纽瑞·琼斯饰。唐·德雷柏的前妻，与唐育有三个孩子：萨莉、鲍比和尤金·史考特。贝蒂在费城的艾金公园市长大，她有着与唐相反的家庭出身、生长环境、社会性别意识等。剧集开始的时候，他们已经结婚七年了，并住在纽约州的奥西宁。在前两季中，贝蒂逐渐意识到丈夫的不忠。如果说唐用放纵来发泄内心的压抑，贝蒂则选择把一切压抑都放在心里，因此她需要看心理医生，说出心中的痛苦。在短暂的分居之后，她发现自己怀孕了，于是允许唐搬回了家。第三季的结尾，在决定与唐离婚之后，贝蒂去了内华达州的里诺。在第四季开始时，贝蒂与唐离了婚，嫁给了亨利·弗兰西斯。她和孩子们还有她的新丈夫搬到了纽约的拉伊市。贝蒂与孩子们的关系，特别是与萨莉的，一直都很紧张。

🔊 Passage 1 📹

剧情介绍：

（第 1 季第 2 集）唐还纠缠在与情人的复杂关系中，新秘书佩奇在打扮上终于不像以前那么寒酸。与罗杰一家吃饭时，唐的妻子贝蒂的手开始不受控制地颤抖。公司策划人员正在为新出的喷雾除臭剂做策划，唐和同事商量把除臭剂用在肯身上。这时公司合伙人库柏走进办公室，他希望唐重新考虑接下为尼克松竞选策划的任务，唐考虑之后答应了他的要求。

Scene 1: Don and Betty were having dinner with the Sterlings. Roger's wife Mona had a short talk with Betty in the dressing room.

唐带着妻子贝蒂与罗杰一家吃饭。罗杰的妻子莫娜与贝蒂在化妆间的对话。

🔊 **Betty:** Mona, could you help me here? I seem to have grown a set of thumbs. Do you ever have that when your hands go **numb**[1]?

贝蒂： 莫娜，能帮帮我吗？我的手有些抖。你手麻了也会这样吗？

Mona: You want me to touch you up?

莫娜： 要我帮你涂口红吗？

Betty: Yeah, I think you'll have to.

贝蒂： 是的，恐怕要麻烦你了。

Mona: Look at those lips. I'll bet it's not hard for you to *hold on*[1] to a man like that.

莫娜： 看看这唇瓣，我敢打赌你抓住男人轻而易举。

(Betty smiled.)

（贝蒂笑起来。）

Mona: Don't smile. It'll make it harder.

莫娜： 别笑，不容易涂。

Betty: It's hard to hold on to anything right now with the... children and running the house and... I don't know if I told you, but my m-mother died two, three months ago.

贝蒂： 现在家里上上下下都得照顾，还有两个孩子，可真不容易。我不知道我有没有告诉你，我妈妈在三个月前去世了。

Waitress: I'm sorry. There are other ladies waiting to use the mirror.

女招待： 很抱歉。还有其他女士等着用镜子。

Scene 2: Don and Betty drank some wine while dining with Roger. They drove home and talked about Don's boss Roger.

在与罗杰的晚餐中，唐与妻子贝蒂饮了一些酒。开车回家的路上，贝蒂与唐谈起老板罗杰。

Betty: I love seeing you like that.

Don: Well, you were sitting on my good side.

Betty: No. I mean, the way other people see you. When you're with strangers, you know exactly what you want.

Don: Well, I like to think I always know what I want.

Betty: Slow down. I'll have to put that in my diary: **lobster**[2] Newburg and **gimlets**[3] should get a divorce. They're not getting along very well.

Don: Once you rounded the corner on number two, I took it for a case of nerves.

Betty: He's your boss. He likes you.

Don: Toots Shor means he likes me. When he gets us to the Four Seasons, then we'll know he trusts me.

Betty: Hmm. He seemed very **forthcoming**[4].

Don: Yeah. When he's *stoned on*[2] martinis.

Betty: I don't know. It all seemed like an invitation to you to con... **confide**[5].

Don: Well, maybe it's just manners, but I was raised to see it as a sin of pride to go on like that about yourself.

Betty: You're so **reverent**[6].

贝蒂：我喜欢那样的你。

唐：你坐的位置能看见我好看的一面。

贝蒂：不，我是说你在其他人面前的样子。你和陌生人一起时，总能知道你想要什么。

唐：我觉得我一直知道自己想要什么。

贝蒂：开慢点儿，我要记到日记里：龙虾沙拉和手钻鸡尾酒不该一起吃。它们混在一起"相处"得不太好。

唐：要第二份的时候，我还觉得你很有勇气呢。

贝蒂：他是你老板，他喜欢你。

唐：去图特肖尔餐厅意味着他喜欢我，如果他请我们去四季酒店，就表示他信任我了。

贝蒂：嗯，他看起来挺随和。

唐：他那是喝马丁尼喝多了。

贝蒂：不知道。像是一种同你深交的邀请。

唐：也许只是出于礼貌，但我从小被教育说，如果向别人吹嘘过去，就太骄傲自满了。

贝蒂：你真是个谦虚的人。

注释 1. numb [nʌm] *adj.* 麻木的，失去知觉的　　4. forthcoming [ˌfɔːˈθkʌmɪŋ] *adj.* 随和的

2. lobster [ˈlɒbstə] *n.* 龙虾　　5. confide [kənˈfaɪd] *v.* 信任，信赖

3. gimlet [ˈɡɪmlɪts] *n.* 鸡尾酒（gimlet 的名词复数）　　6. reverent [ˈrevərənt] *adj.* 恭敬的，谦虚的

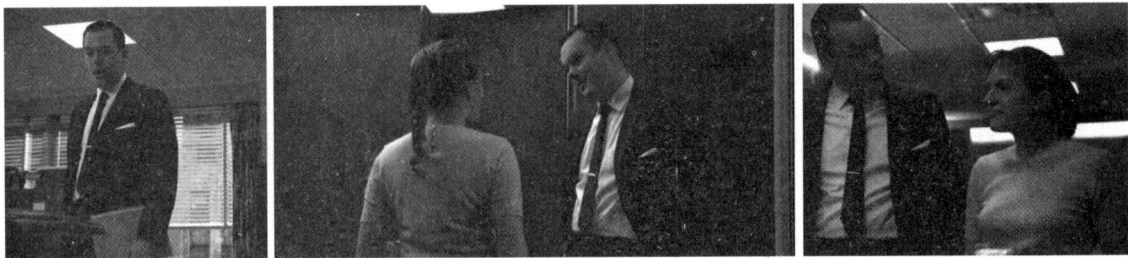

Scene 3: Peggy asked Paul Kinsey about the approval of his ideas and Paul felt quite unsatisfied. They bought lunch together, and then Paul told Peggy about the running of the company and the importance and pressure of copywriters.

佩奇询问保罗的方案是否通过，保罗表示很惋惜。他们一起买午餐，途中保罗向佩奇讲述公司的运转及文案编写人的重要性与压力。

Peggy:	How'd it go?	佩奇：	怎么样？
Paul:	I've still got my novel.	保罗：	这份工作不成，我还可以写小说。
Peggy:	I'm sorry.	佩奇：	抱歉。
Paul:	Buy me lunch?	保罗：	请我吃午餐？
Paul:	Samuel, that Drape man? It's sadder than a map.	保罗：	塞缪尔，那个叫德雷柏的男人，可不好对付。
Samule:	Well, it's **lightweight**[7], and it tells me I'm at work. But you sure can talk, Mr. Kinsey. 60 cents.	塞缪尔：	我还在工作，不能讲闲话。但你可以讲，金西先生。60美分。
Paul:	What are you doing? Keep the change. You *figured*[8] *the place out*[3] yet?	保罗：	你在干什么？不用找了。你摸透这里的状况了吗？
Peggy:	What do you mean?	佩奇：	你指的是什么？
Paul:	How it runs.	保罗：	这里怎么运转的。
Peggy:	I know the copywriters tell the Art Department what to do, and I know the account **executives**[9] tell the copywriters what to do.	佩奇：	我知道是广告文案编写人告诉艺术部门做什么，业务经理告诉文案编写人做什么。
Paul:	What? No one tells the writers what to do except for the Head of Creative, your boss, Donald Draper. Don't think that just because he's good-looking, he's not a writer. Dig. This is the Media Department. They're where 90% of where the client's check goes. They buy space... newspapers, billboards, television, and my favorite aging whore, radio. That's the whole shakedown, actually. All you really need to know. They don't sell ideas or campaigns or **jingles**[10]. They sell media at a 15% markup.	保罗：	什么？没人有权告诉文案做什么，除了创意总监，你上司唐·德雷柏。别以为他长得帅，就不懂写东西。好好想想，这是传媒部门，客户90%的钱都是给这儿的，他们花钱买报纸、广告牌、电视上的空间，还有我最爱的广播，差不多也就这些。你需要知道的也就这么多。他们不卖创意、广告活动或是广告词，他们以高出原价15%的价格对外出售媒体。创意只是对外

Creative is just window dressing that's thrown in for free.

Peggy: Really?

Paul: Accounting, they keep track of how much we're spending **versus**[11] how much we're taking in, and since we're buying futures, if you ever, ever see, um, the man upstairs go in there, grab the lifeboats, baby. We're going down.

Paul: Account Management, where prep schoolers skip arm-in-arm, *Wizard of Oz*[1] style, joined together by their lack of skill and their love of mirrors. Account executives are all good at something, although it's never advertising. **Submitted**[12] for your approval: One Peter Campbell, a man who recently discovered that the only place for his hand is in your pocket. You watch it? Have you seen it? The Twilight Zone?

Peggy: I don't think so. I don't like science fiction.

Paul: I'm gonna pretend you didn't say that. Mitch in Media says CBS might pull the plug. I'll kill myself. And here we have the Creative Department, the talent, home sweet home. Like the Art Department downstairs, they put us far enough away from the elevators so we can't **sneak**[13] out. You know, there are women copywriters.

Peggy: Good ones?

Paul: Sure. I mean, y-you can always tell when a woman's writing copy, but sometimes she just might be the right man for the job, you know?

Peggy: You must be very creatively satisfied.

的一种展示，那并不挣钱。

佩奇： 真的吗？

保罗： 会计们天天算我们值不值工资给的那个数。既然我们在为未来投资，所以如果你看到高层的人到那里去，抓住救生艇吧，亲爱的，我们要完了。

保罗： 财务管理部门，那些还在上预科的人手拉着手，像《绿野仙踪》里那样蹦蹦跳跳地开始旅程，他们因为缺乏技能和对镜子情有独钟而逐渐走到一起。虽然他们从来没做过广告，但业务经理总有他们擅长的。他在恳求你的应允，皮特·坎贝尔。这个男人最近发现，他可以从你身上揩油。你看过吗？《黄昏地带》？

佩奇： 应该没看过，我不喜欢科幻题材的。

保罗： 我装作你没说过，传媒部的米奇说 CBS 电视台准备结束这部剧，我会自杀的。这里就是创作部，天才集中营，我们甜蜜的家，跟楼下的艺术部门一样。他们把我们放在离电梯很远的地方，防止我们溜走。你知道吗，文案编写人也有女的。

佩奇： 优秀吗？

保罗： 当然。我是说女人写的东西总是一眼就能看出来。 但有时候还非得要这种效果。这工作很适合她们，知道吗？

佩奇： 你那么有创意，一定很满意这份工作。

注释

7. lightweight ['laɪtweɪt] *n.* 无关重要的事

8. figure ['fɪgə] *v.* 想出，弄清

9. executive [ɪg'zekjətɪv] *n.* 总经理，负责人

10. jingle ['dʒɪŋgl] *n.* 广告词

11. versus ['vɜːsəs] *prep.* 与……对比，与……对抗

12. submit [səb'mɪt] *v.* 提交

13. sneak [sniːk] *v.* 偷偷溜走

Paul: Let's not lose our heads. Sterling Coop is positively Cro-Magnon[2]. I have a friend... I'm not even going to say what agency... but all they do is to play darts, and honestly, I think they're the best store on the street. You like Ukrainian food? Oxtail dumplings?

Peggy: I still have a lot of work to do. I think he's still in there. Huh.

Paul: *Got it*[4].

Peggy: Thanks for lunch. Sorry about your copy.

Paul: Thanks for reminding me.

保罗： 嘘，小心掉脑袋。斯特林·库柏绝对是来自旧石器时代的人。我有个朋友，我不会说他是哪个公司的，他告诉我他们每天就飞飞镖，但他们绝对是这一带最阔绰的人。你喜欢乌克兰食物吗？比如牛尾水饺？

佩奇： 我还有好多工作要做，我觉得他还在那里。

保罗： 明白了。

佩奇： 谢谢你的午餐，为你的文案惋惜。

保罗： 谢谢你又揭了一次我的伤疤。

📖 文化背景

1. *Wizard of Oz* 《绿野仙踪》

《绿野仙踪》主要讲小姑娘多萝茜被龙卷风刮到奥兹国进行冒险的故事。她陆续结识了没有脑子的稻草人、没有心脏的铁皮人和十分胆小的狮子，他们为了实现各自的心愿，互相帮助，携手协作，历尽艰险，遇到许多稀奇古怪的事情。最终，他们凭借自己非凡的智力和顽强的毅力，都完成了自己的心愿。和《西游记》颇有几分相似之处。

2. Cro-Magnon 克鲁马努人

旧石器时代晚期在欧洲的高加索人种，克鲁马努人被认为是新人的代表。新人阶段，又称晚期智人阶段。新人阶段以后，人类就进入了现代人的发展阶段。

☎ 常用表达

1. hold on 握住，抓牢

例： Despite her aching shoulders, Nancy held on.
南希不顾双肩疼痛，紧抓不放。

2. be stoned on 被……灌醉

例： They get themselves stoned on beer.
他们大喝啤酒，喝得烂醉。

3. figure out 弄明白，想出

例： I simply couldn't figure out his intention.
我简直揣摩不透他的用意。

4. got it 知道了

例： I've got it. It is a quotation.
想起来了，这是一条引语。

Passage 2

剧情介绍：

（第 1 季第 13 集）皮特·坎贝尔的岳父知道他失去了升职的机会后表示他现在应该做的是为家庭负责，生个孩子。达克成为策划主管后第一次接手的广告就是柯达公司的幻灯片放映机。唐·德雷柏和妻子贝蒂吵架，不愿意和她的家人一起过感恩节，贝蒂决定带孩子回家。唐将撰写一款护肤品广告词的任务交给了佩奇，遭到皮特的反对。

Scene 1: Pete was having a talk with his father-in-law Tom. Tom asked about Pete's promotion and having a baby, which made Pete and Trudy embarrassed.

皮特与岳父汤姆一起聊天，汤姆聊到皮特的晋升与孩子一事，这使得皮特与妻子特鲁迪都感到很尴尬。

Tom: Nixon didn't stand a chance. The Browns **trounced**[1] the Redskins[1], 31:10. The result of that last home game has correctly predicted the last six elections.

Pete: I wish someone would have told me that. Of course, it's really a 50/50 chance of being right.

Tom: I want to treat you like a son because... I feel that way towards you.

Pete: OK.

Tom: Trudy told us that you were up for a **promotion**[2] and you didn't get it or something.

Pete: I wish she hadn't.

Tom: Now, she loves you. And honestly, I

汤姆：尼克松根本没有机会。布朗队痛击红肤队（橄榄球队），以 31 比 10 获胜。上次主场比赛的结果准确预测了近6次选举的结果。

皮特：我真希望当时有人告诉我。当然，可能性也就一半一半。

汤姆：我想把你当我儿子看，因为……我觉得你就像我的儿子。

皮特：嗯。

汤姆：特鲁迪告诉我们你本来有机会晋升的，但你却什么都没捞着。

皮特：我真希望她没跟你讲过。

汤姆：现在，她爱你。老实说，

注释 **1. trounce** ['trauns] v. 使大败，痛击
2. promotion [prə'məuʃən] n. 晋升，提升

	think you need to take a little focus off your work.		我觉得你该从工作上转移点儿注意力。
Pete:	This from one of the top salesmen at Vicks Chemical. When you started talking about that Clearasil company you bought…	皮特：	这话居然出自威克斯制药的金牌销售员之口。当你开始谈论你购买克利拉思公司时……
Tom:	Now, that was kind of worth **bragging**[3] about. Did you know that there's a surge in adolescence right now?	汤姆：	那件事很值得夸耀。你知道吗？时下青年人群数量猛增。
Pete:	I'll tell you, Sterling Cooper and yours truly would love to help you deliver that message.	皮特：	我告诉你，斯特林库柏公司会带着您的问候向公众传达这一信息的。
Tom:	See? Now that's what I'm talking about. The only family and business you should be mixing is the production of a child.	汤姆：	明白吗？这就是我想说的。唯一让家庭和事业平衡的方法就是生个孩子。
Pete:	And what did Trudy say about that?	皮特：	特鲁迪是怎么说的？
Trudy:	About what?	特鲁迪：	说什么？
Trudy's mother:	Tom, *loose lips sink ships*[1].	特鲁迪的母亲：	汤姆，多说不宜。
Tom:	I was just saying that work isn't everything, you know. It's like that song says: Um, *tend your own garden*[2].	汤姆：	我就跟他说事业不是男人的一切。像那句歌唱的：照管好你的花园。
Trudy:	What song is that, Daddy?	特鲁迪：	那是什么歌，爸爸？
Tom:	Uh, I don't know. People say it. It's true.	汤姆：	我不知道。人们都这么说，一点儿没错。
Trudy's mother:	It is true.	特鲁迪的母亲：	是一点儿没错。
Tom:	Yeah, tend to your own garden. That means… you know, start growing things.	汤姆：	照管好你的花园，也就是说，种点儿什么出来。
Trudy:	Daddy! You are **embarrassing**[4] us.	特鲁迪：	爸爸！太难为情了。
Tom:	It'll be the best Christmas present this one ever had. And hell, Thanksgiving's Thursday.	汤姆：	这绝对是最棒的圣诞礼物。赶紧啊，周四就是感恩节了。

(Trudy and Peter laughed.) | （特鲁迪和皮特笑起来。）

Scene 2: Don made a projection of his Wedding, his wife Betty's production of a baby and his kids' growing in order to display his ideas about wheels to Kodark company.

唐将自己结婚、妻子生孩子、小孩成长的照片做成幻灯片，向柯达公司展示自己的创意。

Roger: Don Draper and Salvatore Romano. This is Joe Harriman and Lunn Taylor. No Eastmans[2] today, unfortunately. They're all back in the lab.

Lunn: It's a wonderful facility, but they don't take **vacations**[5].

Roger: What do they show, slides of them working?

(Everybody laughed.)

Joe: so, have you figured out a way to work the wheel into it?

Lunn: we know it's hard because wheels aren't seen as exciting technology even though they are the original.

Don: Well, technology is a **glittering**[6] lure. But there is the rare occasion when public can be engaged in a level beyond flash, if they have a **sentimental**[7] bond with the product. My first job, I was in house at a fur company, with this old pro, copywriter. Greek, named Teddy. Teddy told me the most important idea in advertising is, new. Creates an itch. You simply put your products in there as a kind of... calamine lotion. He also talked about the deeper bound with the product. **Nostalgia**[8]. It's delicate... But potent. Sweetheart, Teddy

罗杰：这是唐·德雷柏和萨尔瓦多·罗曼诺。这是乔·哈里曼和林恩·泰勒。很不走运，今天没有研发人员参与。他们都回实验室里去了。

林恩：他们的设备很好，但是不休假。

罗杰：那他们要展示什么，工作场景的幻灯片吗？

（大家都笑起来。）

乔：那么，你想出要怎么把转轮加进去了吗？

林恩：我们知道很难，因为转轮实在不是什么新的技术，即使他们其实是原创。

唐：好吧，技术是赤裸裸的诱惑，但也有极少的情况，人们会关注闪光灯以外的东西，就是当他们与产品有了一种感情联系时。我的第一份工作是我在一个皮草公司内部工作，跟一个职业撰稿人，一个叫泰迪的希腊人共事。泰迪告诉我，广告行业最重要的理念是创新，挑起人们的好奇心。你只是把你的产品摆在那儿，就像一种润肤剂。他还告诉我，一种与产品的深层联系，一种怀旧感，很微妙，但却有力。亲爱的，

注释
3. **brag** [bræg] v. 自夸，吹嘘
4. **embarrass** [ɪm'bærəs] v. 使尴尬，使窘迫
5. **vacation** [və'keɪʃn] n. 假期
6. **glittering** ['glɪtərɪŋ] adj. 光辉灿烂的，闪闪发光的
7. **sentimental** [sentɪ'mentl] adj. 富有情感的，伤感的
8. **nostalgia** [nɒ'stældʒə] n. 对往事的怀恋，怀旧

told me that in Greek, nostalgia literally means the pain from an old wound. It's a **twinge**[9] in your heart, far more powerful than memory alone. This device, isn't a spaceship. It's a time machine. Goes backwards, and forwards. Takes to a place, where we ache to go again. It's not called the wheel. It's called the **carousel**[10]. Let us travel the way, a child travels. Round and round, and back home again. To the place where we know we are loved.

Roger: Good luck at your next meeting.

Scene 3: Don's boss Roger and his colleagues came to cheer for his success about Kodark. Don decided to ask new junior copywriter Peggy to deliver Clearasil to the masses, which made Pete quite depressed.

老板罗杰和创作部的同事来向唐庆祝他的关于柯达公司的创意的成功，唐把皮特从岳父手中接过的新护肤品广告词撰写的任务交给刚升职为初级撰稿人的佩奇，皮特提出反对。

Roger: Don, I have to **warn**[11] you, I'm not alone.

Salvatore: It was beautiful.

Paul: Congratulations, mein Kommandant[3].

Roger: They called from the lobby. They cancelled their other meetings, including DDB. Not just a victory for us. It's a victory for civilization. There's also more **celebrating**[12]. Mr. Campbell, here, your father-in-law called. He'll be in before Christmas.

Ken: I've got to get married.

Don: No, thank you. I'm good.

泰迪告诉我，在希腊语里，怀旧这词的字母意思是旧伤口残留的疼痛，是你心里的一种刺痛，比单独的记忆更具有力量。这个设备，并不是一个太空船，它是一个时间机器，它可以后退，也可以前进，它带着我们去那些我们会再次痛苦的地方。它并不叫转轮，它叫作旋转木马。它让我们像个孩子一样玩耍旅行，转了一圈又一圈，然后再次回到家。回到一个我们感到自己被爱着的地方。

罗杰：祝你下次会议好运。

罗杰：唐，得提醒你，后面还有一群人。
萨尔瓦多：太美了。
保罗：恭喜你。
罗杰：他们从大厅里打来电话。他们取消了其他会议，包括与DDB公司的。这不仅仅是我们的胜利，也是文明的胜利。还有更多值得庆祝的。这位坎贝尔先生，你岳父打电话来，说他圣诞节前会加入我们的股份。
肯：我也得去结婚了。
唐：不，谢谢。我不需要。

Ken:	Here's how.	肯:	庆祝我们的成功。
Everybody:	Cheers.	所有人:	干杯。
Don:	You know what, Pete. I've got a way for you to turn this account into a home run.	唐:	你知道吗，皮特。我有个帮你把这客户变为家族企业的办法。
Paul:	He's on a roll.	保罗:	他可是多次成功。
Don:	Clearasil[4]. You know who buys that? Young girls. What a difference it makes in their lives to be **blemish**[13]-free.	唐:	克利拉思，你知道谁会买它的产品吗？年轻的姑娘们。能完美无瑕，对于她们的生活太重要了。
Pete:	I believe it does.	皮特:	我相信一定是的。
Don:	We have the perfect writer for that. Peggy Olson.	唐:	我们有绝佳的文字创作者，佩奇·奥尔森。
Pete:	That's funny.	皮特:	你真好笑。
Don:	Freddy Rumsen and I were both very **impressed**[14] with her insight.	唐:	我和弗雷迪·拉姆森都很欣赏她的见识。
Pete:	Freddy Rumsen.	皮特:	弗雷迪·拉姆森。
Ken:	If I can *weigh in*[3]…	肯:	如果让我也加入的话……
Pete:	No.	皮特:	不可能。
Ken:	Come on. That Belle Jolie thing. Plus you should have seen her in that **booth**[15] yesterday. She was like Kinsey but with balls.	肯:	不是吧，那个法国女孩。并且你们应该看看她昨天在录音棚的样子。她就像是男版的金西。
(Everybody laughed.)		（大家都笑起来。）	
Pete:	Stop joking already, will you, Don?	皮特:	别开玩笑了，好吗，唐？
Don:	Excuse me?	唐:	你说什么？
Pete:	This is my father-in-law. He's expecting the very best. I am expecting the very best. Not some little girl who'll walk away.	皮特:	这位客户是我岳父。他期望的是最好的人，而不是某个会一走了之的小姑娘。
Don:	You'll have to give back that copy of Ayn Rand.	唐:	那你就把那份稿件还给安·兰德吧。
Pete:	Do you know how hard I worked to get this account?	皮特:	你知不知道我多努力才得到这个客户？
Roger:	Who the hell is she?	罗杰:	她到底是谁？
Pete:	Peggy is not even a copywriter. She's a… a secretary.	皮特:	佩奇甚至都不是一个撰稿人，只是个秘书。

注释
9. twinge [twindʒ] *n.* 刺痛，痛苦
10. carousel [.kærə'sel] *n.* 旋转木马
11. warn [wɔːn] *v.* 提醒
12. celebrating ['selɪbreɪtɪŋ] *adj.* 值得庆祝的
13. blemish ['blemɪʃ] *n.* 瑕疵，污点
14. impressed [ɪm'prest] *adj.* 印象深刻的
15. booth [buːð] *n.* 隔开的小间，小室

Don:	Peggy!	唐：	佩奇！
Peggy:	Yes, Mr Draper?	佩奇：	什么事，德雷柏先生？
Don:	Miss Olsen, you are now a junior copy-writer. Your first account will be delivering Clearasil to the spotted masses.	唐：	奥尔森小姐，现在起你升为初级撰稿人。你的第一个任务是把克利拉思推向目标群体。
Peggy:	What?	佩奇：	什么？
Paul:	Don't act surprised.	保罗：	别装得这么吃惊。
Peggy:	Is this really happening?	佩奇：	您说真的吗？
Don:	Yes, it is.	唐：	是的。
Peggy:	My goodness. I will do my sincere best.	佩奇：	我的天哪。我一定会全力以赴的。
Don:	Good to hear. Mr. Campbell, here, will brief you after the holiday.	唐：	很好。坎贝尔先生会在假日后给你指示。
Peggy:	Of course.	佩奇：	好的。
Don:	That'll be all.	唐：	就这样。
Peggy:	Thank you, Mr Draper.	佩奇：	谢谢你，德雷柏先生。

文化背景

1. The Browns trounced the Redskins 布朗队痛击红肤队

The Browns 与 the Redskins 分别为美国早期的两支橄榄球队，即布朗队与红肤队（或称华盛顿红人队）。

2. Eastmans 伊斯门，暗指研发人员。

Eastman 为美国摄影技术领域的发明家 George（1854–1932）的姓氏。

3. mein Kommandant 我的上司

4. Clearasil 克利拉思，一种专业祛痘护肤品。

常用表达

1. loose lips sink ships 多说不益

例：You'd better keep silent at the top meeting. Loose lips sink ships.

你最好在高层会议上保持沉默。多说无益。

2. tend your own garden 照料好自己的花园，（暗指）生儿育女

例：You are 30, not ever young. You should tend your own garden.

你已经 30 岁了，不再年轻了。你该生儿育女了。

3. weigh in 参与讨论，对……发表意见

例：Cranston and others were improperly trying to weigh in on the decision.

克兰斯顿和其他人都不合时宜地想在这个决定中发表高见。

🔊 Passage 3 🎥

剧情介绍：

（第3季第5集）萨丽在学校出现反常行为，苏珊娜老师请德雷柏夫妇到学校会面。达克暗中联系坎贝尔，约坎贝尔外出吃饭。贝蒂诞下一名男婴，她想用去世父亲的名字给孩子命名。达克约了坎贝尔和佩奇，想说服两人跳槽。佩奇希望德雷柏给自己涨工资，德雷柏拒绝了她的请求。坎贝尔因为在推销过程中牵涉到种族歧视的问题，他被库柏等人严厉斥责。

Scene 1: Don and his wife Betty went to Sally's school. The teacher told them about Sally's fighting with another child and asked if something happened in their family.

唐和妻子来到学校，老师告诉他们萨丽与另一个孩子打架的事，并询问是不是他们家里出了什么变故。

Teacher:	I was expecting the Piersons as well, but they're not coming. Please. My goodness. Of course. Here, take mine. I **appreciate**[1] that both of you are here.	老师：	我本来是在等皮尔森一家人，可他们不来了。请坐。我的天啊。当然，请坐我的椅子。非常感谢你们两个今天都能来。
Don:	What happened?	唐：	出什么事了？
Teacher:	The children were at the water **fountain**[2] during gym. And Sally told Becky Pierson she should save some for the fish. Becky ignored her. Sally hit the back of her head. And her face went into the spigot. And then Becky went after her... Hair pulling, **scratching**[3].	老师：	体育课的时候孩子们在饮水机边喝水。萨丽让贝奇·皮尔森给鱼留点儿，贝奇没有理她。萨丽打了她的后脑勺，而她的脸撞上了水龙头。然后贝奇开始追她，扯头发，用指甲抓她。
Don:	She didn't need stitches in the end, I understand?	唐：	应该没有严重到需要缝针吧？
Betty:	This girl... this Becky Pierson, Sally told me she's a bruiser.	贝蒂：	这个女孩，这个贝奇·皮尔森，萨丽告诉我她很壮。

注释
1. **appreciate** [ə'priːʃɪeɪt] *v.* 感谢
2. **fountain** ['faʊntən] *n.* 喷水器，喷泉
3. **scratching** [sk'rætʃɪŋ] *v.* （scrath 的 ing 形式）抓伤

Teacher:	She's heavy. The children poke pencils into her sides, when she's sitting because they think she can't feel it.	老师：	她块头是有点儿大。她坐着的时候有同学用铅笔戳她，因为他们觉得她感觉不到。
Betty:	Sally doesn't do that, does she?	贝蒂：	萨丽没那么做过吧?
Teacher:	No...But... This bad behavior is new. I know that you're expecting a child, but she already has a little brother. I guess what I'm asking is, has anything changed at home recently?	老师：	没有……不过……这种出格的行为是最近才出现的。我知道你们正在期待一个新生儿的降临，她也已经有个弟弟了。我想问的是，最近您家里有什么变故吗?
Betty:	My... My father *passed away*[1]. Last week... The week before... two weeks now.	贝蒂：	我……我父亲过世了，就在上周。不，已经两周了。
Teacher:	I feel terrible for bringing that up for you.	老师：	我很抱歉提起了您的伤心事。
Betty:	Well, it... it has not been easy.	贝蒂：	的确，这种事很难释怀。
Teacher:	Is this grandpa Gene we're talking about? Oh, that poor thing.	老师：	是她的吉恩外公吗? 很遗憾。
Don:	Sally didn't mention it?	唐：	萨丽没有提起过吗?
Teacher:	Why didn't you call us or send a note? I don't think she missed a day. Did she go to the funeral?	老师：	你们为什么不给我们打个电话或送个信? 她一天都没有缺勤。她去葬礼了吗?
Betty:	Why would we put her through that?	贝蒂：	我们不想让她经历这些。
Don:	I don't think children belong in grave yards.	唐：	我觉得墓地不是孩子该去的地方。
Teacher:	No, of course not. Now I realize why she was asking all those questions about Medgar Evers[1.] murder.	老师：	没错，你说得对。现在我知道她为什么会问关于麦格·艾佛斯的谋杀案的问题了。
Don:	She was?	唐：	她问过吗?
Betty:	I'm... I'm sorry. I have to use the ladies' room again.	贝蒂：	抱歉，我得再去趟洗手间。
Teacher:	We can talk about this another time.	老师：	我们可以下次再谈这些。
Betty:	No, I'm not as upset as I look. I... I can't help this.	贝蒂：	不用，我没有那么悲伤。我只是忍不住了。
Teacher:	I am **mortified**[4].	老师：	我说错话了。
Don:	It's not a good time.	唐：	确实不应该这时候说这些。
Teacher:	No, and... It really should be... shouldn't it? Sally does need more attention. She's grieving. There is a very special pain to losing someone at that age. I don't know if you can understand that.	老师：	没错，本来不应该这样的，对吗? 你们应该多关心关心萨丽，她很悲伤。在那么小的年龄失去祖父，对于一个孩子的打击是很大的。我不知道你是否可以理解。
Don:	I can.	唐：	我理解。

Teacher: Mrs. Draper, I was just talking to your husband, and this really can wait.

Betty: Are you sure? Because I just want to put it behind us. I just really want everything to be okay when the baby comes.

Teacher: It's going to be a beautiful summer.

老师：德雷柏夫人，我刚才和你丈夫谈了，这件事真的可以以后再谈的。

贝蒂：你确定吗？因为我只是想让这件事赶快过去。我希望孩子出生时一切顺利。

老师：这个夏天会非常美好。

Scene 2:   Pete complained to Paul that the guest areas he got was the black while Ken's were successful accounts.

皮特向保罗抱怨艾德蒙电视商分给他的客户都是黑人区的，而肯则是成功客户。

Paul: People forget that Karl Marx[2] was the greatest economist who ever lived. And whatever you think of his solution, the problem he posed was about the **catastrophic**[5] up and down of the marketplace.

保罗：人们已经淡忘了卡尔·马克思是史上最伟大的经济学家，暂且不论他提出的解决方案，但他提出的问题都是关于灾难性的商海浮沉的。

Pete: Tell the folks at Admiral that Karl Marx says everything's okay.

皮特：告诉艾德蒙的人，卡尔·马克思说不必惊慌。

Paul: Boom and bust. Bull and bear. I need a TV. I have a TV.

保罗：繁荣和衰败，牛市或熊市。如果需要电视，该买还是要买的。

Pete: Damn it, Paul, someone helped Ken cherry-pick all of Burt's successful **accounts**[6] and I've been left with the dogs.

皮特：该死，保罗。肯背后有人相助，分到的都是成功客户，而我的客户却很差。

Paul: Admiral is not a dog.

保罗：艾德蒙不差。

Pete: Sales are flat. It's all over their memos. And now I have to look them in the eye with nothing...except maybe new creative.

皮特：他们销售平平，他们的会议备案里写的全是这个，而我现在面对他们却依然脑袋空空，除非有新的创意。

Paul: Stop it.

保罗：别再发牢骚了。

Pete: Now you're interested. There are some areas of growth, and I mean **literally**[7]

皮特：现在你感兴趣。某些地区的销售额是有所增长的，我就事论事。亚

注
释   **4. mortify** ['mɔːtəfi] v. 使受辱，使伤害

5. catastrophic [ˌkætə'strɔfik] adj. 灾难的，惨重的

6. accounts [ə'kaʊnts] n. 账，账目

7. literally ['lɪtərəli] adv. 照字面理解，就事论事

areas... Atlanta, Oakland, Chicago, Detroit, Newark, D. C.

Paul: Great jazz cities.

Pete: And I left out st. Louis and Kansas city... also growing. What does that mean?

Paul: Great jazz musicians?

Pete: Seriously, is it possible that these admirals are being bought by negroes?

Colleague: Lois caught her scarf putting paper in the xerox.

Paul: Maybe when Joan leaves I can finally *get rid of*[2] her.

Pete: Can you pretend like you're back in the media department and tell me what this says to you? Look at the cities. Is it possible that negroes are outbuying other people 2:1?

Colleague: You could jump to that **conclusion**[8], I suppose.

特兰大、奥克兰、芝加哥、底特律、纽瓦克、华盛顿特区。

保罗： 都是些不错的爵士之城。

皮特： 还有圣路易斯和堪萨斯，也在增长。这是什么意思？

保罗： 伟大的爵士音乐家吗？

皮特： 说真的，有没有可能成为艾德蒙电视机的主要消费群体呢？

同事： 露易丝往复印机里放纸时，把围巾卡进去了。

保罗： 估计琼走后我就能彻底摆脱她了。

皮特： 能否劳驾你借用你的专业背景，帮忙分析一下这些图表说明了什么问题？看看这些城市，有可能的购买力是其他人的两倍吗？

同事： 单从图表，的确可以得出这样的结论。

Scene 3: Roger called Don to ask about his new-born baby's name. Don said it had no name yet. Roger told Don his importance in the company.

罗杰与唐通电话问起唐刚出生的小儿子的名字，唐说还没起。罗杰表示唐不在时很多工作处于停滞状态。

Secretary: Did you get any sleep?

Don: No, and I don't expect to for the next six months.

Secretary: I wasn't sure where to put it all. Mr. Draper's office. Please hold. It's Mr. Sterling. *Are you in*[3]?

Don: Roger.

Roger: Dada.

秘书： 你昨晚睡觉了吗？

唐： 没有，估计以后六个月都睡不好了。

秘书： 我不知道把这些放在哪里好。德雷柏先生办公室。等等。是斯特林先生，要接吗？

唐： 罗杰。

罗杰： 爸爸。

Don:	Where are you?		唐:	你在哪里？
Roger:	Down the hall. How's Betty? Did she perform like a **champ**⁹?		罗杰:	会议室。贝蒂怎么样？她表现得非常好吧？
Don:	She did.		唐:	她确实很棒。
Roger:	I need his **initials**¹⁰. Jane's gonna put them on the back of her **yacht**¹¹ or something for him.		罗杰:	我需要他名字的首字母。简想刻在她的游艇后面，还有给你们的贺礼上。
Don:	No name yet.		唐:	还没起名字。
Roger:	There's a lot of guys **twiddling**¹² their thumbs down in art.		罗杰:	美工部很多人闲得发慌。
Don:	Why were you in the art department?		唐:	你怎么会知道美工部的情况？
Roger:	Lane was. **Apparently**¹³ we're all backed up. No one will move forward without your **approval**¹⁴.		罗杰:	是莱恩。显然我们现在陷入停滞状态了，没有你的参与，我们无法正常运作。
Don:	I missed half a day.		唐:	我只请了半天假。
Roger:	Betty had the baby, not you.		罗杰:	是贝蒂生孩子，不是你。
Don:	I'll see what I can do.		唐:	我看看能做些什么。
Roger:	Good. That guy's a tick. See you at the traffic meeting.		罗杰:	很好。那家伙是个讨厌鬼。会上再见。

📚 文化背景

1. Medgar Evers 麦格·艾佛斯

密西西比州的黑人民权领袖麦格·艾佛斯，1963 年 6 月 12 日遭到杀害。

2. Karl Marx 卡尔·马克思

世界上无产阶级的伟大导师、科学社会主义的创始人。伟大的政治家、哲学家、经济学家、革命理论家、社会学家、革命家。主要著作有《资本论》《共产党宣言》。他是无产阶级的精神领袖，是当代共产主义运动的先驱。马克思最广为人知的哲学理论是他对于人类历史进程中阶级斗争的分析。他认为几千年以来，人类发展史上最大的矛盾与问题就在于不同阶级之间的利益掠夺。依据历史唯物论，资本主义终将被共产主义所取代。

注释

8. **conclusion** [kən'kluːʒn] *n.* 结论
9. **champ** [tʃæmp] *n.* 冠军
10. **initials** [ɪ'nɪʃəls] *n.* （姓名或组织名称等的）首字母
（initial 的名词复数）
11. **yacht** [jɒt] *n.* 快艇，游艇
12. **twiddling** ['twɪdlɪŋ] *v.* （心不在焉地）捻弄
（twiddle 的现在分词）
13. **apparently** [ə'pærəntlɪ] *adv.* 显然地；表面上
14. **approval** [ə'pruːvl] *n.* 同意，批准

常用表达

1. **pass away** 去世，过世

   例：He unfortunately passed away at an early age last year.

   他去年不幸英年早逝。

2. **get rid of** 摆脱，除掉

   例：He latched onto us and we couldn't get rid of him.

   他缠着我们，甩也甩不掉。

3. **Are you in?** 你要不要参加？你要不要接（电话）？

   例：The call is from your guest. Are you in?

   这个电话是你的客户打来的，要接吗？

Chapter 7

青春偶像剧
Tendy Drama / Idol Drama

　　偶像剧，又称青春偶像剧。是指集数不多（一般 30 集以内）、大量采用面貌俊美的演员、符合社会流行的造型服饰、适合年轻人的偶像艺人、以细腻爱情戏为主、以现代的时装电视剧为主要场景、以青少年为主要收视对象的剧种。一般来说，偶像剧起源于日本的诸如《东京爱情故事》《101 次求婚》等偶像明星主演的 12 集日剧。不过也有人认为，偶像剧应该是来自美国的电视系列剧《飞越比佛利》。还有人认为，偶像剧其实早就在菲律宾、印度有类似的剧种。

　　偶像剧与稍早流行于电视的"肥皂剧"或"时装剧"的最大不同是，该剧种最先强调的并非剧本的张力，也不是演员的演技表现，而是演员的外貌，主角多为年轻演员。随着近年来偶像剧的数量越来越多，观众口味不断提高，收视压力也越来越大，偶像剧不再像以前那样只局限于一段纯粹的爱情，两个尽善尽美的偶像，一座梦幻的校园，而是开始在情节、人物、制作、包装等各个方面不断升级。像中国观众熟悉的《绯闻女孩》《吉尔莫女孩》《秘社》等都属于这个范畴。

19

The Secret Circle

《秘社》

入选理由：

　　《秘社》是美国哥伦比亚及华纳兄弟联合电视网于 2011 年 9 月开播的一部新剧。该剧改编自美国女作家丽莎·简·史密斯的同名小说，是一部带有魔幻色彩的青春偶像剧。故事的背景设定在华盛顿附近一个虚构的小镇——命运港，讲述了 16 岁的少女凯西·布兰克发现自己是一个百分之百纯正血统的女巫后加入秘社的故事。《秘社》开播伊始即受到青少年观众的欢迎，收视率在 2011 年秋季开播的新剧中排名第一，获得了多项大奖的提名。遗憾的是，尽管《秘社》的平均收视率在联合电视网的全部在播剧集中排名第三，却未能获得第二季的续订。联合电视网的这一决定让《秘社》的忠实观众极为失望，他们建立了一个名为"拯救《秘社》"的网站，希望能改变《秘社》的命运。虽然 2012 年秋季，《秘社》未能回归荧屏，但诸多民意调查结果依然显示《秘社》是观众们最为怀念的剧集。

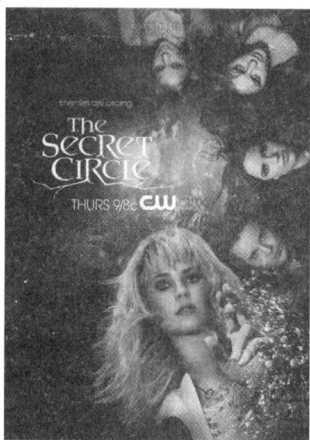

Section 1　剧情特点：

　　凯西·布兰克是一个快乐、普通的少女，直到她母亲艾米利亚突然死于一场火灾。成为孤儿的凯西心情低落，无处容身，只好搬回母亲的家乡——华盛顿郊区一个叫命运港的小镇，与慈祥和蔼的外祖母简共同生活。凯西的母亲多年前离开这里后再也没有回来过，但奇怪的是，镇上的人对凯西了解颇多，甚至比她自己还要了解她。 亚当很快帮助凯西解开了体内禁锢的魔法能力，凯西不得不承认他们所说的一切都是真的。凯西在母亲童年时住过的房间里发现了一本古老的咒语书，还发现母亲竟然给自己留下了一条消息。母亲的"解释"让凯西明白了自己的命运——真实而又危险的命运。凯西和她的朋友们并不知道，她们并非世上唯一的魔法生物，一股黑暗力量正蠢蠢欲动。这股力量可能和镇上的成年人有关，包括戴安娜的父亲查尔斯和菲伊的母亲张伯伦。更重要的是，凯西母亲的死亡可能并不是一起意外，而是一场延续了数个世纪的正邪大战战火重燃的开篇。

Section 2　对白特点：

　　本剧是根据《吸血鬼日记》原著小说作者丽莎·简·史密斯另一套三卷本同名小说改编。作为一部具有奇幻色彩的青春剧，本剧剧情像逻辑思维游戏般充满悬疑，加上主人公大都是十六七岁的学生，因此对白生动有趣、扣人心弦。此外主要演员的语速、语调和发音都是地道的美式英语，相对简单易学，非常适合英语学习者模仿练习。

Section 3　角色分析：

凯西·布兰克 (Cassie Blake)：从小就没有父亲，母亲也在她刚满16岁时意外身亡。凯西不得不从繁华的加州首府搬到宁静的小镇命运港与外祖母共同生活。她身边总是发生一些难以理解的怪事，但这些事情在她发现母亲的魔法书后逐渐变得清晰起来。在原著中，凯西是个很害羞的女孩，但在电视剧集中，凯西是个"很酷但是很怪"的女孩。

亚当·科南特 (Adam Conant)：17岁，巫师社团成员。亚当见到凯西后不久便把新塞勒姆的秘密（巫师社团）告诉了她。两人经常交谈，而且总是"挑战"对方。在原著中，亚当和戴安娜青梅竹马，一起长大。但是亚当第一眼见到凯西便对她产生了好感。亚当很强壮，深褐色的头发，蓝眼睛。

戴安娜·米德 (Diana Meade)：18岁，聪明、性感、美貌出众。戴安娜对初来乍到的凯西十分友好，并成为她在命运港结识的第一个朋友。凯西很喜欢戴安娜，认为她关心自己纯粹是出于好心。戴安娜现在的男友是亚当，这让凯西感觉不安。戴安娜和另一名女同学菲伊是死对头，两人经常为凯西发生争吵。在原著中，戴安娜是巫师社团的领袖，但菲伊一直觊觎这个位置。戴安娜与凯西亲如姐妹，一方面是因为她确实喜欢凯西，另一方面是因为她在凯西身上看到了魔法潜力。其实在秘社第20集已经证实戴安娜和凯西是同父异母的姐妹。戴安娜个子很高，留着又长又亮的金棕色头发，绿眼睛。

菲伊·钱柏林 (Faye Chamberlain)：17岁，性感、时尚，是校长的女儿。菲伊对新来的凯西十分好奇，但是对杰克与凯西之间的关系持反对意见。菲伊和戴安娜关系一直不好。菲伊经常干一些出格的事情。在原著中，菲伊是戴安娜的表妹，拥有强大的魔力。菲伊在凯西刚来学校的第一天就找她的麻烦，直到戴安娜出手干预，凯西才得以脱身。菲伊体态健美，身材窈窕，皮肤很白。

梅丽莎·格拉塞 (Melissa Glaser)：17岁。梅丽莎是菲伊的好友，巫师社团成员。她性格偏冷，原著中没有这个角色。

尼克·阿姆斯特朗 (Nick Armstrong)：17岁，坏男孩，巫师社团成员，在校园里向低年级学生兜售违禁药物。尼克和凯西是邻居，两人的关系可以用"既爱又恨"来形容（两人的卧室正好隔窗相对）。在原著中，巫师社团里的女孩子都称尼克叫"蜥蜴"。他外表冷漠，性格叛逆，对什么事情都不关心。尼克长相帅气，头发和眼睛都是棕色的。他特别喜欢摆弄自己的车。

杰克·阿姆斯特朗 (Jake Armstrong)：尼克的哥哥，尼克死后杰克代替他加入秘社，因为父母的死，跟猎巫师混在一起，想要杀死命运港所有的巫师，对凯西有好感。

Passage 1

剧情介绍：

（选自第1季第1集）凯西在回家的路上突然发生了爆胎，她下车求救未果，只能通知家里的妈妈，告诉她她会自己换好轮胎回去。然而与此同时，一辆黑色汽车，停在凯西家厨房的后面，一个神秘男子，通过一股神秘的力量用水和火柴将凯西的母亲烧死。孤身一人的凯西，来到母亲的家乡——华盛顿州一个名叫命运港的小镇，和外祖母生活在一起。在这里，凯西遇到了一系列她自己无法解释的奇异事件，她向自己的新同学——友善的戴安娜述说了自己的困惑。戴安娜把凯西带到郊外树林中一个无人居住的旧房子里，在这里凯西惊诧地见到了自己的其他几个同学：亚当、菲伊、尼克和梅丽莎。他们告诉凯西：她和他们一样都是百分百纯正血统的巫师，她在小镇的种种怪异的遭遇都是黑魔法在作祟，所以他们希望和凯西联手组成秘社。

Scene 1: Diana guided Cassie through the woods into a deserted house.

戴安娜带着凯西穿过树林到了一个废弃的房子。

Cassie:	What is this place?	凯西：	这是哪里啊？
Diana:	Come on.	戴安娜：	跟我来。
Faye:	Finally.	菲伊：	总算来了。
Nike:	Hey, neighbor. I'm Nick, also known as the guy in the window.	尼克：	你好，邻居。我叫尼克，就是你家对面窗户里的那个家伙。
Adam:	Hi!	亚当：	你好！
Cassie:	OK. What are all of you doing here? What's going on?	凯西：	你们都在这干吗呢？这是怎么了？
Adam:	We want to explain.	亚当：	听我们解释。
Diana:	I didn't want to tell you like this, but I didn't have a choice...	戴安娜：	我不想以这种方式告诉你，但我别无选择……
Faye:	She has a right to know.	菲伊：	她有权知道。
Cassie:	Know what?	凯西：	知道什么？
Diana:	Who you are.	戴安娜：	你的身世。
Cassie:	OK. This is getting really **weird**[1]. I...	凯西：	够了，越说越离谱了……
Adam:	Hey, you don't have to be scared.	亚当：	嘿，别害怕。
Cassie:	Somebody tell me what's going on.	凯西：	那就告诉我到底怎么了。
Diana:	Look, Cassie, I know this is going to sound	戴安娜：	凯西，我知道这听起来不可思议。

	crazy. Ok, but... that fire yesterday...I don't know how to say this. Um...We're different. You're different.		不过……昨天的那场大火……不知道如何说起……呃，我们不是普通人。你也不是普通人。
Faye:	Oh, for God's sake, **spit it out**[2]! You're a witch. You're a full-blooded, 100% witch. We all are. There. Done.	菲伊：	哦，天哪，痛快点儿说吧！你是个女巫，一个有着百分百纯正血统的女巫。我们全都是。好了，说完了。
Cassie:	This is beyond crazy.	凯西：	这太不可思议了！
Faye:	The truth works that way.	菲伊：	事实就是这么不可思议。
Adam:	Cassie, I know how this sounds. The truth is, our **ancestry**[3] is part of a **legacy**[4] that *dates* as far *back* as 1692.	亚当：	凯西，我知道这听起来不可思议。事实上，我们的世系可以追溯到 1692 年，是先辈遗留下来的。
Cassie:	You guys are saying I'm a witch.	凯西：	你们说我是个女巫！
Melissa:	Like your mother and her mother.	梅丽莎：	你母亲，还有你外婆也都是。
Diana:	It's all in here, Cassie. Each family has a book like this one, a journal that lays down each family line. I found mine…	戴安娜：	全都记录在这里了，凯西。每个家族都有一本这样的书，记录了每个家族的族谱。我找到了我家的……
Faye:	Which explains her air of **superiority**[5].	菲伊：	这也是为何她总是一副高人一等的姿势。
Melissa:	The book contains thousands of spells. We've been practicing, but without a full circle, we can only do really lame ones.	梅丽莎：	书中有成千上万条咒语。我们一直都在练习，但如果没有一个完整的秘社，我们只能玩些小儿科的把戏。
Faye:	Like open locked doors.	菲伊：	比如打开上锁的门。
Nick:	Or curtains.	尼克：	或者窗帘。
Cassie:	Or set cars on fire.	凯西：	或者让车着火。
Faye:	I'm sorry about that. I got a little **out of hand**[6].	菲伊：	我很抱歉，我有点失控了。
Adam:	Complete circle is 6... one from each of the 6 families	亚当：	一个完整的秘社是六个人……分别来自六个家族。
Diana:	You're the sixth. You complete the circle.	戴安娜：	你是第六个，秘社因你而完整。
Melissa:	Now we're whole.	梅丽莎：	现在我们齐了。
Faye:	We have more power now.	菲伊：	力量也更强大了。
Diana:	But there's a ritual that will bind us so we can control our power.	戴安娜：	我们需要进行一个联合的仪式，这样我们就可以控制自己的力量了。

注释

1. **weird** [wɪəd] *adj.* 离奇的；古怪的；怪异的
2. **spit out** 吐出，说出
3. **ancestry** ['ænsəstrɪ] *n.* 祖先
4. **legacy** ['ænsəstrɪ] *n.* 遗赠物
5. **air of superiority** 有优越感的样子
6. **out of hand** 相当于 **out of control** 失控

Cassie: You are seriously **messed up**[7]. Get out of my way.	**凯西：** 你们真是一群疯子。给我让开!
Faye: Don't pretend you don't believe us. Deep down, you know it's true.	**菲伊：** 别装作你根本不信我们，你的内心深处知道都是真的。
Cassie: What's true is how crazy you are.	**凯西：** 你们全疯了才是真的。
Adam: Hey, take it easy.	**亚当：** 别激动，放松点儿。
Faye: She can't just **waltz**[8] out of here. She'll run to her grandmother.	**菲伊：** 她不能就这么一走了之，她会去找她外婆的。
Diana: No one can know about us, not even our families. We have to stay secret.	**戴安娜：** 不能让任何人知道我们的秘密，即使是家人。我们必须保密。
Cassie: Fine.	**凯西：** 好吧。
Melissa: Great. I knew it.	**梅丽莎：** 好极了，我就知道会这样。
Faye: Nicely done, Diana.	**菲伊：** 干得不错，戴安娜。

Scene 2: Cassie ran out of the house into the woods, followed by Adam.
凯西从房子里跑了出来，亚当也跟了过去。

Adam: Cassie, Cassie, wait. It's not as crazy as it seems.	**亚当：** 凯西，凯西，等一下。这其实没有你想象得那么荒唐。
Cassie: Yes, it is. This is **insane**[9]. All of you are insane.	**凯西：** 不，这太荒唐了。你们都疯了。
Adam: Our parents had a circle just like ours.	**亚当：** 我们的父母也有过和我们一样的秘社。
Cassie: Oh, my God! Can you hear yourself? My mother was not a witch. I would have known.	**凯西：** 天哪! 你知道自己在说什么吗? 我妈妈不是女巫，不然她一定会告诉我的。
Adam: No, 'cause it was all covered up. 'cause something went wrong. People were hurt. They were killed. So they **abolished**[10] witchcraft.	**亚当：** 不会，因为所有的一切都被掩盖起来了。因为曾经出过事，有人受过伤，他们都被杀了。因此巫术才会被禁止。
Cassie: I don't believe you.	**凯西：** 我不信你的话。
Adam: You're not the only one who's lost a parent, Cassie. We all have.	**亚当：** 并不是只有你一个人失去了父母，凯西。我们都是一样。

Cassie: There's no such thing as witches and magic. I don't believe it. I can't.

Adam: Let me show you.

(Adam picked up a leaf with dewdrops and handed it to Cassie.)

Adam: Here. It's OK. Trust me. Close your eyes. Ok. Now, concentrate on how your hand is connecting with the leaf, then how the leaf is connecting with the water, and say "A drop of water, as light as air" and keep repeating it.

Cassie: A drop of water, as light as air. A drop of water, as light as air. A drop of water, as light as air. I don't feel anything.

Adam: Feel that? That **tingling**[11] when my hand is touching yours? That's your energy connecting with mine. Now, try again.

C&A: A drop of water, as light as air. A drop of water, as light as air. A drop of water, as light as air.

Cassie: Are you doing this?

Adam: We are. This has never happened before.

Diana: You did magic with her?

Adam: I thought if she knew what she was capable of, she wouldn't be as afraid of it

Melissa: You made water **float**[12]?

Faye: How romantic.

Nick: And then, you let her just run away.

Adam: I lost control.

Faye: Sounds like it.

Adam: No, I lost control of the magic. With Cassie here, our power is **magnified**[13] a hundred times over.

Diana: Which is why we need to perform the ritual.

凯西：这个世上不存在什么女巫或者法术。我不相信。我无法相信。

亚当：那我给你看。

（亚当从地上捡起一片带着露珠的树叶，递给凯西。）

亚当：给你。不会有事的，相信我。闭上眼睛。好的，现在集中精力，想着你的手与这片叶子相连在一起，而叶子又与水珠相连，说"小小一滴水，轻轻如空气"，然后不停地重复。

凯西：小小一滴水，轻轻如空气。小小一滴水，轻轻如空气。小小一滴水，轻轻如空气。我什么也感觉不到啊!

亚当：感觉到了吗？我的手碰到你的手时那种刺痛的感觉？这是我们的能量连接起来了。现在，再试试。

凯和亚：小小一滴水，轻轻如空气。小小一滴水，轻轻如空气。小小一滴水，轻轻如空气。

凯西：这是你做的吧?

亚当：是我们。以前从来没这样过。

戴安娜：你跟她一起施了魔法?

亚当：我想如果她知道她的能力，她就不会怕了。

梅丽莎：你们让水滴浮起来了？

菲伊：好浪漫啊……

尼克：然后你就让她一个人跑了?

亚当：我失去控制了。

菲伊：听起来的确是这样的。

亚当：不，我对魔法失去控制了，有了凯西，我们的能力能放大百倍。

戴安娜：这就是我们要举行仪式的原因。

注释
7. be messed up 神经错乱，心智不清
8. waltz [wɔːlts] v. 跳华尔兹舞；轻快地或跳着舞走
9. insane [ɪnˈseɪn] adj. 疯狂的；精神错乱的
10. abolish [əˈbɒlɪʃ] v. 废止，废除
11. tingle [ˈtɪŋgəl] n. 刺痛；激动
12. float [fləʊt] v. 飘动，漂浮
13. magnify [ˈmæɡnɪfaɪ] v. 放大

Melissa:	Yeah, and the sooner, the better, before she **blabs**[14] to her grandmother and anyone else that would listen.	梅丽莎：	是啊，越快越好否则她告诉她外祖母了怎么办，然后其他人也有可能听到。
Adam:	She's not going to tell anybody.	亚当：	她不会告诉其他人的。
Faye:	Oh, and he would know. They made magic together.	菲伊：	哦，他知道的，他们可一起施法了呢。
Nick:	All right, I'll **swing by**[15] her grandmother's.	尼克：	好的，我会顺路去她家。
Faye:	You guys have fun.	菲伊：	你们玩得开心点。
Diana:	I certainly will. Where are you going?	戴安娜：	我肯定会很开心的。你要去哪儿?
Faye:	We have to find Cassie. I'm not interested in your little ritual. We have real power now. The last thing I want to do is control it. And I'm not going to.	菲伊：	我们得找到凯西，我对你的小仪式可不感兴趣，我们现在有了真正的魔法，我才不想去控制它呢。我也不准备这样做。
Diana:	This is exactly what I was afraid of. You know what she's like.	戴安娜：	这就是我最怕的事情。你知道，她就是这样。
Adam:	Let's just find Cassie.	亚当：	我们还是找凯西吧。

文化背景

1. witch 女巫

无论是在欧洲的古老传说中还是欧美近代的艺术童话里，女巫都是一个经常出现的形象。在大多数传说中，这些会魔法的女人通常被描述为鹰钩鼻的老太婆，相貌奇丑无比，披着黑色的斗篷、带着尖尖的帽子、骑着扫把在夜空中飞来飞去，会念邪恶的魔法，会用蜥蜴、蝙蝠、蜘蛛、毒蛇等材料配各种古怪的药水。不幸的是，女巫不仅出现在童话和传说中，在中世纪的欧洲，人们深信女巫真实存在，从15世纪至18世纪，人们对女巫展开猎杀，无数女性被诬为"女巫"，或被斩首示众，或惨遭火刑。后人对于葬身灭巫狂潮之中的"女巫"数量一直无法给出一个准确的数字。

常用表达

1. date back 回溯至

例： This castle dates back to Roman times.

这个城堡可追溯到罗马时代。

These plant fossils date back to the age of the dinosaurs.

这些植物化石可追溯至恐龙时代。

注释 **14. blab** [blæb] *v.* 泄密；胡扯
15. swing by 拜访

Passage 2

剧情介绍：

（选自第 1 季第 2 集）凯西在母亲住过的卧室里发现了一封信和一本写满奇怪咒语的书。母亲在信中告诉凯西，她体内拥有不可估量的法力，并且有人会因为这股力量来找她。在学校化学课上，大家做金属碳酸盐反应的实验，菲伊再次操纵法力，让溶液加热，凯西的烧杯爆裂。凯西控制不住自己体内的能量，心里很生气无意把菲伊的烧杯也爆裂。凯西告诉亚当她为此感到抱歉，亚当告诉她他可以帮助她控制法力。 在废弃的建筑屋内，亚当告诉凯西，每个巫师家族都有一本书，而现在只有戴安娜从母亲那里找到《影之书》，过去曾发生一场严重的意外让所有人都禁止使用巫术，凯西表示不明白。亚当解释说：一个人无法控制力量，曾经的事故可能是因为他们联结秘社造成的，联结秘社不仅会强大他们的力量，也会更好控制他们每个人的力量。

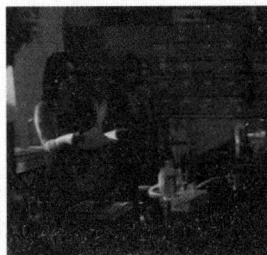

Scene 1: In a chemistry class, the teacher asks students to do an experiment, and Faye uses her magic power on Cassie.

化学课上老师让做实验，菲伊运用魔法念起了咒语，凯西面前的玻璃瓶爆炸了。

Teacher: So I have two big rules in my classroom. Rule number one—do not breathe in the vapors of these **chemicals**[1]. Rule number two—always wear **goggles**[2]. Ok, let's get it started. Got a big day today. First and foremost, safety goggles on, please. Afterwards, I want you to pour 300 milliliters of solution "A" and two drops of solution "B" into your beakers, please. Now, take in mind that many of these carbonates are very **toxic**[3], which, for those you who don't know, that means dangerous. Now, remember that the point of this experiment is to compare the reactivity of these different metal carbonates...

老师： 在我的课上有两点要求你们要注意：第一点，不要把这些化学物品的蒸气给吸进去；第二点，不要摘护目镜。好吧，我们开始吧，今天事情很多。首先，请把护目镜戴上，然后，把 300 毫升的 A 溶液倒入烧杯，再往烧杯中加两滴 B 溶液。记好，这些硝酸盐中有很多都是有毒的。你们中可能有人不知道，这些东西是很危险的。现在，记住实验的目的是比较这些金属硝酸盐的反应能力。

注释
1. chemicals ['kemɪkəl] *n.* 化学药品；化学制品
2. goggle ['gɒgl] *n.* 眼睛睁视；护目镜
3. toxic ['tɒksɪk] *adj.* 有毒的

Faye:	Fire without **flame**[4] bring me heat.	菲伊：	炙热如火。
Melissa:	What are you doing?	梅丽莎：	你干什么呢？
Faye:	Experimenting. Try it. Fire without flame...	菲伊：	做实验呢。试试看，炙热……
Melissa:	Bring me heat.	梅丽莎：	如火。
Faye:	Fire without flame...	菲伊：	炙热……
Melissa:	Bring me heat.	梅丽莎：	如火。
Teacher:	Is anybody hurt? Is anybody hurt?	老师：	有人受伤吗？有人受伤吗？
Adam:	Cassie. Cassie, wait a minute.	亚当：	凯西，凯西，等等!
Cassie:	I did that. I got mad and that's what happened. I didn't *mean to*[1]. Why is this happening? How do I stop it?	凯西：	那是我干的，我一生气然后杯子就碎了，我不是有意的，怎么会这样？我该怎么做才能控制？
Adam:	That's the thing, you can't. But if you let me, I can help.	亚当：	就是这样，你控制不了的，但如果你愿意的话，我可以帮你。

Scene 2: Cassie is led to the deserted house by Adam.

亚当又将凯西带到那座废弃的房子里。

Cassie:	Why do you guys come here?	凯西：	你们为什么选这个地方？
Adam:	Because no one else does.	亚当：	因为没有别的人会来。
Cassie:	Condemned **buildings**[5] are like that.	凯西：	这就像凶宅一样。
Adam:	Well, it's important that no one find out about us. Especially our families.	亚当：	不能让别人发现我们的秘密，尤其是我们的家人。
Cassie:	How did you discover...	凯西：	你怎么发现……
Adam:	We're <u>witches</u>[1]? Diana found her mom's book of shadows. That's how we know about all of us.	亚当：	我们是巫师的？戴安娜发现了她妈妈的《影之书》，我们就是从那本书中知道的。
Cassie:	She's the only one with a book?	凯西：	只有她一个人有那本书？
Adam:	**Technically**[6] each family has a book, but hers is the only one we have access to.	亚当：	其实每个家庭都应该有一本书，但是目前我们当中只有她有。
Cassie:	Why?	凯西：	为什么？

Adam: Because witchcraft is forbidden. It was abolished.	亚当： 因为巫术是被禁止的，巫术被废除了。
Cassie: Because of what happened years ago.	凯西： 因为多年前发生的意外。
Adam: It's when my mom died. And Diana's mom. Faye's dad. Melissa's mom. Nick lost both of his parents.	亚当： 我妈妈就是在那时候死的，还有戴安娜的妈妈，菲伊的爸爸，梅丽莎的妈妈，尼克的父母都死了。
Cassie: And my dad. I don't know much about him. Just that there was some big accident.	凯西： 还有我爸爸，我不太了解他，只知道发生了个大意外。
Adam: Well, the **official**[7] story was some teens were partying on an old boat and there was a fire. Some didn't get out.	亚当： 官方给出的解释是：一群年轻人在旧船上开派对，结果引起了火灾，有些人没来得及逃走。
Cassie: A fire.	凯西： 一场火灾。
Adam: Diana thinks it's because they didn't bind the circle.	亚当： 而戴安娜认为是因为他们没有限制自己的力量。
Cassie: I don't understand.	凯西： 我不明白。
Adam: Every witch is born into a circle. Ours is made up of our 6 families. The circle has more power than any one person can handle. Binding it is the only way we can **utilize**[8] the power, but keep it controlled.	亚当： 每个巫师都是生来要加入某个秘社的，我们的秘社由六个家庭组成，秘社的力量超过了每一个人的能力，限制它是我们唯一可以利用这种力量同时又得以控制的办法。
Cassie: Faye says that it will link us together.	凯西： 菲伊说这会成为我们的羁绊。
Adam: Yes. It will limit our individual abilities, but *strengthen*[2] us as a group. That way no one can have too much power.	亚当： 没错，这会限制我们个人的巫力，但是能增加整个秘社的力量。这样一来，就不会有人过于强大。
Cassie: It's like living in a *Harry Potter*[1] movie.	凯西： 感觉就像活在《哈利·波特》电影里一样。
Adam: He has a wand. It is not all bad. Just let me show you.	亚当： 人家有魔杖。也不全是坏事，我做给你看。

注
释
4. flame [fleɪm] *n.* 火焰
5. condemned building ［法］被宣布为危险的建筑
6. technically ['teknɪkəlɪ] *adv.* 严格说来；准确来说
7. official [ə'fɪʃəlɪ] *adj.* 正式的；官方的
8. utilize ['juːtɪlaɪz] *vt.* 利用；使用

📖 文化背景

1. *Harry Potter* 《哈利·波特》

英国著名魔法题材小说，是英国女作家 J. K. 罗琳创作的系列奇幻小说集，全书共 7 本，描写主角哈利·波特在霍格沃茨 7 年学习生活中的冒险故事；该系列被翻译成 67 种语言，所有版本的总销售量逾 5 亿本（2013 年 10 月），名列世界上最畅销小说之首。美国华纳兄弟电影公司把这 7 本小说改拍成 8 部同名电影，哈利·波特电影系列是史上最卖座的电影系列，总票房收入达 76 亿美元。

☎ 常用表达

1. mean to 打算；意指；故意

例：I didn't mean to take a taxi but I had to, as I was late.

我虽然不想坐计程车，但因为太迟了所以非坐不可。

I didn't mean to offend you.

我不是故意冒犯你。

I'm sorry I hurt you; I didn't mean to.

对不起，我弄伤了你；我不是故意的。

2. strengthen 加强；变坚固

例：He has been brought in to strengthen the defence.

已请他来加强后卫力量。

Every effort was made to strengthen unity.

大家尽力加强团结。

We want to strengthen our tie with them.

我们想加强与他们的关系。

Passage 3 🔊 📹

剧情介绍:

（选自第 1 季第 12 集）杰克突然回来，他告诉凯西和亚当，猎巫人会回来通过仪式杀死凯西，如果凯西想知道真相，可以让他看看他的记忆，因为 16 年前的大火，他就在现场。亚当约戴安娜商量到底要不要回到 16 年前的场景，戴安娜认为回去就能找到真相。杰克和凯西念咒语回到 16 年前的船上，在船上，凯西看到了父亲，以及父亲被猎巫人放火烧死的情形。但到最后的时候，父亲的一条项链救了他，大火将猎巫人反噬，凯西的父亲离开。

Scene: Jake tells Cassie he was present when the accident which killed their parents occurred.

杰克告诉凯西那场杀死他们父母的火灾发生时他在现场。

Jake: Did you get Adam's permission to come here?	**杰克:** 亚当允许你来这儿了吗?
Cassie: Did you come back to kill me?	**凯西:** 你回来是要杀我的吗?
Jake: You wouldn't be here all by yourself if you really thought that.	**杰克:** 如果你真这样想，就不会独自过来了。
Cassie: Actually, while you've been gone, I've been really **getting a hang of**[1] this dark magic thing[1]. So, yeah, I would.	**凯西:** 事实上，在你离开的这段时间，我掌握了一些黑魔法的诀窍，所以我会独自过来。
Jake: If I wanted to kill you, I would have left you in the burning school. I'm here to save your life.	**杰克:** 如果我想杀你，就不会在学校那场火灾中救你了，我是来救你的。
Cassie: By figuring out how they killed my father?	**凯西:** 通过找出他们杀我父亲的方法来救我。
Jake: Yes.	**杰克:** 是的。
Cassie: How? You can't ask anyone's parents and you can't ask the witch hunters. So who's left to tell us what happened that day?	**凯西:** 怎么做? 你不能问家长，也不能去问猎巫人，那天晚上幸存下来的还有谁呢?
Jake: Me.	**杰克:** 我。
Cassie: What does that mean?	**凯西:** 你什么意思?

注释 1. get a hang of （口语）练习，熟练掌握

Jake: I was there.

Cassie: At the fire? How? You would have been so young.

Jake: I was hiding in my parents' car. They didn't know I was there.

Cassie: Why didn't you say anything before?

Jake: I don't remember much. I must have **blocked it all out**[2].

Cassie: So... what?

Jake: I think you can help me remember. Or maybe even see what happened for yourself.

Cassie: How?

Jake: You can connect with others in ways the rest of us can't.

Cassie: You want me to go into your memory?

Jake: On the day of the fire, my parents were going out. I didn't want them to go without me, So I **snuck**[3] into the backseat and hid under a blanket. When we got to the boat yard, they parked, went onto the ferry. I waited until they couldn't see me and followed them. I snuck up onto the boat, and that's the last thing I can remember.

Adam: Diana said you were here. She didn't mention you brought along your pet **psychopath**[4].

Cassie: Adam, he was at the fire 16 years ago. Whatever he saw was bad enough that he's blocked it out completely.

Adam: So?

Jake: For years I've been *working on*[1] a memory spell that can take me back to that day so we can *find out*[2] what really happened.

Adam: So what makes you think the spell will work now?

Jake: Cassie and her dark magic.

Cassie: See, there's a disconnect between Jake's memories and the consciousness of it. So if I can link to him and experience his memory, maybe I can see what he's blocked out.

Adam: You hear how **ridiculous**[5] that sounds?

Cassie: I did it with Faye at her grandfather's cabin. I

杰克：我当时在场。

凯西：那场火灾？怎么会？你那时还是个小孩吧。

杰克：我躲在父母的车里，他们不知道。

凯西：之前为什么没听你说过。

杰克：我记不太清了，一定是这段记忆被封闭了。

凯西：那又怎样？

杰克：你可以帮助我回忆，甚至你可以亲自目睹我的记忆。

凯西：怎么做？

杰克：你可以与其他人互相感应，而这种事其他人都做不到。

凯西：你想让我进入你的记忆？

杰克：火灾那天，我父母都出去了，我想跟他们一起，所以我就钻到后座底下，藏在一条毯子下面。到船坞后，他们停好车来到渡口。等他们看不到我了，我就跟上他们溜到了船上，我就只记得这些。

亚当：戴安娜说你在这儿，但没提到你把这个神经病也带来了。

凯西：亚当，他目睹了6年前的那场大火，当时发生的事肯定非常糟糕，以至于他把那段记忆都封存了。

亚当：所以呢？

杰克：多年来我一直在练一个记忆咒语，能让我想起那天的事。这样我们就能知道到底发生了什么。

亚当：那你又凭什么认为现在这个咒语能有效？

杰克：因为凯西和她的黑魔法。

凯西：杰克无法意识到他有这段记忆，如果我能跟他相连，经历那段回忆，也许就能知道被隐藏的真相。

亚当：你知道这主意听起来有多离谱吗？

凯西：我和菲伊在她爷爷的木屋试过，我

saw Faye's memory of herself as a little girl. It was like she was standing right in front of us.

Adam: Is this spell safe?

Jake: The only risk is if the mind disconnects from what's real. By us experiencing it together, we'll be **grounded**[6] to each other.

Adam: I barely understand what that means. Cassie, please, it's too much of a risk.

Cassie: I can't. I can't just wait around for these witch hunters to come at me with some super special dark magic killing plan. I have to find out what happened that day. We all do. This is our only chance.

能看到菲伊小时候的记忆，真实得如同她就站在我们眼前。

亚当： 这咒语安全吗？

杰克： 唯一的风险是思想连接可能会从现实断开，我们俩因为一起回忆而被彼此禁锢。

亚当： 我不太明白这意味着什么。凯西，别这么做，太危险了！

凯西： 不行，我不能就这么束手就擒，等着猎巫人带着什么疯狂的封杀黑魔法计划找上门来。我必须查出真相，我们都必须这么做，否则就没机会了！

📖 文化背景

1. black magic thing 黑魔法

黑魔法主要的来源属性是黑暗的且大都是跟恶魔借的力量，所以被叫作黑魔法。因为黑暗的力量比较邪恶，所以通常都被大家拿去当诅咒。

🗣 常用表达

1. work on 对……起作用；企图影响或说服；忙于

例： This medicine will work on the affected part.

这种药能对患部起作用。

Can you work on him to change his mind?

你能说服他改变主意吗？

She is working on a new dictionary.

她一直在忙着编写一本新词典。

2. find out 发现；找出；揭发出来

例： We must find out the truth of this incident.

我们一定要把这件事情的真相找出来。

Don't just accept his say-so; find out for yourself.

别听他信口开河，你得自己去弄清楚。

注释
2. **block out** 遮住；遮挡
3. **sneak** [sni:k] snuck 为 sneak 的过去式，偷偷溜走
4. **psychopath** ['saɪkə,pæθ] n. 精神变态者，精神病患者

5. **ridiculous** [rɪ'dɪkjʊləs] adj. 可笑的，荒谬的；荒唐的
6. **ground** [graʊnd] vi. 搁浅，停飞；此处指两人因互相联系而无法单独活动

One Tree Hill
《篮球男孩》

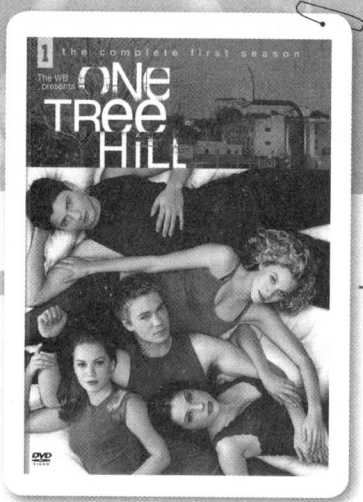

20

入选理由：

这部青春偶像剧又名《篮球兄弟》，由美国 The CW 电视台从 2003 年 9 月 23 日开播，一共出了九季，2004 年、2005 年《篮球男孩》分别获得 "最受青少年欢迎奖" 和 "最受欢迎电视新人奖"中男艺人、女艺人奖提名。扎德·麦克·默里获得 "最受欢迎电视男艺人" 奖。该剧结合青春无敌的偶像剧情节，新生代俊男美女组合，以 TreeHill 小镇所发生的故事为主轴，讲述年轻人成长的故事，引出一段段亲情、友情、爱情。它所描写的成长中的问题是时时刻刻发生在我们身边的问题。每个人的成长经历都会有所不同，有的人也许一辈子一帆风顺，而有的人经历了风风雨雨，但是我们需要学会面对人生中形形色色的问题，学会面对解决而不是怯懦逃避。

Section 1　剧情特点：

这部剧主要描述的是两位同父异母的兄弟内森与卢卡斯，内森有完整的家庭，性格傲慢、自信，家境富裕，是高中篮球队的明星球员；而卢卡斯则是一个安静孤僻的、由妈妈独自抚养的普通男孩。两人之前一直保持着距离，但自从卢卡斯也进入内森的篮球队后，从小就困扰两人的传闻，随着他们争夺队中的地位及女友而愈演愈烈，但也使他们发现了自我，并意识到两人有许多共同点，由相互敌视、排斥到包容、接受，开始注重兄弟情谊，最后成为默契极佳的队友，也成了真正的兄弟。

Section 2　对白特点：

《篮球男孩》在每集的开始和结尾，都会引用作家的名言，作为引入和总结。那富有哲理的句子，通过卢卡斯这位对写作一直抱有热情的男主角的旁白，娓娓道来。在叙事手法上，它同众多优秀的美剧一样，悬念丛生，前后呼应，情节紧凑。每一集都很精致，人物对白值得回味，服装、陈设赏心悦目，背景音乐是它一贯的亮点。

Section 3　角色分析：

卢卡斯·斯科特 (Lucas Eugene Scott)：单亲家庭背景，以及长久以来背负的私生子的传闻，让他把全部的爱都给了母亲，也让他比别人更渴望一份矢志不渝的爱情。她为了母亲放弃了篮球，也为了母亲重新追求自己的梦想。他对柏敦的爱，从高中时就深藏心底。他把这份爱情写在信纸上，和好友哈利一起把他们的梦想储藏在"时光盒"中。他和一群志同道合的好友打街边篮球，他们最终都如愿加入了学校的篮球队。

内森·斯科特 (Nathan Scott)：在父亲丹的教育下，心中只有篮球和胜利的欲望，甚至因此遗忘了自己真正的追求，把父亲的指令当作自己的梦想。直到卢卡斯的出现，他才重新审视自己的人生，开始为自己赢得胜利。特别是他和哈利的爱情，转变了他的人生。他变得积极进取，负有责任心，并慢慢摒弃了对卢卡斯的敌意。

柏敦·索耶 (Peyton Sawyer)：是一个美丽的女孩儿，这是大家都知道的。但并不是每个人都知道，这个看似一点都不活泼的冷美人，内心却对音乐和绘画情有独钟。后来，在卢卡斯的鼓励下，她试着向出版社发画稿。虽然被出版社器重，却因为不愿为迎合大众而改变自己的风格而被辞退。柏敦用漫画来表达内心的感受，她喜欢把自己沉浸在音乐中。她是个孤单的孩子，投身艺术或许就是她寻求安慰的方式。

🔊 Passage 1 📷

剧情介绍：

（选自第 1 季第 1 集）在本集中，内森的篮球教练怀蒂邀请卢卡斯加入篮球队，丹意识到卢卡斯的到来是对内森的威胁，要求内森警告卢卡斯。卢卡斯接受内森的挑战，相约午夜在河边比赛，赌约不仅包括篮球队的主控权，还包括内森的女朋友柏敦。

Scene:　At the park, Mouth is getting ready to announce the game.

在公园，莫斯正准备开始解说比赛。

Mouth: Good evening, ladies and gentlemen, and welcome to an historic night of basketball. I'm Mouth McFadden, **along with**[1] my gamey partner, Jimmy Edwards, and, Jimmy, we're **in for**[2] a treat tonight.

Jimmy: And who doesn't love a treat, Mouth? I know I do—s'mores, ice cream, cake.

(Nathan and Peyton walk out of Nathan's home and talk about the game .)

Peyton: So, if you're not doing it for your dad, then why are you doing it?

Nathan: You wouldn't **get it**[3].

Peyton: I **guess not**[4]. So what if this guy plays? Are you really that threatened?

Nathan: I'm not threatened by anyone.

Peyton: Well, then, why do it?

Nathan: To prove I'm the best.

Peyton: Okay, so, **what if**[5] he wins? What does he get?

Nathan: He gets you.

(At the park, spectators are talking indistinctly)

Mouth: Just moments before the stroke of 12:00, and still no Nathan Scott.

Jimmy: The natives are getting restless, Mouth, judging by the crowd that envelops our booth.

Junk: You don't have a booth.

Mouth: Junk Moreti joins us now. Junk, you care to make a **prediction**[6]?

Junk: I predict you guys will be the two biggest morons out here.

Mouth: And it looks like Nathan Scott has arrived, driven by car right onto the court.

(Chanting)

Crowd: Nathan! Nathan! Nathan! Nathan!

Boy : **By the way**[7], I hope you don't mind, but I told a few people.

(Chanting continues, cheers and applause as the game starts.)

Boy : Come on, let's go, baby. Let's go, Nathan!

(Spectators cheer)

莫斯: 女士们先生们，晚上好，欢迎来到篮球史上最有意义的今晚。我是莫斯·马克费顿，旁边是我的搭档吉米·爱德华。吉米，今晚这里会有一场盛宴。

吉米: 有谁不喜欢盛宴，莫斯？我只知道我喜欢棉花糖、冰激凌、蛋糕。

（内森和柏敦边从内森家往出走，边讨论一会儿的篮球赛。）

柏敦: 如果不是为了你爸爸，那你为什么要这样做？

内森: 你不会明白的。

柏敦: 我可不这么想。那如果他真的很会打球呢？你真的感到那么大的威胁吗？

内森: 我不会被任何人威胁。

柏敦: 好吧，那你为什么这么做？

内森: 为了证明我是最好的。

柏敦: 那么如果他赢了呢？他会得到什么？

内森: 他会得到你。

（公园内，观众们议论纷纷。）

莫斯: 很快就到十二点了，内森·斯科特还没有出现。

吉米: 人们开始喧闹了，莫斯，包围了我们场地的人议论纷纷。

庄克: 你们根本没有场地。

莫斯: 庄克·莫爱提来了。庄克，你介意预测一下结果吗？

庄克: 我预测你们俩会是这里最大的傻瓜。

莫斯: 好像内森·斯科特到了，驾车直接进入了场地。

（喊叫声）

人群: 内森！内森！内森！内森！

甲: 顺便说一句，我希望你不介意，但是我告诉了几个人。

（喊叫声继续着，欢呼声和掌声预示着比赛的开始。）

甲: 加油，上啊，宝贝！上啊，内森！

（观众欢呼）

Mouth: Okay, folks, *here we go*[1]—15 by ones. Make it, take it, win by one, and you can feel the intensity in the air.

(Lucas first strike, Nathan defense.)

Nathan : You ready for this?

Lucas : Why not?

Nathan : It's your life.

Lucas : Yeah. It is.

(The game begins. Lucas make a long shot.)

Mouth : Oh-ho! A 25-footer rips the silk like Jimmy Edwards in a size 3 dress.

Nathan : Go ahead, man. I'll give you that all night.

(Lucas again into a ball.)

(Cheers and applause)

Lucas: What happened to all night?

(Nathan steals)

Nathan : Is that all you got, man? If that's all you got, this is over.

(Nathan layups and makes a point.)

Peyton: Yeah! All right!

Jimmy: This looks to be a battle, mouth. Uhh! Yeah! Yeah!

(The game goes on with both boys making great shots. Nathan elbows Lucas in the face.)

Lucas : No foul. Basket counts. Besides... You won't score again.

Mouth: Oh, the basket counts, and it's 14:12, game point for Nathan. He could win it all right here. Nathan for the win.

(Lucas makes an unbelievable block.)

Mouth: Holy crap! Did you see that?! Someday men will write stories about that block. Children will be **named after**[8] it. Argentinean women will *weep for*[2] it. Luke gets a basket, and he's down by one.

莫斯： 好了，观众们，现在开始了。每场 15 分，领先一分就算赢。你能感觉到空气中的紧张气氛。

（卢卡斯先攻，内森防守。）

内森： 你准备好了吗？

卢卡斯： 为什么不？

内森： 这关系到你的一生。

卢卡斯： 是呀，确实。

（游戏开始，卢卡斯远投先进一球。）

莫斯： 哦耶！一个 25 英尺外远射，球穿过网，就像吉米·爱德华穿了大号衣服。

内森： 继续呀，我今晚就让你这么干。

（卢卡斯又进一球。）

（欢呼声和掌声）

卢卡斯： 要是我真的一晚上都如此呢？

（内森断球）

内森： 你就只有这点本领？如果你就这点本领，你就输定了。

（内森上篮得一分。）

柏敦： 好的，漂亮！

吉米： 看来很快要变成真的战斗了，莫斯。哦耶！

（游戏继续进行着，两人都投中了不少球。内森用手肘打了卢卡斯的脸。）

卢卡斯： 不计犯规，进了就算。另外，你不会再得分了。

莫斯： 哦，得分有效，现在是 14 比 12，内森获得了赛点。他马上就能获胜。内森投篮了。

（卢卡斯送出一记不可思议的大帽。）

莫斯： 天哪！你看到了吗？！有一天人们要为这记球立传。孩子们会以它命名。阿根廷的女人会为它哭泣。卢卡斯得分啦，他还落后一分。

注释	
1. **along with** 沿（顺）着；连同……一起；与……一道	5. **what if** 假使……将会怎么样
2. **be in for** 必定遭到；参加	6. **make a prediction** 做预测
3. **get it** 明白了；做到	7. **by the way** 顺便说说，顺便问一下；在途中
4. **I guess not** 我不这么想	8. **name after** 以……命名

Nathan:	You're down by one, man. Don't choke now.	内森：	还落后一分，不要喘不上气哦。
Mouth:	Another dagger, and it's all tied up! I think I'm gonna puke.	莫斯：	又一记重击，现在平分了！我想我要吐了。
Crowd:	Come on, Nate! Come on, shut him down, Nathan!	人群：	加油，内森，加油，打败他，内森。
Mouth:	This is it, folks—no going back now. The next basket wins it.	莫斯：	观众们，现在没有退路了，下一个球定胜负。
Nathan:	He's never mentioned you, man—not once in all these years.	内森：	他从来没有提到过你，这么多年来一次都没有。
Lucas:	This is for my mom.	卢卡斯：	这球是为了我妈妈。
Mouth :	Luke for the win!	莫斯：	卢卡斯投篮了!
(Lucas makes the winning shot!)		（卢卡斯投入了决定胜负的一球！）	
Mouth:	It's good! It's good! Lucas Scott takes it 15:14, and there is bedlam and delirium and felicity for all!	莫斯：	太棒了！卢卡斯·斯科特以 15 比 14 获胜，混乱、惊喜、幸运交织在一起!

常用表达

1. Here we go

鼓舞型：比如你的车子发动不起来了，摆弄许久后成功，可以说 "Here we go"。

泄气型：比如你刚刚坐过山车坐得头晕眼花，你朋友一定要你陪他再坐一次，你可以叹道 "Here we go again..."。

如果在"鼓舞型"中是你朋友帮你发动的车，他可以说 "There you go!"，直译当然是"（让我们）走吧，出发，开始（干）"，但在具体句子里要看上下文。

2. weep for 为……而哭泣

例：weep not for the past

不要为过去担忧

weep not for the memories

不要为回忆哭泣

Passage 2 📷 🔊

剧情介绍：

（选自第 2 季第 3 集）本集中，内森和海莉的婚礼顺利举行了，他们经历了波折，终于还是走到了一起。然而，事情还不算完，为了他们的事情而费尽心机的朋友们不甘心就这样放过他们，提姆提议要举办一次告别单身生活的派对，布鲁克也张罗着办一个专属于未婚女子的派对，让海莉最后疯狂一把。

Scene: At Nathan's and Haley's home, Peyton is standing at one end of the wedding wall while Haley stands at the other; Brooke is looking at it critically, directing where it should go.

在内森和海莉的家里，柏敦站在婚礼照片墙的一边，海莉站在另一边，布鲁克则指挥着如何摆放。

🔊 **Peyton:** I think it needs to **come down**[1] on the **left some**[2].

Brooke: No, it's **gotta**[3] come down on the right.

Haley: Our left is your right.

Brooke: Oh...then why are we arguing?

(Camera pans and we see Tim sitting at the counter looking through the yellow pages.)

Tim: Hey Nathan! What do you think?

(Haley and Peyton straighten the Wedding Wall and place it up against a wall.)

Tim: Thai, Mexican, Chinese is always good.

Brooke: (Nodding at the position of the Wedding Wall.) Yeah.

Haley: Tim, you just ate! How is it possible that you're still hungry?

Tim: I'm not ordering food, I'm ordering **strippers**[4].

柏敦： 我想左边要往下一点儿。

布鲁克： 不，应该是右边要往下。

海莉： 我们的左边就是你的右边。

布鲁克： 那我们干什么要争？

（镜头切换，我们看到提姆坐在吧台前翻看着电话薄。）

提姆： 嘿，内森，你觉得呢？

（海莉和柏敦摆正照片墙，紧贴墙面放置。）

提姆： 泰国的，墨西哥的，中国的向来不错。

布鲁克： （点点头确定了照片墙的位置）不错。

海莉： 你才刚吃过怎么会还饿啊？

提姆： 我不是要叫外卖，我是在找脱衣

注释 1. come down 下来，降落；流传下来；倒塌；落魄，失势 3. gotta=have got to 必须
2. left some 左边一点 4. stripper 脱衣舞女郎

(Brooke, Peyton and Haley look at him.)

Brooke: Ooo.

Tim: What?! (Haley and Peyton lower the Wall onto the floor.) You guys got married *so*[1] fast, I got screwed **outta**[5] being the best man and I am not getting screwed outta the Bachelor party[1].

(Nathan appears with only a towel wrapped around his waist.)

Haley: Tim.

Tim: (To Nathan.) I-I was gonna be the best **man**[6] right?

Nathan: (To Haley.) He's like a dog with a bone, Hales.

Haley: (Half serious.) Great, lets get him neutered.

Tim: Come on Haley! It's just a stripper! It's harmless fun.

Brooke: You know, Tim's right. See…(She yanks Nathan's towel off, he dashes off to the bedroom, embarrassed.)…fun!

(The girls laugh, Tim looks away.)

Peyton: Yes, but *so*[1] much more fun when you haven't seen it before.

Brooke: Nice! (Slaps hands with Peyton.)

Peyton: (Realising his wife's there.) Sorry.

Haley: Yeah.

Brooke: (Awkward for only a moment.) Haley, let the boys have their fun. Besides, what's good for the goose is even better for you. But you get to have a bridal shower[1] and rake in tonnes of loot from all the guests. This is *so*[1] a fair trade.

Haley: Wow, I *so*[1] don't need loot.

Brooke: (Displays Haley's hand towel.) OK, Sunny Hill Lodge?

Haley: It's Kichey.

Peyton: So's this thing.

Brooke: Oh no. No, no, that is bridal shower code red. **I'm on it.**[7]

舞娘。

（布鲁克、柏敦和海莉一起盯着他。）

布鲁克： 啊。

提姆： 干什么？（海莉和柏敦将照片墙放到地上）你们这么快就结婚，还骗我当伴郎，休想不让我办单身派对。

（内森腰间围着条毛巾出现在大家面前。）

海莉： 提姆。

提姆： （对着内森）我会是伴郎，对吧？

内森： （对着海莉）他像狗看到骨头一样满心欢喜，海莉。

海莉： （半认真）好的，那就把他阉了。

提姆： 拜托，海莉！不过是脱衣舞娘！无伤大雅又好玩。

布鲁克： 你知道吗？提姆说得对，看……（她掀掉了内森的浴巾，内森尴尬地躲回了浴室。）真有趣！

（女孩子们大笑，提姆把脸扭到一边。）

柏敦： 对，但要是以前没看过会更好玩。

布鲁克： 说得好（和柏敦击掌！）

柏敦： （意识到他的妻子就在这儿。）对不起。

海莉： 没关系。

布鲁克： （尴尬片刻。）海莉，让他们男生玩去吧。再说，让那些傻瓜去玩对你来说更好。你会有一场新娘送礼会，从所有客人身上搜刮战利品。这真是个公平的交易。

海莉： 哇！我可不需要什么战利品。

布鲁克： （展示海莉的浴巾）是吗？那阳光山庄呢？

海莉： 真俗气。

柏敦： 这也是哦。

布鲁克： 哦，不，不，那新婚送礼会是红色警戒。算我一份。

文化背景

1. bachelor party & bridal shower 单身汉舞会和新娘送礼会

西方国家有一种传统，会在婚礼前夕为新郎举行告别单身的"单身汉舞会"，当然女生也有类似告别单身的派对叫"新娘送礼会"。在结婚前夜，准新人会和他（她）的朋友们一起出去狂欢，地点大多设在舞厅，以此作为婚前最后一次狂欢。根据传统，派对的费用都是新郎的朋友们掏钱。"新娘送礼会"与会的每个姐妹会送准新娘一件礼物。

常用表达

1. so 的用法

(1) so 做副词，意为"这样""如此"，常用来代替整个句子或某一情况的全部，在口语中常与 think, hope, say, be afraid 等词语连用，表示客气、委婉的答语。

例：—I think English is more useful than Chinese. What about you?

—我认为英语比汉语更有用，你说呢?

—I don't think so.

—我不这样认为。

—Will it be fine tomorrow? 明天天气会好吗?

—I hope so. 但愿如此。

(2) so 做连词，意为"因而""所以""为了""以便"等。

例：Wang Tao's pen was broken, so he needed a new one.

王涛的钢笔坏了，所以他需要买支新的。

提醒注意：用英语表达"因为……，所以……"时，用了 because 就不能再用 so，用了 so 就不能再用 because。请注意下面汉语句子的英语译法：

例：因为他病了，所以没去上学。

误：Because he was ill, so he didn't go to school.

正：Because he was ill, he didn't go to school.

正：He was ill, so he didn't go to school.

(3) so 做副词，在句中可以修饰形容词或副词。

a. so 表示程度，意为"这么""那么""如此地"。

例：When he came back, I was so tired.

当他回来的时候，我疲劳极了。

b. so 常用于口语，意为"非常""很"。

例：A: I found it in my bag five minutes ago. 五分钟前我在我的包里找到了它。

B: I'm so glad. 我很高兴。

c. 在"so+ 助动词 /be 动词 / 情态动词 + 主语"的倒装结构中，表示前面所述的肯定情况也适合于后者。

注释 5. get screwed outta=get screwed out of 受骗的　　7. I'm on it. 算我一个；交给我吧
6. the best man 伴郎

例：I'm good at English, and so is my sister.

我英语学得好，我妹妹学得也好。

I like English and so does she.

我喜欢英语，她也喜欢。

We can speak Chinese, so can Kate.

我们会讲汉语，凯特也会。

提醒注意：在这一结构中的主语可以是名词或人称代词，但它和上文的主语不是同一个"人"或"物"。

例：—She bought a computer. 她买了一台电脑。

—So did I. 我也买了一台。

另外，这一结构的否定式是"neither/nor+ 助动词 /be 动词 / 情态动词 + 主语"。

例：—He doesn't know Lin Tao's address. 他不知道林涛的地址。

—Neither do I. 我也不知道。

这里的 neither/nor 意为"也不"或"也没有"。

(4) 在 "so+ 主语 + 助动词 /be 动词 / 情态动词"结构中，so 用于对前面事实的肯定，有"的确如此"之意。

例：—He will go to Hangzhou for a holiday tomorrow. 他明天要去杭州度假。

—So he will. 的确如此。

提醒注意：在这一结构中的主语和上文中的主语通常是同一个"人"或"物"。

例：—It's her turn now. 现在轮到她了。

—So it is! 是呀！

(5) 在"主语 +do（动词某种形式）+so"结构中，so 用以避免重复前文提到的情况。

例：The teacher asked us to read the text and we did so.

老师让我们读这篇课文，我们就读了。

Passage 3

剧情介绍：

（选自第3季第12集）今晚篮球队与黑鸦队有一场比赛，某篮球俱乐部的知名顾问来到镇上，要从篮球队中挑选几个人。凯伦和基斯决定开始约会，并一起观看今晚的篮球比赛。

Scene: Lucas enters the room, buttoning his cuffs. He looks down and laughs. Karen is sitting at her vanity mirror, putting make-up on.

卢卡斯边扣袖口的扣子边走进凯伦的卧室，他低头看着凯伦笑了。凯伦正坐在她的化妆镜前补妆。

Lucas: (bends down) So, tonight's the big **night**[1]. Are you excited? I mean, Keith is like the most popular kid in school.

(Karen looks at him for a long moment.)

Karen: Don't **make fun of**[2] me.

(Lucas laughs.)

Karen: I'm too **nervous**[3].

(Lucas pats her on the arm and walks further into the room. Karen puts lipstick on and Lucas sits on her bed.)

Karen: Right, now, (pause) how do I look?

Lucas: (shrugs) Like my mom.

Karen: (sighs forcefully) I'm serious!

Lucas: You look great, ma.

(Karen smiles.)

Lucas: You looked great the last time you asked me and the time before that.

Karen: And, what about the time before that?

Lucas: (thinks hard) Oh, **so-so**[4].

(Karen smiles and looks down.)

卢卡斯：（弯下身子）今晚很重要，你兴奋吗？我的意思是，基斯就像是学校里最受欢迎的孩子。

（凯伦盯着他看了好一阵。）

凯伦：别笑话我了。

（卢卡斯笑了。）

凯伦：我太紧张了。

（卢卡斯拍了拍她的胳膊往屋子里面走。凯伦涂了些口红，卢卡斯坐到了她的床上。）

凯伦：好吧，（停顿了一下）现在我看上去怎么样？

卢卡斯：（耸耸肩）像我妈妈。

凯伦：（用力地叹了口气）我是认真的！

卢卡斯：你看上去好极了，妈妈。

（凯伦笑了。）

卢卡斯：你上次问我的时候就棒极了，再上次也一样。

凯伦：那再上一次呢？

卢卡斯：（认真地想了想）马马虎虎。

（凯伦笑着向下瞭了一眼。）

注释
1. the big night 重要的夜晚
2. make fun of 开玩笑；取笑某人
3. nervous ['nɜːvəs] *adj.* 紧张的；不安
4. so-so 一般的；马马虎虎的

Karen: (nervously) Shouldn't dating get easier?

(The doorbell rings.)

Karen: (frantic) Oh, um,... OK. (gets off the stool)

Lucas: Do you want me to have a little talk with him? *You know*[1], *make sure*[2] his intentions are **honourable**[5].

Karen: I got it from here.

Karen: Alright, um,... (takes her bag) **good luck**[6] at the game. You will be joining us for dinner afterwards?

Lucas: I'll be there.

(Karen smiles.)

Karen: OK.

(She walks out of the door.)

Lucas: (calling after her) You know, this is getting pretty serious, huh – bringing him home to meet the **fam**[7]?

Karen: (pokes her head in for a beat) Enough !

(Lucas laughs and stands. She opens the front door to Keith. She smiles delightedly.)

Karen: Keith. You look…

Keith: You look… too. (smiles nervously)

(Karen bites her lip and Keith laughs. She shuts the door behind her and walks down the front porch with him.)

Karen: I, uh,… **have a confession**[8],I was, uh,… pretty nervous about tonight.

Keith: Oh, yeah, me too. I actually changed my shirt three times and… I was gonna change again and then I realized I only have three shirts.

(Karen laughs.)

Karen: *Well*[3], I like that one.

(Karen looks at the car, stunned.)

Karen: This is yours?

Keith: This is the car I've always **dreamed about**[9]… which… makes it prefect for tonight.

Karen: What made you finally decide to buy it?

(Keith holds open the door for her.)

Keith: Lately I've been… less about talking and more about doing.

(They smile and Karen gets into the car. Keith drives away.)

凯伦：　　（紧张地）约会怎么就这么难呢？

（门铃响起。）

凯伦：　　（抓狂）噢，好了。（离开凳子）

卢卡斯：　要不要我跟他谈一谈？看看他有没有打什么坏主意？

凯伦：　　还是我来吧。

凯伦：　　好吧，嗯，（拿起她的包）比赛好运。赛完后跟我们一起吃晚饭，好吗？

卢卡斯：　我会去的。

（凯伦微笑。）

凯伦：　　好的。

（她走出房门。）

卢卡斯：　（在她身后喊道）看来你是来真的了，带他来见家里人？

凯伦：　　（回过头）够了!

（卢卡斯边笑边起身。凯伦为基斯打开家门。高兴地笑了。）

凯伦：　　基斯，你看上去……

基斯：　　你看上去……也是。（紧张地笑）

（凯伦咬了一下嘴唇，基斯笑了。凯伦关上了身后的门与基斯并肩走到一起。）

凯伦：　　我，哦，……我得承认，今晚我比较紧张。

基斯：　　哦，我也是。我换了三件衬衫，准备再换的时候才意识到我只有三件。

（凯伦笑了。）

凯伦：　　我喜欢这件。

（凯伦震惊地看着车。）

凯伦：　　这是你的？

基斯：　　这是我做梦都想要的车，有了它今晚就完美了。

凯伦：　　你是怎么决定买下的？

（基斯为她打开车门。）

基斯：　　最近我说的比较少，做的比较多。

（他们同时笑了，凯伦坐进车里。基斯开车离去。）

常用表达

1. you know 口头语，没有实在意义。相当于"你知道的""你也知道"。

例：He is, you know, kind of shy.

你也知道，他有点害羞。

2. make sure 确保；务必；确信

例：Make sure you are good for her and help her out, whenever you can.

你要确保对她好，要时时刻刻尽你所能去帮助她。

Make sure you have the truth on your side, and that your idea makes sense.

要保证让真相站在你这一边，这样你的见解才能站得住脚。

3. well 的用法作为开头语在英语中经常出现，主要有：

(1)（用于表示想要开口说话）嗯，唔

例：Sylvia shook hands, "Well, you go get yourselves some breakfast."

西尔维娅摆了摆手说："嗯，你们自己去吃些早餐吧。"

(2)（用于表示想要继续话题）这个，不过

例：The trouble with city is that they do not have enough quality players. Well, that can easily be rectified.

难题在于他们缺乏优秀球员。不过，这种情况很容易改变。

(3)（用于转换话题）对了，好了

例：Thank you, Lionel, for singing that for us. Well, we'd better tell you what's on the show between nine and midnight.

谢谢你的歌声，莱昂内尔。好了，我们来看看从 9 点到午夜都播出什么节目。

注
释

5. honourable ['ɒnərəbl] *adj.* 荣誉的；值得尊敬的；表示尊
敬的

6. good luck 好运

7. fam=family 家里人

8. have a confession 承认

9. dream about 梦想；梦到

21

Skins
《皮囊》

入选理由：

《皮囊》是 2007 年以来英国 E4 频道推出的一个新晋剧集，至今已播出六季，第七季于 2012 年 10 月到 1 月在曼彻斯特和伦敦拍摄，于 2013 年 1 月 21 日回归荧幕。《皮囊》于 2011 年摘得年度"最佳电视节目奖"。国内将其贴切地翻译为《皮囊》，因为这部剧或许想告诉我们，我们都生活在精致的皮囊中，用彼此依偎、亲肤取暖的方式来慰藉这迷乱而孤独的青春。剧中一群青春癫狂的英国花样少年不停狂欢派对，纸醉金迷，过着不同寻常的生活。透过小小的镜头可以看到他们的生活及感情的起起落落，感受并温习不可复制的青春。但在这颓废和荒谬生活的外表下，我们更能看到他们细腻的内心世界和无奈。

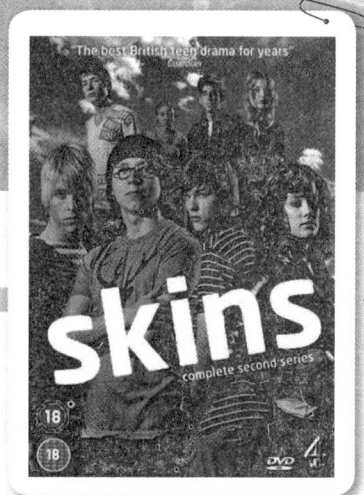

Section 1　剧情特点：

这部剧主要描述了英国的一群高中生在成长过程中面临的压力、爱情和友情等的考验和抉择、家庭矛盾的困扰等。这部剧虽算是一部青春偶像剧，但它更倾向于展示当代青少年成长过程中精神世界的种种问题。

Section 2　对白特点：

《皮囊》的台词极为口语化，英语学习者可以从中学到很多经典的英式口语。同时，也能帮助英语学习者熟悉优美但难懂的英音。但因为剧情的需要，剧中对白有一些不雅的口头禅，希望英语学习者能够辨别。

Section 3   角色分析：

托尼·斯通 (Tony Stone): 埃菲·斯通的哥哥，米歇尔·理查森的男朋友。他长得最帅，是小镇里最受欢迎的男孩。帅气的外表也让他变得"贪婪"，他不满足于与米歇尔·理查森谈恋爱，所以与本校的另一个女孩关系暧昧，并因此招惹了麻烦。后来与米歇尔·理查森感情受挫，在车祸后也遇到了不少的困难，终于从一个稚嫩的男孩走向成熟。

埃菲·斯通 (Effy Stone): 托尼·斯通的妹妹，她总是摆出很酷的样子，不爱搭理人，不与人交朋友，行为乖张叛逆。她是托尼·斯通真正关心的人，但她却总是带来托尼·斯通不想看到的结果。

席德·詹金斯 (Sid Jenkins): 席德·詹金斯是一个毫无自信的男孩，他交过女朋友，却对托尼·斯通的女友米歇尔·理查森爱慕有加，而他的朋友托尼·斯通总是把他当作傻瓜戏弄，但这并不能阻止席德·詹金斯对托尼·斯通美丽女友持之以恒的追求。但是席德·詹金斯要比他自己所想的聪明得多，而这也使得他最后能勇敢面对托尼·斯通并且赢得自己的梦中情人，但这个女孩却并不是他以前所追求的那一个。

克里斯·迈尔斯 (Chris Miles): 总是玩各种把戏以博人一笑，他藐视世间的一切事物，但没有任何事情能阻止他去参加心理学课程，因为他热爱心理学课的安吉老师。对他来说，安吉就是脱俗于世间的天使。在安吉的未婚夫出现后感情彻底破灭，不过又与杰兰德·菲瑟结下了姻缘……

马可西·奥利弗 (Maxxie Oliver): 一个同性恋者。他的双手双脚如同有着魔力，非常擅长踢踏舞与绘画。

米歇尔·理查森 (Michelle Richardson): 托尼·斯通的女朋友。她美貌与智慧并存，让每个人都自惭形秽，除了托尼·斯通。而米歇尔·理查森也深知这一点，她只是不知道怎样从他的掌控中脱离出来。

凯西·安斯沃思 (Cassie Ainsworth): 一个厌食症患者。她喜欢席德·詹金斯，而席德·詹金斯却喜欢米歇尔·理查森。一直不为之所动的席德·詹金斯激怒了凯西·安斯沃思，于是她对席德·詹金斯采取了报复行动。而席德·詹金斯慢慢发现自己真正喜欢的人是凯西·安斯沃思，于是他又回过头来找凯西·安斯沃思，最终他们走到了一起。

杰兰德·菲瑟 (Jalanda Fazer): 非常阳光的女孩，她是这个国家最有天赋的青年单簧管演奏者。杰兰德·菲瑟不能忍受任何不公平的事情，特别是托尼·斯通对待她最好的朋友米歇尔·理查森的方式。她在第二季爱上了克里斯·迈尔斯，并怀上了他的孩子，在克里斯·迈尔斯死后打掉了孩子。

🔊 Passage 1 📷

剧情介绍：

（选自第1季第4集）克里斯·迈尔斯的妈妈离家出走了，把家里所有的东西都带走了，只给克里斯·迈尔斯留下一千块钱。以为妈妈只是出去度假的克里斯·迈尔斯很快就把这一千块钱花光了，一直不见妈妈回来的克里斯·迈尔斯发现了空空的衣柜，这时他才恍然大悟，是妈妈不要他了。这时他想起了爸爸，于是就和好友杰兰德·菲瑟一起去了爸爸的住处……

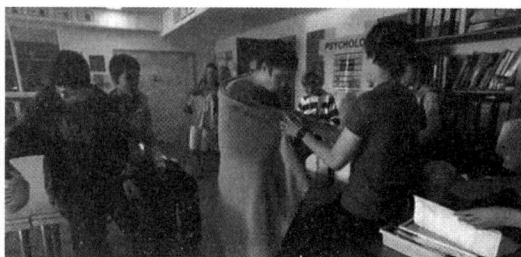

Scene 1: Chris Miles is homeless. He goes to school naked. His friends help to provide clothes for him.

克里斯·迈尔斯无家可归了。他光着身子来到了学校。好友帮他找衣服。

🔊**Friend:**	Hey, Chris, trousers! How good are we?	朋友:	嘿，克里斯，裤子！看我们对你多好！
Friend:	Don't tell him.	朋友:	别告诉他。
Tony:	Everyone's talking about some naked guy who just walked through school.	托尼:	大家都在谈论大摇大摆进了学校的裸男。
Sid:	People are trying to work out whether you've made a political statement.	席德:	他们在想你是不是有什么政治见解。
Michelle:	This **top**[1] any good?	米歇尔:	这件上衣怎么样?
Cassie:	I think you'll like it.	凯西:	我觉得你会喜欢的。
Chris	I didn't think anyone would notice.	克里斯:	我还以为没人会注意。
Sid:	Yeah. Maybe a few did.	席德:	或许有些人注意到了。
Tony:	Pull yourself **together**[2]. Chris, you need a mum, you big baby.	托尼:	振作起来，天哪，你需要个妈妈，大婴儿。

Jalanda: Tony!	杰兰德: 托尼!
Tony: Fucking hell, he's not **pathetic**³. You can take a joke, can't you, Chris?	托尼: 走开，他还没那么可怜，你还能接受玩笑，能吗，克里斯?
Jalanda: Look, you try it, OK? No Mum, no Dad, on your own.	杰兰德: 听着，有本事你试试，没爹没妈，孤苦伶仃。
Tony: Sounds brilliant to me.	托尼: 妙绝!
Chris: I've got... I've got a Dad.	克里斯: 我有……我有爸爸。

Scene 2: Chris Miles and Jalanda Fazer go to Chris Miles' father's home. The doorbell rings.
克里斯·迈尔斯和杰兰德·菲瑟去了克里斯·迈尔斯的爸爸家。门铃响了。

Chris: There's no-one in.	克里斯: 家里没人。
Jalanda: You'll be fine, Chris, OK?	杰兰德: 会好的，克里斯，好吗?
(The door opens and a woman, the stepmother of Chris Miles, Mary, appears.)	(门开了，克里斯·迈尔斯的继母玛丽开了门。)
Mary: Chris?	玛丽: 克里斯?
Mary: Oh, Chris! What a...	玛丽: 克里斯! 多……
Mary: What a lovely surprise!	玛丽: 多好的惊喜!
Chris: Look, we weren't **planning on**⁴...	克里斯: 我们不是要……
Jalanda: Hi, I'm Jal.	杰兰德: 你好，我是吉奥。
Mary: Jal, I'm Mary.	玛丽: 吉奥，我是玛丽。
Mary: Won't you come in?	玛丽: 你们进来吧。
Mary: Your dad'll be back soon. But I can **give him a ring**⁵ anyway, shall I?	玛丽: 你爸爸很快就回来了，但我可以给他打个电话，好吗?
Chris: What, he's not here? We could come back ano...	克里斯: 什么，他不在? 我们可以下次再……
Mary: Wonderful!	玛丽: 好极了!
Mary: Wonderful.	玛丽: 好极了。

注释
1. **top** [tɒp] *n.* 上衣
2. **pull together** 齐心协力（这里指"振作起来"）
3. **pathetic** [pəˈθetɪk] *adj.* 令人同情的，可怜的
4. **plan on** 打算

Mary:	And this is little Sammy.	玛丽：	这位是小萨米。
Mary:	Do you want to come and say hello, Chris?	玛丽：	你想来打个招呼吗，克里斯？
Chris:	Er, no, I'll, um, leave him to **sleep**[6].	克里斯：	不了，让他睡觉好了。
Mary:	Well...	玛丽：	好吧。
(They three sit in silence.)		（他们三个一阵沉默。）	
Mary:	How's your mum, Chris?	玛丽：	你妈妈好吗？克里斯？
Jalanda:	Actually, that's the reason...	杰兰德：	其实这就是我们来……
Chris:	Yeah, she's getting better.	克里斯：	好，她好多了。
Mary:	Oh, no!	玛丽：	噢，不！
Mary:	She hasn't had another turn?	玛丽：	她是不是又吸毒了吗？
Chris:	Um, no. Not really. She's fine.	克里斯：	没有。没有。她很好。
Mary:	Good. Well, send her my best.	玛丽：	那很好，代我问她好。
Mary:	Why don't we look for some baby photos of Chris? That could be fun.	玛丽：	我们找找克里斯小时候的照片。看吧，会很有趣的。
Mary:	Graham **labels**[7] them by year.	玛丽：	格拉汉姆按年份归类的。
Mary:	I'm trying to encourage him to label by mood, but...	玛丽：	我想让他以心情归类，但……
Chris:	You won't find any of me.	克里斯：	你不会找到我的。
Mary:	Worried we might find something embarrassing?	玛丽：	怕我们看到尴尬的照片吗？
Mary:	Ah, **bingo**[8]!	玛丽：	啊，找到了！
Mary:	Look, he's even sweeter than Sammy.	玛丽：	看，他比萨米还可爱呢！
Mary:	I don't think I'm supposed to say that as a mum, but you are!	玛丽：	作为妈妈本不该这么说，不过你的确很可爱！
Mary:	Have a look at him!	玛丽：	看看他！
Jalanda:	You do look quite cute.	杰兰德：	你看起来的确很可爱。
Chris:	That's not me.	克里斯：	那不是我。
Mary:	It is.	玛丽：	怎么不是？
Chris:	No, it's not. It's Peter.	克里斯：	不，不是，那是彼得。
Mary:	Well, we can still say he looks sweet, can't we?	玛丽：	不过他还是很可爱的，不是吗？
Jalanda:	Who's Peter?	杰兰德：	彼得是谁？
Chris:	Um, he's my brother.	克里斯：	他是我哥哥。
Jalanda:	Your brother?	杰兰德：	你哥哥？
(Graham comes back and Mary goes to the door.)		（格拉汉姆回来了，玛丽走向门去。）	
Mary:	Graham!	玛丽：	格拉汉姆？
Mary:	You'll never guess who's here!	玛丽：	你肯定猜不到谁来了！
Mary:	It's Chris! Isn't that great!	玛丽：	是克里斯！这简直太棒了！
Graham:	I need a shower. I'm going for a shower.	格拉汉姆：	我要洗澡，我要去洗个澡。
Mary:	I've just had to sit with him for the last half	玛丽：	我刚刚不得不和他坐了半个钟

hour!

Graham: Well, **get rid of**[9] him.

Mary: Don't do this to me, Graham, he's your son.

Graham: Can't help that. He's a **fuck-up**[10], just like his mum.

Graham: I don't want him here, OK? I'm taking a shower.

(Chris Miles' baby brother cries. Chris Miles goes to comfort him. At this moment, Mary comes back to them.)

Mary: Everything's fine, he's just got a couple of calls to make.

Jalanda: He's calmed down. You look nice together, Chris.

Mary: Just wants to suckle on something, probably. Give me your finger.

(Chris Miles drops the baby by accident.)

Mary: Come on, Sammy. Come on.

Jalanda: Listen. His mum has...

Mary: Does he want money?

Jalanda: No. He doesn't.

(Chris Miles runs out of his Dad's home.)

Jalanda: Chris!

(Jalanda Fazer runs after Chris Miles and they arrive at a tomb.)

Jalandar: You OK?

Chris: I could never do them knots at <u>Cubs</u>[1], you know, and they said, "Ah, he's not got the fingers for it," or whatever. But look what my fucking fingers can do now, eh? Hey, do you... do you wanna hear about the best day of my life? Cubs. I'd **pissed myself**[11] by accident. They'd had us sitting down for ages

头呢!

格拉汉姆: 把他弄出去!

玛丽: 别这么对我,格拉汉姆,他是你儿子。

格拉汉姆: 没办法,他是个混蛋,和他妈一样!

格拉汉姆: 我不想看到他,好吗?我就想洗澡。

(克里斯·迈尔斯的小弟弟哭闹,克里斯·迈尔斯去哄他。玛丽回到了他们身边。)

玛丽: 一切正常,只是他得打几通电话。

杰兰德: 他不哭了,你俩看上去合得来,克里斯。

玛丽: 也许他想吸什么东西,试试你的手指。

(克里斯·迈尔斯不小心把弟弟掉地上了。)

玛丽: 抱抱,萨米,抱抱。

杰兰德: 听着,他妈妈……

玛丽: 他想要钱吗?

杰兰德: 不,不是的。

(克里斯·迈尔斯跑出了门。)

杰兰德: 克里斯!

(杰兰德·菲瑟追上克里斯·迈尔斯,他们跑到一块墓地处。)

杰兰德: 你还好吗?

克里斯: 童子军的时候我总学不会打结,他们就说"他那破手就那样"或是其他什么的。看看我的手指究竟能干什么?你想……你想听听我这辈子最好的一天吗?参加童子军的时候,我一不小心尿了裤子,他

注释
5. **give him a ring** 打电话给他; **ring** *n.* =phone call
6. **leave him to sleep** 让他睡吧,不打扰他了;
　　leave *vt.* 使或允许在或保持某一特定状态
7. **label** ['leɪbl] *v.* 把……归类、描述
8. **bingo** ['bɪŋɡəʊ] *interj.* (感叹词)看吧!嘿!(用于表达活

动中突然出现的结果或结局)

9. **get rid of** 摆脱
10. **fuck-up** 一团糟,一场糊涂
11. **pissed myself** 尿湿自己

and, um, I was trying... trying to get out like to leave the room but this kid kept blocking me, stopping me leaving, he was playing a game or something and, um... So I told him, right, that he was a **dickhead**[12], and that he's gonna get out of my way, dickhead... ...and then the whole place went quiet cos I'd said "dickhead". And then they was all laughing, everyone, and I couldn't work out if it was cos I'd swore or if they'd seen that my shorts were wet, so I tried to cover my shorts with my hands, right, but that meant they all definitely noticed and then there was more laughing. But, yeah, Peter, my brother, he was, um, he was youngest-ever **sixer**[13] or something. They're the ones in charge, sixers. He could do all the knots, him. Him and Dad would practice. He loved it. Anyway, he stands up, yeah, sixer, and, um, and they all liked him, and, um, he takes my hand, and took me to the toilet. And then he had me take my shorts off, and then he cleaned me up. And then he took off his shorts and put them on me. And then... he kissed me on the cheek, and took my hand, and we both went out there. Him just in his pants. No-one laughed. Best day of my life.

Chris: Look, don't, um, don't tell the others, yeah, about...

Jalanda: No, I won't. Do you know what you're gonna do?

Chris: What, me? No, I...

Jalanda: You think your mum's gonna come back?

Chris: Not if she's still around.

Jalanda: How do you know?

Chris: She left flowers by the grave again.

们让我们整天坐着，我想……想离开屋子，但有个孩子一直挡着我，不让我出去，他在玩什么游戏。所以，我就告诉他，他是个笨蛋白痴，他得给我闪开，笨蛋白痴。然后整个屋子都静了下来，因为我说了笨蛋白痴，他们都笑话我，所有的人，我根本不知道是因为我说了脏话还是因为我裤子湿了，所以我试着用手挡住短裤，那样他们才都看到了。然后笑得更欢了。但是，彼得，我哥哥，他是……他是最年轻的击球手之类的。他们管着我们，他什么结都会系，他和爸爸经常练习，他喜欢那样。不管怎样，他站起来了，击球手，大家都喜欢他，然后，他拉着我的手，领我进厕所，然后他让我脱掉短裤，为我清洗干净，然后他把自己的短裤脱下来给我穿上。然后……他亲了我的脸，拉起我的手双双走了出去，他只穿着内裤，没人笑话他，这辈子最好的一天。

克里斯： 听着，别告诉别人关于……

杰兰德： 放心，我不会的。你知道自己要做些什么吗？

克里斯： 什么，我吗？不，我……

杰兰德： 你认为你妈妈还会回来吗？

克里斯： 不会了，她就在附近。

杰兰德： 你怎么知道？

克里斯： 她又给我哥献花了。

文化背景

1. Cubs 童子军

童子军，又称童军运动，英文为 Scouting，是一个国际性的、非政治性非军事性的、非政府性的、非营利性的青少年运动组织。其目的是通过强调野外实践活动的非正规教育，在身体、精神和智力上培训青少年，使他们成为快乐、健康、有用的公民，能对未来社会做出贡献。童子军运动开始于 1907 年，创始人是英国爵士罗伯特·贝登堡。贝登堡先生鉴于当时英国青年道德堕落，体格衰弱，恐遭古代罗马帝国亡国的覆辙，故而研发出一套可行的训练方法试图挽救这种危机。

常用表达

1. fun 有趣的事；开心的事

例：Sailing is (good/great) fun.

帆船运动是一大乐趣。

🔊 Passage 2 📷

剧情介绍：

（选自第 2 季第 8 集）杰兰德·菲瑟怀了克里斯·迈尔斯的孩子，杰兰德·菲瑟不知怎么处理这件事，因为杰兰德·菲瑟的爸爸对她期望很高，要求很严格，而且他一直不看好整天不务正业的克里斯·迈尔斯，然而杰兰德·菲瑟和克里斯·迈尔斯是真心相爱的。杰兰德·菲瑟还是把怀孕这件事告诉了爸爸。一天，从学校回到家的杰兰德·菲瑟发现妈妈竟然来了……

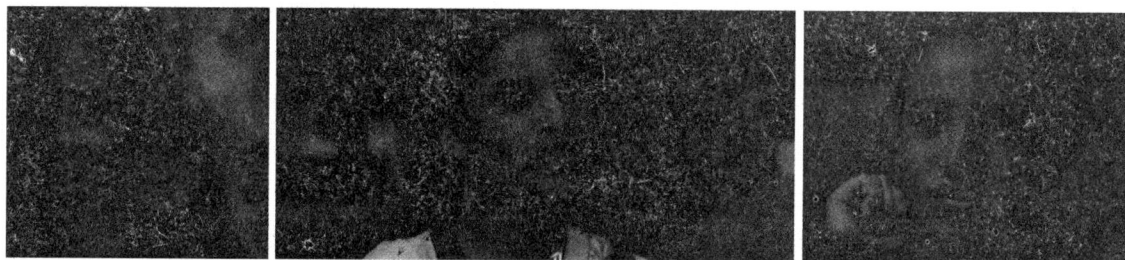

Scene:	Outside Jalanda Fazer's home.
	在杰兰德·菲瑟家外面。

🔊 **Chris**	You all right?	克里斯：	你还好吗？
Jalanda:	Chris.	杰兰德：	克里斯……
Chris:	I thought you were coming round last night.	克里斯：	我以为你昨晚会过来的。
Jalanda:	Yeah, sorry.	杰兰德：	是啊，抱歉。
Chris:	Cassie says that I should talk to you.	克里斯：	凯西说我应该和你谈谈。
Jalanda:	I can't. Chris. I've gotta go to London for my **audition**[1] and back for my **oral**[2].	杰兰德：	现在不行，克里斯，我得赶去伦敦面试，回来还得考口试。
Chris:	I know, but you need to hear this.	克里斯：	我知道，不过你得听好……
Jalanda:	No.	杰兰德：	不要。
Chris:	I waited for you and...	克里斯：	我一直在等你……
Jalanda:	Not now!	杰兰德：	现在不是时候！
Chris:	Hold on, look, listen... What are we waiting for? Come and live with me. We're gonna *run out of time*[1] if you don't stand still...	克里斯：	等等，听好了，我们还等什么？搬过来和我住吧！我快没时间了！如果你还站在原地不动……
Jalanda:	I've gotta go. I'm gonna be late.	杰兰德：	我得走了，我要迟到了。
Chris:	Yeah, I know.	克里斯：	我知道。
Jalanda:	You... You know?	杰兰德：	你……你知道？
Chris:	I know that if you go to that audition, then you'll get in, and then, sooner or later, we'll be over.	克里斯：	我知道如果你去面试，你肯定会通过的，然后迟早我们之间会玩完的。

Jalanda: You don't know what you're talking about.	杰兰德： 你不知道自己在说什么。
Chris: No? Look, my **pad's**[3] this way.	克里斯： 是吗？我的公寓在这边。
Jalanda: My music audition.	杰兰德： 我要去音乐学院面试……
Chris: Don't go.	克里斯： 别走。
Jalanda: What?!	杰兰德： 什么？
Chris: I need you.	克里斯： 我需要你。
Jalanda: It's not like I've got in yet.	杰兰德： 去面试不代表我就会通过。
Chris: You'll get in! And then you'll probably move in with some fucking music student called Terry from East **Anglia**[4], who blows a fucking **trombone**[5], and then you'll sit up discussing your blowing techniques.	克里斯： 你肯定会通过的，到时候你可能会和从东英格兰来的音乐系学生特里住在一起，那个人还是吹长笛的，然后你们会坐在一块讨论吹笛的技巧。
Jalanda: Huh? What?	杰兰德： 啊……什么？
Chris: And I fucking love you. Yeah, you'll move in with him and I could be, like, dying, yeah, and you wouldn't even know about it.	克里斯： 我真的爱你，你和他住在一起，我就会痛不欲生，你甚至都不会知道。
Jalanda: I'm just going to an audition. Then we're gonna talk, Chris. Wish me luck.	杰兰德： 我只是去面试而已，面试完我就和你谈，克里斯，祝我好运吧！
Chris: Luck. All right, no blowing trombones, then, yeah?	克里斯： 好运。但是不准找吹长笛的！
Chris: Yeah.	克里斯： 好吧。
(Jalanda Fazer goes to her audition.)	（杰兰德·菲瑟去试音了。）
Judge: Jalanda Fazer. Which of the four pieces are you playing for us today?	评委： 杰兰德·菲瑟，四首曲子中你要演奏哪首？
Jalanda: The <u>Brahms</u>[1].	杰兰德： 勃拉姆斯。
Judge: Brahms? A bit of a **cop out**[6].	评委： 勃拉姆斯？有点保守哦……
Jalanda: Cop out?	杰兰德： 保守？
Judge: It's the easiest piece out of the four, and we're about challenge. We need to know if you are, too.	评委： 这是四首中最简单的一首了，我们喜欢挑战，我们想知道你是不是也喜欢挑战。
Jalanda: But...	杰兰德： 不过……
Judge: So we'll give the <u>Weber</u>[2] a **crack**[7], unless you feel you aren't up to it.	评委： 那么我们来试试韦伯，除非你觉得自己没这个能力。
Judge: Oh, let her play the easy piece.	评委： 让她演奏那首简单的好了。
Jalanda: I'll play the fucking Weber. What are you lookin' at?	杰兰德： 我就演奏韦伯，你们看什么呢？

注释		
1. audition [ɔ:'dɪʃn] *n.* 试音	**5. trombone** [trɒm'bəʊn] *n.* 长号
2. oral ['ɔ:rəl] *n.* 口试	**6. cop out** 逃避
3. pad [pæd] *n.* ＜俚＞公寓，卧室	**7. crack** [kræk] *n.* 试图，尝试
4. Anglia 英格兰的拉丁名称	

(Michelle Richardson goes to Cassie Ainsworth's place.)

Michelle: Hi, Cassie.

Cassieh: Hi, Chelle.

Michelle: Um... I was just wondering if Jal was here. Thought we could go to the oral together.

Cassie: She's not here. OK?

Michelle: Cassie. Has she told him yet?

Cassie: It's none of our business, Chelle.

Michelle: Look, I want to talk to him.

Cassie: Chris went to bed. He's not feeling well again. She'll be at the oral. She always does what she's supposed to do.

Michelle: Look, Cassie... I'm really sorry about me and Sid.

Cassie: He saw sense.

Michelle: Yeah, I'm glad.

Cassie: Good luck, Chelle.

(The audition is over. Jalanda Fazer goes home.)

Jalanda: Hello? Hello?

Mother: Hello, Jalanda.

Jalanda: Mum?

Jalanda: Is this real?

Mother: Everything's real, darling. You'd better **tuck in**[8] before Ace and Lynton come.

Jalanda: You won't be here when Ace and Lynton come.

Mother: Sit down. I hear you've got a boyfriend.

Jalanda: Who said...? Right, Dad told you.

Mother: Ronnie tells me a lot of things.

Jalanda: No, he doesn't. He doesn't talk about you, you don't exist for him.

Mother: Well, you know all about it, don't you?

Jalanda: Dad wouldn't. He hates you.

Mother: One thing I know for certain about Ronnie is that he doesn't hate me. Jalanda, there is a reason for everything. Whatever you do now about this baby... will have a reason. You'll understand it, maybe nobody else will. But

（米歇尔·理查森去了凯西·安斯沃思家。）

米歇尔：　嗨，凯西。

凯西：　　嗨，米歇尔。

米歇尔：　我想知道杰奥是不是在这里，我们一起去口试。

凯西：　　她不在这里。好吧!

米歇尔：　凯西。她跟他说了吗？

凯西：　　这事跟我们无关，米歇尔。

米歇尔：　我想跟他说说。

凯西：　　克里斯睡觉了，他又不舒服了。她会去口试的，她总会做自己的份内事。

米歇尔：　对啊，听着凯西，我很抱歉和席德之间的事情。

凯西：　　他开始懂事了。

米歇尔：　对，我很高兴。

凯西：　　祝你好运，米歇尔。

（试音结束，杰兰德·菲瑟回到了家。）

杰兰德：　有人吗？有人吗？

妈妈：　　你好，杰兰德。

杰兰德：　妈妈？

杰兰德：　这是真的吗？

妈妈：　　一切都是真的，亲爱的。在埃斯和林顿来之前，你最好好好吃一顿。

杰兰德：　埃斯和林顿来的时候你就不会在这了。

妈妈：　　坐。听说你有了男朋友。

杰兰德：　你听谁说的？对，是爸爸。

妈妈：　　罗尼和我讲了很多事。

杰兰德：　他才没有。他不会说起你，你对他而言是不存在的。

妈妈：　　你什么都知道，对吗？

杰兰德：　爸爸不会这么做的，他恨你。

妈妈：　　关于他，我有件事十分确定，那就是他不恨我。杰兰德，每件事的发生都是有原因的。不管你现在怎么处理这个孩子，都是有原因的，也许别人不会理解，但你

you can **live with**[9] that, can't you?

Jalanda: Where *the fuck*[1] were you?!

Mother: I remember standing... in this kitchen one Tuesday. I scraped **sauce off**[10] Lynton's coat and wiped **snot**[11] off Ace's knee. And I re-did the **plaits**[12] in your hair. And I watched you go off to school. And I knew that your Dad was **coming in**[13] from the afternoon flight from New York.

Jalanda: We needed you.

Mother: I couldn't stand that. It was easy to go upstairs and pack a bag, walk to the bus stop, get on. I had some choices. I had some choices, and that's what I did.

Jalanda: Did you know the maximum text charge from one mobile phone network to another is 30p? And you couldn't even **spare**[14] 30 **fucking**[15] pence to check I was OK, to say happy birthday! Talking now is gonna achieve what? Tell me, because my network's fucking cheap! You made your choice.

Mother: Jalanda...

Jalanda: It's Jal.

Mother: Jalanda... The one thing that your father couldn't forgive was... I wasn't honest. I didn't tell him. That was all.

Jalanda: You'd better go before Ace and Lynton get back.

自己会。你可以接受这一点，不是吗？

杰兰德： 你算什么？

妈妈： 我记得一天星期二，我站在这个厨房里，我把调料汁从林顿身上擦掉，把鼻涕从埃斯的膝盖上抹掉，我重新给你梳理头发，我眼看着你上学去，我知道你爸爸要搭下午航班从纽约回来。

杰兰德： 我们当时需要你。

妈妈： 我接受不了这个事实，走上楼去，打包行李，走去汽车站，开始新生活，这很容易，我有我自己的选择。我有我自己的选择，我也就这么做了。

杰兰德： 你知道吗？一条短信的价格最多是 30 便士？你都不能花 30 便士问问我还好吗？都不会跟我说一声"祝你生日快乐"！现在我们谈话了又会怎么样？告诉我，因为我的手机网便宜死了！你做了你的选择了！

妈妈： 杰兰德。

杰兰德： 我叫杰奥。

妈妈： 杰兰德，你爸爸不原谅我，是因为，我不诚实，我没有告诉他，就是这样。

杰兰德： 你最好在埃斯和林顿回来前离开。

注释
8. **tuck in** 饱吃
9. **live with** 忍受；顺应
10. **scraped off** 擦去，刮掉
11. **snot** [snɒt] *n.* <粗>鼻涕
12. **plait** [pleɪt] *n.* 辫子
13. **coming in** 到达
14. **spare** [speə] *v.* 提供；抽出
15. **fucking** ['fʌkɪŋ] *adj.* 该死的（用于加强语气）

📖 文化背景

1. Brahms 勃拉姆斯

Johannes Brahms（1833 年 5 月 7 日—1897 年 4 月 3 日），约翰内斯·勃拉姆斯，德国十九世纪浪漫主义作曲家、钢琴家、乐队指挥家，也是德国近代最重要的浪漫派音乐家之一。勃拉姆斯的作品兼有古典手法和浪漫精神，交响作品中模仿贝多芬，气势宏大，然而笔法细腻，情绪变化多端，很多作品都是世界名曲，与巴赫、贝多芬并称德国音乐史上的"三 B"。

2. Weber 韦伯

Carl Maria Von Weber（1786 年 11 月 18 日—1826 年 6 月 5 日）韦伯，德国作曲家。他出生于一个戏剧之家，从小随父母在各地旅行演出，对戏剧非常熟悉，对德国民间音乐、风俗也有很深的体验。韦伯十岁学钢琴，之后又学作曲，十二岁开始写作歌剧音乐。代表作是歌剧《自由射手》（《魔弹射手》），其浓郁的德国风格和浪漫气息，被认为是德国第一部浪漫主义歌剧。此外，他还写了歌剧《奥伯龙》，以及少序曲、协奏曲、奏鸣曲。其中，钢琴曲《邀舞》最为脍炙人口，人们已将此改编成管弦乐曲和芭蕾舞演出。

🖋 常用表达

1. run out of time 时间用完了；run out of 用完，耗光，用尽

例：I'll have to stop you there, we've run out of time.

我只好让你在那里打住，我们的时间已经用完了。

Passage 3

剧情介绍:

（选自第 2 季第 10 集）克里斯·迈尔斯和他哥哥一样，死于一种先天性疾病。在准备克里斯·迈尔斯的葬礼时，克里斯·迈尔斯的爸爸为了自己所谓的"面子"，禁止克里斯·迈尔斯的"死党"参加克里斯·迈尔斯的葬礼。于是克里斯·迈尔斯的朋友偷走了克里斯·迈尔斯的尸体，但在克里斯·迈尔斯的女友杰兰德·菲瑟的斥责下，他们最终还回了尸体。在克里斯·迈尔斯葬礼的当天，仍旧没有受到邀请的他们依然来到了葬礼上，不过是远远地站在高处……

Scene:	At Chris Miles' funeral.
	在克里斯·迈尔斯的葬礼上。

Jalanda: I've been thinking about what Chris would have wanted me to say today. The advice he'd give me. Which would be something like, "*You know what*[1], **babe**[1]", "These guys know all about me. Tell them about someone different." So I thought I'd say something about a hero of Chris's. A man called captain Joe Katanga. In 1960, climbing into a **foil**[2] balloon, Captain Joe **ascended**[3] 32 kilometres into the **stratosphere**[4]. And then, armed only with a parachute, he jumped out. He fell for four minutes and 36 seconds, reaching 740 mph before opening his parachute five kilometres above the earth. It had never been done before. And has never been done since. He did it just because he could... **Keep going**[5].

杰兰德: 我曾想过克里斯·迈尔斯会希望我在今天说什么，他能给我的建议，应该会是"知道吗？宝贝""这些人了解我的全部，跟他们说点儿与众不同的"，所以我决定说说克里斯·迈尔斯偶像的事迹，一位叫作乔·加丹加的上校。1960 年他爬进了一个热气球，乔上校在大气层中上升到 32 千米，然后只背着一个降落伞就跳了出去，他下跌了 4 分钟 36 秒，速度达到每小时 740 英里。离地面只有 5 公里的时候他才打开降落伞，这种行为，前所未有。他这么做，只是因为他有能力……继续。这就是克里斯·迈尔斯崇

注释

1. **babe** [beɪb] *n.*（US 俚）姑娘；少女；妞儿
2. **foil** [fɔɪl] *n.* 箔
3. **ascend** [ə'send] *v.* 上升；升高

4. **stratosphere** ['strætəsfɪə] *n.* 平流层，同温层（距地表约 10 至 60 公里之间的大气层）
5. **keep going** 继续

...and that's why Chris loved him. Because the thing about Chris was he said yes. He said yes to everything. He loved everyone. He was the bravest boy... man, I knew. And that was... He flung himself out of a foil balloon every day. Because he could. Because he was. And that's why... and that's why... We... We loved him.

拜他的原因，因为克里斯·迈尔斯的特别之处就在于他接受了现实，他接受了一切，他热爱每一个人，他是我认识的最勇敢的男孩，男人。他每天都跳出热气球，因为他有这个能力，因为他这么做了，这就是为什么，这就是为什么我们，我们爱他。

常用表达

1. you know what 你知道么，你猜怎么着（用于句首，主要是引出想说的话或事情）

例：You know what, I'm not gonna be able to enjoy this.

你猜怎么着，我欣赏不了这个。

Chapter 8

史诗剧
Epic Drama

　　好莱坞不太喜欢拍历史剧，近年来拍过的描写历史的电视系列剧屈指可数。这也难怪，美国两百多年的时间，两场几万人参加的战争，实在翻不出太多的花样。本国史既然没有太多可挖掘的素材，美剧的编剧们通常会把视线投向欧洲大陆：帝国政治的权力角逐，重重宫帏后的阴谋诡计，冷兵器时代的金戈铁马，等等。而一旦有剧本能打动制片商投资，就一定是大手笔。近年来的几部历史题材的系列剧每一集的制作费都高达几百万，堪比一部电影。所以美剧中历史题材的剧目走的是少而精的路线，无论是服装道具，还是人物塑造，都既注重历史，又不失当代视角，而且气势恢宏，场景壮观。例如描写凯撒和屋大维的《罗马》、描写英王亨利八世的《都铎王朝》、描写意大利 15 世纪教皇家族的《波吉亚家族》等，都是其中的佼佼者。

　　最近几年，特效技术的进步给好莱坞的史诗剧带来了新的变化，《魔戒》等魔幻题材电影的走红也影响了电视剧的选材，一批依托虚拟世界杜撰出来的传奇也出现在电视屏幕上。这些剧目摆脱了历史和现实的束缚，编剧可以充分发挥想象力，魔法、僵尸、神龙等都可以成为剧情的一部分。这些剧目虽然在现实中不可能发生，但是倚仗好莱坞高超的特技效果，观众看到的场景却是真实可信，《冰与火之歌》就是这样的代表。看了这种无中生有、天马行空的历史剧，真让人不得不佩服好莱坞的造梦功能。

The Borgias

《波吉亚家族》

22

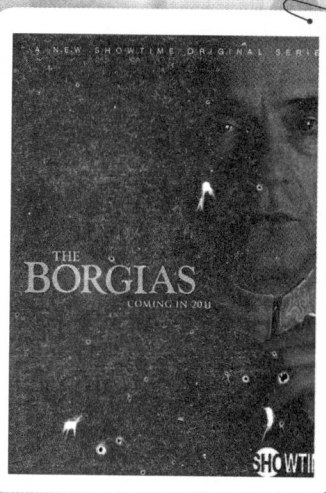

入选理由：

　　《波吉亚家族》是美国娱乐时间电视台 2011 年开播的一部以历史为题材的系列剧，描述对象是意大利历史上最臭名昭著的黑手党家族。该剧迄今已完成两季，是一部大制作、大投入的名家精品，获得多项艾美奖提名。该剧的主创团队以欧洲班底为主，担当剧本创始人、监制和编剧的是著名爱尔兰电影导演尼尔·乔丹，他导演的讲述爱尔兰共和军创始人生平的电影《迈克尔·柯林斯》曾荣获 1996 年威尼斯电影节金狮奖。他的加盟使得该剧备受关注，第一季第一集的观众人数就达到创美国娱乐时间电视台记录的 140 万。

　　另一位加盟的大牌明星是男主角教皇亚历山大六世的扮演者，英国著名演员杰瑞米·艾恩斯。他早在 1990 年就凭借《命运的逆转》夺得当年的奥斯卡影帝称号，如今演技更加纯熟老练。在塑造这个以行为放荡、不择手段闻名的教皇时，并没有渲染其张狂、霸气的一面，而是采用相对内敛的方式，通过细微的面部表情和目光来透露人物内心的杀机，细致刻画了教皇内心的老谋深算、狡猾凶残，以及对亲人的温情。剧组其他演员的表现也同样精彩，这使得本剧顺利续约，目前第三季正在拍摄中。

Section 1　剧情特点：

　　波吉亚家族是文艺复兴后期意大利的实际统治者，家族中先后出了两位教皇，更积累了巨大的权势和财富，比权势和财富更出名的是他们为获得财富、权势而使用的血腥手段。1492 年，这个家族的族长罗德里戈·波吉亚在难以服众的情势下通过大规模贿选，从而登上教皇宝座，为了维持家族的长期统治，他们开始了残酷的党同伐异，对政敌，一方面是谋杀和追捕，一方面是联姻和媾和；而家族内部也异常混乱，本应独身终生的教皇罗德里戈竟然有四个私生子，这些孩子彼此间或兄妹乱伦、或弟兄仇杀，罗德里戈本人也会拿自己孩子的婚姻做筹码来换取政治利益。

　　总之，本剧详尽描述了波吉亚家族统治意大利三十年的历史，充分展示了 15 世纪末期教廷的腐败、堕落，剧情充斥着骄奢淫逸、纵欲贪婪、乱伦、谋杀和谎言，更将宗教的虚伪与残忍刻画得淋漓尽致，有助于我们深入了解中世纪欧洲的人文和历史。

Section 2　对白特点：

《波吉亚家族》并不适合所有人观看。从语言方面来讲，一方面该剧描绘的是神权至上的中世纪罗马教廷，对白中有大量祷告词和拉丁文，还会引用很多圣经上的典故，不熟悉天主教的人可能会难以理解；另一方面，剧中的政治人物之间的对话，语速快、声音小、句子简练、古雅，其含义往往分表面意思和实际意图两种层面，不熟悉历史的人很可能听懂了对话的每个单词，但不能理解句子背后的意思。

然而事物总有两面性，以上的不利因素换一个角度可以视为对英语水平提高的帮助，而且三大宗教之一的基督教至今仍是欧洲社会的主流文化，通过观剧，提高对那些祷告词和与宗教有关的拉丁词汇的理解，可以帮助我们更好地和信仰基督教的欧美人交流。如果在看剧的过程中，多花些时间在历史背景的搜集上，将有助于理解剧中人物的对话，这也是对欧洲历史的一种知识积累。

虽然该剧包含有太多的暴力、血腥等镜头，但从整体上看，该剧演绎的重点仍在反应历史原貌和发掘人性的光辉上，并非一味渲染暴力。就其思想深度和艺术表现力来说，该剧不失为一出优秀的写实剧目，让我们更深入地了解了欧洲的历史与文化及其黑暗的一面。从这个角度上讲，该剧仍值得一看，特别是对那些英语基础较好的学生。

Section 3　角色分析：

罗德里戈·波吉亚 (Rodrigo Borgia)：罗马教皇一般会被视为上帝在世间的代言人，通常由教会内最德高望重的人出任，但这位亚历山大六世教皇却往往被视为文艺复兴时期教廷腐败堕落的象征。作为一位天主教的神职人员，他违背了一个神父应该"忠贞、服从、安于清贫"的誓言，生活上他穷奢极欲、疯狂敛财，政治上他野心勃勃、玩弄权术，此人甚至有四个公开的子女，并将这些子女作为政治筹码为自己的野心服务。但是，这个铁石心肠的恶人也并非没有温柔的一面，对儿女的疼爱、特别是对小女儿卢克雷齐娅的关心展现了他慈父的一面，他总是对子女强调"我们是一家人"。当然这种慈爱并不能阻止他为了政治利益把小女儿嫁给一个粗野、残暴的性虐狂，也没能阻止自己两个儿子间的仇杀。在位十一年后，亚历山大六世死于政敌的毒杀，倒是应了"恶有恶报"的老话。

切泽尔·波吉亚 (Cesare Borgia)：切泽尔·波吉亚是教皇亚历山大六世的私生子。作为长子，他继承了父亲的野心、残忍、狡猾和淫乱。这个英俊的公爵下手凶狠毒辣、冷酷无情，尤其擅长用毒，他最为人诟病的是与亲妹妹的乱伦之恋及杀死自己的亲兄弟。剧本并没有回避他的这些恶行，但描写的却是让人感觉他这么做理由充分。但无论如何美化，切泽尔·波吉亚都是一个名声狼藉的野心家和双手沾满鲜血的刽子手，这点连他自己都不否认。

卢克雷齐娅·波吉亚 (Lucrezia Borgia)：虽然有乱伦的恶名和众多的情人，卢克雷齐娅·波吉亚在欧洲历史上的名声其实不恶。这位颇具才气的美人，很热衷于赞助艺术家，对意大利的文艺复兴运动贡献良多。不幸的是她是教皇的女儿，为了父亲的野心她曾三次出嫁，又反复被父兄从丈夫们手中夺走，原因是教皇需要更有利可图的政治联盟。丈夫被夺走、情人被杀、还眼看着自己的孩子被害，有了这样的经历，任何人都会发生改变。该剧的前两季就集中描绘了她是如何从一个天真无邪的美丽少女蜕变成工于心计的人。要想在那样的乱世里生存，就必须学会保护自己，而要在乱世保护自己，就得学会如何伤害别人。令人宽慰的是卢克雷齐娅最终找到了一个真心爱自己的人，善良总会有回报，她算是黑手党家族中结局最好的一个。

🔊 Passage 1 📷

剧情介绍：

（选自第 1 季第 1 集）1492 年，教皇英诺森八世谢世，下一任教皇将在几位枢密主教中通过闭门选举选出。波吉亚家族的罗德里戈并不是最有希望的，但是凭借着手中的财富进行的大规模的贿选，他一步步逼近权利的中心。为了让家族的权势时代延续，他让自己的两个儿子一人从戎一人从教。但是权势从来都是有代价的。自此，波吉亚家族就开始与凶杀和阴谋为伴了。

Scene 1: The cardinals were holding a meeting in a church to elect next Pope, but without any result. One night in the corridor, Rodrigo met Della Rovere, who also was a candidate as promising as himself. Although the two enemies tried not to give the slightest indication, the hatred could still be felt between their dialogues.

枢密主教们在一处教堂里举行选举教皇的会议，会议迟迟没有结果。这天晚上，罗德里戈与跟他同样有希望当选的候选人德拉·罗韦雷在走廊里相遇了，这两个政治死敌间的对话虽然不动声色，但仍不掩彼此间的憎恶。

🔊 **Rovere:** Cardinal[1] Borgia.

Rodrigo: My Lord Cardinal.

Rovere: Whoever wins this **contest**[1]...

Rodrigo: Election.

Rovere: If you were a different man, I might vote for you. You've performed your duties as Vice-Chancellor **admirably**[2]. The Church has need of your organizational genius. But, She has other needs as well.

Rodrigo: And they would be?

Rovere: Honesty. **Probity**[3]. Goodness.

Rodrigo: You find me lacking in those qualities?

Rovere: Yes. And so I shall fight you to the end, and beyond that, if need be, with any means at my disposal.

罗韦雷： 波吉亚主教。

罗德里戈： 我的主教大人。

罗韦雷： 无论谁赢得了这场竞争……

罗德里戈： 是选举。

罗韦雷： 如果你是另外一个人，我也许会投你一票。做为教区副秘书长，你的表现非常出色。教廷需要你天才的组织能力。但是，她同样还需要其他品质。

罗德里戈： 那是哪些呢？

罗韦雷： 诚实、廉洁、善行。

罗德里戈： 你发现我缺乏这些品质吗？

罗韦雷： 是的，因此我将会与你抗争到最后一刻，甚至更久，如果有必要的话，我会竭尽我的所有来反对你。

Rodrigo: I do tend to win whatever battles I fight. But what talk we of fighting? It is all in God's hands. Good night, My Lord.

罗德里戈： 我会赢得我所参与的所有斗争。但是我们如此的口舌之争又有何用？所有的一切都在上帝的掌握之中。晚安，我的大人。

Scene 2: Rodrigo Borgia finally became Pope Alexander VI, his illegitimate son Cesare came to confess to the newly elected pope. Actually, the son was reporting the bribery progress to the father, and they discuss face to face what to do next step.

罗德里戈·波吉亚终于成了教皇亚历山大六世，他的私生子切泽尔来到忏悔室向新任教皇忏悔，实际是儿子向父亲汇报贿选工作，当面商讨下一步的行动安排。

Cesare: I ask to **confess**[4] to you, Holy Father, because I have **sinned**[5].

切泽尔： 我要向你忏悔，圣父，因为我有罪。

Rodrigo: How have you sinned, my son?

罗德里戈： 你有何罪了，我的孩子？

Cesare: I have **corrupted**[6] my soul. I have **pledged**[7] estates, castles, **benefices**[8] to your brother cardinals. I have transferred the documents in the **innards**[9] of **roasted**[10] beasts and **fowls**[11]. All to secure your election as **pope**[12].

切泽尔： 我亵渎了我的灵魂。我典当了土地、城堡、俸禄向你的其他枢机兄弟们行贿。我将财产转让文件塞进了烤牛排和烤鹅的内脏里。所有这些都是为了确保让你当选教皇。

Rodrigo: And God will repay us tenfold.

罗德里戈： 上帝会十倍奉还给我们的。

Cesare: But you must set my soul *at ease*[1], Father. Can a family such as ours survive such a prize? We are **Spaniards**[13]. They hate us.

切泽尔： 但你必须使我的灵魂得到解脱，神父。像我们这样的人家，能承受得起这种荣耀吗？我们是西班牙人，他们痛恨我们。

注释

1. **contest** ['kɒntest] *n.* 竞赛，角逐
2. **admirably** ['ædmərəblɪ] *adv.* 极好地；令人钦佩地
3. **probity** ['prəʊbətɪ] *n.* 廉洁；正直
4. **confess** [kən'fes] *v.* 忏悔
5. **sin** [sɪn] *n.* 犯罪，犯过错
6. **corrupt** [kə'rʌpt] *v.* 使腐败，亵渎
7. **pledge** [pledʒ] *n.* 抵押；典当
8. **benefice** ['benɪfɪs] *n.* 圣俸
9. **innards** ['ɪnədz] *n.* 内脏
10. **roast** [rəʊst] *v.* 烤
11. **fowl** [faʊl] *n.* 家禽；鸟
12. **pope** [pəʊp] *n.* 罗马教皇；教宗
13. **Spaniard** ['spænɪəd] *n.* 西班牙裔人

The enemies we have at present will be multiplied tenfold.

Rodrigo: God will protect his **Vicar**[14] on Earth, Cesare, and those dearest to him.

Cesare: And will you inform God as to his duties in this regard?

Rodrigo: Why this **blasphemous**[15] tone, my son?

Cesare: Because I swear, if God does not protect us, I shall.

Rodrigo: You are a **bishop**[16], Cesare. You have no need of such **temporal**[17] thoughts.

Cesare: You placed this collar round my neck, Father. You made God my **calling**[18]. But the sins I've committed for you must convince you, surely, that the Church is not my calling. I beg you now to release me of my **vows**[19]. Let me live as a **layman**[20], as a soldier. I can then protect our family from the storm that surely must **engulf**[21] it.

Rodrigo: You are my eldest son, Cesare. You *were always destined*[2] to be a prince of the Church.

Cesare: I would be a prince of state, Father, and I think you know that.

Rodrigo: The **papal**[22] army is small, Cesare. The battles I will fight will be within these sacred walls. This is where I will need your help. Juan can bear arms for the Borgia family, and lead whatever army the pope has, and I will not have my authority questioned further on this. Ego te absolvo ab omnibus censuris, et peccatis, in nomine Patris, et Filii, et Spiritus Sancti. Amen.

罗德里戈：上帝会保护他在人间的代理人，切泽尔，还有他最亲爱的人。

切泽尔：你会告诉上帝这件事是他的职责吗？

罗德里戈：为何你的口气对上帝如此不敬，我的孩子？

切泽尔：因为我发誓，如果上帝不保护我们，我就自己保护。

罗德里戈：你是个主教，切泽尔。没必要想这些世俗之事。

切泽尔：是你把主教的衣领套在我脖子上的，父亲。你使得上帝成了我的追求。但是我为你而犯下的这些罪孽应该已让你确信，真的，教会并非我的使命。我求你让我放弃我的誓言，让我做一个俗人，做一个战士。我能保护我们的家人免于这场吞噬一切的风暴。

罗德里戈：你是我的长子，切泽尔。你注定要成为教会的亲王。

切泽尔：我更想成为一个国家的亲王，父亲，我想你是知道的。

罗德里戈：教廷的军队规模太小，切泽尔。我要进行的战争将在这些神圣的围墙之内。在这里，我需要你帮我。乔瓦尼可以为波吉亚家族去当兵，统领教皇的军队，我不允许你在这些问题上再质疑我的权威。以圣父、圣子、圣灵之名赦免你的罪，阿门。

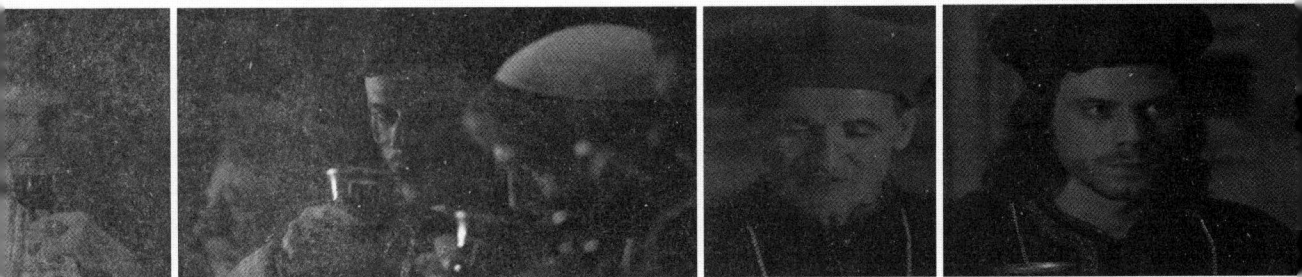

Scene 3: Success in the pope election did not mean everything had been settled. In a banquet hosted by a bishop Orsini in honor of the Pope, alert Cesare found that someone intend to poison him and his father, then he left that poisonous wine to the suspect…

当选教皇并不意味着一切都尘埃落定。在一次主教奥尔西尼宴请教皇的晚宴上，机警的切泽尔就发现有人要毒死他们父子俩，于是他把毒酒留给了凶手……

Orsini:	I propose a **toast**[23] to harmony, amongst us, servants of God.	奥尔西尼： 我提议大家干一杯，为了和谐，上帝的信徒，和谐共处。
Rodrigo:	To the communion of saints, and the forgiveness of sins.	罗德里戈： 与神圣为伍，宽恕罪愆。
All:	Amen.	众人： 阿门。
Rovere:	I'd like to propose a second toast. To **metaphor**[24].	罗韦雷： 我想敬第二轮酒，为了"隐喻"。
Cesare:	Why metaphor?	切泽尔： 为什么是"隐喻"？
Rovere:	Because she's so **infinitely**[25] **pliable**[26]. A prince one minute, a monkey the next. And what her hidden meaning is only God in his infinite wisdom knows.	罗韦雷： 因为她是如此完美圆滑。前一分钟还是王子，转眼就变成猴子。而它隐藏在背后的真正含意，只有全能的上帝懂得。
Cesare:	I propose another toast. To monkeys.	切泽尔： 我也要祝一次酒。敬猴子。
Orsini:	Monkeys?	奥尔西尼： 猴子？
Cesare:	They lick your hand one minute, bite your neck the next. And everyone knows what you do with the monkey that bites you.	切泽尔： 一分钟之前它还在舔你的手，转眼就咬你的脖子。每个人都知道你会怎么对待那只咬你的猴子。
Rovere:	And what do you do with the monkey that bites you?	罗韦雷： 那该对那只咬你的猴子做什么？
Cesare:	You **wring**[27] its neck.	切泽尔： 你该拧断它的脖子。

注释
14. vicar ['vɪkə(r)] *n.* 牧师；代理人	21. engulf [ɪn'gʌlf] *v.* 吞没；席卷
15. blasphemous ['blæsfəməs] *adj.* 亵渎神明的；不敬神的	22. papal ['peɪpl] *adj.* 教廷的；罗马教皇的
16. bishop ['bɪʃəp] *n.* 主教	23. toast [təʊst] *n.* 祝酒词
17. temporal ['tempərəl] *adj.* 暂时的；当时的；现世的，世俗的	24. metaphor ['metəfə(r)] *n.* 暗喻，隐喻；比喻说法
18. calling ['kɔːlɪŋ] *n.* 职业；欲望	25. infinitely ['ɪnfɪnətli] *adj.* 无限的；完美的
19. vow [vaʊ] *n.* 誓言	26. pliable ['plaɪəbl] *adj.* 柔韧的；圆滑的
20. layman ['leɪmən] *n.* 门外汉；俗人	27. wring [rɪŋ] *v.* 绞，拧

文化背景

1. Cardinal 枢机主教

枢机主教，因穿红衣、戴红帽，故也称为红衣主教，在罗马天主教廷中的地位仅次于教皇，俗称教会亲王。当教皇去世十五天后，枢密主教们要进入一个与外界隔绝的选举处，每天进行两次无记名投票，直到有人赢得三分之二的选票。

常用表达

1. at ease 舒服，自在

例: He didn't feel completely at ease in the strange surroundings.

他在陌生的环境中感到不那么自在。

2. be destined 命中注定的

例: He is destined to be the ruler of the kingdom.

他注定要成为这个王国的统治者。

Passage 2

（选自第2季第1集）参选教皇失败的德拉·罗韦雷不甘心就此投降波吉亚家族，为躲避亚历山大六世的追杀，他逃亡至法国，并随法王查理八世反攻罗马。面对兵临城下的窘境，亚历山大六世演出了一出空城计，成功的化解了危机，地位反而更加稳固。

Scene 1: France King Charles VIII led his army to Rome, and paid the courtesy call on Pope Alexander VI with Lucrezia's guidance. There was nobody else except for Pope Rodrigo, praying in his shabby monk robe.

法王查理八世领兵来到罗马，在卢克雷齐娅的引领下单独面见教皇亚历山大六世，教堂里空荡荡的，只有教皇罗德里戈穿着寒酸的修士袍在祈祷……

Rodrigo: Miserere mei, Deus, secundum magnam miseri- cordiam ...

Charles: Forgive me, **Friar**[1]. I am seeking an audience with the pope. I have been interrupted at prayer.

Rodrigo: Our prayers are ended. And perhaps they will be answered.

Charles: Can this really be the Pope of Rome? Pope Alexander?

Rodrigo: **Sextus**[2]. At your service, my lord. And you, my lord, are?

Charles: King Charles of France. It is not as we expected.

Rodrigo: Does the Pope of Rome disappoint Your Highness? Had you hoped for gold and silver **vestments**[3]? Display has its purpose.

罗德里戈：吾主慈悲，怜悯于我……

法王查理：原谅我，修士，我是想觐见教皇，我打扰了你的祈祷。

罗德里戈：我们的祈祷已经完成了，而也许祈祷就会实现。

法王查理：这当真是罗马教皇吗？教皇亚历山大？

罗德里戈：六世，为您效劳，我的大人。那您呢，大人，您是谁？

法王查理：查尔斯，法国国王。这可不是我所期待的。

罗德里戈：罗马教皇让你失望了吗，陛下？您期望见到璀璨的金银法袍吗？外表固有其意义所在，但

But simplicity must rule our hearts. We are all of us naked before God. Even the Pope of Rome. Even...the King of France.

简朴必得是我们内心的规则。在上帝的面前，我们皆是赤裸的。即使是罗马教皇，即使是……法国国王。

Scene 2: In the church, King of France and Pope of Rome continued their negotiation, and all the conspiracies and transactions were carried out in the sacred name. In the first round of negotiation, King Charles promised not to force Pope Alexander to abdicate…

教堂里，法王查理在继续和教皇亚历山大六世进行谈判。当然，所有的阴谋和交易都是以神圣的名义进行的，谈判的第一回合，法王表示不逼迫教皇亚历山大退位……

Rodrigo: I am sure you too, Your Highness, sometime long to be free of the burden of kingship.

Charles: To walk as a man among men. It would be sweet relief, Your Holiness.

Rodrigo: Just as we **long**[4] to be free of the burden of the **papacy**[5]. The papal **robes**[6] are such a weight upon our shoulders. One longs to be *relieved of*[1] the burden, to be a simple **priest**[7] again, praying to the God of Abraham.

Charles: We understand, Your Holiness.

Rodrigo: Then perhaps Your Highness knows one who would relieve us of this burden?

Charles: The very thought **appalls**[8] me, Your Holiness.

Rodrigo: Really? Why?

Charles: We do not choose our calling, Your Holiness. It is chosen for us. When called to serve, as King of France, and, I am sure,

罗德里戈：您想必也是如此，陛下，有时会渴望卸下王位的重担。

法王查理：在普通人中，像普通人一样生活。那会是一个甜蜜的解脱，教皇陛下。

罗德里戈：像我一样，渴望摆脱这教廷的负担，教皇的法袍使我不堪重负。我渴望从这重担中解脱，做回一名单纯的教士，向亚伯拉罕的上帝祈祷。

法王查理：我理解，教皇陛下。

罗德里戈：那么也许陛下您知道谁能使我摆脱这个负担？

法王查理：我对这种想法深感震惊，教皇陛下。

罗德里戈：真的？为什么？

法王查理：我们无法选择自己的使命，教皇陛下，是这些使命选择了我们。当我们受到召唤时，作为

you as Pope of Rome, we can only have one response: <u>serviam</u>[1].

Rodrigo: I will serve.

法国国王，我相信你作为罗马教皇，我们只有一种选择：献身。

罗德里戈： 我将献身。

Scene 3: In the second round of negotiation, King Charles expressed euphemistically his thirst for the throne of Naples. It would cost nothing, so Pope Alexander agreed immediately.

查理与教皇谈判第二回合的内容，是法王委婉地提出对那不勒斯王位的要求。对这个惠而不费的要求，教皇自然一口答应下来……

Rodrigo: Then perhaps, what is needed is a renewal of one's **vows**[9].

Charles : One's vows?

Rodrigo: A renewal of your vows of kingship before the Pope of Rome. The papal **investiture**[10] of the Kingdom of France.

Charles : France, as you must know, Your Holiness, has traditional **claims**[11] upon the Kingdom of Naples.

Rodrigo: But of course! Even better. The papal investiture of the kingdoms of France and Naples. And your **solemn**[12] oath, before God to rule them *in His holy name*[2].

罗德里戈： 那也许我们要做的只是修改一下我们的誓言。

法王查理： 我们的誓言?

罗德里戈： 你需要在罗马教皇面前，重新宣讲你作为法国国王的誓言。教廷会为法国国王加冕。

法王查理： 法国，你是知道的，教皇陛下，一直以来都主张拥有那不勒斯王国的主权。

罗德里戈： 那当然，更好的办法是，教廷将为法国和那不勒斯国王加冕。而您，则在上帝面前庄严宣誓，以上帝的神圣名义统治。

注释

4. long [lɒŋ] *v.* 渴望，极想

5. papacy ['peɪpəsɪ] *n.* 罗马教皇职位；教皇权

6. robe [rəʊb] *n.* 长袍，礼服

7. priest [priːst] *n.* 牧师；神父；教士

8. appall [ə'pɔːl] *v.* 使惊骇，惊吓

9. vow [vaʊ] *n.* 许愿，誓言

10. investiture [ɪn'vestɪtʃə(r)] *n.* 加冕；授权仪式

11. claim [kleɪm] *n.* 要求承认（权利、所有权等）；声称有权

12. solemn ['sɒləm] *adj.* 庄严的，严肃的；隆重的，郑重的

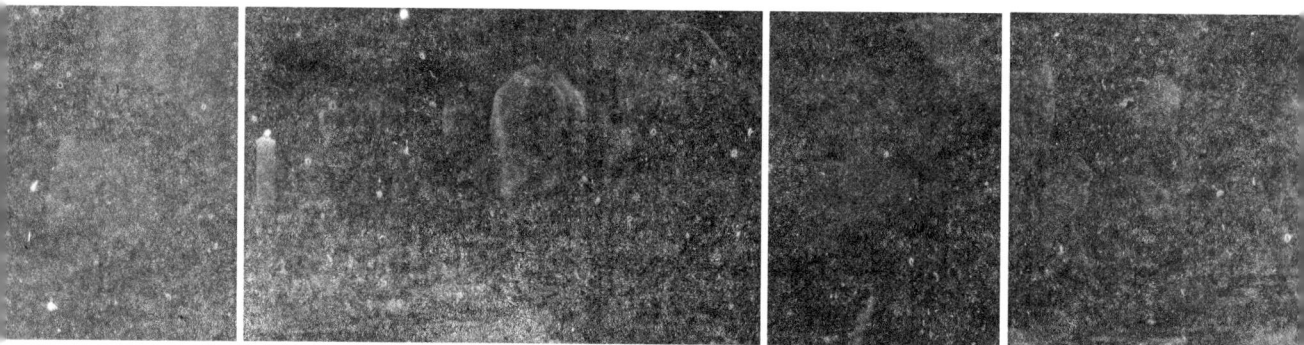

Scene 4: Obviously, crafty King Charles could not be satisfied only by an empty promise, so he put forward another request in the dinner…

一个空头的承诺显然不能满足老奸巨猾的法王查理，在晚宴上，法王查理向亚历山大提出了另一个要求……

Charles:	We would make a request of Your Holiness.	法王查理：	我们想对陛下您提个要求。
Rodrigo:	We will respectfully hear it.	罗德里戈：	我洗耳恭听。
Charles:	We would have you **nominate**[13] a papal **legate**[14] to accompany our armies to the Kingdom of Naples, to remain with us for the duration of our visit.	法王查理：	我们希望陛下您指派一位教会使节，随同我们军队前往那不勒斯王国，并且在我们拜访那不勒斯期间和我们在一起。
Rodrigo:	Very well. We will nominate a legate of our choice…	罗德里戈：	很好。那我为你指派的那位使节是……
Charles:	Oh, no! Not of your choice, Holy Father. Of ours.	法王查理：	噢，不，不是您来选择，教皇陛下，我们来选。
Rodrigo:	Who would you choose?	罗德里戈：	那您选择的是哪位？
Charles:	Your son. Cardinal Cesare Borgia.	法王查理：	您儿子，凯撒·波吉亚枢机主教。
Cesare:	You would have me accompany your army as… a **hostage**[15]?	切泽尔：	你是要我跟随你的部队，做……人质？
Charles:	No. God forbid. A hostage implies **enmity**[16].	法王查理：	当然不是，看在上帝的份上，人质这个词充满了敌意。
Cesare:	And what does legate imply?	切泽尔：	那么使节又是什么意思？
Charles:	Friendship, surely. And a **guarantee**[17] that such friendship will continue.	法王查理：	友谊，当然了，一个让友谊地久天长的保证。

注释

13. **nominate** ['nɒmɪneɪt] *v.* 指定，指派
14. **legate** ['legət] *n.* 使节
15. **hostage** ['hɒstɪdʒ] *n.* 人质；抵押品
16. **enmity** ['enməti] *n.* 仇恨，敌意
17. **guarantee** [ˌgærən'ti:] *v.* 保证；担保

📖 文化背景

1. serviam 拉丁语，献身

中世纪的欧洲，教皇权与各国王权是并存于世的两种权力体系。国王是世俗的统治者，维持社会的稳定和正义，保证人民的幸福；教会则负责信徒的精神生活和宗教生活，让教徒得到天堂的幸福。国王的统治经过天主教廷的承认才具备合法性，而教皇没有军队，他的统治要靠各个国王的支持，但权力无限膨胀的本性使得这两种权力之间充满了矛盾。世俗王权与宗教神权的斗争贯穿了长达 10 个世纪的中世纪。

📠 常用表达

1. relieve...of... 解除（某人）的（负担、困难等）

例：It will relieve her of a tremendous burden.

这将给她解决一个巨大的负担。

2. in one's name 以……名义

例：He published that novel in his own name.

他以自己的真名发表了那部小说。

Passage 3

剧情介绍:

（选自第 2 季第 10 集）波吉亚家族无论对内对外，手段的残忍是一致的。对外，他们残酷迫害谴责教皇堕落、腐败的教士，并将他烧死在火刑柱上；对内，教皇的两个儿子彼此仇视，最终老二乔瓦尼被老大切泽尔杀死，尸体被抛进了台伯河。等教皇意识到是自己的溺爱毁掉了二儿子时，一切都已经太晚了。1503 年，教皇亚历山大六世死于政敌投毒。似乎只有卢克雷齐娅是幸运的，她终于找到了一个真心爱自己的人。

Scene 1: In the church, Lukrezia encountered Alfonso[1], who was from d'Este Family and came to propose to her. However, Alfonso did not recognize the beauty in front of him was Lukrezia herself, and took her as a maid who just came to assess him. Lukrezia took the opportunity to tease this naive young man, only to find that he did love herself...

卢克雷齐娅在教堂里偶遇前来向自己求婚的埃斯特家族的阿方索，而阿方索并没有认出眼前的美女就是卢克雷齐娅本人，还以为只是一个奉命考察他的宫女，卢克雷齐娅借机捉弄着这个天真的年轻人，却发现他是真心喜欢自己……

Alfonso: When you speak of me to the Lady Borgia, if your account is favorable, can you and I...?

Borgia: Never. We must never see each other again. If you are hers, you are hers alone.

Alfonso: So, tell her I was **inept**[1], or **coarse**[2] or beyond ugly. And come with me and be mine alone.

Borgia: You would *turn down*[1] the pope's own daughter for me? Why?

Alfonso: Because I have never known a woman so lovely.

Borgia: Poor boy.

阿方索: 当你向卢克莱琪娅小姐提到我时，如果你的描述令她满意，你和我还能……?

波吉亚: 绝不可能。咱俩永远也不能再见面了。如果你是属于她的，你只能属于她一个人。

阿方索: 那么，告诉她我愚蠢无能，或者举止粗俗，或者相貌奇丑。然后你和我走，做只属于我的人。

波吉亚: 你会为了我拒绝教皇的女儿? 为什么?

阿方索: 因为我从未见过如此可爱的女人。

波吉亚: 可怜的男孩。

Scene 2: Cesare and Borgia were enjoying precious tranquility, then Borgia asked Cesare to marry her but was rejected…

切泽尔和波吉亚在她的卧室里享受着难得的宁静,波吉亚提出要让哥哥做她的主婚人,但是切泽尔拒绝了妹妹的要求……

Borgia: Cesare?

Cesare: Little sister.

Borgia: I would ask you something.

Cesare: Then ask, and it is yours.

Borgia: I would ask you to marry me.

Cesare: As you wish. My word is my word. We shall *run away*[2], change our names perhaps. Live out our days in some small fishing village by the coast, where no one will ever guess who we once were.

Borgia: To Alfonso.

Cesare: Yes, yes, I know. You would have me marry you to him.

Borgia: Yes.

Cesare: Do you love him?

Borgia: I think he is good. I believe I can love him.

Cesare: So you have a good man at last. But I cannot marry you.

Borgia: I truly wish it.

Cesare: These hands have seen too much of blood and sin to join two such tender creatures.

Borgia: These hands bear a cardinal's ring.

Cesare: Until today they have.

波吉亚：切泽尔?

切泽尔：小妹妹。

波吉亚：我有点事要求你。

切泽尔：说吧，任你予求。

波吉亚：我希望你能为我证婚。

切泽尔：如你所愿。我说话算话。我们得跑得远远的，或许还得改名。在某个海边的小渔村住下来，在那儿没人会揣度我们曾经是谁。

波吉亚：把我嫁给阿方索。

切泽尔：是的，没错，我知道。你想让我做你们的证婚人。

波吉亚：是的。

切泽尔：你爱他吗?

波吉亚：我想他是个好人，我相信我可以爱上他。

切泽尔：所以你最终会有一个好归宿，但是我不能给你证婚。

波吉亚：我是真的非常希望。

切泽尔：这双手已然沾染了太多的鲜血和罪孽，不能去把你们那么温柔的手牵到一起。

波吉亚：这双手是因为主教的戒指而受困。

切泽尔：直至今日他们依然如此。

注释 1. inept [ɪ'nept] *adj.* 无能的，愚蠢的
2. coarse [kɔːs] *adj.* 粗糙的；粗俗的；下等的

Scene 3: Pope Alexander buried with his own hands his second son, then prepare to carry out a frank father-and-son talk with Cesare. But before the conversation started, the Pope drank a cup of wine the servant handed him. He didn't know the servant was a spy placed in his side by his political opponnts for a long time, also did not know what was put into the wine.

教皇亚历山大六世亲手埋葬了自己死去的二儿子，然后准备与大儿子切泽尔进行一场父子间的坦诚交流。可惜在谈话前，教皇喝下了侍者递过来的一杯酒。他不知道的是这名侍者是政敌安插在他身边多时的，也不知道酒里放了些什么。

Cesare:	What's happened to your hands, Father?	切泽尔： 你的手怎么了，父亲？
Rodrigo:	We have buried our son. And we realize now that we have brought this upon ourselves.	罗德里戈： 我的儿子，已经埋葬好了。现在我才意识到这一切都是自作自受。
Cesare:	Father?	切泽尔： 父亲？
Rodrigo:	You are our own doing. What you've done is our doing also. We brought you to this. You say we granted every favor to him. But our favors fell on him so easily, of their own accord. You are too much like me. A man feels less favor for his own image reflected.	罗德里戈： 你是我培养造就的。你做的，就等于是我做的。是我把你带到了这里。你说我把所有的宠爱都给了他。但我对他的宠爱就是这么自然而然地落到他身上的，像是他们自己给予的。你太像我了。人对自己的影子总会少爱几分的。
Cesare:	If I cannot have your affection, can you at least grant me your forgiveness?	切泽尔： 如果我得不到您的喜爱，那我能不能至少得到您的赦免？
Rodrigo:	I...	罗德里戈： 我……
(Pope Alexander stopped in the middle of his sentence because the poison showed its effect. The servant was poisoned to death quickly, and Pope fell down to the ground soon.)		（教皇话没出口就毒发了，一旁侍立的侍者中毒死去，而教皇很快也在儿子的呼唤中倒下了。）
Cesare:	Father. Father! No! Father! Help!	切泽尔： 父亲，父亲！不！父亲！救命啊！

📖 文化背景

1. Alfonso d'Este 埃斯特家族的阿方索

埃斯特家族是一个显赫的意大利贵族家庭，是费拉拉（Ferrara，1240 年—1597 年）和摩德纳（Modena，1288 年—1796 年）的统治者和著名的文艺复兴时期的艺术赞助人，也是教皇亚历山大六世极力拉拢的对象。阿方索，即费拉拉公爵阿方索一世，是卢克雷齐娅的第三任，也是最后一任丈夫。1519 年 6 月 24 日卢克雷齐娅在费拉拉生下她的第八个孩子染上产后并发症去世，她被葬在科尔布斯·多米尼修道院里，阿方索于 1534 年 10 月 31 日去世，死后夫妻合葬。

📒 常用表达

1. turn down 舒服，自在

例：There's no reason whatsoever to turn down this suggestion.

没有任何理由拒绝这个建议。

2. run away 逃跑

例：Three years ago I ran away to Mexico to live with a circus.

三年前我逃到墨西哥，在一个马戏团生活。